Microsoft SQL Server 2014 Business Intelligence Development Beginner's Guide

Get to grips with Microsoft Business Intelligence and data warehousing technologies using this practical guide

Reza Rad

BIRMINGHAM - MUMBAI

Microsoft SQL Server 2014 Business Intelligence Development Beginner's Guide

First published: May 2014

Production Reference: 2220514

Published by Packt Publishing Ltd.
Livery Place
35 Livery Street
Birmingham B3 2PB, UK.

ISBN 978-1-84968-888-8

www.packtpub.com

Cover Image by Artie Ng (artherng@yahoo.com.au)

Credits

Author

Reza Rad

Reviewers

John Heaton

Goh Yong Hwee

Raunak T. Jhawar

Francesco Quaratino

James Serra

Acquisition Editor

James Jones

Content Development Editor

Madhuja Chaudhari

Technical Editors

Pragnesh Bilimoria

Taabish Khan

Pooja Nair

Copy Editors

Sayanee Mukherjee

Aditya Nair

Alfida Paiva

Project Coordinator

Amey Sawant

Proofreaders

Simran Bhogal

Maria Gould

Ameesha Green

Paul Hindle

Indexer

Priya Subramani

Graphics

Valentina Dsilva

Disha Haria

Yuvraj Mannari

Abhinash Sahu

Production Coordinator

Komal Ramchandani

Cover Work

Komal Ramchandani

About the Author

Reza Rad has more than 10 years of experience in databases and software applications. Most of his work experience is in data warehousing and business intelligence. He has worked with Microsoft technologies from SQL Server 7 and Visual Basic 6 to the latest versions of SQL Server and .NET. He has a Bachelor's degree in Computer Engineering.

Reza is a DW/BI architect and consultant. He has worked with large enterprises around the world and delivered high-quality data warehousing and BI solutions for them. He has worked with industries in different sectors, such as Health, Finance, Logistics, Sales, Order Management, Manufacturing, Telecommunication, and so on.

Reza has been awarded the Microsoft Most Valuable Professional in SQL Server from 2011 to 2014. He is an international speaker in SQL Server, BI, and DW conferences around the world. He speaks in SQL PASS Summits, Microsoft TechEd, SQL Saturdays, SQL Server user groups, and code camps.

Reza has written books on SQL Server and databases. One of his most recent books is *SQL Server 2012 Integration Services: An Expert Cookbook, Packt Publishing*.

Reza is a big fan of data-related technologies, his expertise is in EIM, ETL, Data governance, big data, data warehousing, BI, data visualization, Master Data Management, OLAP, and so on. He is the author of Webcast series on the RADACAD website (http://www.radacad.com). He writes articles and blog posts on his technical blog (http://www.rad.pasfu.com); he writes about most of the Microsoft technologies, such as SSIS, MDS, DQS, SSAS, Power BI, HDInsight, and so on. His blog contains the latest information on his presentations and publications.

Reza is a Mentor and a Microsoft Certified Trainer. He has been in the professional training business for many years. He conducts extensive 400 handed-level training for many enterprises around the world via both remote and in-person training. He is an active member of MSDN forums, especially those on SQL Server and Power BI. He is also the leader of the New Zealand Data Warehousing and Business Intelligence user group, which is a registered chapter of PASS.

About the Reviewers

John Heaton graduated top of his class with a Diploma in Information Technology from Technikon Witwatersrand in South Africa (equivalent to a Bachelor's degree in Computer Science). He has worked for more than 10 years with Oracle Corporation and has held various positions, including that of a Practice Manager. He had been co-running the North Business Intelligence and Warehouse Consulting practice, delivering business intelligence solutions to Fortune 500 clients. During this time, he steadily added business skills and business training to his technical background.

In 2005, John decided to leave Oracle and become a founding member in a small business named iSeerix. This allowed him to focus on strategic partnerships with clients to design and build Business Intelligence and data warehouse solutions.

John's strengths include the ability to communicate the benefits of introducing a Business Intelligence solution to a client's architecture. He has gradually become a trusted advisor to his clients. His philosophy is based on responsibility and mutual respect. He relies on the unique abilities of individuals to ensure success in different areas and strives to foster a team environment of creativity and achievement.

Today, John specializes as a Solution / Technical Architect assisting customers in designing large complex data warehouses. Through the years, he has worked in numerous industries with differing technologies. This broad experience base allows him to bring a unique perspective and understanding when designing and developing a data warehouse. The strong business background, coupled with technical expertise, and his certification in Project Management makes him a valued asset to any data warehouse project.

John has authored *Business Intelligence Cookbook: A Project Lifecycle Approach Using Oracle Technolog*, Packt Publishing.

Goh Yong Hwee is a database specialist, systems engineer, developer, and trainer based in Singapore. He is a Microsoft Certified Trainer and a Certified Novell Instructor. Some of the courses that he is authorized to deliver and has delivered include Microsoft SQL Server Business Intelligence, Microsoft Windows Server, Microsoft SharePoint, Microsoft Exchange Server, and Suse Linux Enterprise Server. Throughout his training, he has consistently maintained a Metrics that Matter score exceeding 8 out of 10. He has also been instrumental in customizing and reviewing his training center's training for its clients.

When imparting knowledge, his objective has been to make technologies easy and simple for everyone to learn. His no-frills approach to training has gained him recognition over the years from both clients and employers, where his clinching of the Best Instructor Award, an accolade conferred by his employer, bore testimonial. He has been in the training industry for five years, and prior to that, he was associated with a Japanese MNC in Singapore as a Systems Analyst, specializing in data warehousing on Microsoft SQL Server, RPG programming on the IBM iSeries, and BPCS ERP. Over the years, he has chosen to focus his work and specialization on Microsoft SQL Server and is currently in full-time employment with a Fortune 500 company in Singapore, taking up the specialist, consultancy, developer, and management roles.

Raunak T. Jhawar is a graduate in Computer Science from the University of Pune and has more than five years of experience working as a software professional working with BI, data visualization, and Hadoop.

Raunak is presently working with Aditi Technologies in Bangalore as a Technical Leader, working with clients and consulting them for their BI and analytics engagements.

Francesco Quaratino has been enjoying working with SQL Server since 2000, as either a Developer or an Administrator. He currently leads an ambitious BI project for Betgenius Ltd. in London, where he lives with his family. The last certification he achieved was MCSE: 2012 Data Platform.

James Serra is an independent consultant with the title of Data Warehouse/Business Intelligence Architect. He is a Microsoft SQL Server MVP with over 25 years of IT experience. He started his career as a software developer, and then he was a DBA for 12 years. For the last seven years, he has been working extensively with Business Intelligence using the SQL Server BI stack. He has been a permanent employee, consultant, contractor, and owner of his own business. All these experiences, along with continuous learning, have helped him to develop many successful data warehouse and BI projects. He is a noted blogger and speaker, having presented at the PASS summit and the PASS Business Analytics Conference.

James has earned the MSCE: SQL Server 2012 Business Intelligence, MSCE: SQL Server 2012 Data Platform, MCITP: SQL Server 2008 Business Intelligence Developer, MCITP: SQL Server 2008 Database Administrator, and MCITP: SQL Server 2008 Database certificates. He has a Bachelor of Science degree in Computer Engineering from UNLV.

James resides in Houston, TX with his wife Mary and three children, Lauren, RaeAnn, and James.

This book is dedicated to my wonderful wife Mary and my children Lauren, RaeAnn, and James, and my parents Jim and Lorraine. Their love, understanding, and support are what made this book possible. Now, if they only understood the content!

---

www.PacktPub.com

Support files, eBooks, discount offers, and more

You might want to visit www.PacktPub.com for support files and downloads related to your book.

Did you know that Packt offers eBook versions of every book published, with PDF and ePub files available? You can upgrade to the eBook version at www.PacktPub.com and as a print book customer, you are entitled to a discount on the eBook copy. Get in touch with us at service@packtpub.com for more details.

At www.PacktPub.com, you can also read a collection of free technical articles, sign up for a range of free newsletters and receive exclusive discounts and offers on Packt books and eBooks.

http://PacktLib.PacktPub.com

Do you need instant solutions to your IT questions? PacktLib is Packt's online digital book library. Here, you can access, read and search across Packt's entire library of books.

Why subscribe?

- Fully searchable across every book published by Packt
- Copy and paste, print and bookmark content
- On demand and accessible via web browser

Free access for Packt account holders

If you have an account with Packt at www.PacktPub.com, you can use this to access PacktLib today and view nine entirely free books. Simply use your login credentials for immediate access.

Instant updates on new Packt books

Get notified! Find out when new books are published by following @PacktEnterprise on Twitter, or the *Packt Enterprise* Facebook page.

Table of Contents

Preface	**1**
Chapter 1: Data Warehouse Design	**7**
Understanding Business Intelligence	**7**
The architecture and components of a BI system	**9**
The data warehouse	9
Extract Transform Load	10
Data model – BISM	10
Data visualization	12
Master Data Management	12
Data Quality Services	12
Building the data warehouse	**13**
Dimensional modeling	14
Fact or measure	15
Dimension	15
The Fact table	15
Grain	15
The star schema	16
An example of Internet sales	16
FactSales	18
The customer dimension	19
DimDate	20
DimProduct	22
DimStore	22
Types of facts	22
The Factless Fact table – The Bridge table	23
Types of dimensions	23
Slowly Changing Dimension	24
SCD type 0	24
SCD type 1	25
SCD type 2	25
Summary	**26**

Chapter 2: SQL Server Analysis Services Multidimensional Cube Development 27
Why is OLAP required? 27
Understanding the SQL Server Analysis Services engine 29
Developing your first cube 31
Time for action – creating an Analysis Services project 31
Time for action – creating the first cube 33
Time for action – viewing the cube in the browser 37
Dimensions and measures 39
Time for action – using the Dimension Designer 39
Time for action – change the order of the Month attribute 42
Time for action – modifying the measure properties 43
Data Source View 44
Time for action – creating a Named Calculation 45
Time for action – using a Named Query 46
Using dimensions 46
Time for action – adding a Fact relationship 46
Hierarchies 49
Time for action – creating a hierarchy 50
Multidimensional eXpression, calculated members, and Named Sets 51
Time for action – writing an MDX query 51
Time for action – calculated members 53
Deploying and processing 54
Time for action – deploying an SSAS project 54
Time for action – processing the data 57
Summary 61

Chapter 3: Tabular Model Development of SQL Server Analysis Services 63
Introducing SSAS Tabular 64
Developing a tabular project 65
Time for action – creating a tabular project 65
Time for action – creating measures 68
Creating hierarchies 69
Time for action – creating a hierarchy from a single table 70
Time for action – creating a hierarchy from multiple tables 71
Data Analysis eXpression, calculated columns, and measures 73
Time for action – using time intelligence functions in DAX 73
Securing the data 76
Time for action – security in tabular 77
Storage modes 79

Time for action – creating a model with the DirectQuery storage mode   80
Tabular versus Multidimensional SSAS   81
Summary   82

Chapter 4: ETL with Integration Services   83
Understanding ETL and data consolidation   84
  Staging   84
SQL Server Integration Services   85
Integration Service projects and packages   86
Time for action – creating your first SSIS project   87
The Control Flow tab   88
Time for action – working with Control Flow tasks   88
The Data Flow tab   96
Time for action – loading customer information from a flat file into a database
table with a Data Flow Task   96
Containers and dynamic packages   107
Time for action – looping through CSV files in a directory and loading them
into a database table   107
Deploying and executing   112
Time for action – deploying an SSIS project   113
Time for action – executing an SSIS package from a catalog   114
Summary   117

Chapter 5: Master Data Management   119
Understanding Master Data Management   119
Master Data Services   121
Time for action – configuring MDS   122
Comparing WebUI with the Excel Add-in   123
Time for action – installing Excel Add-in   124
Creating models and entities   125
Time for action – creating a model and an entity   125
Time for action – creating an entity with data from the Excel Add-in   126
Time for action – change tracking   127
The entity relationship   129
Time for action – creating a domain-based relationship   129
Business rules   131
Time for action – creating a simple business rule   131
Working with hierarchies   133
Time for action – creating a derived hierarchy   133
Security and permission   135
Time for action – permission walkthrough   135

Integration management | 136
Time for action – a subscription view | 137
Time for action – entity-based staging | 138
Summary | 141

Chapter 6: Data Quality and Data Cleansing | **143**
Understanding data quality | 143
Data Quality Services | 145
Time for action – installing Data Quality Services | 147
Knowledge Base Management | 149
Time for action – creating a Knowledge Base | 149
Knowledge discovery | 151
Time for action – knowledge discovery | 151
Data cleansing with Data Quality Projects | 153
Time for action – using Data Quality Project for cleansing | 153
Domain and composite domain rules | 157
Time for action – composite domain rules | 157
Synonyms and standardization | 159
Time for action – creating synonyms and setting standardization | 160
Matching | 162
Time for action – matching policy | 163
Time for action – matching projects | 165
Integrating with MDS and SSIS | 166
Time for action – the DQS cleansing component in SSIS | 166
DQS integration with MDS | 169
Summary | 170

Chapter 7: Data Mining – Descriptive Models in SSAS | **171**
An introduction to data mining | 171
The Microsoft Decision Tree algorithm | 174
Time for action – creating a data mining solution with the Microsoft
Decision Tree algorithm | 174
Microsoft association rules | 184
Time for action – the Microsoft association rule | 184
Algorithm parameters | 190
Summary | 191

Chapter 8: Identifying Data Patterns – Predictive Models in SSAS | **193**
Finding the best algorithm | 193
Time for action – finding the best mining model with Lift Chart and Profit Chart | 194
Predicting data with DMX | 207

Time for action – predicting prospective bike buyers   207
Microsoft Time Series   214
Time for action – predicting future sales with Microsoft Time Series   214
Summary   218

Chapter 9: Reporting Services   **219**
The Reporting Services architecture   219
Developing a basic report   221
Time for action – creating our first report using SSRS   221
Extended report development   226
Parameters   226
Time for action – adding parameters to a report   226
Printing and page configuration   232
Time for action – changing a page's properties   232
Sorting and grouping   234
Time for action – applying ordering and grouping on the data rows   234
Expressions   237
Time for action – changing the background color of data rows based
on expressions   237
Adding charts   240
Time for action – working with charts in Reporting Services   240
Deploying and configuring   242
Time for action – deploying a report   242
Time for action – using Report Manager   245
Summary   246

Chapter 10: Dashboard Design   **247**
The PerformancePoint service   247
Time for action – configuring PerformancePoint in SharePoint   248
The Dashboard Designer utility   250
Time for action – creating your first dashboard with PerformancePoint
Dashboard Designer   250
The dashboard pages   253
Time for action – creating a dashboard page   253
PPS dashboard's on-the-fly features   256
Time for action – exploring on-the-fly features   256
Filters   259
Time for action – working with filters   259
PerformancePoint Wrap Up   262
Power View   262

Time for action – enabling Power View in Excel   263
Time for action – creating the first Power View dashboard   264
    Map   266
Time for action – geographical data visualization using Power View   266
    Scatter chart   269
Time for action – visualizing time-based information with a scatter chart   269
    Filtering data   273
Time for action – using Filter in Power View   273
    Wrapping up Power View   274
Summary   274

Chapter 11: Power BI   **275**
Self-service ETL with Power Query   275
Time for action – self-service ETL with Power Query   276
Power Map   285
Time for action – data visualization with Power Map   285
Summary   292

Chapter 12: Integrating Reports in Applications   **295**
Designing .NET applications with reports   296
Time for action – installing AdventureWorks SSRS sample reports   296
Developing reports in a web application   297
Time for action – working with reports in web/Windows applications   297
Developing reports in a Metro application   301
Time for action – working with reports in Metro applications   302
Working with ReportViewer in a local processing mode   303
Time for action – designing reports and working with the local processing mode 304
Passing parameters to a report   308
Time for action – changing a report configuration with a ReportViewer
Object through code behind   308
Using the results of a mining model in an application   313
Time for action – running DMX queries from a .NET application   313
Summary   321

Index   **323**

Preface

Business Intelligence (BI) is one of the hottest topics nowadays in the Information Technology field. Many companies and organizations intend to utilize a BI system to solve problems and help decision makers make decisions. This high demand for BI systems has raised the number of job openings in this field.

The following is Gartner's definition of Business Intelligence (`http://www.gartner.com/it-glossary/business-intelligence-bi/`):

> *Business Intelligence (BI) is an umbrella term that includes the applications, infrastructure and tools, and best practices that enable access and analysis of information to improve and optimize decisions and performance.*

There are various reasons to have a BI system in place, but helping decision makers to make better decisions is one of the main purposes of BI. As an example, a director of a manufacturing company would like to understand the trend of sales in past months (or years) on specific products. This trend would be helpful for him to decide any changes in that product or to create some other editions of that product. A bank directory might like to use data mining solutions to distinguish suspicious or fraudulent transactions. A board of directors would be interested to see Key Performance Indicators (KPIs) of their business.

BI could help in all the scenarios mentioned here and many more. A BI system usually uses a data warehouse as a core tool. The data warehouse is an integrated dimensional data structure. Data from a variety of sources will be fed into the data warehouse and some data quality and governance would be applied on the data. The dimensional model of data warehousing is optimized for reporting and analysis, so data visualization tools can directly query against the data warehouse. Another layer of modeling might be added to the BI architecture, OnLine Analytical Processing (OLAP), or the tabular model. These models will improve data access in terms of speed and performance of queries. BI systems have one or more data visualization frontends that will be the GUI for the end user.

In this book, we will go through the BI architecture and explore the Microsoft technologies that can implement and deliver BI solutions.

What this book covers

Chapter 1, Data Warehouse Design, explains the first steps in thinking and designing a BI system. As the first steps, a developer needs to design the **data warehouse (DW)** and needs an understanding of the key concepts of the design and methodologies to create the data warehouse.

Chapter 2, SQL Server Analysis Services Multidimensional Cube Development, explains how an OLAP multidimensional structure is required to provide fast query response and aggregated data from a data warehouse. In this chapter, readers will learn what OLAP provides and how to design OLAP with Microsoft SSAS Multidimensional.

Chapter 3, Tabular Model Development of SQL Server Analysis Services, explains that SSAS Tabular is a new method of presenting data in Microsoft BI 2012 and is very useful in small BI systems and when a developer wants to create POC. In this chapter, the reader will learn about SSAS Tabular and how to use it in BI projects.

Chapter 4, ETL with Integration Services, describes how ETL is an operation of transferring and integrating data from source systems into the data warehouse. ETL needs to be done on a scheduled basis. In this chapter, readers learn how to think about ETL processes and use SSIS to perform data transfers.

Chapter 5, Master Data Management, guides readers on how to manage reference data. Master Data Management (MDM) is very critical in all integrated systems, especially in BI and data warehouse. In this chapter, the reader will learn how to use Master Data Services (MDS) to implement an MDM solution.

Chapter 6, Data Quality and Data Cleansing, explains that data quality is one of the biggest concerns of database systems. The data should be cleansed to be reliable through the data warehouse. In this chapter, readers will learn about data cleansing and how to use Data Quality Services (DQS), which is one of the new services of SQL Server 2012, to apply data cleansing on data warehouse.

Chapter 7, Data Mining – Descriptive Models in SSAS, provides a descriptive model on historical events. In this chapter, readers will understand data mining concepts and how to use data mining algorithms to understand the relationship between historical data, and how to analyze it using Microsoft technologies.

Chapter 8, Identifying Data Patterns – Predictive Models in SSAS, focuses on predicting future outcomes based on a pattern recognized in the existing data. In this chapter, readers will become familiar with algorithms that help in prediction, and how to use them and customize them with parameters. Users will also understand how to compare models together to find the best algorithm for the case.

Chapter 9, Reporting Services, explores Reporting Services, one of the key tools of the Microsoft BI toolset, which provides different types of reports with charts and grouping options. In this chapter, readers will learn when and how to use SSRS to create and design reports from data warehouses, SSAS Multidimensional, or SSAS Tabular.

Chapter 10, Dashboard Design, describes how dashboards are one of the most popular and useful methods of visualizing data. In this chapter, readers will learn when to use dashboards, how to visualize data with dashboards, and how to use PerformancePoint and Power View to create dashboards.

Chapter 11, Power BI, explains how predesigned reports and dashboards are good for business users, but power users require more flexibility. Power BI is a new self-service BI tool. In this chapter, you will learn about Power Query as a self-service ETL tool and Power Map as a 3D geospatial data visualization tool.

Chapter 12, Integrating Reports in Applications, begins with the premise that reports and dashboards are always required in custom applications. This chapter explains different ways to integrate SSRS reports and other dashboards into C# or VB.NET applications in web or Metro applications to provide reports on the application side for the users.

What you need for this book

This book will explain the features of Microsoft SQL Server 2014 Enterprise Edition. However, you can also download and install MS SQL Server 2014 Evaluation Edition, which has the same functionalities but is free for the first 180 days, from the following link:

`http://technet.microsoft.com/en-US/evalcenter/dn205290.aspx`

There are many examples in this book and all of the examples use the following databases as a source:

- AdventureWorks2012
- AdventureWorksDW2012
- AdventureWorksLT2012

You can download the database files from the following link:

`http://msftdbprodsamples.codeplex.com/releases/view/55330`

After downloading the database files, open SQL Server Management Studio and enter the following scripts to create databases from their data files:

```
CREATE DATABASE AdventureWorks2012 ON (FILENAME = '{drive}:\
  {file path}\AdventureWorks2012_Data.mdf')
  FOR ATTACH_REBUILD_LOG;
```

```
CREATE DATABASE AdventureWorksDW2012 ON
   (FILENAME = '<drive>:\
   <file path>\AdventureWorksDW2012_Data.mdf')
   FOR ATTACH_REBUILD_LOG ;
CREATE DATABASE AdventureWorksLT2012 ON
   (FILENAME = '<drive>:\
   <file path>\AdventureWorksLT2012_Data.mdf')
   FOR ATTACH_REBUILD_LOG ;
```

Who this book is for

This book is very useful for BI professionals (consultants, architects, and developers) who want to become familiar with Microsoft BI tools. It will also be handy for BI program managers and directors who want to analyze and evaluate Microsoft tools for BI system implementation.

Conventions

In this book, you will find several headings that appear frequently.

To give clear instructions on how to complete a procedure or task, we use:

Time for action – heading

1. Action 1
2. Action 2
3. Action 3

Instructions often need some extra explanation so that they make sense, so they are followed with:

What just happened?

This heading explains the working of tasks or instructions that you have just completed.

You will also find a number of styles of text that distinguish between different kinds of information. Here are some examples of these styles, and an explanation of their meaning.

Code words in text, database table names, folder names, filenames, file extensions, pathnames, dummy URLs, user input, and Twitter handles are shown as follows: "Expand the `Chapter 02 SSAS Multidimensional` database and then expand the dimensions."

A block of code is set as follows:

```
SELECT [<axis_specification>
       [, <axis_specification>...]]
   FROM [<cube_specification>]
[WHERE [<slicer_specification>]]
```

New terms and **important words** are shown in bold. Words that you see on the screen, in menus or dialog boxes for example, appear in the text like this: "On the **Select Destination Location** screen, click on **Next** to accept the default destination."

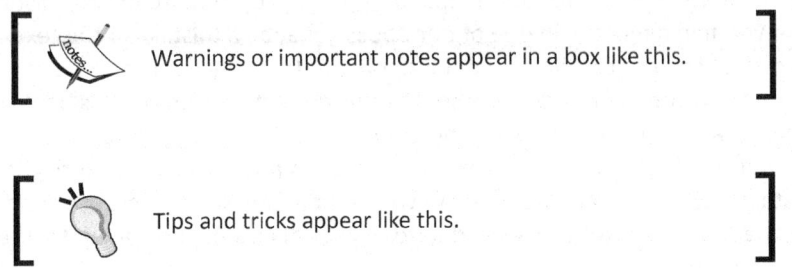

> Warnings or important notes appear in a box like this.

> Tips and tricks appear like this.

Reader feedback

Feedback from our readers is always welcome. Let us know what you think about this book—what you liked or may have disliked. Reader feedback is important for us to develop titles that you really get the most out of.

To send us general feedback, simply send an e-mail to feedback@packtpub.com, and mention the book title through the subject of your message.

If there is a topic that you have expertise in and you are interested in either writing or contributing to a book, see our author guide on www.packtpub.com/authors.

Customer support

Now that you are the proud owner of a Packt book, we have a number of things to help you to get the most from your purchase.

Downloading the example code

You can download the example code files for all Packt books you have purchased from your account at http://www.packtpub.com. If you purchased this book elsewhere, you can visit http://www.packtpub.com/support and register to have the files e-mailed directly to you.

Downloading color versions of the images for this book

For your convenience we have also provided a PDF that contains higher resolution color versions of the images used in this book. These can be extremely useful as you work through various stages of the project when working with materials or examining small detail changes as we tweak individual parameters. You can download the PDF from `https://www.packtpub.com/sites/default/files/downloads/8888EN_ColoredImages.pdf`.

Errata

Although we have taken every care to ensure the accuracy of our content, mistakes do happen. If you find a mistake in one of our books—maybe a mistake in the text or the code—we would be grateful if you would report this to us. By doing so, you can save other readers from frustration and help us improve subsequent versions of this book. If you find any errata, please report them by visiting `http://www.packtpub.com/submit-errata`, selecting your book, clicking on the **errata submission form** link, and entering the details of your errata. Once your errata are verified, your submission will be accepted and the errata will be uploaded to our website, or added to any list of existing errata, under the Errata section of that title.

Piracy

Piracy of copyright material on the Internet is an ongoing problem across all media. At Packt, we take the protection of our copyright and licenses very seriously. If you come across any illegal copies of our works, in any form, on the Internet, please provide us with the location address or website name immediately so that we can pursue a remedy.

Please contact us at `copyright@packtpub.com` with a link to the suspected pirated material.

We appreciate your help in protecting our authors, and our ability to bring you valuable content.

Questions

You can contact us at `questions@packtpub.com` if you are having a problem with any aspect of the book, and we will do our best to address it.

1

Data Warehouse Design

Nowadays, **Business Intelligence** *(BI) is one of the hot topics in most of the job markets around the world. Most companies are establishing or planning to establish a Business Intelligence system and a* **data warehouse** *(DW). Knowledge related to the BI and data warehouse are in great demand in the job market. This chapter gives you an understanding of what Business Intelligence and data warehouse is, what the main components of the BI system are, and what the steps to create the data warehouse are.*

This chapter focuses on the designing of the data warehouse, which is the core of a BI system. The following chapters are about other BI components such as visualization, data integration, data governance, and so on. A data warehouse is a database designed for analysis, and this definition indicates that designing a data warehouse is different from modeling a transactional database. Designing the data warehouse is also called dimensional modeling. In this chapter, you will learn about the concepts of dimensional modeling.

Understanding Business Intelligence

Based on Gartner's definition (`http://www.gartner.com/it-glossary/business-intelligence-bi/`), Business Intelligence is defined as follows:

Business Intelligence is an umbrella term that includes the applications, infrastructure and tools, and best practices that enable access to and analysis of information to improve and optimize decisions and performance.

As the definition states, the main purpose of a BI system is to help decision makers to make proper decisions based on the results of data analysis provided by the BI system.

Nowadays, there are many operational systems in each industry. Businesses use multiple operational systems to simplify, standardize, and automate their everyday jobs and requirements. Each of these systems may have their own database, some of which may work with SQL Server, some with Oracle. Some of the legacy systems may work with legacy databases or even file operations. There are also systems that work through the Web via web services and XML. Operational systems are very useful in helping with day-to-day business operations such as the process of hiring a person in the human resources department, and sale operations through a retail store and handling financial transactions.

The rising number of operational systems also adds another requirement, which is the integration of systems together. Business owners and decision makers not only need integrated data but also require an analysis of the integrated data. As an example, it is a common requirement for the decision makers of an organization to compare their hiring rate with the level of service provided by a business and the customer satisfaction based on that level of service. As you can see, this requirement deals with multiple operational systems such as CRM and human resources. The requirement might also need some data from sales and inventory if the decision makers want to bring sales and inventory factors into their decisions. As a supermarket owner or decision maker, it would be very important to understand what products in which branches were in higher demand. This kind of information helps you to provide enough products to cover demand, and you may even think about creating another branch in some regions.

The requirement of integrating multiple operational systems together in order to create consolidated reports and dashboards that help decision makers to make a proper decision is the main directive for Business Intelligence.

Some organizations and businesses use ERP systems that are integrated, so a question may appear in your mind that there won't be a requirement for integrating data because consolidated reports can be produced easily from these systems. So does that mean that these systems still require a BI solution? The answer in most cases is yes. The companies or businesses might not require a separate BI system for internal and parts of the operations that implemented it through ERP. However, they might require getting some data from outside, for example, getting some data from another vendor's web service or many other protocols and channels to send and receive information. This indicates that there would be a requirement for consolidated analysis for such information, which brings the BI requirement back to the table.

The architecture and components of a BI system

After understanding what the BI system is, it's time to discover more about its components and understand how these components work with each other. There are also some BI tools that help to implement one or more components. The following diagram shows an illustration of the architecture and main components of the Business Intelligence system:

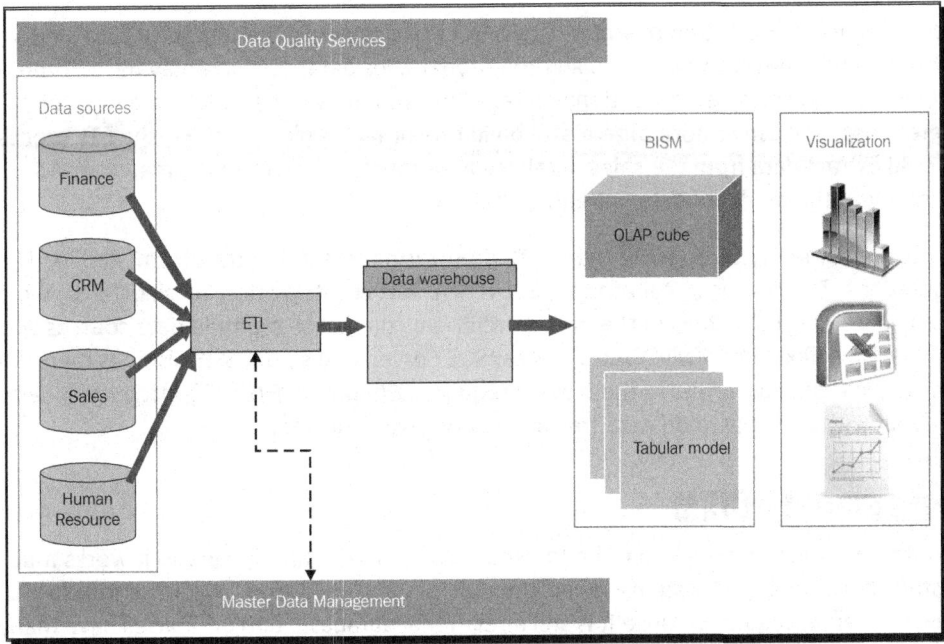

The BI architecture and components differ based on the tools, environment, and so on. The architecture shown in the preceding diagram contains components that are common in most of the BI systems. In the following sections, you will learn more about each component.

The data warehouse

The data warehouse is the core of the BI system. A data warehouse is a database built for the purpose of data analysis and reporting. This purpose changes the design of this database as well. As you know, operational databases are built on normalization standards, which are efficient for transactional systems, for example, to reduce redundancy. As you probably know, a 3NF-designed database for a sales system contains many tables related to each other. So, for example, a report on sales information may consume more than 10 joined conditions, which slows down the response time of the query and report. A data warehouse comes with a new design that reduces the response time and increases the performance of queries for reports and analytics. You will learn more about the design of a data warehouse (which is called dimensional modeling) later in this chapter.

Extract Transform Load

It is very likely that more than one system acts as the source of data required for the BI system. So there is a requirement for data consolidation that extracts data from different sources and transforms it into the shape that fits into the data warehouse, and finally, loads it into the data warehouse; this process is called **Extract Transform Load** (ETL). There are many challenges in the ETL process, out of which some will be revealed (conceptually) later in this chapter.

According to the definition of states, ETL is not just a data integration phase. Let's discover more about it with an example; in an operational sales database, you may have dozen of tables that provide sale transactional data. When you design that sales data into your data warehouse, you can denormalize it and build one or two tables for it. So, the ETL process should extract data from the sales database and transform it (combine, match, and so on) to fit it into the model of data warehouse tables.

There are some ETL tools in the market that perform the extract, transform, and load operations. The Microsoft solution for ETL is **SQL Server Integration Service** (**SSIS**), which is one of the best ETL tools in the market. SSIS can connect to multiple data sources such as Oracle, DB2, Text Files, XML, Web services, SQL Server, and so on. SSIS also has many built-in transformations to transform the data as required. *Chapter 4, ETL with Integration Services*, is about SSIS and how to do data transformations with this tool.

Data model – BISM

A data warehouse is designed to be the source of analysis and reports, so it works much faster than operational systems for producing reports. However, a DW is not that fast to cover all requirements because it is still a relational database, and databases have many constraints that reduce the response time of a query. The requirement for faster processing and a lower response time on one hand, and aggregated information on another hand causes the creation of another layer in BI systems. This layer, which we call the data model, contains a file-based or memory-based model of the data for producing very quick responses to reports.

Microsoft's solution for the data model is split into two technologies: the OLAP cube and the In-memory tabular model. The OLAP cube is a file-based data storage that loads data from a data warehouse into a cube model. The cube contains descriptive information as dimensions (for example, customer and product) and cells (for example, facts and measures, such as sales and discount). The following diagram shows a sample OLAP cube:

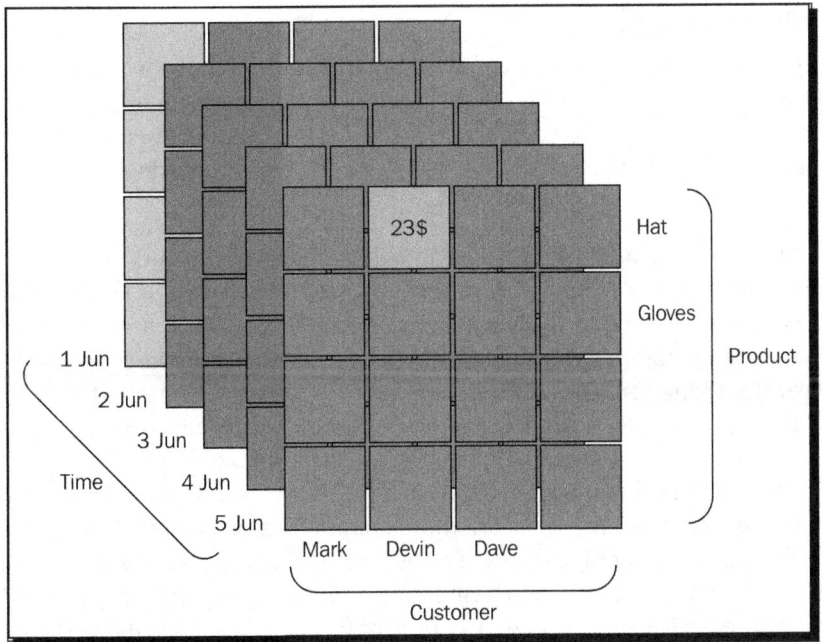

In the preceding diagram, the illustrated cube has three dimensions: **Product**, **Customer**, and **Time**. Each cell in the cube shows a junction of these three dimensions. For example, if we store the sales amount in each cell, then the green cell shows that **Devin** paid **23$** for a **Hat** on June 5. Aggregated data can be fetched easily as well within the cube structure. For example, the orange set of cells shows how much **Mark** paid on June 1 for all products. As you can see, the cube structure makes it easier and faster to access the required information.

Microsoft SQL Server Analysis Services 2012 comes with two different types of modeling: multidimensional and tabular. Multidimensional modeling is based on the OLAP cube and is fitted with measures and dimensions, as you can see in the preceding diagram. The tabular model is based on a new In-memory engine for tables. The In-memory engine loads all data rows from tables into the memory and responds to queries directly from the memory. This is very fast in terms of the response time. You will learn more about SSAS Multidimensional in *Chapter 2*, *SQL Server Analysis Services Multidimensional Cube Development*, and about SSAS Tabular in *Chapter 3*, *Tabular Development of SQL Server Analysis Services*, of this book. The **BI semantic model (BISM)** provided by Microsoft is a combination of SSAS Tabular and Multidimensional solutions.

Data visualization

The frontend of a BI system is data visualization. In other words, data visualization is a part of the BI system that users can see. There are different methods for visualizing information, such as strategic and tactical dashboards, **Key Performance Indicators** (**KPIs**), and detailed or consolidated reports. As you probably know, there are many reporting and visualizing tools on the market.

Microsoft has provided a set of visualization tools to cover dashboards, KPIs, scorecards, and reports required in a BI application. PerformancePoint, as part of Microsoft SharePoint, is a dashboard tool that performs best when connected to SSAS Multidimensional OLAP cube. You will learn about PerformancePoint in *Chapter 10, Dashboard Design*. Microsoft's **SQL Server Reporting Services** (**SSRS**) is a great reporting tool for creating detailed and consolidated reports. SSRS is a mature technology in this area, which will be revealed in *Chapter 9, Reporting Services*. Excel is also a great slicing and dicing tool especially for power users. There are also components in Excel such as Power View, which are designed to build performance dashboards. You will learn more about Power View in *Chapter 9, Reporting Services*, and about Power BI features of Excel 2013 in *Chapter 11, Power BI*. Sometimes, you will need to embed reports and dashboards in your custom written application. *Chapter 12, Integrating Reports in Application*, of this book explains that in detail.

Master Data Management

Every organization has a part of its business that is common between different systems. That part of the data in the business can be managed and maintained as master data. For example, an organization may receive customer information from an online web application form or from a retail store's spreadsheets, or based on a web service provided by other vendors.

Master Data Management (**MDM**) is the process of maintaining the single version of truth for master data entities through multiple systems. Microsoft's solution for MDM is **Master Data Services** (**MDS**). Master data can be stored in the MDS entities and it can be maintained and changed through the MDS Web UI or Excel UI. Other systems such as CRM, AX, and even DW can be subscribers of the master data entities. Even if one or more systems are able to change the master data, they can write back their changes into MDS through the staging architecture. You will learn more about MDS in *Chapter 5, Master Data Management*.

Data Quality Services

The quality of data is different in each operational system, especially when we deal with legacy systems or systems that have a high dependence on user inputs. As the BI system is based on data, the better the quality of data, the better the output of the BI solution. Because of this fact, working on data quality is one of the components of the BI systems. As an example, Auckland might be written as "Auck land" in some Excel files or be typed as "Aukland" by the user in the input form.

As a solution to improve the quality of data, Microsoft provided users with DQS. DQS works based on Knowledge Base domains, which means a Knowledge Base can be created for different domains, and the Knowledge Base will be maintained and improved by a data steward as time passes. There are also matching policies that can be used to apply standardization on the data. You will learn more about DQS in *Chapter 6, Data Quality and Data Cleansing*.

Building the data warehouse

A data warehouse is a database built for analysis and reporting. In other words, a data warehouse is a database in which the only data entry point is through ETL, and its primary purpose is to cover reporting and data analysis requirements. This definition clarifies that a data warehouse is not like other transactional databases that operational systems write data into. When there is no operational system that works directly with a data warehouse, and when the main purpose of this database is for reporting, then the design of the data warehouse will be different from that of transactional databases.

If you recall from the database normalization concepts, the main purpose of normalization is to reduce the redundancy and dependency. The following table shows customers' data with their geographical information:

Customer first name	Last name	Suburb	City	State	Country
Devin	Batler	Remuera	Auckland	Auckland	New Zealand
Peter	Blade	Remuera	Auckland	Auckland	New Zealand
Lance	Martin	City Center	Sydney	NSW	Australia

Let's elaborate on this example. As you can see from the preceding list, the geographical information in the records is redundant. This redundancy makes it difficult to apply changes. For example, in the structure, if **Remuera**, for any reason, is no longer part of the **Auckland** city, then the change should be applied on every record that has **Remuera** as part of its suburb. The following screenshot shows the tables of geographical information:

Custom▼	Father ▼	Geo ▼
Devin	Batler	11
Peter	Blade	11
Lance	Martin	12

Suburb ▼	City ▼	State ▼	Country ▼	Key ▼
Remuera	Auckland	Auckland	New Zealand	11
City Cente	Sydney	NSW	Australia	12

So, a normalized approach is to retrieve the geographical information from the customer table and put it into another table. Then, only a key to that table would be pointed from the customer table. In this way, every time the value **Remuera** changes, only one record in the geographical region changes and the key number remains unchanged. So, you can see that normalization is highly efficient in transactional systems.

This normalization approach is not that effective on analytical databases. If you consider a sales database with many tables related to each other and normalized at least up to the third normalized form (3NF), then analytical queries on such databases may require more than 10 join conditions, which slows down the query response. In other words, from the point of view of reporting, it would be better to denormalize data and flatten it in order to make it easier to query data as much as possible. This means the first design in the preceding table might be better for reporting.

However, the query and reporting requirements are not that simple, and the business domains in the database are not as small as two or three tables. So real-world problems can be solved with a special design method for the data warehouse called dimensional modeling. There are two well-known methods for designing the data warehouse: the Kimball and Inmon methodologies.

The Inmon and Kimball methods are named after the owners of these methodologies. Both of these methods are in use nowadays. The main difference between these methods is that Inmon is top-down and Kimball is bottom-up. In this chapter, we will explain the Kimball method. You can read more about the Inmon methodology in *Building the Data Warehouse, William H. Inmon, Wiley* (http://www.amazon.com/Building -Data-Warehouse-W-Inmon/dp/0764599445), and about the Kimball methodology in *The Data Warehouse Toolkit, Ralph Kimball, Wiley* (http://www.amazon.com/The -Data-Warehouse-Toolkit-Dimensional/dp/0471200247). Both of these books are must-read books for BI and DW professionals and are reference books that are recommended to be on the bookshelf of all BI teams. This chapter is referenced from *The Data Warehouse Toolkit*, so for a detailed discussion, read the referenced book.

Dimensional modeling

To gain an understanding of data warehouse design and dimensional modeling, it's better to learn about the components and terminologies of a DW. A DW consists of Fact tables and dimensions. The relationship between a Fact table and dimensions are based on the foreign key and primary key (the primary key of the dimension table is addressed in the fact table as the foreign key).

Fact or measure

Facts are numeric and additive values in the business process. For example, in the sales business, a fact can be a sales amount, discount amount, or quantity of items sold. All of these measures or facts are numeric values and they are additive. Additive means that you can add values of some records together and it provides a meaning. For example, adding the sales amount for all records is the grand total of sales.

Dimension

Dimension tables are tables that contain descriptive information. Descriptive information, for example, can be a customer's name, job title, company, and even geographical information of where the customer lives. Each dimension table contains a list of columns, and the columns of the dimension table are called attributes. Each attribute contains some descriptive information, and attributes that are related to each other will be placed in a dimension. For example, the customer dimension would contain the attributes listed earlier.

Each dimension has a primary key, which is called the surrogate key. The surrogate key is usually an auto increment integer value. The primary key of the source system will be stored in the dimension table as the business key.

The Fact table

The Fact table is a table that contains a list of related facts and measures with foreign keys pointing to surrogate keys of the dimension tables. Fact tables usually store a large number of records, and most of the data warehouse space is filled by them (around 80 percent).

Grain

Grain is one of the most important terminologies used to design a data warehouse. Grain defines a level of detail that stores the Fact table. For example, you could build a data warehouse for sales in which Grain is the most detailed level of transactions in the retail shop, that is, one record per each transaction in the specific date and time for the customer and sales person. Understanding Grain is important because it defines which dimensions are required.

The star schema

There are two different schemas for creating a relationship between fact and dimensions: the snow flake and star schema. In the start schema, a Fact table will be at the center as a hub, and dimensions will be connected to the fact through a single-level relationship. There won't be (ideally) a dimension that relates to the fact through another dimension. The following diagram shows the different schemas:

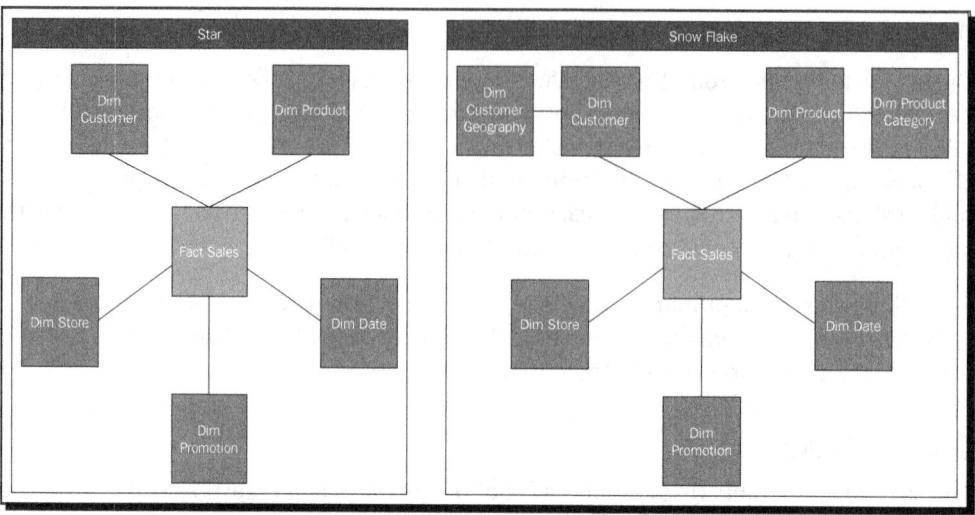

The snow flake schema, as you can see in the preceding diagram, contains relationships of some dimensions through intermediate dimensions to the Fact table. If you look more carefully at the snow flake schema, you may find it more similar to the normalized form, and the truth is that a fully snow flaked design of the fact and dimensions will be in the 3NF.

The snow flake schema requires more joins to respond to an analytical query, so it would respond slower. Hence, the star schema is the preferred design for the data warehouse. It is obvious that you cannot build a complete star schema and sometimes you will be required to do a level of snow flaking. However, the best practice is to always avoid snow flaking as much as possible.

An example of Internet sales

After a quick definition of the most common terminologies in dimensional modeling, it's now time to start designing a small data warehouse. One of the best ways of learning a concept and method is to see how it will be applied to a sample question.

Assume that you want to build a data warehouse for the sales part of a business that contains a chain of supermarkets; each supermarket sells a list of products to customers, and the transactional data is stored in an operational system. Our mission is to build a data warehouse that is able to analyze the sales information.

Before thinking about the design of the data warehouse, the very first question is what is the goal of designing a data warehouse? What kind of analytical reports would be required as the result of the BI system? The answer to these questions is the first and also the most important step. This step not only clarifies the scope of the work but also provides you with the clue about the Grain.

Defining the goal can also be called requirement analysis. Your job as a data warehouse designer is to analyze required reports, KPIs, and dashboards. Let's assume that the decision maker of a particular supermarket chain wants to have analytical reports such as the comparison of sales between stores, or the top 10 customers and/or top 10 bestselling products, or he wants to compare the sale on weekdays with weekends.

After requirement analysis, the dimensional modeling phases will start. Based on Kimball's best practices, dimensional modeling can be done in the following four steps:

1. Choosing the business process.
2. Identifying the Grain.
3. Designing dimension.s
4. Designing facts.

In our example, there is only one business process, that is, sales. Grain, as we've described earlier, is the level of detail that will be stored in the Fact table. Based on the requirement, Grain is to have one record per sales transaction and date, per customer, per product, and per store.

Once Grain is defined, it is easy to identify dimensions. Based on the Grain, the dimensions would be date, store, customer, and product. It is useful to name dimensions with a `Dim` prefix to identify them easily in the list of tables. So our dimensions will be `DimCustomer`, `DimProduct`, `DimDate`, and `DimStore`. The next step is to identify the Fact table, which would be a single Fact table named `FactSales`. This table will store the defined Grain.

After identifying the Fact and dimension tables, it's time to go more in detail about each table and think about the attributes of the dimensions, and measures of the Fact table. Next, we will get into the details of the Fact table and then into each dimension.

FactSales

There is only one Grain for this business process, and this means that one Fact table would be required. Based on the provided Grain, a Fact table would be connected to **DimCustomer**, **DimDate**, **DimProduct**, and **DimStore**. To connect to each dimension, there would be a foreign key in the Fact table that points to the primary key of the dimension table.

The table would also contain measures or facts. For the sales business process, facts that can be measured (numeric and additive) are SalesAmount, DiscountAmount, and QuantitySold. The Fact table would only contain relationships to other dimensions and measures. The following diagram shows some columns of the **FactSales**:

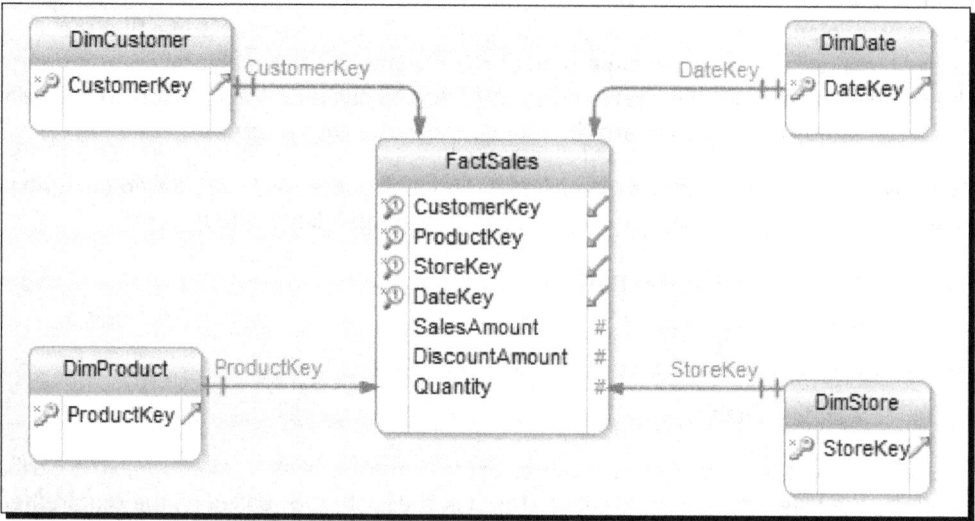

As you can see, the preceding diagram shows a star schema. We will go through the dimensions in the next step to explore them more in detail. Fact tables usually don't have too many columns because the number of measures and related tables won't be that much. However, Fact tables will contain many records. The Fact table in our example will store one record per transaction.

As the Fact table will contain millions of records, you should think about the design of this table carefully. The String data types are not recommended in the Fact table because they won't add any numeric or additive value to the table. The relationship between a Fact table and dimensions could also be based on the surrogate key of the dimension. The best practice is to set a data type of surrogate keys as the integer; this will be cost-effective in terms of the required disk space in the Fact table because the integer data type takes only 4 bytes while the string data type is much more. Using an integer as a surrogate key also speeds up the join between a fact and a dimension because join and criteria will be based on the integer that operators works with, which is much faster than a string.

If you are thinking about adding comments in this made by a sales person to the sales transaction as another column of the Fact table, first think about the analysis that you want to do based on comments. No one does analysis based on a free text field; if you wish to do an analysis on a free text, you can categorize the text values through the ETL process and build another dimension for that. Then, add the foreign key-primary key relationship between that dimension to the Fact table.

The customer dimension

The customer's information, such as the customer name, customer job, customer city, and so on, will be stored in this dimension. You may think that the customer city is, as another dimension, a Geo dimension. But the important note is that our goal in dimensional modeling is not normalization. So resist against your tendency to normalize tables. For a data warehouse, it would be much better if we store more customer-related attributes in the customer dimension itself rather than designing a snow flake schema. The following diagram shows sample columns of the DimCustomer table:

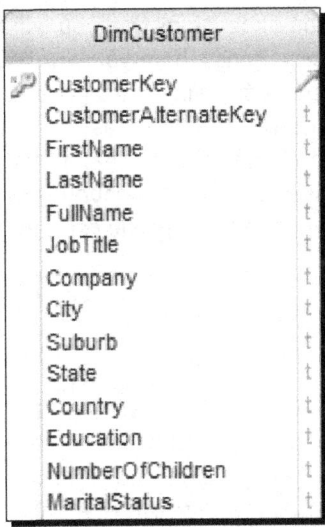

The DimCustomer dimension may contain many more attributes. The number of attributes in your dimensions is usually high. Actually, a dimension table with a high number of attributes is the power of your data warehouse because attributes will be your filter criteria in the analysis, and the user can slice and dice data by attributes. So, it is good to think about all possible attributes for that dimension and add them in this step.

As we've discussed earlier, you see attributes such as **Suburb**, **City**, **State**, and **Country** inside the customer dimension. This is not a normalized design, and this design definitely is not a good design for a transactional database because it adds redundancy, and making changes won't be consistent. However, for the data warehouse design, not only is redundancy unimportant but it also speeds up analytical queries and prevents snow flaking.

You can also see two keys for this dimension: `CustomerKey` and `CustomerAlternateKey`. The `CustomerKey` is the surrogate key and primary key for the dimension in the data warehouse. The `CustomerKey` is an integer field, which is autoincremented. It is important that the surrogate key won't be encoded or taken as a string key; if there is something coded somewhere, then it should be decoded and stored into the relevant attributes. The surrogate key should be different from the primary key of the table in the source system. There are multiple reasons for that; for example, sometimes, operational systems recycle their primary keys, which means they reuse a key value for a customer that is no longer in use to a new customer.

`CustomerAlternateKey` is the primary key of the source system. It is important to keep the primary key of the source system stored in the dimension because it would be necessary to identify changes from the source table and apply them into the dimension. The primary key of the source system will be called the business key or alternate key.

DimDate

The date dimension is one of the dimensions that you will find in most of the business processes. There may be rare situations where you work with a Fact table that doesn't store date-related information. `DimDate` contains many generic columns such as **FullDate**, **Month**, **Year**, **Quarter**, and **MonthName**. This is obvious as you can fetch all other columns out of the full date column with some date functions, but that will add extra time for processing. So, at the time of designing dimensions, don't think about spaces and add as many attributes as required. The following diagram shows sample columns of the date dimension:

It would be useful to store holidays, weekdays, and weekends in the date dimension because in sales figures, a holiday or weekend will definitely affect the sales transactions and amounts. So, the user will require an understanding of why the sale is higher on a specific date rather than on other days. You may also add another attribute for promotions in this example, which states whether that specific date is a promotion date or not.

The date dimension will have a record for each date. The table, shown in the following screenshot, shows sample records of the date dimension:

DateKey	DateFullName	DateFull	Year	Quarter	QuarterName	QuarterKey	Month	MonthKey	MonthName	DayOfMonth	NumberOfDaysInTheMonth	DayOfYear	WeekOfYear
20130521	21 May 2013	2013-05-21	2013	2	QTR 2	20132	5	201305	May	21	31	141	21
20130522	22 May 2013	2013-05-22	2013	2	QTR 2	20132	5	201305	May	22	31	142	21
20130523	23 May 2013	2013-05-23	2013	2	QTR 2	20132	5	201305	May	23	31	143	21
20130524	24 May 2013	2013-05-24	2013	2	QTR 2	20132	5	201305	May	24	31	144	21
20130525	25 May 2013	2013-05-25	2013	2	QTR 2	20132	5	201305	May	25	31	145	21
20130526	26 May 2013	2013-05-26	2013	2	QTR 2	20132	5	201305	May	26	31	146	22
20130527	27 May 2013	2013-05-27	2013	2	QTR 2	20132	5	201305	May	27	31	147	22
20130528	28 May 2013	2013-05-28	2013	2	QTR 2	20132	5	201305	May	28	31	148	22
20130529	29 May 2013	2013-05-29	2013	2	QTR 2	20132	5	201305	May	29	31	149	22
20130530	30 May 2013	2013-05-30	2013	2	QTR 2	20132	5	201305	May	30	31	150	22
20130531	31 May 2013	2013-05-31	2013	2	QTR 2	20132	5	201305	May	31	31	151	22
20130601	01 Jun 2013	2013-06-01	2013	2	QTR 2	20132	6	201306	June	1	30	152	22
20130602	02 Jun 2013	2013-06-02	2013	2	QTR 2	20132	6	201306	June	2	30	153	23
20130603	03 Jun 2013	2013-06-03	2013	2	QTR 2	20132	6	201306	June	3	30	154	23
20130604	04 Jun 2013	2013-06-04	2013	2	QTR 2	20132	6	201306	June	4	30	155	23
20130605	05 Jun 2013	2013-06-05	2013	2	QTR 2	20132	6	201306	June	5	30	156	23
20130606	06 Jun 2013	2013-06-06	2013	2	QTR 2	20132	6	201306	June	6	30	157	23
20130607	07 Jun 2013	2013-06-07	2013	2	QTR 2	20132	6	201306	June	7	30	158	23

As you can see in the records illustrated in the preceding screenshot, the surrogate of the date dimension (DateKey) shows a meaningful value. This is one of the rare exceptions where we can keep the surrogate key of this dimension as an integer type but with the format of YYYYMMDD to represent a meaning as well.

In this example, if we store time information, where do you think would be the place for time attributes? Inside the date dimension? Definitely not. The date dimension will store one record per day, so a date dimension will have 365 records per year and 3650 records for 10 years. Now, we add time splits to this, down to the last minute, and then we would require *24*60* records per day. So, the combination of the date and time for 10 years would have *3650*24*60= 5265000* records. However, 5 million records for a single dimension are too much; dimensions are usually narrow and they occasionally might have more than one million records. So in this case, the best practice would be to add another dimension as DimTime and add all time-related attributes in that dimension. The following screenshot shows some example records and attributes of DimTime:

TimeKey	Hour24	Hour24ShortString	Hour24MinString	Hour24FullString	Hour12	Hour12ShortString	Hour12MinString	Hour12FullString	AmPmCode	AmPmString	Minute
200201	20	20	20:00	20:00:00	8	08	08:00	08:00:00	1	PM	2
200202	20	20	20:00	20:00:00	8	08	08:00	08:00:00	1	PM	2
200203	20	20	20:00	20:00:00	8	08	08:00	08:00:00	1	PM	2
200204	20	20	20:00	20:00:00	8	08	08:00	08:00:00	1	PM	2
200205	20	20	20:00	20:00:00	8	08	08:00	08:00:00	1	PM	2
200206	20	20	20:00	20:00:00	8	08	08:00	08:00:00	1	PM	2
200207	20	20	20:00	20:00:00	8	08	08:00	08:00:00	1	PM	2
200208	20	20	20:00	20:00:00	8	08	08:00	08:00:00	1	PM	2
200209	20	20	20:00	20:00:00	8	08	08:00	08:00:00	1	PM	2
200210	20	20	20:00	20:00:00	8	08	08:00	08:00:00	1	PM	2
200211	20	20	20:00	20:00:00	8	08	08:00	08:00:00	1	PM	2
200212	20	20	20:00	20:00:00	8	08	08:00	08:00:00	1	PM	2
200213	20	20	20:00	20:00:00	8	08	08:00	08:00:00	1	PM	2
200214	20	20	20:00	20:00:00	8	08	08:00	08:00:00	1	PM	2
200215	20	20	20:00	20:00:00	8	08	08:00	08:00:00	1	PM	2
200216	20	20	20:00	20:00:00	8	08	08:00	08:00:00	1	PM	2
200217	20	20	20:00	20:00:00	8	08	08:00	08:00:00	1	PM	2
200218	20	20	20:00	20:00:00	8	08	08:00	08:00:00	1	PM	2
200219	20	20	20:00	20:00:00	8	08	08:00	08:00:00	1	PM	2

Usually, the date and time dimensions are generic and static, so you won't be required to populate these dimensions through ETL every night; you just load them once and then you could use them. I've written two general-purpose scripts to create and populate date and time dimensions on my blog that you can use. For the date dimension, visit the `http://www.rad.pasfu.com/index.php?/archives/95-Script-for-Creating-and-Generating-members-for-Date-Dimensions-General-Purpose.html` URL, and for the time dimension, visit the `http://www.rad.pasfu.com/index.php?/archives/122-Script-for-Creating-and-Generating-members-for-Time-Dimension.html` URL.

DimProduct

The product dimension will have a `ProductKey`, which is the surrogate key, and the business key, which will be the primary key of the product in the source system (something similar to a product's unique number). The product dimension will also have information about the product categories. Again, denormalization in dimensions occurred in this case for the product subcategory, and the category will be placed into the product dimension with redundant values. However, this decision was made in order to avoid snow flaking and raise the performance of the join between the fact and dimensions.

DimStore

We are not going to go in detail through the attributes of the store dimension. The most important part of this dimension is that it can have a relationship to the date dimension. For example, a store's opening date will be a key related to the date dimension. This type of snow flaking is unavoidable because you cannot copy all the date dimension's attributes in every other dimension that relates to it. On the other hand, the date dimension is in use with many other dimensions and facts. So, it would be better to have a conformed date dimension. `Outrigger` is a Kimball terminology for dimensions, such as date, which is conformed and might be used for a many-to-one relationship between dimensions for just one layer.

Types of facts

In the previous example, you learned about transactional fact. Transactional fact is a fact table that has one record per transaction. This type of fact table usually has the most detailed Grain.

There is also another type of fact, which is the snapshot Fact table. In snapshot fact, each record will be an aggregation of some transactional records for a snapshot period of time. For example, consider financial periods; you can create a snapshot Fact table with one record for each financial period, and the details of the transactions will be aggregated into that record.

Transactional facts are a good source for detailed and atomic reports. They are also good for aggregations and dashboards. The Snapshot Fact tables provide a very fast response for dashboards and aggregated queries, but they don't cover detailed transactional records. Based on your requirement analysis, you can create both kinds of facts or only one of them.

There is also another type of Fact table called the accumulating Fact table. This Fact table is useful for storing processes and activities, such as order management. You can read more about different types of Fact tables in *The Data Warehouse Toolkit*, *Ralph Kimball*, *Wiley* (which was referenced earlier in this chapter).

The Factless Fact table – The Bridge table

We've explained that Fact tables usually contain FKs of dimensions and some measures. However, there are times when you would require a Fact table without any measure. These types of Fact tables are usually used to show the non-existence of a fact.

For example, assume that the sales business process does promotions as well, and you have a promotion dimension. So, each entry in the Fact table shows that a customer X purchased a product Y at a date Z from a store S when the promotion P was on (such as the new year's sales). This Fact table covers every requirement that queries the information about the sales that happened, or in other words, for transactions that happened. However, there are times when the promotion is on but no transaction happens! This is a valuable analytical report for the decision maker because they would understand the situation and investigate to find out what was wrong with that promotion that doesn't cause sales.

So, this is an example of a requirement that the existing Fact table with the sales amount and other measures doesn't fulfill. We would need a Fact table that shows that store S did the promotion P on the date D for product X. This Fact table doesn't have any fact or measure related to it; it just has FKs for dimensions. However, it is very informative because it tells us on which dates there was a promotion at specific stores on specific products. We call this Fact table as a Factless Fact table or Bridge table.

Types of dimensions

Using examples, we've explored the usual dimensions such as customer and date. When a dimension participates in more than one business process and deals with different data marts (such as date), then it will be called a conformed dimension.

Sometimes, a dimension is required to be used in the Fact table more than once. For example, in the **FactSales** table, you may want to store the order date, shipping date, and transaction date. All these three columns will point to the date dimension. In this situation, we won't create three separate dimensions; instead, we will reuse the existing `DimDate` three times as three different names. So, the date dimension literally plays the role of more than one dimension. This is the reason we call such dimensions role-playing dimensions.

There are other types of dimensions with some differences, such as junk dimension and degenerate dimension. The junk dimension will be used for dimensions with very narrow member values (records) that will be in use for almost one data mart (not conformed). For example, the status dimensions can be good candidates for junk dimension. If you create a status dimension for each situation in each data mart, then you will probably have more than ten status dimensions with only less than five records in each. The junk dimension is a solution to combine such narrow dimensions together and create a bigger dimension.

You may or may not use a junk dimension in your data mart because using junk dimensions reduces readability, and not using it will increase the number of narrow dimensions. So, the usage of this is based on the requirement analysis phase and the dimensional modeling of the star schema.

A degenerate dimension is another type of dimension, which is not a separate dimension table. In other words, a degenerate dimension doesn't have a table and it sits directly inside the Fact table. Assume that you want to store the transaction number (string value). Where do you think would be the best place to add that information? You may think that you would create another dimension and enter the transaction number there and assign a surrogate key and use that surrogate key in the Fact table. This is not an ideal solution because that dimension will have exactly the same Grain as your Fact table, and this indicates that the number of records for your sales transaction dimension will be equal to the Fact table, so you will have a very deep dimension table, which is not recommended. On the other hand, you cannot think about another attribute for that dimension because all attributes related to the sales transaction already exist in other dimensions connected to the fact. So, instead of creating a dimension with the same Grain as the fact and with only one column, we would leave that column (even if it is a string) inside the Fact table. This type of dimension will be called a degenerate dimension.

Slowly Changing Dimension

Now that you understand dimensions, it is a good time to go into more detail about the most challengeable concepts of data warehousing, which is **slowly changing dimension (SCD)**. The dimension's attribute values may change depending on the requirement. You will do different actions to respond to that change. As the changes in the dimension's attribute values happen occasionally, this called the slowly changing dimension. SCD depends on the action to be taken after the change is split in different types. In this section, we only discuss type 0, 1, and 2.

SCD type 0

Type 0 doesn't accept any changes. Let's assume that the **Employee Number** is inside the Employee dimension. **Employee Number** is the business key and it is an important attribute for ETL because ETL distinguishes new employees or existing employees based on this field. So we don't accept any changes in this attribute. This means that type 0 of SCD is applied on this attribute.

SCD type 1

Sometimes, a value may be typed wrongly in the source system, such as the first name, and it is likely that someone will come and fix that with a change. In such cases, we will accept the change, and we won't need to keep historical information (the previous name). So we simply replace the existing value with a new value. This type of SCD is called type 1. The following screenshot shows how type 1 works:

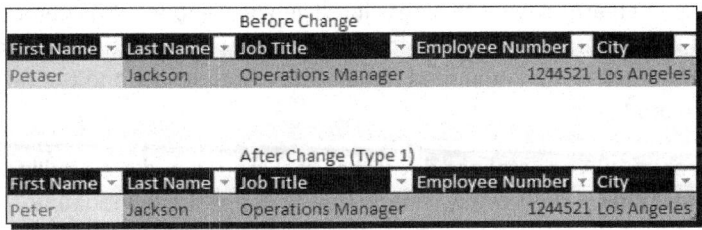

SCD type 2

In this type, it is a common requirement to maintain historical changes. For example, consider this situation; a customer recently changes their city from Seattle to Charlotte. You cannot use type 0 because it is likely that someone will change their city of living. If you behave like type 1 and update the existing record, then you will miss the information of the customer's purchase at the time that they were in Seattle, and all entries will show that they are customers from Charlotte. So the requirement for keeping the historical version resulted in the third type of SCD, which is type 2.

Type 2 is about maintaining historical changes. The way to keep historical changes is through a couple of metadata columns: `FromDate` and `ToDate`. Each new customer will be imported into `DimCustomer` with `FromDate` as a start date, and the `ToDate` will be left as null (or a big default value such as 29,990,101). If a change happens in the city, the existing records in `ToDate` will be marked as the date of change, and a new record will be created as an exact copy of the previous record with the new city and with a new `FromDate`, which will be the date of change, and the `ToDate` field will be left as null. Using this solution to find the latest and most up-to-date member information, you just need to look for the member record with `ToDate` as null. To fetch the historical information, you would need to search for it in the specified time span whether the historical record exists. The following screenshot shows an example of SCD type 2:

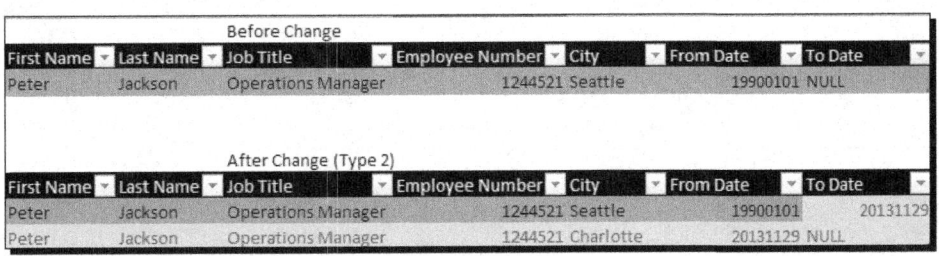

There are other types of SCD that are based on combinations of the first three types and cover other kinds of requirements. You can read more about the different types of SCD and methods of implementing them in *The Data Warehouse Toolkit* referenced earlier in this chapter.

Summary

In this chapter, you learned what Business Intelligence is and what its components are. You studied the requirement for BI systems, and you saw the solution architecture to solve the requirements. Then, you read about data warehousing and the terminologies in dimensional modeling.

If you come from a DBA or database developer background and are familiar with database normalization, then you will know that in dimensional modeling, you should avoid normalization in some parts and you would need to design a star schema. You've learned that the Fact table shows numeric and additive values, and descriptive information will be stored in dimensions. You've learned different types of facts such as transactional, snapshot, and accumulating, and also learned about different types of dimensions such as outriggers, role playing, and degenerate.

Data warehousing and dimensional modeling together constitute the most important part of the BI system, which is sometimes called the core of the system. In the following chapters, we will go through some of the BI system components such as ETL, OLAP, Dashboards, and reports.

2

SQL Server Analysis Services Multidimensional Cube Development

*In the previous chapter, you learned how to design a data warehouse. In this chapter, you will learn how to create an **OnLine Analytical Processing (OLAP)** cube with the help of Microsoft **SQL Server Analysis Services (SSAS)** from an existing data warehouse. OLAP means loading data from a data warehouse into a file structure that makes it much faster to access measures in different granular levels. OLAP cubes also provide much better navigation through hierarchical structures, and slicing and dicing becomes much easier.*

In this chapter, you will understand how to develop SSAS cubes and how to create hierarchies and calculated measures. MDX, which is the query and calculation language of SSAS Multidimensional, will be introduced. You will also read about the deployment of OLAP cubes on the server and the processing of cubes to get data loaded into the OLAP structure. Creating an OLAP cube is an important step in a BI system because it will provide the just mentioned benefits.

Why is OLAP required?

OLAP is a data structure that provides multidimensional cubes from data and provides useful information for decision makers. While designing an OLAP system, the most important factor is reporting requirements. Compared to **OnLine Transactional Processing (OLTP)**, OLAP provides faster reports because it reshapes data in cube structures rather than the traditional relational structure based on tables.

As an example, assume that you want to create a report in a BI system for sales based on products and dates. You might need to get the sales amount per day, per month, or per year. You might also have categories of products. So, it will be helpful if you have a graph with two dimensions, **Product** as one dimension and **Date** as another dimension:

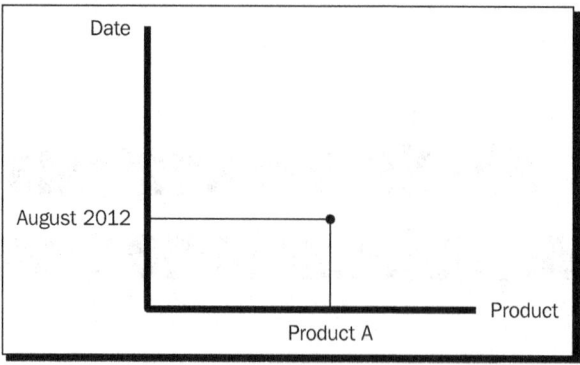

Having two dimensions helps to achieve each granular point and each conjunction of both dimensions easier and faster. For example, point **A** shows the total sales amount of **ProductA** in **August 2012**. Each point in the preceding graph is a measure, and each line shows a dimension attribute.

Now, assume that the report needs another dimension, **Store**. Also, the **Store** dimension might have its own attributes and hierarchies as well, for example, types of stores and branches of stores. So, you will need a graph with three axes as shown in the following diagram:

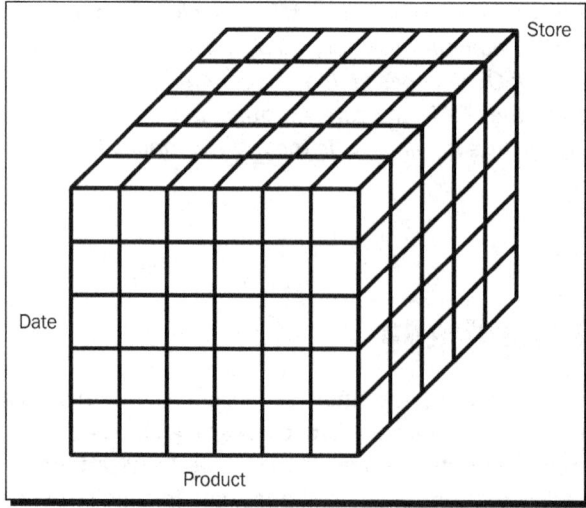

The structure shown in the previous diagram helps you to find the junction of the three dimensions in every granular level of the defined attributes. For example, the total sales amount of ProductA in August 2012 in a New Zealand store is a point of junction of three axes of each value represented together in the cube shown in the previous diagram. This structure is also called a cube. This is how the OLAP cube is named: the dimensions are axes of the cube and the measures are connection points of it.

In real-world requirements, you might need many more than three dimensions for some reports and analytics, so the real-world structure of cubes will have more than three dimensions, but they cannot be illustrated on paper so we cannot show you a sample of cube with eleven dimensions.

The OLAP tools are utilities that provide the ability to create an OLAP cube structure, and then data will be loaded into that structure. After loading data into that structure, which is called processing, information can be easily gathered from data by querying each point or conjunction of the cube axis.

Understanding the SQL Server Analysis Services engine

Microsoft SQL Server released Analysis Services in 2000 as an OLAP cube tool. This tool is a mature service of Microsoft technologies in BI that provides the ability to develop cubes and create dimensions and measures. Creating hierarchies (such as the product category hierarchy) based on attributes of dimensions are also possible within SSAS.

Microsoft introduced a new language named MDX to query the SSAS cube. This querying language has the ability to query cube-structured data and work with hierarchies. Also, many Microsoft-reporting and dashboard tools support this language.

Bottom of text cut off **BI Semantic Model (BISM)** in SQL Server 2012. BISM is the data modeling layer between the source database/data warehouse and the data visualization layer. There are two methods for modeling data in BISM, of which SSAS Multidimensional will be covered in this chapter and SSAS Tabular will be covered in the next chapter.

Take a look at the following diagram:

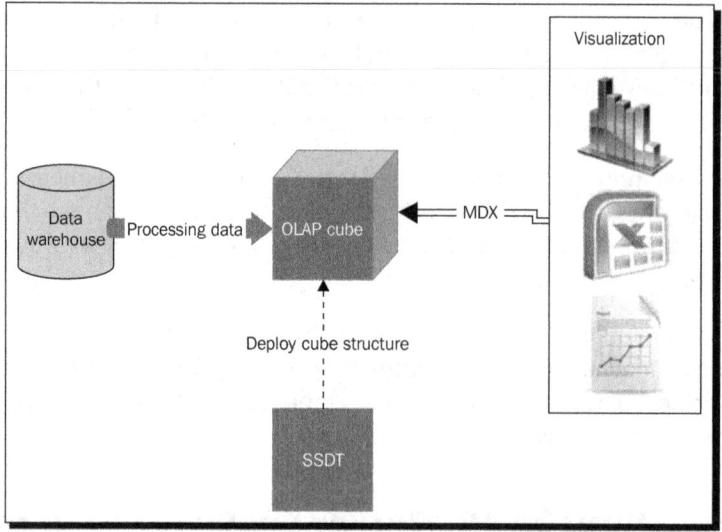

Analysis Services is an engine that runs SSAS databases on the server. After the deployment of an SSAS database (which contains cubes, dimensions, measures, security, and some other information that you will dig into in chapters related to data mining), the metadata and structure of cubes will reside on the SSAS server. Then, a processing step is required to load data from a data warehouse into the SSAS cube structure. This step usually runs on a schedule at the end of ETL processing after loading data into the data warehouse (we will talk about ETL in *Chapter 4, ETL with Integration Services*.

This process will take place when a client wants to get data from a cube. The client tool queries data from the SSAS cube using MDX queries. MDX queries will be compiled, parsed, and executed in the SSAS engine. Hence, some results in a multidimensional format will be returned to the client tools. Then, the reporting client tools, for example, SSAS, will show information to the user as the report and dashboard layout are formatted.

Note that the query will get data from the cube structure and not from the source data warehouse. So the data will be too important in order to load data from the data warehouse into the SSAS cube with a processing step because it will keep data updated and more accurate.

MDX queries will be resolved from the SSAS cube in the MOLAP storage mode. There are other storage modes for SSAS, which are ROLAP and HOLAP. ROLAP resolves queries directly from the source database, while HOLAP is a hybrid method. A detailed discussion on storage modes are outside the scope of this book. You can read more about them at `http://msdn.microsoft.com/library/ms174915.aspx`.

As the data entries will be stored in the cube, data security will be an important aspect. Fortunately, SSAS provides an extensive security mechanism that delivers role-based and row-level security on each cell of the cube, and security can be applied through the administration or development tools. You can read more about SSAS security at `http://technet.microsoft.com/en-us/library/ms174840.aspx`.

Developing your first cube

When you install Microsoft SQL Server BI services such as Analysis Services, you can also install **SQL Server Data Tools (SSDT)**. SSDT is a designer and developer tool for SSAS cubes. SSDT was formerly known as **Business Intelligence Development Studio (BIDS)** in SQL Server 2008R2 and earlier versions.

Time for action – creating an Analysis Services project

In this example and other examples of this book, we will use SSDT for Visual Studio 2012. You can download and install it from `http://www.microsoft.com/en-us/download/details.aspx?id=36843`.

After installation, perform the following steps:

1. Open SQL Server Data Tools by clicking on **Start**, then navigate to your Microsoft SQL Server 2012 folder and under that, choose **SQL Server Data Tools for Visual Studio 2012**.

2. Go to the **File** menu and under **New**, select **Project**.

3. In the **New Project** window, under templates in the left-hand side pane, click on **Analysis Services** and from the list of templates in the main pane, choose **Analysis Services Multidimensional and Data Mining Project**. Name the project Chapter 02 SSAS Multidimensional, as shown in the following screenshot:

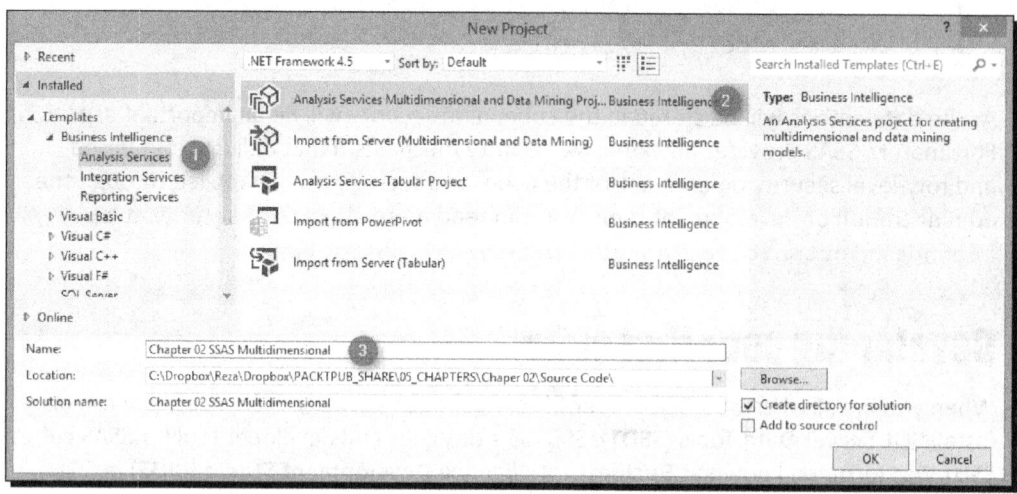

What just happened?

In this example, we used SQL Server Data Tools to create our first Analysis Services project. After creating the project, you will see an empty project with folders listed as follows:

Folder name	Description
Data Sources	This contains source connections to databases
Data Source Views	This contains diagrams of tables and views with relationship and metadata information
Cubes	The OLAP cube
Dimensions	The SSAS database dimensions
Mining Structures	Data Mining structures (refer to *Chapter 7, Data Mining – Descriptive Models in SSAS* and *Chapter 8, Identifying Data Patterns – Predictive Models in SSAS* for more information)
Roles	Security roles and permissions
Miscellaneous	Any other file that is related to this project

Time for action – creating the first cube

There are two ways to create a cube: through **Cube Wizard** or by creating an empty cube. When we create a cube from the wizard, the relationships between measures and dimensions will be created automatically based on the underlying **Data Source View** (DSV) after choosing it. However, if we create a cube from an empty one, we need to set up a relationship between the measure groups and dimensions in the cube designer. In the next example, we create the cube using Cube Wizard.

1. The first step is to create a data source connection. To create a data source connection, right-click on a data sources folder.

2. Open the SSAS project and select **New Data Source**. As shown in the next screenshot, create a connection to the **AdventureWorksDW2012** database. In the **Impersonation Information** field, enter the username and password of a domain/ windows account that has the appropriate permissions for that database. Name the data source `AdventureWorksDW2012`.

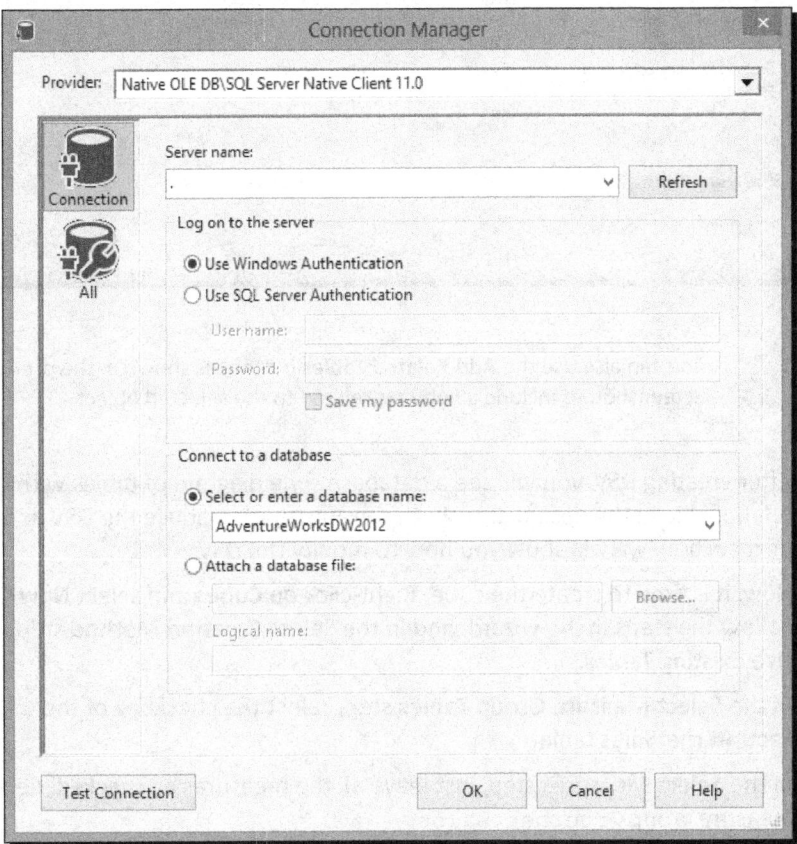

3. There is one more step before creating the cube, and that step is the creation of the Data Source View. Right-click on the `Data Source Views` folder and choose `New Data Source View.` Choose the data source from step 1. In the **Select Tables and View** step, choose the tables as shown in the next screenshot and name the data source view `AdventureWorksDW2012`:

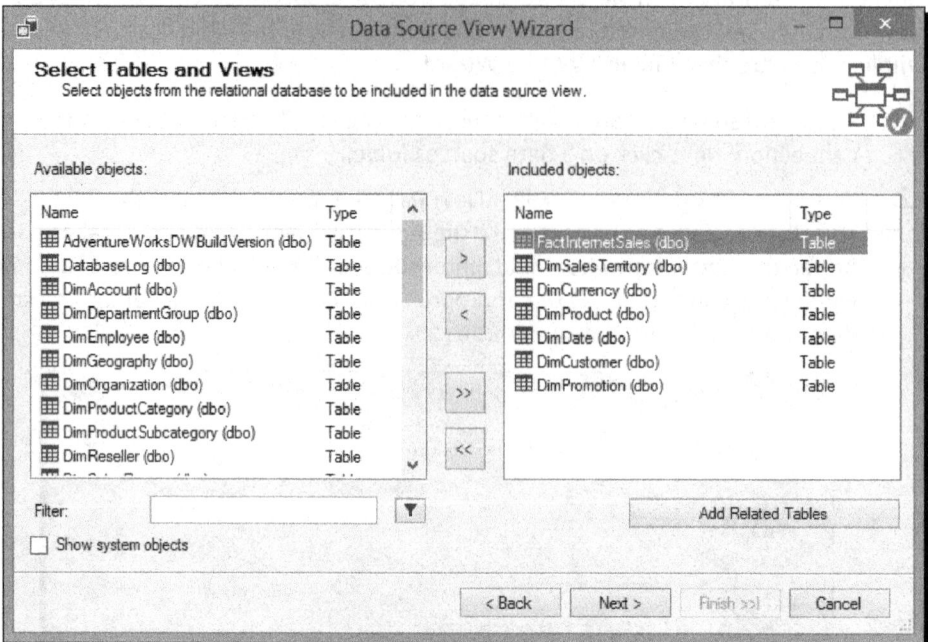

 You can also use the **Add Related Tables** button, as shown in the previous screenshot, to include all objects related to the selected object.

4. After creating DSV, you will see a database style diagram of tables with their relationship in the design area. In this example, we just use the DSV as is, but in the next section, we will show you how to modify the DSV.

5. Now, it is time to create the cube. Right-click on **Cubes** and select **New Cube**. Follow the steps in the wizard, and in the **Select Creation Method** step, choose **Use Existing Tables**.

6. In the **Select Measure Group Tables** step, select the checkbox of the **FactInternetSales** table.

7. In the **Select Measures** step, just leave all the measures as checked. Rename the measure group `Internet Sales`.

8. In the **Select New Dimensions** step, leave all the tables as checked except for **Fact Internet Sales**. Rename all the options in **Dimension** in this step, and remove **Dim** from their name, as shown in the following screenshot:

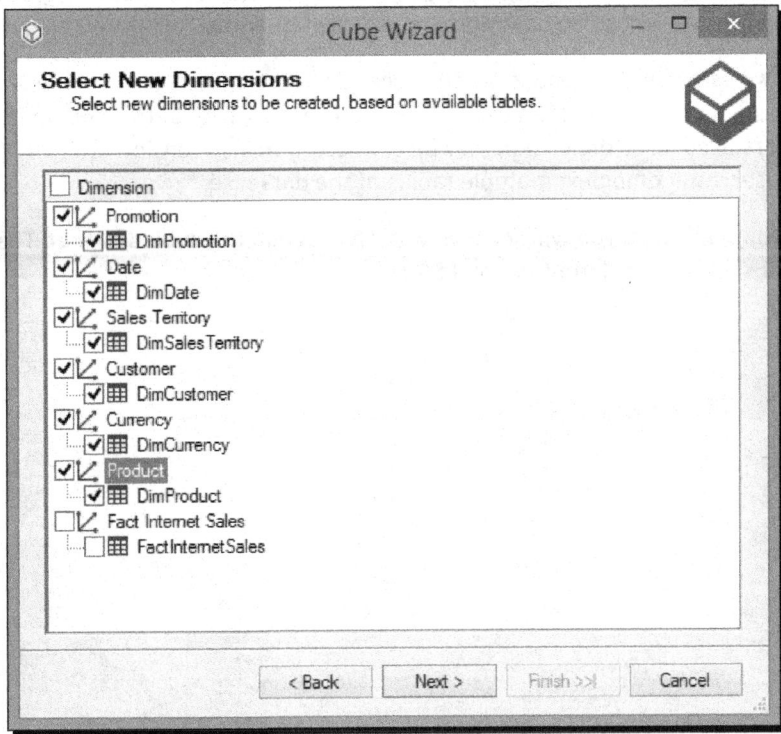

9. Rename the cube Internet Sales.

What just happened?

In the first step of your example, you created a data source connection to a data warehouse. The credential used to create this connection is important because SSAS will use that credential to connect to the underlying database.

In the next step, a DSV is created from the data source. You can add as many tables and views as you want to the data source view; the data source view creates the base structure for cube development.

In steps 4, 5, and 6, you created a cube through **Cube Wizard** from the existing tables in the data source view. To create cubes, you should define your measure groups and dimensions. Measure groups are similar to the Fact tables, each measure group may contain one or more facts. In this example, the **FactInternetSales** table is selected as a measure group, and it contains measures such as **Sales Amount** and **Order Quantity**.

In step 7, we saw that dimensions are the second important items that should be defined when you create the cube. In the example, dimensions such as **Date**, **Product**, and **Sales Territory** are used. Each dimension may be connected to a dimension table in DSV or to a view that is a result of joining multiple tables of the database.

After creating the cube, you will see a view of the cube in the cube designer. The following screenshot shows the different parts of SSDT:

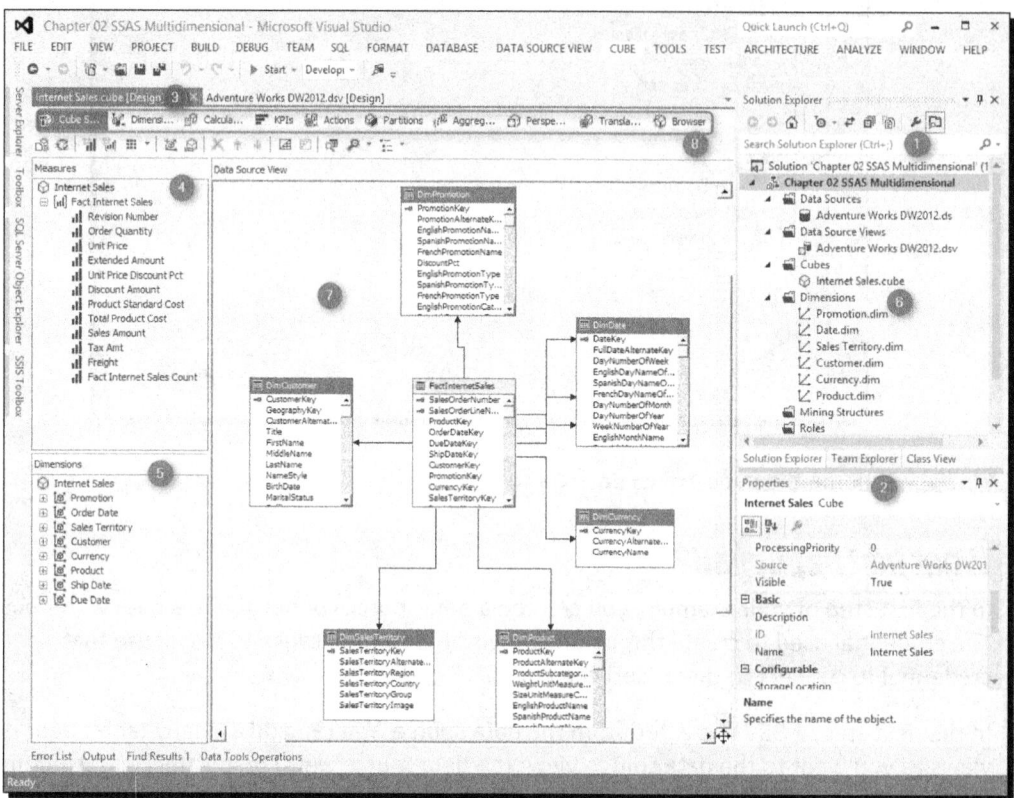

The **Solution Explorer** pane (number **1** in the screenshot) is part of SSDT that shows projects and files, data sources, DSVs, cubes, and other project-related items.

The **Properties** window (number **2** in the screenshot) is the place where you can view and change the properties of the selected object; for example, in the previous screenshot, the **Properties** window shows the properties of the **Internet Sales** cube.

The cube designer (number **3** in the screenshot) is the main designer in the SSDT in which you will spend most of your time as an SSAS developer. Here, you can view the layout of the cube's measure group and dimensions (number **7** in the screenshot); you can go to different tabs (number **8** in the screenshot), such as **Dimension Usage**, **Partitions**, **Browser**, and **KPIs**. We will walk through many of these tabs in this chapter.

A list of the **Measure** groups and their measures (number **4** in the screenshot) can be viewed in the **Cube Structure** tab. You can also see two different lists of dimensions: first is the database's dimensions (number **6** in the screenshot) and second is the cube's dimensions (number **5** in the screenshot). The difference between the cube's and the database's dimension is that there might be some dimensions in the database that are not used in this cube (for example, consider an SSAS project with multiple cubes). On the other hand, there might be a single database dimension that is used multiple times in one cube, which we will call the role-playing dimension (for example, there is only one database dimension, **Date**, but there are three role-playing dimensions in the cube, which are named **Order Date**, **Ship Date**, and **Due Date**).

One of the benefits of creating a cube from a wizard is that it will automatically create all the relationships between the database dimensions and the measure groups, based on the relationship defined in the DSV.

Time for action – viewing the cube in the browser

After creating the cube, you can view it in the cube browser. There are two ways to open the cube browser: through SQL Server Management Studio and through the built-in cube browser in the SSDT. The SSMS cube browser will be useful when we deploy the cube to an SSAS Server (for details on deployment, refer to the *Deploying and processing* section of this chapter). For this example, we use the SSDT cube browser.

To browse the cube, processing is required. Processing is the process of extracting data from a data warehouse, applying the cube's calculations and structures to it, and loading it into the OLAP cube's structure. Perform the following steps to view the cube:

1. In **Solution Explorer**, right-click on the project **Chapter 02 SSAS Multidimensional** and choose **Process**.

2. You will see a dialog box stating **The Server contents appears to be out of date. Would you like to build and deploy the project first?**. Answer it by clicking on **Yes**.

3. In the **Process** window, leave all the configurations as the default and click on **Run**.

4. After completing the **Process Progress** step, close the **Process** window.

5. Go to the **Browser** tab, which is the last tab in the cube designer.

6. If you've got a message saying that the database does not exist or the cube is not up to date, try to reconnect the browser. You can click on the **Reconnect** button, which is the third icon from the top left-hand side of the **Browser** tab.

7. In the **Browser** tab, from the **Metadata** pane, under the **Internet Sales** measures, drag-and-drop **Sales Amount** into the main empty pane in the middle. Do the same for the **Order Quantity** measure.

8. You will see a grand total of **Sales Amount** and **Order Quantity** calculated from the cube.

9. From the **Metadata** pane, under the **Sales Territory** dimension, drag-and-drop **Sales Territory Key** into the main pane as shown in the following screenshot:

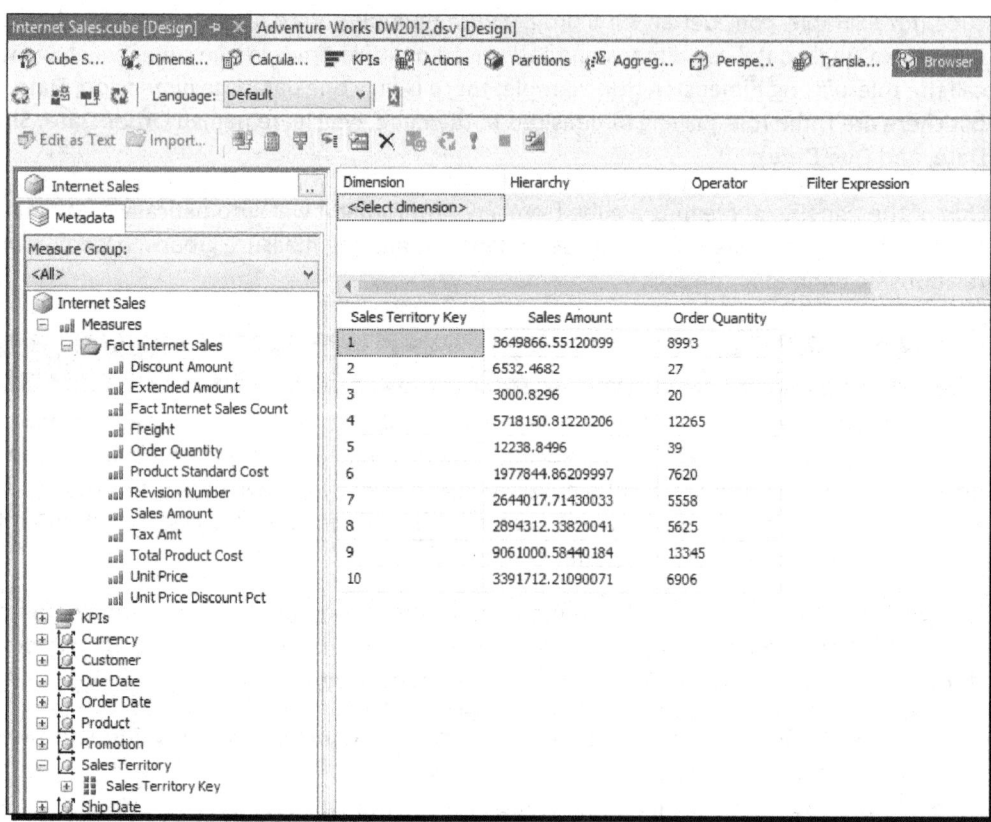

What just happened?

You deployed and processed the cube in the previous example in order to be able to view the cube in the browser. In the last section of this chapter, we will discuss deployment and processing in more detail.

Viewing the cube in the browser of SSDT helps SSAS developers to check the frontend view of the cube from the user's perspective. In this example, you've seen the grand total of **Sales Amount** shown easily with a drag-and-drop in the browser window.

Slicing and dicing the **Sales Amount** by **Sales Territory** is also easily done by dragging-and-dropping the **Sales Territory Key** dimension in the browser. However, you probably noticed that the **Sales Territory** dimension only has one attribute, which is a key, and the key numbers don't make sense for a business user. So, for the next section, we need to bring descriptive information as additional attributes in the **Sales Territory** dimension and other dimensions of the cube.

On the other hand, the **Sales Amount** and **Order Quantity** dimension scan be shown with thousand separators and with a suitable format (for example, currency for the sales amount) in order to be more appropriate from the user's point of view. In the next section, we will change the display format of measures.

Dimensions and measures

At the time of cube development in the SSAS, there might be many times when you would need to make changes to the dimensions and measures. For example, you might need to change the display format of a measure or change the aggregation function of it. For dimensions, you might also need to add/remove an attribute or change the relationship between the attributes. In this section, we will add some attributes to the **Sales Territory** dimension and also make changes in the display format of the measures.

Time for action – using the Dimension Designer

The **Dimension Usage** tab is a specific designer for dimensions in the SSDT. In the next example, you will see how to create new attributes using the Dimension Designer:

1. In the **Solution Explorer**, right under dimensions, double-click on **Sales Territory**.
2. A new designer window will be opened; this designer is called a Dimension Designer.
3. In the **Dimension Structure** tab, drag-and-drop **Sales Territory Region** from the **Data Source View** pane to the **Attributes** pane.
4. Do this for **Sales Territory Group** and **Sales Territory Country** as well.

5. Select **Sales Territory Key** in the **Attributes** pane, and then in the **Properties** window, change the **AttributeHierarchyVisible** property of this attribute to **false**.

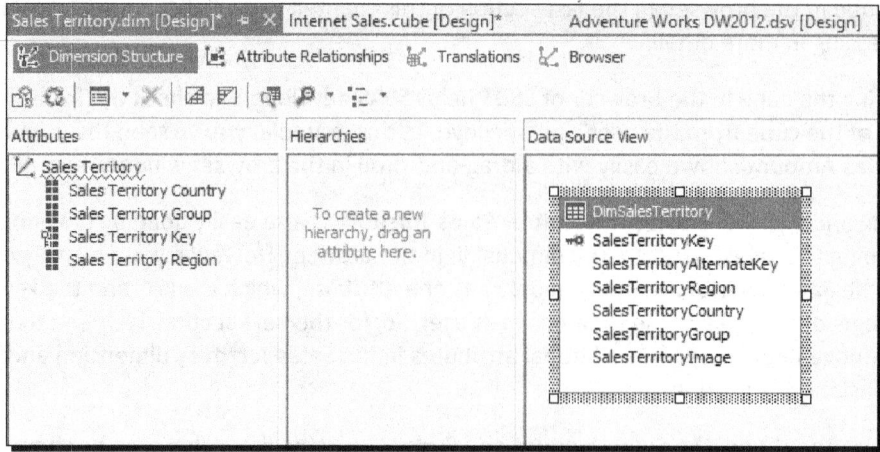

6. Save the changes and process the dimension. You can process the dimension with the **Process** button, which is the second button from the top left-hand side of the dimension structure tab.

7. Go to the **Browser** tab in the Dimension Designer and then reconnect to a process (you can see how to reconnect to a process in the next screenshot). Select **Sales Territory Country** in the hierarchy drop-down list and you will then see the dimension member values listed in the browser:

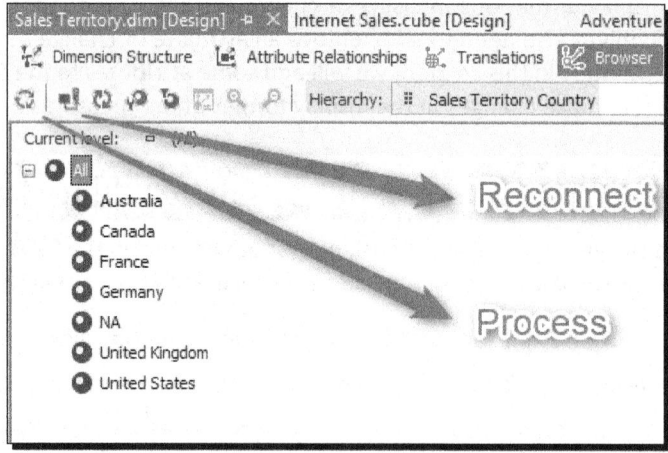

What just happened?

The Dimension Designer used in this example adds new attributes to the **Sales Territory** dimension. To create a new attribute, you can simply drag-and-drop it from the data source view, but sometimes the data source view doesn't contain the appropriate column, which forces you to change the data source view (in the next chapter, you will see how to make changes in the DSV).

You can also change the properties of the dimension attributes in the **Dimension Structure** tab. For example, we changed `AttributeHierarchyVisible` of **Sales Territory Key** to false, and as a result, this attribute was not shown directly in the browser. There are some properties and configurations for each attribute. The following list shows the most useful properties of attributes:

Property	Description
`AttributeHierarchyDisplayFolder`	You can specify a folder name, and the attribute will be listed under that folder name under **Dimension** in the browser.
`AttributeHierarchyEnabled`	As a default function, each attribute creates a hierarchy. Which hierarchy will create separate aggregations is based on each member value. This feature is very useful when you apply it on attributes that have a number of unique values, which is much lower than the number of all the dimension members' values (such as city), but it will be better to disable it for attributes such as the address line that might be different on each record of the dimension.
`AttributeHierarchyVisible`	Controls the visibility of the attribute in the browser for the client tools, but this attribute is still accessible from MDX queries.
`DiscritizationBucketCount`	Number of buckets when you want to discretise a continuous attribute.
`DiscritizationMethod`	Used to choose a discretization method.
`IsAggregatable`	Defines whether the given attribute is aggregatable or not.
`OrderBy`	Defines how to place the attributes in hierarchy according to the order.
`OrderBy Attribute`	Defines the related attributes for which the type of ordering will be executed..
`NameColumn`	This column acts as a label for each member.
`KeyColumns`	This column(s) acts as a key for each member.

To run this example, you need to deploy the changes and the process again; this step is required after each change that you make in the metadata of the SSAS cube, dimension, or measures. For the next example, we will use the `OrderBy` and `OrderBy Attribute` properties to change the ordering of a dimension attribute.

Time for action – change the order of the Month attribute

For this example, we will add some attributes to the date dimension, such as a month attribute, and we will then change the ordering of that attribute to show the correct order as shown in the following steps:

1. Double-click on the **Date** dimension in **Solution Explorer**.

2. In the **Dimension** designer, go to the **Browser** tab; you can see all the members of the **Date Key** attribute there. Members of the **Date Key** attribute are integer values with the YYYYMMDD format. This format is not well formed from the business user's perspective. In this example, we will change this format and also add two other attributes for the year and month.

3. Go to the **Dimension Structure** tab, select **Date Key** in the **Attributes** pane, then in the **Properties** window, click on the ellipsis button of the **NameColumn** property. In the **Name Column** dialog box, select **FullDateAlternateKey** and click on **OK**.

4. Then rename the `Date Key` attribute to `Date`.

5. Drag-and-drop **CalendarYear** from the **Data Source View** pane to the **Attributes** pane.

6. Drag-and-drop **MonthNumberOfYear** from the **Data Source View** pane to the **Attributes** pane.

7. As the **Month Number of Year** view only shows values such as **1, 2,...** **12**, we need to change it to show the month names. So, change the **NameColumn** property of this attribute to **EnglishMonthName**. Also, rename this attribute to `Month`.

8. Process the dimension and go to the **Browser** tab; if you choose **Date** in the hierarchy drop-down list, you will see values such as **2005-01-01**, which is what we want.

9. If you choose **Month** in the hierarchy drop-down list, you will see that the month names are visible, but they are not in the correct order.

10. Go back to the **Dimension Structure** tab. Select the **Month** attribute, and then in the **Properties** window, change the **OrderBy** property to **Key**.

11. Process the dimension and go to **Browser**, and you will see that the month's values are shown in the correct order this time.

What just happened?

In this example, you used two other properties of the dimension attributes. You used those properties to change the order of the values and also to change the display values of an attribute. You also learned how to make changes in the dimension structure and check results in the browser.

In step 3 and step 7, we changed the label value of the attributes with the help of **NameColumn**. While configuring the **NameColumn** property to another column in the data source view, the value of that column will be shown in **Browser**, but the value of the **KeyColumn**(s) will be used in aggregations and calculations. You did that for **Month** and **Date** full format in the preceding example.

Using the **OrderBy** attribute, you changed the order of the **Month** attribute to **Key**. This means that this attribute will be sorted based on **KeyColumn**, and because the **KeyColumn** is **MonthNumberOfYear** and it is an integer value, it will be ordered correctly (refer to step 10). It is also possible to sort one attribute based on another attribute's **Name** or **Key** column (using the **OrderByAttribute** property).

Time for action – modifying the measure properties

After modifying the dimension attribute's properties, it is time to change the measure's properties. Properties such as display format, display folder, and aggregation function can be changed in the **Properties** window. Perform the following steps:

1. In SSDT, go to the **Cube** designer, and in the **Cube structure** tab, select the **Sales Amount** measure. Change the **FormatString** property of this measure to **Currency**.

2. Select the **Order Quantity** measure and change **FormatString** of this measure to **#,##**.

3. Go to the Excel browser; there is an option to view the cube in Excel, and you need to click on **Analyze** in the Excel icon in the browser.

4. In the Excel browser, choose **Sales Amount** and **Order Quantity**, and from **Order Date**, choose **Calendar Year** as shown in the following screenshot:

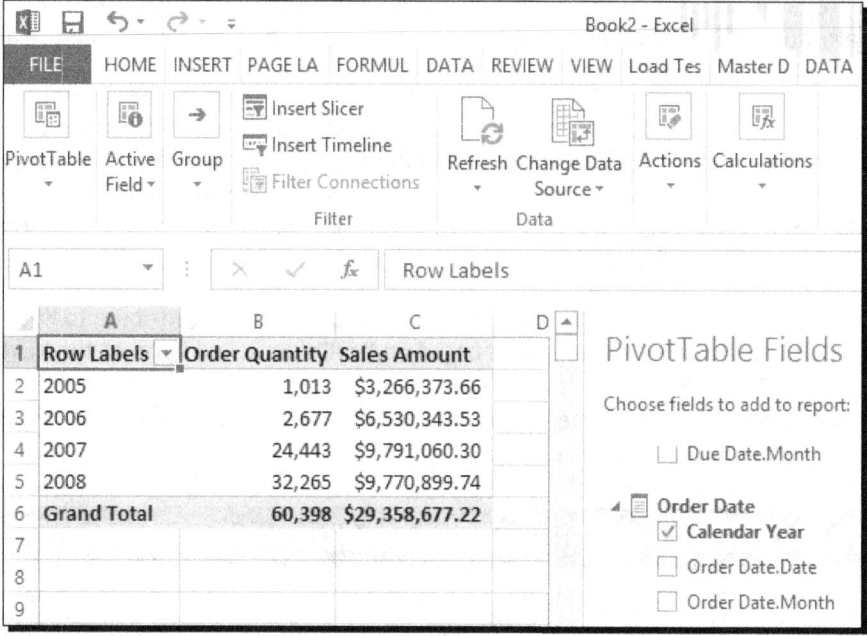

What just happened?

You changed the display format of the measures by configuring the **FormatString** property. You can also change the `AggregationFunction` to `Sum`, `Average`, `Count`, and so on. Also, in this example, you saw a new browser for the Analysis Service cube.

Excel is a great tool for business users; it can connect to the SSAS cube and shows measures and dimension attributes as formatted. Business users are quite familiar with Excel because it can be easily found on every system that has Microsoft Office installed. Also, Excel has many features for filtering and charting, which makes it more comfortable for users to work with data.

Data Source View

In the previous sections, we explained what the **Data Source View** (**DSV**) is and how to create DSV. However, sometimes, there is a requirement to change the DSV. For example, you might want to add a calculated column in the DSV with SQL commands and functions, you might want to create a relationship between two views, or you might need to write a query and create a DSV table based on that query. All of these modifications can be done in the DSV, and in this section, we will go through some of them.

Time for action – creating a Named Calculation

In this exercise, we will create a new calculated column in the DSV for the full name because the customer dimension only contains the first name and last name separately. You will see how we can use T-SQL commands to create a Named Calculation. Perform the following steps to create a Named Calculation.

1. Go to the **Adventure Works DW2012 DSV** designer.

2. In the **Customer** dimension, you can see that there are three name columns as **First name**, **Middle name**, and **Last name**, but there is no full name. We want to have the full name shown as the main customer attribute of the customer dimension in the cube. So, we will create a column in DSV for that.

3. Right-click on **DimCustomer** and select **New Named Calculation**.

4. Set the column name as **Full Name**, and write the following code in the **expression** area:

```
FirstName+' '+ISNULL(MiddleName+' ','')+LastName
```

5. Click on **OK** and you will see the new column added to the table. Right-click on **DimCustomer** and select **Explore Data**. Some sample data rows from the **Customer** table will be shown in another window and you can also see the **Full Name** column populated at the end of the column's list as well.

6. Go to the **Customer** Dimension Designer, select the **Customer Key** attribute, and change the **NameColumn** to **Full Name** from **DimCustomer**. Also, rename the `Customer key` to `Customer`.

7. Browse the **Customer** dimension (after deploying and processing), and you will see that the full name of the customer appears as **Customer Values** in the browser.

What just happened?

Named Calculations are very useful when you want to add calculated columns to the underlying database, but for some reason, you cannot do that in the database. For example, your user account only has read-only permissions on the database. In such cases, you can benefit by creating Named Calculations.

As you've seen in this example, Named Calculations are created based on the **expression** area. The language of the expression is based on the underlying database. This means that if the underlying database is an Oracle database, you can use functions such as `rownum` or `decode`, which work in an Oracle environment. If the underlying database is SQL Server, you can use functions and T-SQL codes that are acceptable in that SQL Server version.

You also saw how to check the result of the execution of Named Calculations with the **Explore Data** option. You can also change the sampling settings for the explored data.

Time for action – using a Named Query

Sometimes, you need to write queries instead of bringing tables and views as is from the database (assume that we don't have access to the underlying database in order to create views or change the structure of tables there). Named Query is a query that runs on the database and its result will be shown as a table in DSV. In this example, we will use a Named Query to bring the product category and subcategory along with the product table columns, by performing the following steps:

1. In the **Data Source View** designer, right-click on the **DimProduct** table and under **Replace Table**, choose **With New Named Query**.

2. In the **Create Named Query** window, add the **ProductCategory** and **ProductSubCategory** tables, and the designer will write joined statements itself.

3. After that step, choose **EnglishProductCategoryName** and **EnglishProductSubcategoryName** from the columns list.

4. Explore data of the **DimProduct** Named Query and review the result.

What just happened?

In this example, we used a Named Query and a query designer to write customized queries on the database. The query language used is T-SQL because the underlying database is SQL Server. However, it can be different based on the database.

You can also create logical keys for Named Queries or views. You can also create relationships between tables, views, and Named Queries in the DSV. These features in the DSV will provide the ability to develop a powerful base for the cube.

Using dimensions

The junction between dimensions and measure groups is defined in the dimension usage area. There are multiple types of relationships between a measure group and dimension. In this section, we will go through the dimension usage and create a new connection for a business requirement.

Time for action – adding a Fact relationship

As a business requirement, you need to add the order line number as a dimension attribute and show it in the browser. As you know, in the current cube, we have an **Internet Sales** measure group, which has some measures such as order quantity and sales amount, but we need to fetch the order line number from **FactInternetSales** as a dimension attribute (this is degenerate dimension, which is explained clearly in *Chapter 1, Data Warehouse Design*).

Perform the following steps to add a Fact relationship:

1. Open the **Data Source View** designer and explore data in the **FactInternetSales** table. You will see that there is a **SalesOrderNumber** and **SalesOrderLineNumber** column there. In this exercise, we will create a dimension based on these columns.

2. Add a Named Calculation in the **FactInternetSales** table and name it `Order Number`. Write the following expression to calculate the concatenation of the order line and order number:

```
'Order Number: '+SalesOrderNumber+', Order Line Number:
  '+convert(varchar(max),SalesOrderLineNumber)
```

3. Explore data in the **FactInternetSales** table. You will see that **Order Number** creates a concatenation of two order line columns such as `Order Number: SO43697` and `Order Line Number: 1`.

4. In the **Solution Explorer** option, right-click on the **dimensions** folder and select **New Dimension**.

5. In the **Select Creation Method** step, choose **use an existing table**.

6. Choose **FactInternetSales** as the table, leave the **SalesOrderNumber** and **SalesOrderLineNumber** columns in the key column area, and choose **Order Number** as **Name column**, as shown in the following screenshot:

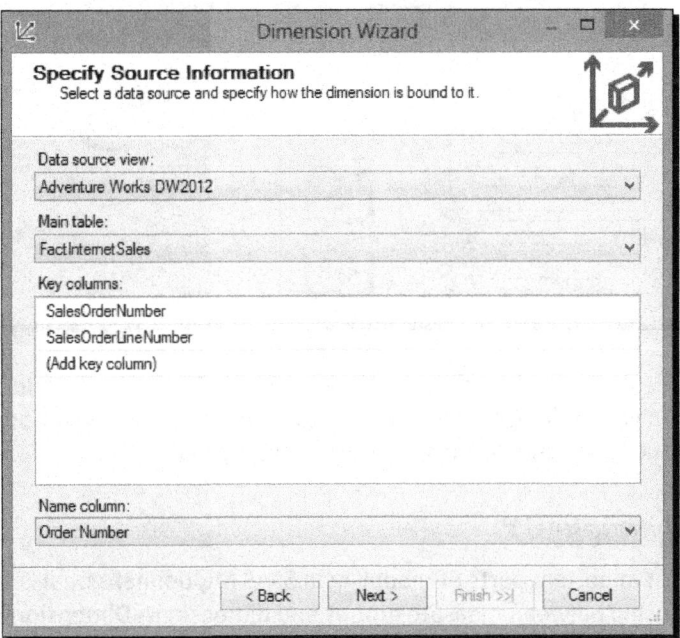

7. In the **Select Related Tables** step, uncheck all the tables.

8. In the **Select Dimension Attributes** step, uncheck all the attributes and only check the **Sales Order Number** option.

9. In the last step, rename the dimension to `Dim Internet Sales Order`.

10. The new dimension will be created under the **dimensions** folder in **Solution Explorer**. Go to the cube designer; in the **Cube Structure** menu, you will see that the new dimension does not exist there. We will add this dimension to the cube in the next steps.

11. Go to the **Dimension Usage** tab in the cube designer (the second tab). Click on the third icon on the top left-hand side, which is **Add Cube Dimension**.

12. In the **Add Cube Dimension** dialog box, choose **Dim Internet Sales Order**.

13. In the matrix, you will see that this dimension is related to the **Internet Sales** measures group based on the **Sales Order Number**. When you double-click on the **Sales Order Number** measure group, you will see that the relationship type is already set as **Fact**, as shown in the following screenshot:

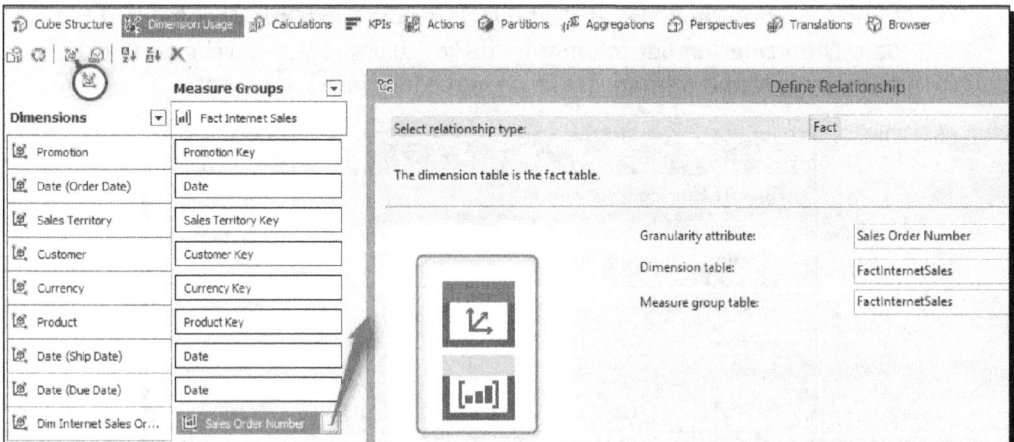

14. After deploying and processing the dimension, check the result in the cube **Browser**. You can view **Sales Order Number** as a dimension attribute and see **Sales Amount** and other measures sliced and diced by this attribute.

What just happened?

One of the most important parts of modeling in SSAS Multidimensional is setting up the correct relationship between measure groups and dimensions. **Dimension Usage** is a tab where we can create, modify, or remove this kind of a relationship.

In this example, we used a descriptive column in the **FactInternetSales** table, and named it **Sales Order Number** (which is a concatenation of the order number and order line number). If you read *Chapter 1, Data Warehouse Design*, you will know about the degenerate dimension and you know that they are in Fact table's granularity but they don't have their own separate dimension table. This is an example of a degenerate dimension.

In this example, we created a SSAS database dimension based on the **FactInternetSales** table. In step 6, we set the key columns and the name column for the same. Then, we created a relationship in the cube between the **Internet Sales** measure group and this new dimension (step 11 and 12). As the source table for both the dimension and measure group is the same, the cube designer considered this relationship as a Fact table and set the granularity of the relationship as the key column of the dimension (step 13).

There are different types of relationships. In the previous example, you saw the **Fact** relationship, which is useful when the dimension is made up of a Fact table. The next table shows information about other relationships. By choosing each relationship, you will see an image that illustrates the relationship between the measure group and dimension (look at the red surrounded area in the screenshot of step 13).

Relationship Type	Description
None	There is no relationship between the measure group and the dimension.
Regular	This is the most common relationship as it shows shows the start schema relation between the fact and the dimension in a one-to-many diagram.
Referenced	The relation between a measure group and a dimension based on an intermediate dimension is observed. This relationship is for snowflake diagrams, which is not recommended usually.
Many to many	This is used when a measure group relates to a dimension based on an intermediate dimension and measure group.
Fact	This is used when dimension is created based on a Fact table.
Data mining	This type relates data mining dimension to a measure group.

Hierarchies

There are two kinds of hierarchies in SSAS Multidimensional: user hierarchies and attribute hierarchies. Each attribute creates a single-level hierarchy that can be used in the designer/ browser with a combination of other attributes to create a multilevel hierarchy. A user hierarchy is a predefined multilevel hierarchy that provide easier access for the end user in the frontend. One of the most important benefits of hierarchies is the ability to drill down and drill up in many MDX client tools such as Excel and PerformancePoint.

Time for action – creating a hierarchy

In this example, we will see how a user can create hierarchies in the browser and how a developer can create a predefined hierarchy for business requirements by performing the following steps:

1. Go to the cube **Browser**, drag-and-drop **Calendar Year**, **Month**, and **Date**, one after another. Then, drag-and-drop **Sales Amount** and **Order Quantity**. You will see a hierarchy created dynamically from the browser.

2. Now, go to the product's Dimension Designer, drag-and-drop the **EnglishProductCategory** name into the **Attributes** pane, and rename it `Product Category`. Do the same for **EnglishProductSubcategoryName** and rename it `Product Subcategory`. Rename the **Product Key** attribute `Product` and change its name column to **EnglishProductName**.

3. Drag-and-drop **Product Category** from the **Attributes** pane into the **Hierarchies** pane.

4. A new hierarchy will be created; rename it `Product Category Hierarchy`.

5. Drag-and-drop the product **Subcategory** under the **Product Category** option (in the **<new level>** area), and then add **Product** under that.

6. Select **Product Category** and change the **AttributeHierarchyVisible** option of this attribute to false. Do this for the **Product Subcategory** and **Product** attributes as well.

7. In the **Dimension** browser, you will see that only **Product Category Hierarchy** is listed, and the values of this hierarchy have created a tree of **Product Category**, **Subcategory** and **Product**.

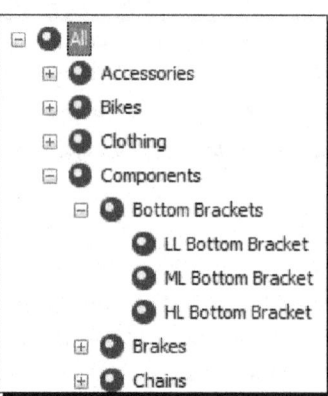

What just happened?

In this example, you created a user hierarchy easily with just a few drag-and-drops. The hierarchy of this example is created from one table. Creating hierarchies from multiple related tables is as simple as creating a hierarchy from a single table; you just need to import attributes from the **Data Source View** pane into the attributes area and you can then create a hierarchy based on the attributes.

You also saw that after creating **Product Category Hierarchy**, we set the visibility of the attributes to false. As the user can access the **Product Category**, **Subcategory**, and **Product** attributes through **Product Category Hierarchy**, there is no need to have separate attributes. Making them invisible from the user's perspective will reduce the user's confusion with regards to too many attributes.

Multidimensional eXpression, calculated members, and Named Sets

In every business, you will face situations where something new came from the business requirements that you didn't consider while designing the data warehouse. On the other hand, sometimes the requirements cannot be fulfilled in the data warehouse and should be fulfilled in the cube.

SSAS provides a way to create calculated members based on an expression language named **Multidimensional eXpression (MDX)**. MDX is the query language for SSAS; all queries from the client applications are sent to the SSAS server as an MDX query, and the result of that query will be returned in a multidimensional format.

As an example for calculation of the members, assuming that you want to calculate the product of the unit price and the item quantity, you can create a calculated member for that. Also, sometimes you might require a subset of a dimension attribute, for example, a list of the top 10 customers in a specific area. The Named Set in SSAS provides the ability to create these kinds of subsets.

Time for action – writing an MDX query

In this example, you will learn more about the MDX structure and how to write queries in the MDX language.

1. Open SQL Server Management Studio, connect to the Analysis Services instance, and click on **Chapter 02 SSAS Multi Dimensional**, and then click on **New Query**.

2. In the **New Query** window, write the following expression:

```
select [Order Date].[Calendar Year].members on 0
from [Internet Sales]
```

You will see a list of the years, the sales amount for each year, and the grand total.

3. Now, run the following statement:

```
select [Sales Territory].[Sales Territory Country].members on 0,
[Order Date].[Calendar].[Calendar Year].members on 1
from [Internet Sales]
```

4. Check the result and you will see the years listed in each row, the countries listed in each column, and the **Sales Amount** measure shown in each cell, which represents the sales amount of that country in that year.

	All	Australia	Canada	France	Germany	NA	United Kingdom	United States
2005	1013	394	47	59	76	(null)	96	341
2006	2677	859	226	233	233	(null)	265	861
2007	24443	5335	3086	2291	2254	(null)	2966	8511
2008	32265	6757	4261	2975	3062	(null)	3579	11631
2009	(null)	(null)	(null)	(null)	(null)	(null)	(null)	(null)
2010	(null)	(null)	(null)	(null)	(null)	(null)	(null)	(null)

What just happened?

MDX is a query language that returns the results in a multidimensional format. In this example, you saw how we define an axis in the output result set. In the first query (step 2), there is only one axis used, which is the column axis. In the second query (step 5), two axes are used, the column axis shows the countries and the row axis shows the years.

An MDX query is not limited to only two axes; you can write an MDX query with 128 axes , for example. However, the client tools are limited to show more than two axes for example, in SSMS, you cannot write a query with more than two axes because it cannot be shown as a result.

The MDX select query structure consists of the SELECT clause on multiple axes, FROM clause, and the WHERE clause.

```
SELECT [<axis_specification>
        [, <axis_specification>...]]
   FROM [<cube_specification>]
 [WHERE [<slicer_specification>]]
```

There are many MDX functions to work with time, hierarchies, and other common applications that are helpful when writing MDX queries. You will work with a few of them in the following examples.

Time for action – calculated members

Calculated members help to perform calculation based on measures, dimension hierarchies, and MDX functions. They are very helpful for covering business requirements with the help of a cube. In this example, we will create a new calculated member for **Profit**.

1. In the cube designer, go to the **Calculations** tab.

2. Create a new calculated member by clicking on the button that is magnified in the next screenshot.

3. Rename the calculated member to [Profit].

4. Write the following expression in the **Expression** field:

   [Measures].[Sales Amount] - [Measures].[Total Product Cost]

5. Set the format string as **"Currency"**.

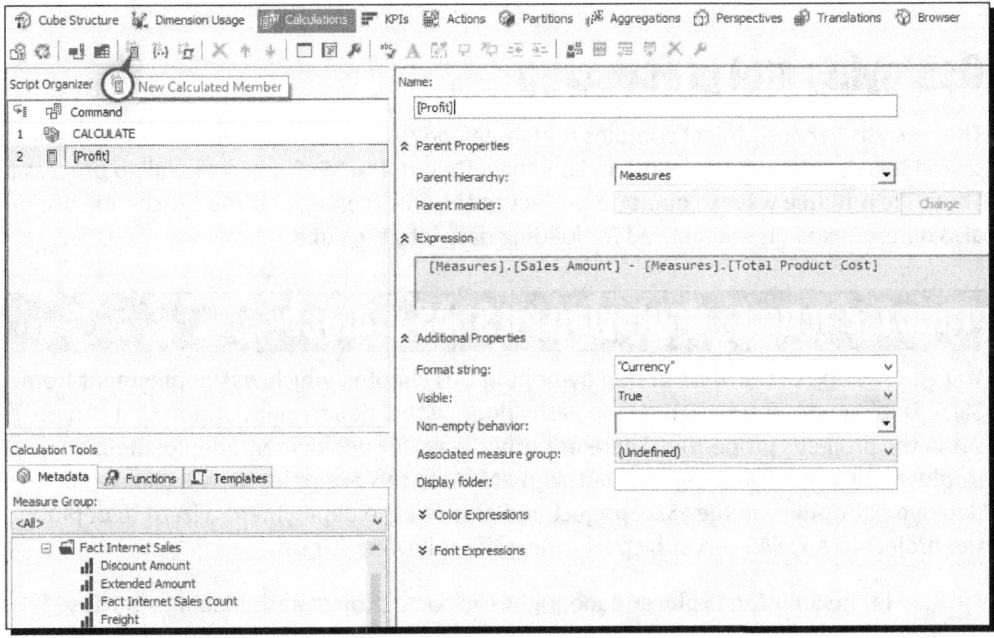

6. Deploy and process this procedure, and then browse the cube with the **Product Category** hierarchy and a **Profit** measure.

What just happened?

In this extremely simple example, we created a profit column based on the total product cost and the sales amount. The MDX expression used here is very simple; as you can see, you don't need to write the whole `select` statement, you just need to write the expression that calculates or applies conditions.

The MDX expression can be made more complex with the help of functions and metadata information listed in the bottom-left side of the preceding screenshot. You can drag-and -drop functions or measures or dimension hierarchies in the expression box and create the expression easily. There are also some properties for calculated columns, such as font, color, and format string, which can be set in this window.

You can also create Named Sets in this window, which can be a subset of the dimension attribute members, for example, a list of the top 50 customers based on the sales amount. You can write MDX scripts to create a Named Set again.

As you've seen in this section, MDX plays an important role in creating calculations and writing complex query scripts on the SSAS Multidimensional cube, so our recommendation for SSAS developers is to improve their MDX skills. The more professionally you can write MDX, the better you will be able to create more powerful cubes for business requirements.

Deploying and processing

The Analysis Service project contains metadata and data. The metadata of the project can be stored to a server with deployment. Loading data into the SSAS project is called processing. There are multiple ways to deploy a project to the SSAS server, and the processing options also differs based on the method for loading data into the cube.

Time for action – deploying an SSAS project

You've seen one of the ways of deployment in this chapter, which was deployment from SSDT. Deployment from SSDT can be easily done with a deployment option that can be set in the project's properties. There are other ways for deployment: deployment with **Deployment Wizard** and deployment with XMLA. In this example, we will change some deployment options in the SSDT project and also use the deployment wizard to deploy the project to an SSAS server by performing the following steps:

1. In the **Solution Explorer** pane, right-click on a project and select **Properties**.
2. In the project's **Configuration Properties** window, go to the **Deployment** tab. You can see some of the deployment options there, such as the server and database name.

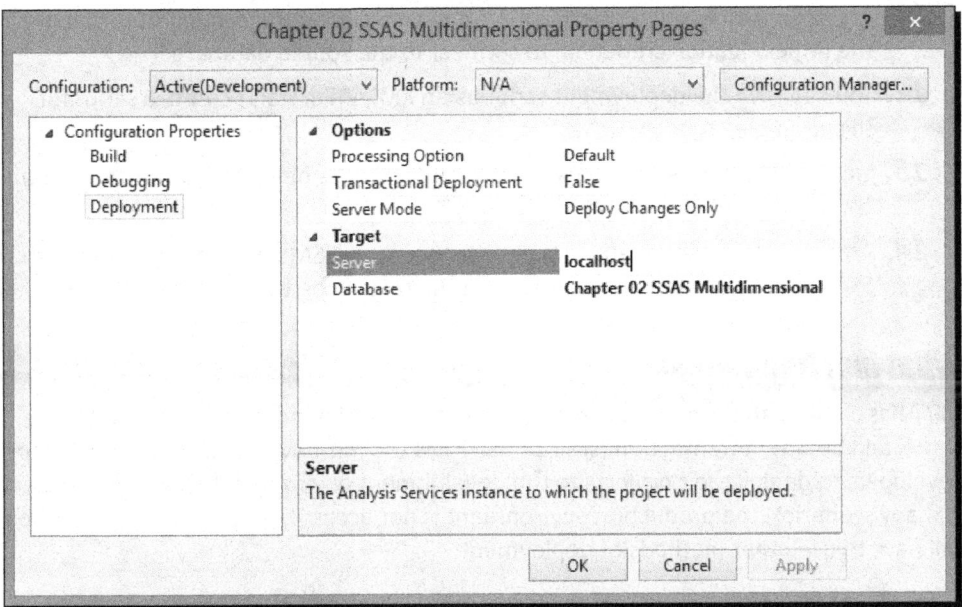

3. Close the project's properties window.

4. Right-click on the project in **Solution Explorer** and build the project.

5. Then, go to the `project` folder in Windows Explorer; under the `bin` folder, you will find four files. These files are deployment files that are created after a successful build action.

6. Go to **Start** and under Microsoft SQL Server 2012, and under **Analysis Services**, click on **Deployment Wizard**.

7. In the **Deployment Wizard** step, choose the `Chapter 02 SSAS multidimensional.asdatabase` file from the `bin` directory of the project.

8. Set the server name and the database name. Note that the database will be created if the database name doesn't exist in that server. You can set the server as a localhost and the database name as `Chapter 02 SSAS Multidimensional`, which are deployed from the wizard (the database can hold one or more cubes, and each database can also have its own security model and a set of conformed dimensions).

9. You can choose whether you want to keep partitioning on the destination database or you want to overwrite them with partitioning defined in this deployment kit. Leave this option as default.

10. You can also choose to keep the existing roles and membership in the destination database or overwrite them with security settings in the deployment kit. Leave this option as the default.

11. In the **Specify Configuration Option** tab, you can set the configurations, for example, the impersonation credential to connect to the source database.

12. You can save the deployment script as an XMLA file. Don't create a script for this example.

13. You can also choose a processing method after the deployment; for this example, choose **default processing**.

14. After the deployment and processing step, open SSMS and you will see the new SSAS project created; you can browse the sales cube there to check it.

What just happened?

SSDT has configurations for deployment, such as the deployment server, the database name, and deploy in transaction (step 2). SSDT is a tool for developers and it is good for developers to deploy their projects to the development environment servers. However, in many scenarios, the production environment is not accessible for developers. So, you will have to use other methods of deployment.

Deployment Wizard is a deployment tool that will be installed with the SSAS service. There are four files required to deploy an SSAS project. These files can be created while building the project (step 4). Each file consists of specific information about deployment. The DBA or the gatekeeper of the production environment can easily run the Deployment Wizard and give the *.asdatabase file path (step 7); follow the steps in the wizard and deploy the project easily.

One of the main benefits of deploying the project with **Deployment Wizard** is that you can choose to retain roles and membership or retain partitioning on the destination database (steps 9 and 10). When you conduct deployment through SSDT, the partitioning and roles will be overwritten. This is an important option because in the production environment, partitioning might be set up in the database, and security and role settings might be different from the security configuration in the SSAS project in SSDT.

XMLA is the language for metadata scripts in SSAS. Running the deployment wizard will produce and run an XMLA command on the SSAS server. If you want to overlook all the wizard steps, you can create an XMLA deployment script (step 12), modify it as you wish to make it run on the production environment, and then just pass this script to the DBA and ask them to run it.

Time for action – processing the data

Deployment will load metadata from an existing Analysis Services project into the SSAS Server, but it won't load data. To load data, another step is required, which is called processing. As there are different requirements to load data, there are multiple types of processing. Sometimes, you just need to populate the changes, but in some cases, such as populating dimensions, you want to populate everything again. In this example, we will go through the processing options by performing the following steps:

1. Open SQL Server Management Studio and connect to the Analysis Services instance.

2. Expand the `Chapter 02 SSAS Multidimensional` database, and then expand the dimensions.

3. Right-click on the **Product** dimension and click on **Process**.

4. In the **Process** window, you can change the process options to **Clear**. Click on the **Clear** option to process and then view the product dimension in the browser; you will see an error message that states that the dimension doesn't contain any hierarchy . The following screenshot shows the Process Options menu:

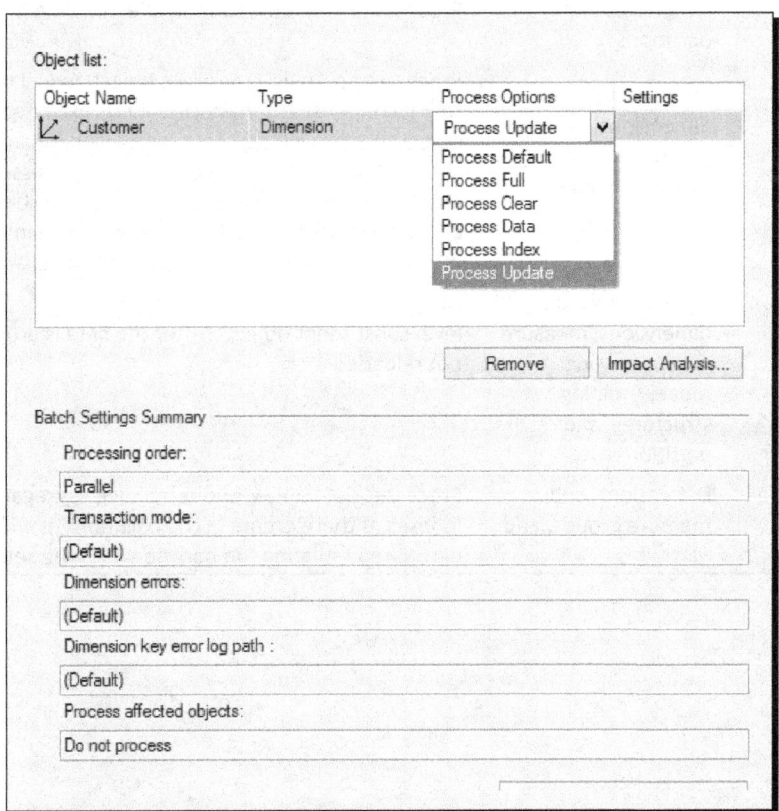

5. Process the **Product** dimension again but with the **Process Full** option. This time, you will see the product category hierarchy with all members.

6. Right-click on the cube and then click on **Process**. You will see the processing options there as well. This shows that processing can be done in the cube or dimensions level.

What just happened?

As you've seen in this example, there are different kinds of processing; some of them are the same as dimensions and partitions. Some of them are only for one of the processing types. The following table (available at `http://technet.microsoft.com/en-us/library/ms174774.aspx`) provides an explanation of the most useful kinds of processing and the SSAS database object that they can be applied to:

Mode	Applies to	Description
Process Default	Cubes, databases, dimensions, measure groups, mining models, mining structures, and partitions	Detects the process state of database objects and performs the necessary processing to deliver unprocessed or partially processed objects to a fully processed state. If you change a data binding, Process Default will do a Process Full operation on the affected object.
Process Full	Cubes, databases, dimensions, measure groups, mining models, mining structures, and partitions	Processes an Analysis Services object and all the objects that it contains. When Process Full is executed against an object that has already been processed, Analysis Services drops all data in the object, and then processes the object. This kind of processing is required when a structural change has been made to an object, for example, when an attribute hierarchy is added, deleted, or renamed.
Process Clear	Cubes, databases, dimensions, measure groups, mining models, mining structures, and partitions	Drops the data in the object specified and in any lower-level constituent objects. After the data is dropped, it is not reloaded.
Process Data	Dimensions, cubes, measure groups, and partitions	Processes data only without building aggregations or indexes. If there is data in the partitions, it will be dropped before repopulating the partition with the source data.

Mode	Applies to	Description
Process Add	Dimensions, measure groups, and partitions	For dimensions, this mode adds new members and updates the dimension attribute captions and descriptions.
		For measure groups and partitions, this mode adds newly available fact data and a process only to the relevant partitions.
		Process Add is not available for dimension processing in Management Studio, but you can write XMLA script performs this action
Process Update	Dimensions	Forces a re-read of data and an update of dimension attributes. Flexible aggregations and indexes on related partitions will be dropped.
Process Index	Cubes, dimensions, measure groups, and partitions	Creates or rebuilds indexes and aggregations for all processed partitions. For unprocessed objects, this option generates an error. Processing with this option is required if you turn off Lazy Processing.
Process Structure	Cubes and mining structures	If the cube is unprocessed, Analysis Services will process, all the cube's dimensions if necessary. After that, Analysis Services will create only cube definitions. If this option is applied to a mining structure, it populates the mining structure with the source data. The difference between this option and the Process Full option is that this option does not iterate the processing down to the mining models themselves.
Process Clear Structure	Mining structures	Removes all training data from a mining structure.

The time taken for processing depends on the structure of data and constraints in the destination database and also depends on the quality of data in the source database; there might be occurrence of some errors. You can catch errors during the processing and do some error configuration. This configuration can be found in the Dimension Designer, cube designer, and also in the **Process** window, as shown in the next screenshot (by clicking on **Change Settings**). The next screenshot shows a sample of the **Dimension key errors** settings.

One of the reasons to use error configuration is to deal with errors that occur during processing. For example, you might want to catch errors such as **key not found** and **log them**, but you still to perform the processing. So, you can use error configuration to perform settings to cover that requirement. Take a look at the following screenshot, which shows the change settings:

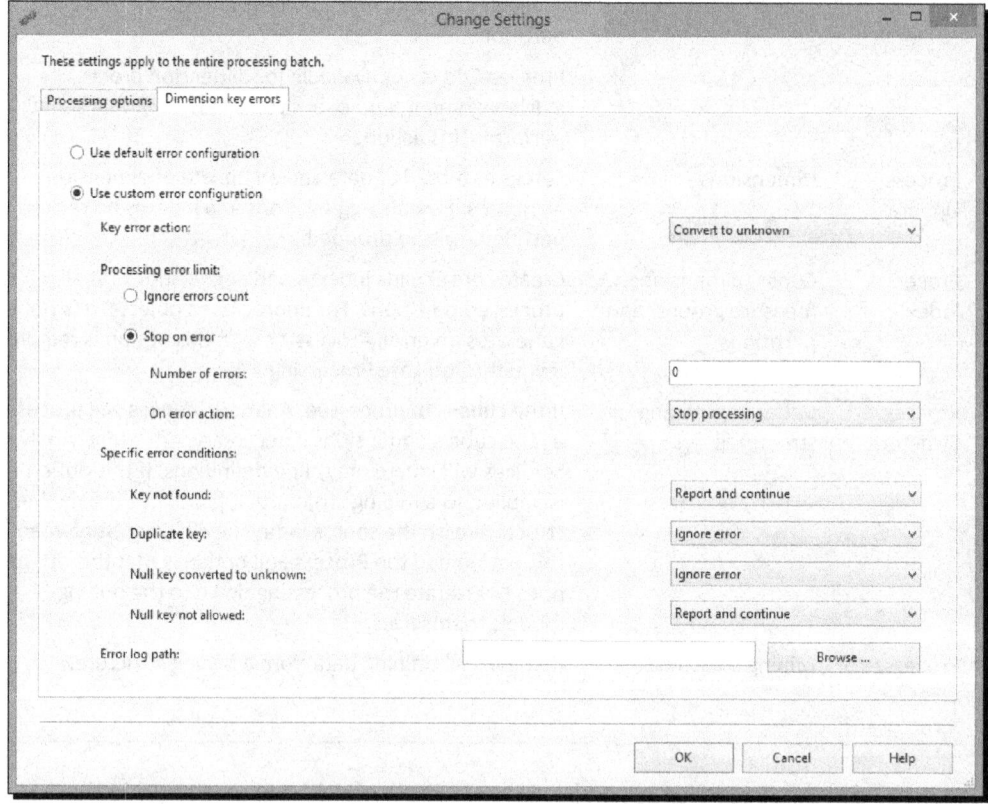

Summary

In this chapter, you learned some of the benefits of having OLAP cube over the data warehouse. Then we learned how to create cubes and dimensions in the SSAS Multidimensional. We've walked through how to create hierarchies and modify dimensions and measure properties. Then we saw how to create calculated columns in the data source view. Some of the changes had to be made in the cube as a calculation; we used MDX, which is a query language for SSAS Multidimensional, to create calculated measures and a named set. Finally, we saw how to deploy an analysis services project to the SSAS Server and how to load data into the database while processing.

There are still many aspects in Analysis Services multidimensional that need to be studied in a more detailed way. We strongly recommend that you use one of the good books written on SQL Server Analysis Services in order to dive deep in to all the aspects of Analysis Services and learn how to face real-world scenarios with SSAS Multidimensional.

3

Tabular Model Development of SQL Server Analysis Services

SQL Server Analysis Services comes with two modeling technologies: multidimensional and tabular. In the previous chapter, you learned how to model a multidimensional OLAP cube. In this chapter, you will learn about tabular modeling.

SSAS Tabular loads data into an In-Memory engine called xVelocity (previously known as Aka Vertipaq). The In-Memory engine provides high-speed access to data, which helps provide very fast reports and dashboards. Tabular modeling allows you to create a table-based model from existing data (that comes from a data warehouse or any other source) and create a relationship between models. Note that the tabular model doesn't require a start schema relation, but this is always recommended if you wish to create a tabular model on the top of your data warehouse and start schema. **Data Analysis Expression (DAX)** *is an expression language for SSAS Tabular, which helps you create calculations and measures based on existing columns and relationships.*

In this chapter, you will learn how to create an SSAS Tabular project and how to create hierarchies from one table or from nested tables. You will learn about the language structure of DAX and how to use DAX functions to create calculations and measures. You will also learn about two different storage models that are supported in the tabular model. Finally, you will see how to apply security and perform deployment.

Introducing SSAS Tabular

SSAS Multidimensional, as you have seen in the previous chapter, is a very powerful modeling tool that provides all the features of OLAP cubes. However, working with multidimensional requires a learning curve; you will need to read a book or some articles, or watch online videos to learn how to work with SSAS Multidimensional.

On the other hand, nowadays, the In-Memory engine is a new technology that provides a very fast response to a client's queries. As you learned from the previous chapter, SSAS Multidimensional loads data into a disk-based storage as long as it is much faster than a database engine, but it will be much faster if it is loaded into memory.

Self-Service BI is another reason why SSAS Tabular comes to help. Earlier, Microsoft provided a tabular solution named Excel PowerPivot. Excel PowerPivot is a tabular modeling technology added in Excel, which helps power users to create models based on their requirements, load data into the In-Memory engine, and solve their business needs easily without requiring a big BI solution.

The SSAS Tabular technology was created as a response to these main reasons: the In-Memory engine, less development time, and the ability to work as a corporate BI solution that can import PowerPivot models. There are other reasons but the main rationales of this technology are those that have just been mentioned. The next diagram shows the comparison of the position of Microsoft analytics solutions with each other.

PowerPivot is the first released tabular modeling technology; it is very powerful and very good for power users because they can connect to data sources and create a model based on their business requirements. PowerPivot could be enhanced for Team BI when it comes with SharePoint. SharePoint can be host for the PowerPivot model. Finally, SSAS Tabular brings the features of corporate BI and tabular together to fill this gap. As a corporate BI, the SSAS Tabular model is scalable and can be deployed to the SSAS Server (more details will be given later in this chapter). Take a look at the following diagram that shows the comparison of SSAS Tabular and Multidimension:

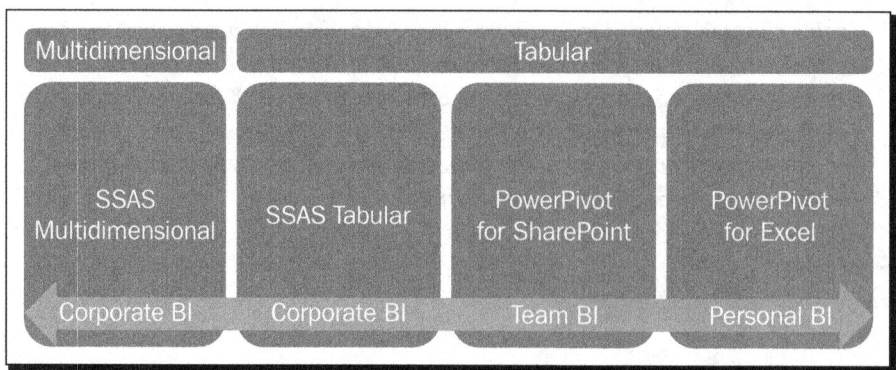

The SSAS Tabular technology that was released with SQL Server 2012 comes with Microsoft's In-Memory engine called xVelocity. xVelocity is a column store engine and provides high performance, In-Memory caching, highly parallel data scanning, and compression.

SSAS Tabular and SSAS Multidimensional cannot reside in a single instance; in other words, a single instance of Analysis Services can be tabular or multidimensional, not both. Therefore, you would need to install two instances of Analysis Services or use two different machines if you want to have both tabular and multidimensional side by side.

Developing a tabular project

To create a tabular project, you need to have SSDT installed. SSDT, as you read in the previous chapter, is a part of the SQL Server installation. After opening SSDT, there are three ways to create a tabular project, such as an empty tabular project, by connecting to a tabular project on the SSAS server, and by importing an existing PowerPivot model.

In this section, you will learn how to create a tabular project from the beginning; you will also see different kinds of data sources supported in tabular.

Time for action – creating a tabular project

In this example, based on data in the AdventureWorksDW2012 database, we will create a tabular project with SSDT from an empty project. You will see a variety of data sources that are supported and how easy it is to work in the tabular modeling environment.

1. Open SSDT, and from the **Files** menu, choose a new project, and then from the **Business Intelligence** templates under **Analysis Services**, choose **Analysis Services Tabular Project**. Name this project `Chapter 03 Tabular`.

2. You might see a dialog box titled **tabular model designer** that asks for a tabular connect option, so enter the SSAS Tabular server's connection details and click on **OK**.

3. A new tabular project will be created. Now, from the **Model** menu, choose **Import** from **Data Source**.

4. In the **Import Table Wizard**, you will see a list of data source types that can be used to import data. Choose Microsoft SQL Server and continue.

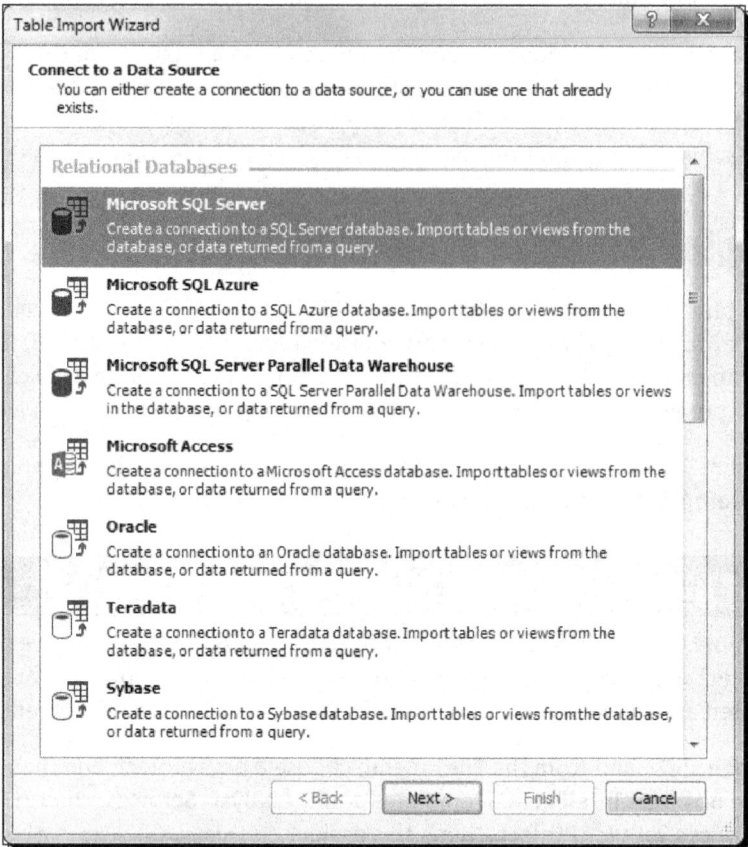

5. Create a connection to AdventureWorksDW2012. In the **Impersonation Information** option, enter the credential details that have the appropriate permission on the underlying database and continue.

6. Choose **Select from a List of Tables and Views to import data** in the next step.

7. In the **Select Tables and Views** option, select **FactInternetSales**, and then click on **select related tables**. Change the name of **FactInternetSales** and all dimensions by removing the `fact` or `dim` prefix from their names such as **InternetSales** and **Date**.

 You can filter data with the **preview** and **filter** buttons and use Excel filtering features to filter data and preview and select it when it looks appropriate for use. For this example, just add tables without any filtering.

8. The final step will show importing summary; all records will be loaded into a workspace for further development and modeling.

9. After importing data, you will see the model in the designer. Tabular designer, as you can see, is much simpler than the multidimensional designer.

10. Under the **Model** menu, go to **View** and then **Diagram View**; you will see a diagram of tables that are related to each other.

What just happened?

Creating a tabular model is as simple as importing data rows from tables or views, but the model will require further modification. In the next sections of this chapter, you will see how to change the model with hierarchies, relationships, and calculations.

SSAS Tabular, as you saw in step 4, supports many types of data sources such as SQL Server, Teradata, Web services, Text files, and more. Also, importing tables and views into the model can be customized with filtering, as mentioned in step 7.

Model designer in a tabular project is very simple; it has two different views, **Grid View** and **Diagram View**. The **Grid View** shows some data rows of each table with columns and properties of each column shown in the properties pane (as shown in the next screenshot). The **Diagram View** shows how tables relate to each other in a diagram (step 10):

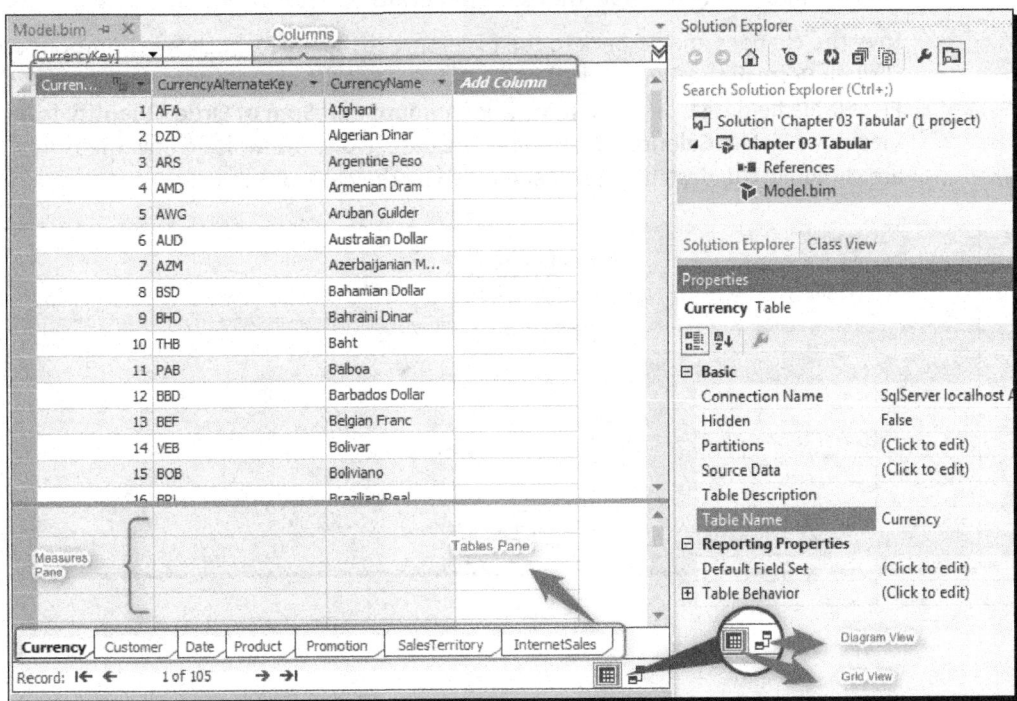

Time for action – creating measures

Tabular doesn't have any measures by default; this means that you need to add measures as required, but don't worry as creating measures is very easy in the model designer. In this example, you will see how to create measures such as **Order Quantity** or **Sales Amount**.

1. Under the **Model** menu, select **Analyze** in Excel; in the dialog box, choose the current Windows user.

2. You will see an Excel spreadsheet open, and in a PivotTable, all the tables from the current tabular model are listed. In the PivotTable fields list under **Internet Sales**, choose **Sales Amount**.

3. You will see distinct values of the **Sales Amount** measure shown instead of a measure with the summary of all the sales amount. This is because there is no measure for the sum of the sales amount, and by default, all the values (even numeric ones) are shown as distinct values.

4. In SSDT, go to the **Grid View** of the **Internet Sales** table. Click on an empty measure cell under the **Sales Amount** column, and then click on the sum icon (this will create DAX in the background, which will be covered later in this chapter). Do the same for **Order Quantity** (look at the following screenshot). Then, select the **Sum of OrderQuantity** measure, and in the **Properties** pane, change the format to a whole number and set **show thousand separator** as **true**.

5. Save the changes and go back to the Excel spreadsheet. Uncheck **Sales Amount** and click on **Refresh** the PivotTable. Now, you will see a list of measures at the top of the PivotTable fields list; select **Sum of SalesAmount** and **Sum of OrderQuantity** from measures. Select **Calendar Year** under the date. Now, you will see how measures are shown in the designer sliced and diced by the calendar year.

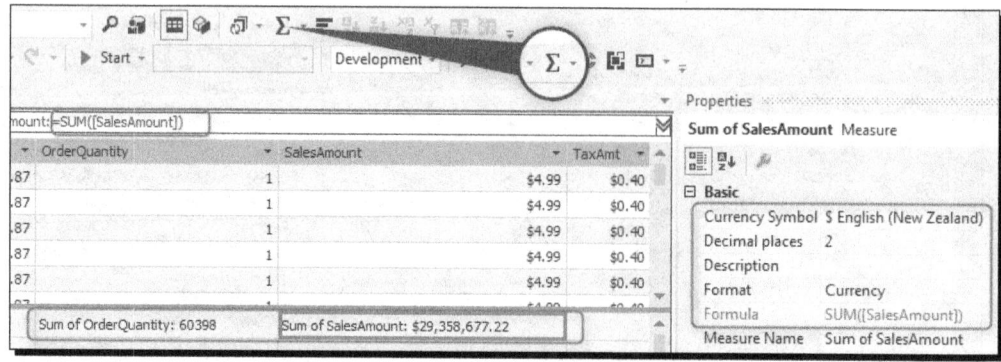

What just happened?

In this example, you learned how to view the results of the tabular model in Excel with **Analyze** in the Excel option. This option will open an Excel spreadsheet with PivotTable that enables you to slice and dice data with different tables and shows measures in comparison to each other (described in steps 1, 2, 3, and 5).

You also saw how easy it is to create measures and configure properties such as format string for measures (step 4). Measures created based on expressions (shown in the screenshot after step 4) are written in the DAX language. DAX provides many functions, and you can enhance them to create complex expressions to create measures, as your business requires.

Creating hierarchies

Creating hierarchies is important in both tabular and multidimensional models. Hierarchies provide a better understanding of data to business users, and help them slice and dice reports and data more easily. Hierarchies can be created from a single table or from nested tables. In multidimensional, creating hierarchies from a single table or multiple tables doesn't make a difference, and both can be done simply with drag-and-drops. But in tabular, there are some differences; examples in this section show how to create hierarchies in a tabular model.

Time for action – creating a hierarchy from a single table

In this example, we want to create a calendar hierarchy in the **Date** table. So, this example shows how to create a hierarchy from a single table. A calendar hierarchy will have the year, quarter, month, and date level:

1. Go to **Diagram View**, maximize the **Date** table (with a maximize icon in the top right-hand side of the **Date** table).

2. Create a hierarchy (the second icon from the top right-hand side of the date table shown in the next screenshot), name the hierarchy as `Calendar`, and drag-and-drop **CalendarYear**, **CalendarQuarter**, **EnglishMonthName**, and **FullDateAlternateKey** as levels of this hierarchy.

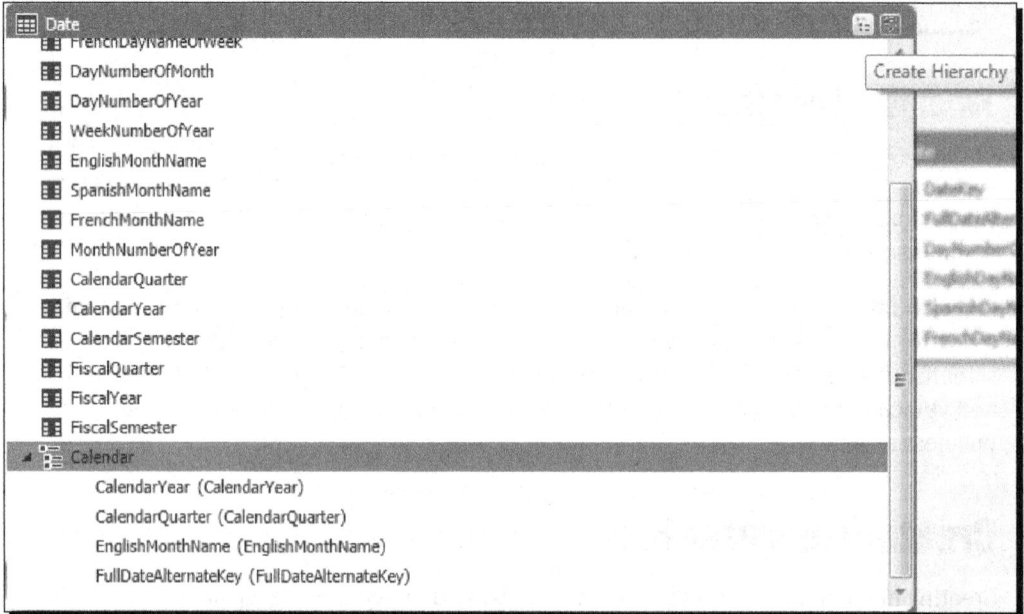

3. Save the changes and view the tabular model in Excel. Select **Calendar** under **Date**. Also, select **Sum of SaleSamount** from measures. You will see that the calendar hierarchy shows the hierarchy of years, quarters, months, and dates.

4. We observe that the order of month in the calendar is not correct; it is already ordered based on the month name, but it should be ordered based on the month number as well.

5. Go to **Grid View** of the **Date** table, select the **EnglishMonthName** column, and then from the tabular toolbox icons on the top, click on the **Sort By Column** icon. Choose **MonthNumberOfYear** as the **Sort By Column**.

6. Save the changes and refresh PivotTable; now you will see that the order of the month shows correctly as January, February, and so on.

What just happened?

Creating hierarchies from a single table is as simple as dragging-and-dropping columns (step 1 to 4). Also, in this example, you saw how you can change the sort order of a column based on other columns (step 5).

Time for action – creating a hierarchy from multiple tables

Creating a relationship between tables in tabular and creating a hierarchy based on inter-related tables are two main parts that you will see in this example. In the first part of this example, we will create a relationship between the product table and the product category and product subcategory. In addition, in the second part, we will create a product category hierarchy based on the columns of these three tables:

1. In the **Model** menu, click on the existing connections and open the current connection. Then, in the **Import Tables** wizard, choose **DimProductCategory** and **DimProductSubcategory**. Change their names to **Product Category** and **Product Subcategory**. Complete the wizard and import the records.

2. Go to **Diagram View**; you will see two new tables added. There is a relationship between the product category and product subcategory. However, there is no relationship between the product subcategory and product. So we need to create a relationship.

3. Drag-and-drop **ProductSubcategoryKey** from the **Product** table to **ProductSubcategoryKey** in the **Product Subcategory** table. A new relationship will be created as a one-to-many relationship. You can double-click on the relationship to change it if you need to.

4. Go to **Grid View** of the **Product** table, add a new column at the end of table, and rename it as Product Subcategory. Write the following expression in the textbox near the fx icon:

   =RELATED(ProductSubcategory[EnglishProductSubcategoryName])

5. Add another column and rename it as `Product Category`, then write the following expression for the new column:

`=RELATED(ProductCategory[EnglishProductCategoryName])`

6. Select the **Product Category** table and change its hidden property to true. Do the same for the **Product Subcategory** table. You will see that these two tables will be shown in gray after the change.

7. Go to **Diagram View**, create a new hierarchy in the **Product** table, and name it as `Product Category Hierarchy`. Drag-and-drop the **Product Category** column (from the **Product** table), the **Product Subcategory** column (from the **Product** table), and **EnglishProductName**.

8. Save the changes and view the model in Excel. You will see that a new hierarchy is created under the **Product** table with category, subcategory, and product names.

What just happened?

Relationships can be created easily in a tabular model. In the previous chapter, you saw that there are multiple kinds of relationships between measure groups and dimensions such as regular, referenced, fact, and so on. However, creating relationships in the tabular mode is as simple as a database relationship. This simplicity when creating relationships and also in other parts of tabular development is the main reason why a tabular model can be developed easier and faster than multidimensional. Steps 1 to 3 showed you how to add new tables into the tabular model and create or edit relationships. Only the one-to-many relationship is supported in the tabular model, but you can create many-to-many relationships with intermediate tables.

As you saw in the previous example, hierarchies can only be created from columns of a single table. As a result, if you want to create a hierarchy from multiple tables, you can use calculated columns. In this example, you saw how we created calculated columns in the product table that shows the corresponding category or subcategory value from the related tables. For creating those columns, a DAX function named RELATED is used; this function will get data from the related table's column (shown in steps 5 and 6).

After creating new calculated columns, there is no need to have two new tables from the user's point of view, so we make them hidden by just changing the hidden properties of those tables to true (step 7). We can also hide columns in each table as required.

Step 8 shows a method that is similar to the method in the previous example, same as the previous example for creating a hierarchy; it just uses columns of the product table to create a hierarchy of product categories.

Data Analysis eXpression, calculated columns, and measures

Data Analysis eXpression (**DAX**) is a query language for tabular models of Microsoft, such as PowerPivot and SSAS Tabular. DAX was introduced in 2010 with PowerPivot and enhanced in SSAS Tabular 2012. The structure of a DAX command is very simple, but a number of built-in functions in DAX is enough to create complex expressions to answer business requirements.

DAX is the language used for creating calculated columns and measures. As you saw in the previous sections, calculated columns are columns added in each table. The value of the calculated columns will be calculated at the time of processing and will be stored in memory. Measures also use DAX expressions for calculations. Measures will be calculated on the fly; their value won't be stored anywhere and will just be visible to the user after calculation. There are two main kinds of evaluation contexts in DAX: row context and filter context. Row context means the current row and is useful for writing expressions that work with the current row, like many of calculated columns. Filter context is a set of records filtered by criteria and is good for creating measures based on a subset of records.

DAX is not the same as MDX. MDX is an expression language that is used to query multidimensional models, as you saw in the previous chapter. MDX supports powerful query features to provide a multidimensional result set. However, DAX is used to query tabular models only. It has many built-in functions that can be used in created measures and calculated members. An SSAS Tabular model works with DAX as the main query language, but it also supports MDX clients (we will go in more details of it in the *Storage Modes* section).

Time for action – using time intelligence functions in DAX

In this example, we will create some measures such as year-to-date, quarter-to-date, fiscal year-to-date, and running total, in order to show you how to use DAX functions and create expressions as you wish. As part of this example, we will use the CALCULATE function, which calculates an expression on a filter context. So, perform the following steps that show the use of time intelligence functions:

1. Go to **Grid View** of the **InternetSales** table and add a new measure using the following expression, and change the format string of this measure to Currency:

```
Sales Amount YTD:=TOTALYTD(SUM(InternetSales[SalesAmount]),
    'Date'[FullDateAlternateKey])
```

2. Save the changes and analyze the model in Excel. Select **Calendar** under **Date**, and **Sales Amount YTD** and **Sum of SalesAmount** under measures. You will see that the new measure is shown but it is not correct (look at the next screenshot). The problem is that the YTD is not calculated correctly; it is because tabular needs to set a date table to time intelligence functions so that it works, as shown in the following screenshot:

Row Labels	Sum of SalesAmount	Sales Amount YTD
⊟2005	$3,266,373.66	$3,266,373.66
⊟3	$1,453,522.89	$1,453,522.89
⊞July	$473,388.16	$473,388.16
⊞August	$506,191.69	$506,191.69
⊞September	$473,943.03	$473,943.03
⊞4	$1,812,850.77	$1,812,850.77
⊞2006	$6,530,343.53	$6,530,343.53

3. Go to **Grid View** of the **Date** table, and then go to the **Table** menu, and under Date, click on **Mark as Date Table**. In the **Mark as Date Table** dialog box, choose **FullDateAlternateKey** column.

4. Save the changes and refresh Excel PivotTable; now, you will see the correct YTD shown under the **Sales Amount YTD** measure, as shown in the following screenshot:

Row Labels	Sum of SalesAmount	Sales Amount YTD
⊟2005	$3,266,373.66	$3,266,373.66
⊟3	$1,453,522.89	$1,453,522.89
⊞July	$473,388.16	$473,388.16
⊞August	$506,191.69	$979,579.85
⊞September	$473,943.03	$1,453,522.89
⊞4	$1,812,850.77	$3,266,373.66
⊞2006	$6,530,343.53	$6,530,343.53

5. Go back to **Grid View** of the **InternetSales** table and add a new measure for **Sales Amount QTD**, and change the format string of this measure to `Currency`:

```
Sales Amount QTD:=TOTALQTD(SUM(InternetSales[SalesAmount]),
  'Date'[FullDateAlternateKey])
```

6. View the model in Excel; you will see that QTD and YTD are shown correctly; QTD restarts at the first of each quarter and YTD restarts at the first of each year.

7. Add another measure in **InternetSales** for YTD based on the fiscal year using the below expression:

```
Sales Amount YTD Fiscal:=TOTALYTD
    (SUM(InternetSales[SalesAmount]),
    'Date'[FullDateAlternateKey],"06-30")
```

8. Add another measure in **InternetSales** for calculating **Running Total** based on the following expression:

```
Running Total:=CALCULATE(SUM(InternetSales[SalesAmount]),
    FILTER(ALL('Date'),'Date'[FullDateAlternateKey]<=MAX
    ('Date'[FullDateAlternateKey])))
```

9. Review the results in Excel as shown in the following screenshot:

Row Labels	Sum of SalesAmount	Sales Amount YTD	Sales Amount QTD	Sales Amount YTD Fiscal	Running Total
⊟2005	$3,266,373.66	$3,266,373.66	$1,812,850.77	$3,266,373.66	$3,266,373.66
⊟3	$1,453,522.89	$1,453,522.89	$1,453,522.89	$1,453,522.89	$1,453,522.89
⊞July	$473,388.16	$473,388.16	$473,388.16	$473,388.16	$473,388.16
⊞August	$506,191.69	$979,579.85	$979,579.85	$979,579.85	$979,579.85
⊞September	$473,943.03	$1,453,522.89	$1,453,522.89	$1,453,522.89	$1,453,522.89
⊞4	$1,812,850.77	$3,266,373.66	$1,812,850.77	$3,266,373.66	$3,266,373.66
⊟2006	$6,530,343.53	$6,530,343.53	$1,327,799.32	$2,724,632.94	$9,796,717.18
⊞1	$1,791,698.45	$1,791,698.45	$1,791,698.45	$5,058,072.11	$5,058,072.11
⊟2	$2,014,012.13	$3,805,710.59	$2,014,012.13	$7,072,084.24	$7,072,084.24
⊞April	$663,692.29	$2,455,390.74	$663,692.29	$5,721,764.40	$5,721,764.40
⊞May	$673,556.20	$3,128,946.94	$1,337,248.48	$6,395,320.59	$6,395,320.59
⊞June	$676,763.65	$3,805,710.59	$2,014,012.13	$7,072,084.24	$7,072,084.24
⊟3	$1,396,833.62	$5,202,544.20	$1,396,833.62	$1,396,833.62	$8,468,917.86
⊞July	$500,365.16	$4,306,075.74	$500,365.16	$500,365.16	$7,572,449.40
⊞August	$546,001.47	$4,852,077.21	$1,046,366.63	$1,046,366.63	$8,118,450.87
⊞September	$350,466.99	$5,202,544.20	$1,396,833.62	$1,396,833.62	$8,468,917.86
⊞4	$1,327,799.32	$6,530,343.53	$1,327,799.32	$2,724,632.94	$9,796,717.18
⊞2007	$9,791,060.30	$9,791,060.30	$4,009,218.46	$6,753,558.94	$19,587,777.48
⊞2008	$9,770,899.74	$9,770,899.74		$50,840.63	$29,358,677.22
⊞2009					$29,358,677.22
⊞2010					$29,358,677.22
Grand Total	$29,358,677.22				$29,358,677.22

What just happened?

You saw a DAX time intelligence expression used in this example. First and foremost, we need to set a **Date** table in order to use time intelligence functions. We set a **Date** table in step 3 and selected a **full date** column as a date column. Note that you cannot use a column with the YYYYMMDD format; it should be a full date type column. Another important note about the date column is that it should contain all the dates from the beginning of the period to the end date of the period; if you have one day missed, you will see incorrect results in the time intelligence functions.

The `TotalYTD` function is used to calculate the YTD sales amount. Using this function is very simple; you just need to set the expression (`SUM(InternetSales[SalesAmount]` in this example) and then set the date column (`Date[FullDateAlternateKey]`), according to step 1. `TotalQTD` is very similar to `YTD` but with different usage.

`TotalYTD` can be used for the fiscal year as well; the only thing you need to do is to pass the last day of the year as the third parameter. In this example (step 7), June 30 is passed as the last day of the year, which means that TotalYTD will restart at July 1 each year.

`Calculate` is a function that works with this signature: `Calculate` (expression, filter1, filter2, and so on). This function will calculate the expression based on the filter context as a result of filters. In this example, the `Calculate` function is used to calculate the running total. There are many usages for the `Calculate` function; you can refer to some MSDN articles for more information about this function at `http://technet.microsoft.com/en-us/library/ee634825.aspx`.

Securing the data

Every data model that contains data needs to be secured. Tabular also provides role-based and row level security, such as multidimensional. Role-based security can be connected to windows domain users as members of this role, and then the permissions on each of the tables can be set. DAX can be used to set the row level security for data.

Time for action – security in tabular

In this example, we will create a role in the tabular model and authorize it to access only the data of the year 2008. We will also show you how to use perspectives to provide a better view for users by performing the following steps:

1. In the **Model** menu, click on **Roles**. Create a new role and name it as `SampleRole`. Set its permission as **Read**.

2. Write the following DAX filter in front of the **Date** row:

   ```
   ='Date'[CalendarYear]=2008
   ```

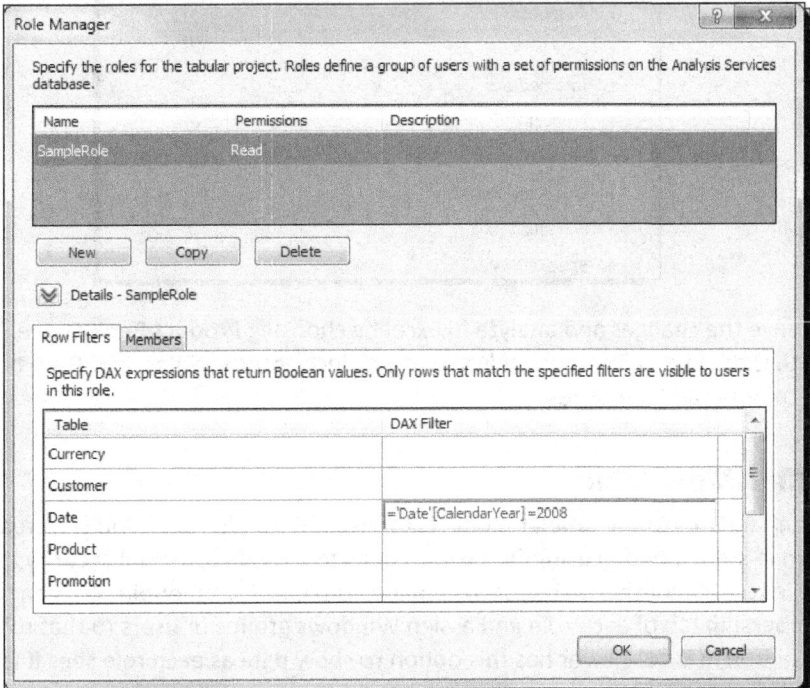

3. Save changes and analyze the model in Excel. In the **Analyze** option in the Excel window, choose **SampleRole** under **Roles**.

4. Select the **Calendar** hierarchy under **Date** and the **Sum of Sales Amount** measure; you will only see data for 2008 shown for this role.

5. Go to SSDT and under the **Model** menu, click on **Perspectives** and then **Create and Manage**. Create a new perspective and name it `Product Perspective`. Select only **Product**, **InternetSales**, and **Date** for this perspective, as shown in the following screenshot:

Fields	Product Perspecti...
− **Tables**	■
− Currency	☐
CurrencyAlternateKey	☐
CurrencyKey	☐
CurrencyName	☐
+ Customer	☐
+ Date	☑
+ InternetSales	☑
+ Product	☑
+ ProductCategory	☐
+ ProductSubcategory	☐
+ Promotion	☐
+ SalesTerritory	☐

6. Save the changes and analyze in Excel by choosing **Product Perspective**. You will see that the Excel PivotTable only shows **Product**, **InternetSales**, and **Date** table-related columns and measures.

What just happened?

Configuring security in the tabular model is robust and simple to do. You can create roles (as shown in steps 1 and 2) using DAX expressions to provide row level security; in this example, only data for the year 2008 was made visible for **SampleRole**. You can go to the **Membership** tab of each role and assign Windows groups or users to that role. The **Analyze** option in Excel viewer has this option to show data as each role sees it (step 3).

Perspectives is not a kind of security, but it provides a way to create different views of the current model for users. This will help in reducing the number of nonrelated tables for a specific view for some business users. As shown in this example (refer to step 5), perspective is used to create a view of the product, date, and measures in order to make it simpler and better to work with rather than having a big list of tables and columns in each table.

 To read more about security in SSAS Tabular, read the article from MSDN available at `http://download.microsoft.com/download/D/2/0/` `D20E1C5F-72EA-4505-9F26-FEF9550EFD44/Securing%20` `the%20Tabular%20BI%20Semantic%20Model.docx`.

Storage modes

Data of the tabular model will be stored in different modes called storage modes. There are two main storage modes in tabular: In-Memory and DirectQuery. The difference between these storage modes is based on the location of the stored data. In-Memory stores data in memory and DirectQuery stores data in the SQL Server database.

In-Memory is the default and recommended storage mode for the tabular model because it loads all the data into the memory and it responds to queries very quickly. Tabular models that work with In-Memory are also accessible from MDX client tools such as Excel Services. All the functionalities of DAX is supported for the In-Memory mode.

DirectQuery stores data into the SQL Server database. It is much slower than In-Memory, but as memory restrictions are much more than disk restrictions, this mode is helpful when the tabular model contains a large dataset that cannot fit into the system's memory (when you try to process the model, you may get an error if it exceeds memory). On the other hand, DirectQuery works directly with data in the SQL Server database and it doesn't require further processing, so another big advantage of this mode is real-time data.

There is also another storage mode, which is a combination of the two modes. This hybrid mode comes with two options: In-Memory with DirectQuery and DirectQuery with In-Memory. In the first option, the queries will be responded from memory, and in the second option, queries will be responded by a relational SQL Server database source. The following table shows all the storage modes and a recommendation about when to use which of these modes:

Query mode	When to use
In-Memory	When full features are available and there is no limitation of resources.
DirectQuery	Used when SSRS and Power View are the only reporting client for a DirectQuery-enabled model. Also used when real-time data is required and/or there are large datasets that don't fit into the memory resources; this is the reason why MDX queries are not supported for a model in the DirectQuery mode.
DirectQuery with In-Memory	Use this mode when MDX-issuing clients, such as Excel, must connect to a model running in the DirectQuery mode. Power View may connect in the DirectQuery mode by using a **Business Intelligence Semantic Model (BISM)** or a **Report Server Data Source (RSDS)** file.
	Use when Power View is the default client to query the model.

Query mode	When to use
In-Memory with DirectQuery	Use when MDX-issuing clients, such as Excel, must connect to a model running in the DirectQuery mode. Power View can only connect in the DirectQuery mode by using an RSDS file if the DirectQuery mode parameter is embedded in the connection string.
	Use when the default client to query the model is an MDX-issuing client. Do not use when BISM files are used to connect to Power View.

Time for action – creating a model with the DirectQuery storage mode

In this example, you will see how to create a model with the DirectQuery mode. Note that in this example, a PowerView viewer is used to show the model, because PowerView is a DAX client that the DirectQuery-enabled tabular model can interact with. Perform the following steps to create the model:

1. Create a new tabular model project and name it DirectQuery Tabular Project.

2. In the **Solution Explorer** pane, choose **model.bim**, and in the **Properties** pane, change the **DirectQuery Mode** property to **On**. Then, right-click on the project in **Solution Explorer** and go to **Properties**. Change **Query Mode** to **DirectQuery**, as shown in the following diagram

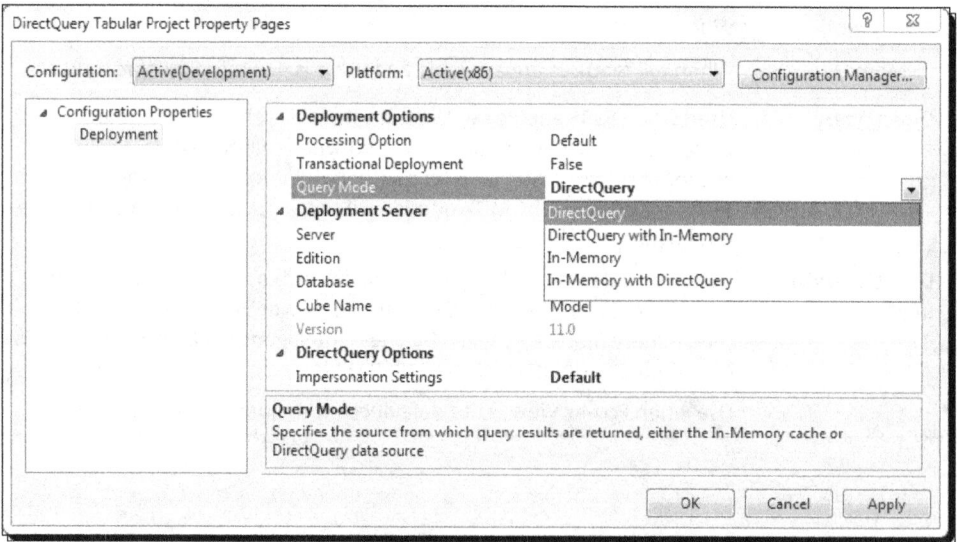

3. Save the changes. Under the **Model** menu, go to **Import from Data Sources**; you will only see SQL Server as the data source. Set **AdventureWorksDW2012** as the source connection.

4. Select **DimDate** and **FactInternetSales** in the list of tables and complete the wizard while loading records.

5. Create a **Sum of OrderQuantity** measure (as described in earlier sections of this chapter).

6. Right-click on **Project** and choose **Deploy**. Deploy the project to SSAS Server.

7. Open Excel; in the **Data** tab, create a connection to SSAS Server and connect to DirectQuery Tabular Project. Try to show data in the PivotTable first. You will see an error message stating that MDX operations are not supported in the DirectQuery mode.

8. Open the data in PowerView and select **Sum of Sales Amount** sliced by calendar year. Now, you can go to AdventureWorksDW2012, change the **FactInternetSales** record's order quantity, and after a simple refresh in Excel, you will see the updated order quantity.

What just happened?

In this example, you saw how to deploy a model with DirectQuery. It is always recommended that you set the DirectQuery mode of the model before further development. In this example, you learned that MDX clients cannot connect to the DirectQuery model. Also, only DAX clients such as PowerView can query these kinds of models (In-Memory supports both MDX and DAX while DirectQuery only supports DAX).

The DirectQuery mode can be used with partitioning to improve scalability, real-time data, and get a fast response together. For example, a partition can be created for data of recent year, which won't be processed and will be in the DirectQuery mode, and another partition (In-Memory) can be created for historical data, which will neither change nor process the data once entered into memory for faster responses.

Tabular versus Multidimensional SSAS

You learned two different analytical-modeling tools and methods in this book: multidimensional and tabular. You might come across a question about which one is better? This is a good question, and the best time to ask this question is before you start modeling, because once you've started modeling in any of these two methods, you cannot convert the project to another model.

You can use both models together in a BI solution for responding to different requirements.

To answer the question, you would need to consider different aspects of the BI system, such as the timeframe for the project to complete, resources for this project, pre-build models in PowerPivot, and many other aspects.

SSAS Multidimensional is like a multifunction modeling tool, and tabular is like a model that is developed for one purpose, that is, performance. You can get a much faster response to a distinct count query in tabular rather than in multidimensional because tabular works with In-Memory's xVelocity engine. However, in multidimensional, you can use actions, translations, and many extended features that are still not available in tabular.

 The article from MSDN shows detailed differences between these two models at `http://download.microsoft.com/download/D/2/0/` `D20E1C5F-72EA-4505-9F26-FEF9550EFD44/SQL2012AS%20` `Multidimensional%20Modeling.docx`.

Summary

SSAS Tabular provides another analytical modeling tool that has a high performance using the xVelocity In-Memory column store engine. This tool is very easy to use rather than multidimensional. However, tabular is in its early stages in comparison with multidimensional that was released in 2000 for the first time. This tool still has room for improvement, but it is good for real-world projects; it will provide higher performance and faster development in BI projects. To be a professional with this tool, your first step is to be a professional in DAX, which is the query language for tabular modeling.

Chapter 2, SQL Server Analysis Services Multidimensional Cube Development and this chapter was about data modeling. The next chapter will explore data transformation and ETL with SSIS. Irrespective of whether you do the data modeling using SSAS Multidimensional or SSAS Tabular, you will definitely need to do ETL and data transformation from the source database to the data warehouse or intermediate tables.

4

ETL with Integration Services

*As you learned in Chapter 1, Data Warehouse Design, a data warehouse is an integrated database with a specific design, which helps us in data analysis and reporting. Chapter 1, Data Warehouse Design was about designing the data warehouse. However, there is always another step, that is, loading the data into the data warehouse. This requirement brings another component of the data warehousing system into play, which is **Extract, Transform, and Load** (**ETL**). The following list explains the function of each process:*

- ◆ *Extract: This is the process of fetching data from the source systems*
- ◆ *Transform: This is the process in which we apply transformations such as aggregation, joining with other datasets, applying rules, splitting or merging results, lookup, join, pivot, and many others*
- ◆ *Load: This process is about loading data into the data warehouse destination tables such as fact and dimensions*

There are a bunch of ETL tools that provide useful features to help in all steps of data transfer and ETL. Microsoft also released SQL Server Integration Services as a part of the Microsoft SQL Server product. Integration Services helps to reduce the amount of work using components and a designed structure for data transfer. Currently, Integration Services is one of the leading ETL tools in the market because of its power and ability to perform data transfer.

In this chapter, we will first go through some ETL concepts and then start working with Integration Services to explore this tool and find out how this tool helps us to implement an ETL scenario.

Understanding ETL and data consolidation

ETL stands for Extract, Transform, and Load. Extract is the process of fetching data from different data sources, Transform is the step where we apply transformation to data, such as aggregation, join with other datasets, applying rules, split or merge result set, and so on. In the Load step, we have data that is ready for the destination table structure, and we load that into the destination fact or dimension table in the data warehouse.

Data transfer or ETL is an important component of the BI and data warehousing system because the source data should be loaded into the data warehouse in a consistent way and be reliable. There are some concerns about data transfer, which makes this process even more important; data might come from different sources such as an Excel file, a DB2 database, or a web service, so the extract step should be able to pick data from all these kinds of data sources. In the transformation step, we should be careful that this data is consistent. Sometimes, we might need to use other data warehousing components such as MDS, to keep the master data consistent; or DQS, to apply data-cleansing rules on the dataset. Data in the source system might be removed or replaced by newer data records, so we should be able to fetch the data in an incremental method as well, because there are some data rows that may appear only once in the data source and be removed from the source system with new data.

Concepts such as **Slowly Changing Dimension (SCD)** and incremental load are challenging situations in the ETL process that we need to be careful about at the time of design and implementation of the ETL scenario. SCD is about loading data into the data warehouse and considering changes in the dimension attributes as well. For example, in customer dimension, if the customer's residing city changes, we might need to keep historical information about the customer's previous city and current city.

Staging

Extracting data from sources into an integrated database comes with some challenges. For example, if datasets are very big, then fetching data from sources shouldn't be combined with any kind of conversion or transformation. The main reason is that it will reduce the performance and slow down the whole ETL process. On the other hand, loading a very large dataset into memory will require a high amount of server resources that are not available at all times. So, the requirement for a staging area is raised; this staging area is an area where we fetch data from different sources exactly as it is into our integrated database. By using a staging area, we can be pretty sure that we don't spend any extra activities to convert or transform data in the extract step, and also, data won't be loaded all at once into the memory.

Using the staging area depends on the data warehouse system's requirement; sometimes, a data warehouse system might be able to perform very well even without a staging area, and sometimes, the staging area cannot be overlooked.

Considering all the concerns and importance of the ETL, different companies have generated tools for the design and implementation of the ETL solution; these tools are called ETL tools. Microsoft also developed a tool named **SQL Server Integration Services (SSIS)**, which is one of the leading ETL tools with lots of powerful features to overcome hardships of the ETL implementation.

SQL Server Integration Services

SQL Server Integration Services is an ETL tool that is part of Microsoft SQL Server. SSIS is a Rapid Application Development tool that comes with a powerful IDE named SQL Server Data Tools (SSDT).

 SSDT is the integrated IDE for SSIS, SSRS, and SSAS.

SSDT was formerly known as **Business Intelligence Development Studio (BIDS)**. There are lots of built-in components in SSIS that help to cover all aspects of an ETL solution. Apart from that, there are many other features such as event handling, buffer configuration, and the ability to work with different types of data sources, thereby making SSIS a great ETL tool.

SSIS was released with this name for the first time in 2005, but prior to that, it was named **Data Transformation Services (DTS)**. DTS was available even in SQL Server 2000, and it improved a lot since that year. As of today, this tool has gone a long way to become a mature technology for ETL and data transformation.

SSIS has an engine that is installed as a part of the Microsoft SQL Server installation media (if you choose the integration services during installation). There is an internal database for SSIS usage that contains logging information, called SSIS projects. Each SSIS project contains packages, shared connection managers, and parameters. Each SSIS package contains parameters, variables, connection managers, and some tasks and containers.
The following diagram shows an architecture diagram of SSIS:

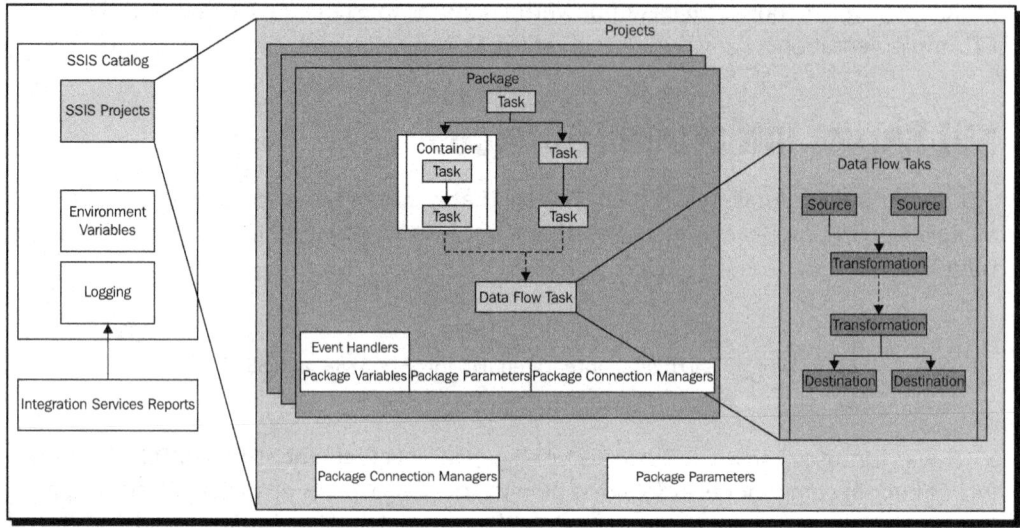

Tasks in SSIS perform a variety of operations such as copying files, sending them via FTP, working with web services, checking a directory for upcoming files, and so on. There is also a specific task named **Data Flow Task**. **Data Flow Task** has three main components: **Source**, **Transformations**, and **Destinations**. These are the main components that are used to deal with datasets, fetching data from sources, transforming them, and loading them into the destination. Each SSIS package can also utilize some event handlers for better control flow execution.

In the following sections of this chapter, we will explore some components and features of SSIS to see how helpful these features are to implement an ETL and data transfer scenario.

Integration Service projects and packages

The very first step in working with SSIS is working with projects and packages. An SSIS project contains one or more packages, connection managers, and parameters. Each package also contains a flow of execution of some tasks. Packages can relate with each other and call each other. Packages accept parameters as an input, and they can also utilize the local variables for using them inside the package.

Time for action – creating your first SSIS project

In this example, we will go through an SSIS project and packages to explore the functionality and structure of these objects. We will create an SSIS package and explore the development environment features in **SQL Server Data Tools** (**SSDT**) for Integration Services. Perform the following steps to create a project:

1. Open SSDT and create a new project of type **Integration Services Project**. Name the project Chapter 04 Integration Services.

2. When the new project opens, you will see **Solution Explorer**, **Package Designer**, and **SSIS Toolbox**:

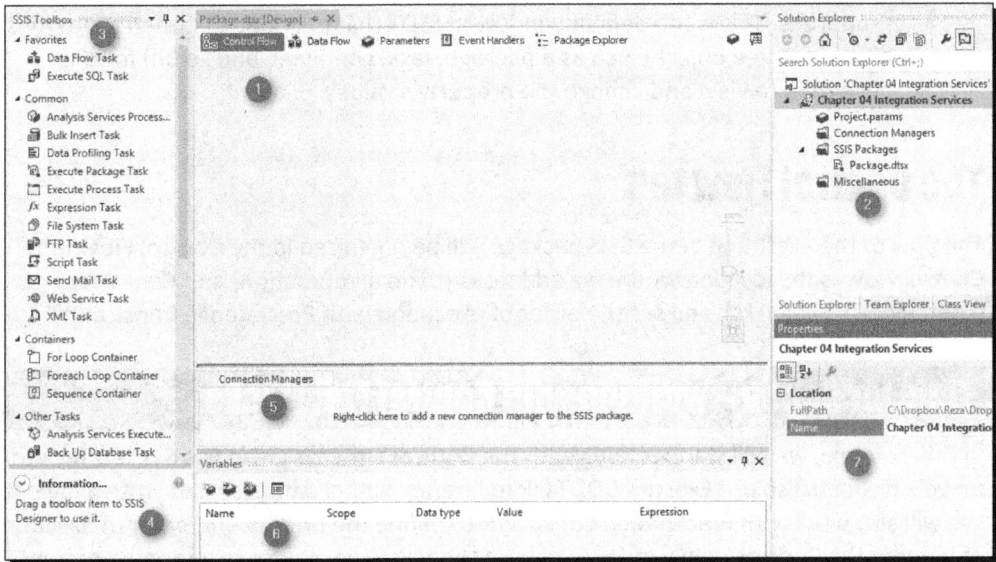

What just happened?

As you've just seen, the SSDT has a special design for the development of SSIS packages. The preceding screenshot shows each part of SSDT, and the description of each part is given as follows:

- **Package Designer**: In the preceding screenshot, the package designer shows the **Control Flow** button.

- **Solution Explorer**: The SSIS projects contain three folders. **SSIS Packages** is used as a location for SSIS package files. **Connection Managers** is used for the project's shared connection managers, which are accessible from all packages in this project. **Miscellaneous** is used for storing any related file, such as documents, to this project and **Project Parameters**, which we will discuss in the following sections.

◆ **SSIS Toolbox**: This toolbox can be different if the package designer is in **Data Flow**. The preceding screenshot shows **SSIS Toolbox** for **Control Flow**. This toolbox shows built-in tasks and components that we can drag-and-drop or double-click in order to add them into the package.

◆ **Information box**: This tab provides more information about each selected item in the toolbox.

◆ **Connection Managers**: This tab is used as a location for the package's connection managers. Connection managers of a package can be used only in that package, and other packages cannot access it. Connections to different data sources can be made using connection managers such as OLE DB, ODBC, flat file, and so on.

◆ **Variables**: The local variables of the package can be managed in this tab.

◆ **Properties**: This is the default window in SSDT that provides the listed properties of the selected object (such as a package, task, container, and so on) for the developer to view and change the property's values.

The Control Flow tab

The flow of the execution in the SSIS package will be organized in the **Control Flow** tab. **Control Flow** is the location where we add tasks (to do an operation) and **Containers** (containers of the tasks), and set the order of execution with **Precedence Constraint**.

Time for action – working with Control Flow tasks

In this example, we will start working with the **Control Flow** task, use **File System Task** to move a file, and also use **Execute SQL Task** to interact with a database and write a log entry. We will also work with **Precedence Constraint** to define the priority and order of execution of items in the **Control Flow** window. Perform the following steps to explore the options in the **Control Flow** window:

1. Create a package-level variable in the **Variables** pane, name it `FilePath` with a string data type, and set its path to the `Customers_1.csv` file.

2. Drag-and-drop a **File System Task** from the SSIS toolbox into the **Control Flow** tab.

3. Double-click on the **File System Task** in the **Package Designer**; the **File System Task Editor** will be opened.

4. Set the **Operation** option as **Move File**, set **IsSourcePathVariable** to **true**, and choose **User::FilePath** as **SourceVariable**:

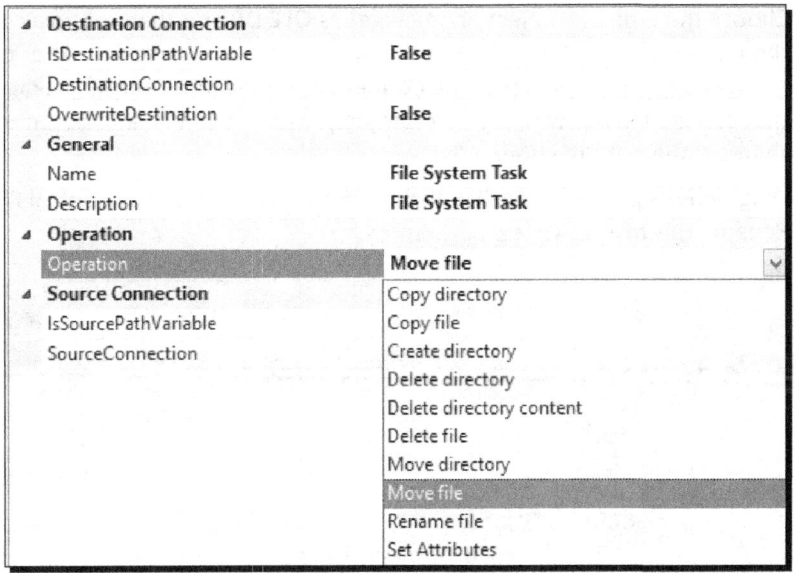

5. Keep **IsDestinationPathVariable** as **False** and create a destination connection to an archive folder (a folder that we use for the purpose of archiving files). Set **OverwriteDestination** to **True**.

6. Name the **File System Task** as `Archive File` and click on **OK**.

   Now, we want to write an entry into a log table after we successfully moved the file.

7. Firstly, create the log table with the following script in the `Packtpub_BI _2014` database:

```
CREATE TABLE [dbo].[LogSourceFile](
  [ID] [int] IDENTITY(1,1) NOT NULL,
  [FileName] [varchar](500) NULL,
  [LoadDateTime] [datetime] NULL,
  CONSTRAINT [PK_LogSourceFile] PRIMARY KEY CLUSTERED
(
  [ID] ASC
)WITH (PAD_INDEX = OFF, STATISTICS_NORECOMPUTE = OFF,
  IGNORE_DUP_KEY = OFF, ALLOW_ROW_LOCKS = ON,
  ALLOW_PAGE_LOCKS = ON) ON [PRIMARY]
) ON [PRIMARY]
```

8. In the SSIS project, under the **Solution Explorer** tab, right-click on the **Connection Managers** folder and create a new connection manager.

9. Choose the type of connection manager as **OLE DB** and then set up a connection to the `Packtput_BI_2014` database on your SQL Server instance. After creating the connection, you will see that the **Connection Managers** pane in **Package** also shows that connection but with a prefix (project), which means that this connection is a shared project connection.

10. Drag-and-drop an **Execute SQL Task** from **SSIS Toolbox** to the **Control Flow** tab. Rename this task as `Write Log Entry`.

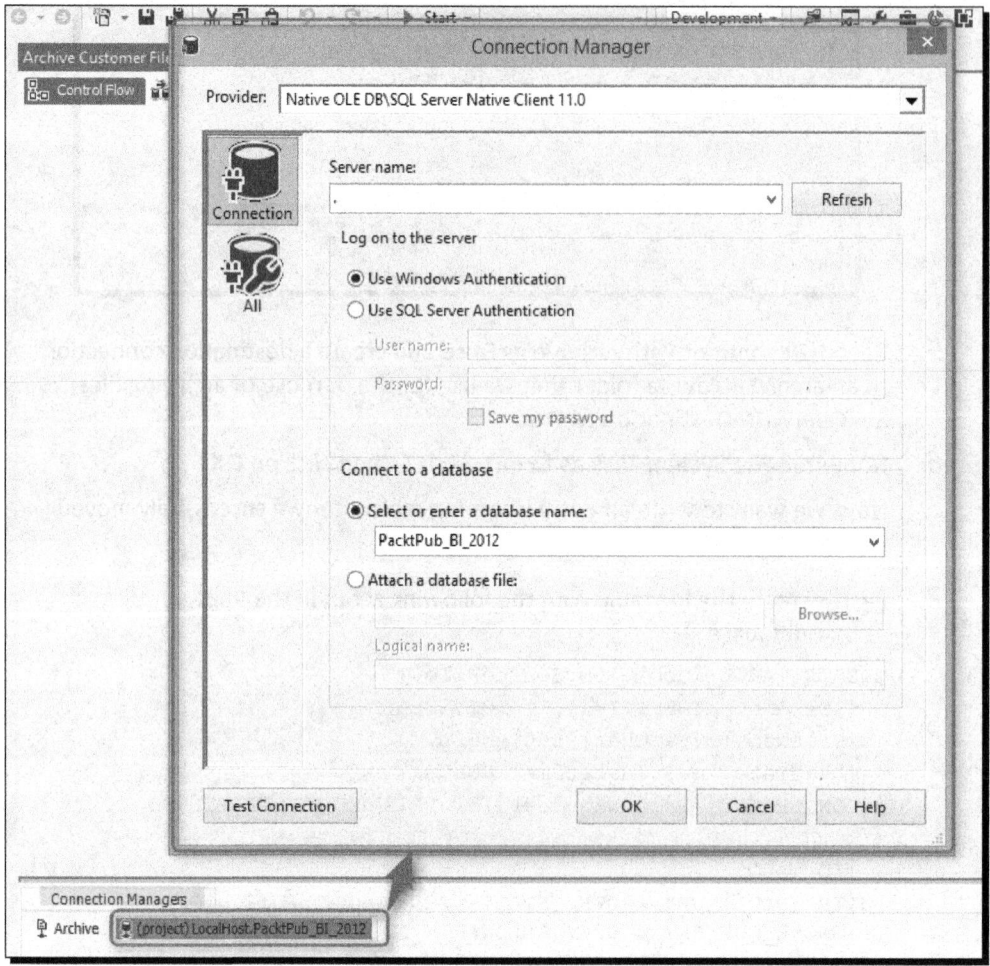

11. Click on the **Archive File** task; you will see a green arrow out of this task. Drag-and-drop this green arrow to the **Write Log Entry** task. This arrow is called **Precedence Constraint**.

12. Double-click on the **Write Log Entry** task. In the **Execute SQL Task Editor** window, keep the **ConnectionType** as **OLE DB**, and choose the Packtpub_BI_2014 database as a connection manager for it, as shown in the following screenshot:

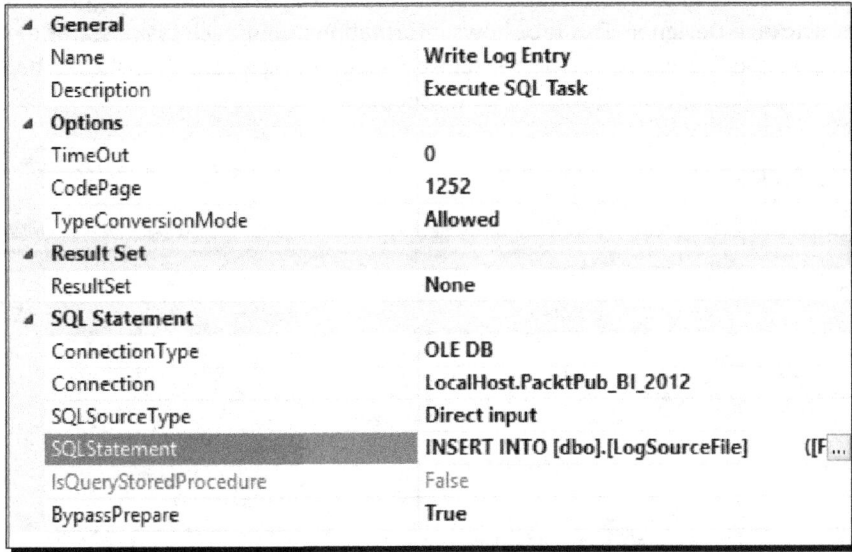

⊿ General	
Name	Write Log Entry
Description	Execute SQL Task
⊿ Options	
TimeOut	0
CodePage	1252
TypeConversionMode	Allowed
⊿ Result Set	
ResultSet	None
⊿ SQL Statement	
ConnectionType	OLE DB
Connection	LocalHost.PacktPub_BI_2012
SQLSourceType	Direct input
SQLStatement	INSERT INTO [dbo].[LogSourceFile] ([F...
IsQueryStoredProcedure	False
BypassPrepare	True

13. Write the following code in the **SQL Statement** property:

```
INSERT INTO [dbo].[LogSourceFile]
        ([FileName]
        ,[LoadDateTime])
    VALUES
        (?
        ,getdate())
```

14. The statement that we wrote in the previous step asks for a parameter, which is the filename; we should set up this parameter in the **Parameters Mapping** tab of the **Execute SQL Task**.

15. Go to the **Parameter Mapping** tab of the **Execute SQL Task Editor** and click on **Add**.

16. Set the **Variable Name** option to the **User::FilePath** variable, set **Data Type** to VARCHAR, and set **Parameter Name** as 0, as shown in the following screenshot:

General	Variable Name	Direction	Data Type	Parameter Name	Parameter Size
Parameter Mapping	User::FilePath	Input	VARCHAR	0	-1
Result Set					
Expressions					

17. Close the **Execute SQL Task Editor** and run the package by pressing the *F5* key or with the run icon in the SSDT.

18. You will see the execution status of each task with icons, which shows a running or successful state. You can also view the execution result in the **Progress** tab of the **Package Designer**. This tab shows information about each task's status along with possible warnings or error messages. The following screenshot shows the execution of the package along with its entire schema:

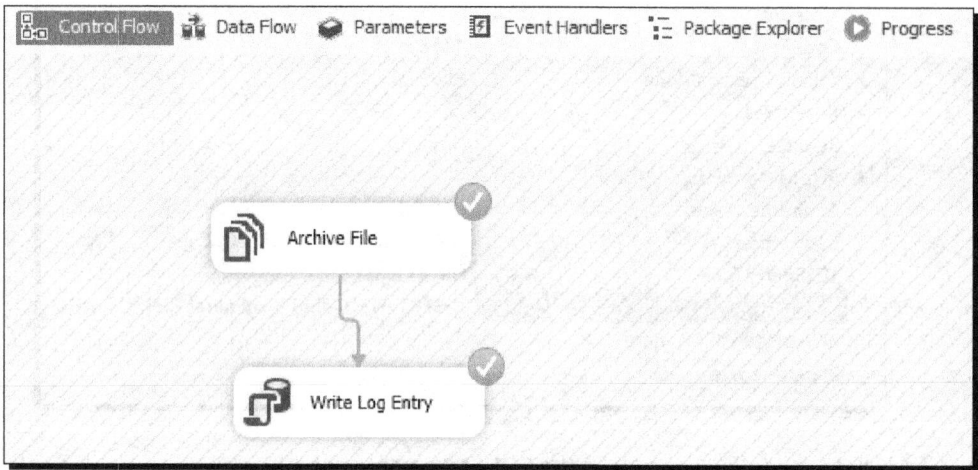

19. Rename the package Archive Customer File.

What just happened?

Congratulations, you've just made your first SSIS package! You've learned how to work with **Control Flow** tasks in this example. However, this example also revealed some other parts of SSIS, such as variables, connection managers, and precedence constraints. We will now dive deep into these parts in these following sections.

Variables

In the first step of this example, we created a package variable. Variables are very important when you want to pass a value between multiple tasks in a package. Variables can have some basic types such as String, Int32, Int64, Boolean, and so on. In this example, we used a variable to store the source file's full path.

File System Task

In steps 2 and 3, we used a **File System Task**. The **File System Task** is useful for file and directory operations. This task uses the System.IO classes to work with files and directories. Some of the operations that we can perform with this task are **Copy file**, **Move file**, **Delete file**, **Create directory**, **Set attributes**, and so on. In steps 4 and 5, we set the operation and the operation's properties such as source and destination.

All the **Control Flow** tasks in SSIS have a **Task Editor** window, similar to what you've seen in **File System Task Editor**; this editor is a GUI that is used to set properties of that task. For the **File System Task**, this GUI provided an opportunity to set the operation, source file, and destination directory. **Source** and **Destination** in the **File System Task** can be an exact connection to a file or folder (as you can see in step 5, we used a direct connection to the destination archive folder), or they can be set with **Variables** (as we've set the source file path with the **User::FilePath** variable in step 4). Working with variables provides us with the ability to make our tasks more dynamic than using static connections and values, because every time that variable's value changes, tasks will work with new values.

Control Flow tasks

As you can see in the SSIS toolbox, there are many control flow tasks, and each of them is suitable for a specific use case in real-world scenarios. The following table briefly explains each task's main duty with a short description (all the tasks are not listed):

Task	Description
Execute SQL Task	This task executes SQL statements on databases, and it may return results
File System Task	This task performs file and directory operations such as copy, move, delete, and others
Data Flow Task	This task performs extensive data transfer operations
FTP Task	This task sends and receives files between local and remote FTP locations
Send Mail Task	This task sends e-mails
Script Task	This task runs .NET scripts
Web Service Task	This task consumes a web service and fetches the result into a file and a variable
XML Task	This task performs XML operations such as XSLT, Xpath, and XML validation
Execute Process Task	This task runs an executable file or application (with or without arguments)
Execute Package Task	This task executes other SSIS packages

Task	Description
Expression Task	This task resolves the result of an SSIS expression into a variable
Bulk Insert Task	This task performs bulk insert operations and loads data from a flat file into a database
Data Profiling Task	This task performs data profiling for a database connection based on existing data rows
CDC Control Task	This task manages working with the change data capture feature in order to get informed about the changes
WMI Event Watcher Task	**Windows Management Instrumentation (WMI)** events can be watched, for example, watching a folder for new upcoming files
WMI Data Reader Task	This task reads WMI information such as the number of drives, disk space, and others
Analysis Service Processing Task	This task processes an SSAS object such as a database, cube, dimension, and partition
Analysis Service Execute DDL Task	This task executes an XMLA command on the SSAS engine, such as synchronizing SSAS databases, backing up an SSAS database, and others

In steps 9 and 10, we created a shared connection manager. Shared connection managers can be created in **Solution Explorer**, and they are visible for all packages in that project. In SSIS, **Connection Managers** are of different types. The **OLE DB** connection, **ADO.NET**, and **ODBC** connections are used for connecting to databases. The **Flat File** connection is used to work with text files such as CSV files. There are many more connection types that you can explore; more information about each connection manager is available at http://msdn. microsoft.com/en-us/library/ms140203%28v=sql.90%29.aspx.

Precedence Constraints

Steps 11 and 12 show us how to set the order of execution with **Precedence Constraints**. A green arrow (which is the default constraint) indicates successful execution of the previous task. So when we connect **Archive File** to **Write Log Entry** with a green arrow, this means that the second file will only be executed if the first task executes successfully. There are other constraints such as Completion and Failure as well. Using the failure precedence constraint is good for error handling. An example of error handling will be sending mail to the system administrator.

Precedence Constraints can also be empowered with expressions. Expression is a special language for an SSIS package, and it provides the ability to use some built-in functions and operators with variables and parameters to generate and calculate something dynamically at the package's run time. Using expressions in **Precedence Constraints** provides the ability to apply IF conditions and change the order of execution based on the result of the expression.

Execute SQL Task

In steps 13 and 14, we created an **Execute SQL Task** to write an entry log record into a database table. As you've seen in the **Control Flow** tasks table, **Execute SQL Task** is used to execute a SQL statement on the underlying database. The standard of writing a SQL statement is based on the database that we are connected to. If we are connected to SQL Server 2012 or a higher database, we can use specific functions such as LAG and LEAD. If we are connected to an Oracle database, we can use functions such as DECODE.

In step 14, we used a question mark sign in the SQL statement. The question mark is a parameter marker in the statement for OLE DB connections. We use the parameter marker to pass a variable value to the SQL statement through Execute SQL Task. In step 15, you can see that we used 0 as the parameter name. Parameter names in OLE DB connections start from 0, and this means that if we had another question mark, we would use 1 for the parameter marker of the second parameter in the **Parameter Mapping** tab.

The following table (sourced from the MSDN page at http://technet.microsoft.com/en-us/library/ms140355.aspx) shows the signature of a parameter marker and parameter names for each connection manager in SSIS for **Execute SQL Task:**

Connection Manager	Parameter Marker	Parameter Name
ADO	?	Param1, Param2, and so on
ADO.NET and SQLMobile	@<parameter name>	@<parameter name>
ODBC	?	1,2,3, and so on
Excel and OLE DB	?	0,1,2,3,...

The **Execute SQL Task** used in this example executes an insert statement and doesn't return any result set. There are some cases in which **Execute SQL Task** returns a result set; in such cases, you can set the ResultSet property of this task to **Single Row** or **Full Result Set** and then set the output variable in the **Result Set** tab.

Progress and execution results

When you run a package in SSDT, you can see the execution status of the tasks with the help of icons that show whether the package is in the running mode, was successful, or failed. Also, there is a **Progress** tab in the run time (which will be named **Execution Results** when SSDT is not in the debug mode), which shows information about each task, container, and package. It also shows if there is a warning in the process of execution or if an error has occurred.

The Data Flow tab

One of the most useful and powerful tasks in **Control Flow** is **Data Flow Task**. The importance of this task is mostly because it functions as the major part of ETL, which extracts data from different sources, transforms it, and loads it into the destination. As this task plays an important role in an SSIS package and in real-world scenarios, there are few packages that don't contain Data Flow task; SSDT has a special designer for **Data Flow**, and the SSIS toolbox's items are different in the **Data Flow** designer.

Time for action – loading customer information from a flat file into a database table with a Data Flow Task

In this section, we will go through an example of fetching information from a CSV file that contains customer information. Then, we will apply a simple transformation to calculate the age of a customer based on their birthday, and finally, we will load the result set into a database table. For this example, we will use a **Data Flow Task** with **Flat File Source**, **Derived Column Transformation**, and **OLE DB Destination**. The following screenshot shows data rows in the `Customers_2.csv` file, which need to be transferred to a database table:

```
"CustomerKey","GeographyKey","CustomerAlternateKey","Title","FirstName","MiddleName","LastName","NameStyle",
"16999","383","AW00016999","","Chloe","M","Kelly","False","1964-04-18","S","","F","chloe64@adventure-works.c
"17000","307","AW00017000","","Miranda","M","Henderson","False","1963-07-03","S","","F","miranda5@adventure-
"17001","638","AW00017001","","Ashley","F","Moore","False","1963-09-02","S","","F","ashley8@adventure-works.
"17002","546","AW00017002","","Dylan","","Martin","False","1963-12-15","S","","M","dylan44@adventure-works.c
"17003","299","AW00017003","","Joanna","M","Dominguez","False","1963-10-28","S","","F","joanna11@adventure-w
"17004","300","AW00017004","","Krista","L","Torres","False","1963-05-08","S","","F","krista12@adventure-work
"17005","307","AW00017005","","Priscilla","R","Anand","False","1963-01-19","S","","F","priscilla21@adventure
```

Perform the following steps to load the information into a database table:

1. Create a new SSIS package; name it `Transfer Customer Data`.

2. Create the destination table for this example by running the following script on the `Packtpub_BI_2014` database:

```
CREATE TABLE [dbo].[Customer] (
    [CustomerKey] [varchar](50) NULL,
    [GeographyKey] [varchar](50) NULL,
    [CustomerAlternateKey] [varchar](50) NULL,
    [Title] [varchar](50) NULL,
    [FirstName] [varchar](50) NULL,
    [MiddleName] [varchar](50) NULL,
    [LastName] [varchar](50) NULL,
    [NameStyle] [varchar](50) NULL,
    [BirthDate] [varchar](50) NULL,
    [MaritalStatus] [varchar](50) NULL,
    [Suffix] [varchar](50) NULL,
```

```
    [Gender] [varchar](50) NULL,
    [EmailAddress] [varchar](50) NULL,
    [YearlyIncome] [varchar](50) NULL,
    [TotalChildren] [varchar](50) NULL,
    [NumberChildrenAtHome] [varchar](50) NULL,
    [EnglishEducation] [varchar](50) NULL,
    [SpanishEducation] [varchar](50) NULL,
    [FrenchEducation] [varchar](50) NULL,
    [EnglishOccupation] [varchar](50) NULL,
    [SpanishOccupation] [varchar](50) NULL,
    [FrenchOccupation] [varchar](50) NULL,
    [HouseOwnerFlag] [varchar](50) NULL,
    [NumberCarsOwned] [varchar](50) NULL,
    [AddressLine1] [varchar](50) NULL,
    [AddressLine2] [varchar](50) NULL,
    [Phone] [varchar](50) NULL,
    [DateFirstPurchase] [varchar](50) NULL,
    [CommuteDistance] [varchar](50) NULL,
    [Age] [int] NULL
) ON [PRIMARY]
```

3. Drag-and-drop a **Data Flow Task** from **SSIS Toolbox** into the package designer. Double-click on the task. You will be redirected to a new tab named **Data Flow**.

4. In the **Data Flow** tab, drag-and-drop a flat file source from **SSIS Toolbox** into the **Package Designer**. Then, double-click on the flat file source.

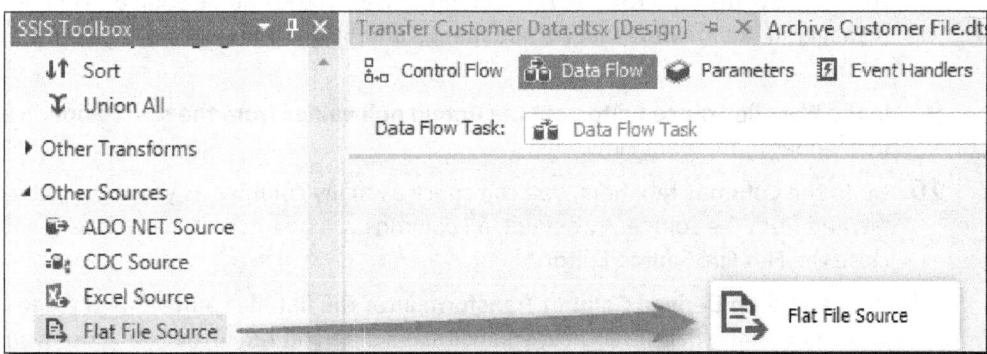

5. In **Flat File Source Editor**, create a new connection. After this step, the **Flat File Connection Manager** menu will be opened.

6. Browse for the `Customers_2.csv` file, and leave the locale and code page configurations as is. Verify the **Format** field to be set as **Delimited**, set **Text qualifier** to " (double quote) as the next screenshot shows, and check the box that says **Column names in the first data row**:

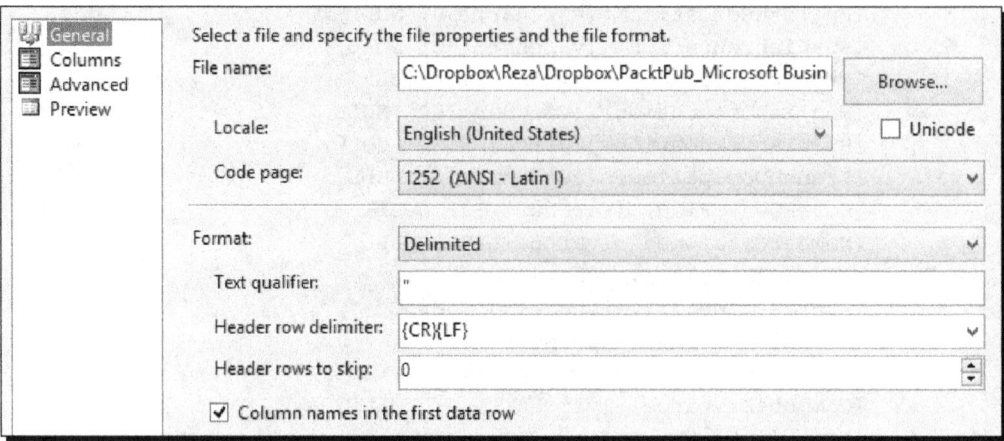

7. Go to the **Columns** tab and you will see how columns are recognized by the settings that we made in the **General** tab. You can also change the row and column delimiters in this tab.

8. The **Advanced** tab shows detailed information about each column; you can set the data type, length, and some other properties for each column in that tab. Finally, you can view the data rows as they are processed in the flat file source's connection manager in the **Preview** tab. Do not change anything in the **Advanced** tab and click on **OK**.

9. In the **Flat File Source Editor**, set the **Retain null values from the source** option as **null values** in the Data Flow.

10. Go to the **Columns** tab; here, you can check as many columns as you want to be fetched from the source. By default, all columns will be fetched. Leave it as is and close the **Flat File Source Editor**.

11. Drag-and-drop **Derived Column Transform** after the flat file source is processed and then click on the flat file source; you will see a blue and red arrow going out from the component; connect the blue arrow to the **Derived Column Transform**. These arrows are called data paths because they are moving data rows.

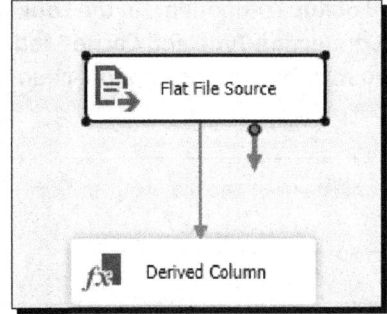

12. In the derived column transform, we can apply calculations with expressions. In this transform example, we want to calculate the age of the customer based on the current year and birth year.

13. Double-click on the **Derived Column Transformation** and write the following expression in the **Expression** box of the first row in the grid:

```
YEAR(GETDATE()) - YEAR((DT_DATE)BirthDate)
```

14. Set the **Derived Column Name** as **Age** and close the derived column transform. The following screenshot shows how a new derived column is added:

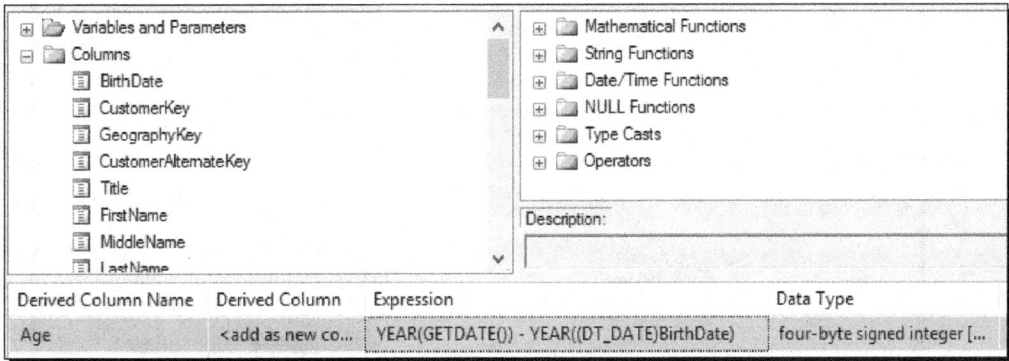

15. Now, we want to check the existence of the record with a **CustomerKey** in the destination table. So, we use a lookup transformation to do this.

16. Drag-and-drop a lookup transform after the **Derived Column**, and connect the data path (the blue arrow) from **Derived Column** to the lookup transform.

17. Double-click on the **Lookup** component. In the **Lookup Transformation Editor**, in the General tab, leave **Connection Type** and **Cache Mode** as is. In the **Specify how to handle rows with no matching entries** option, choose **Redirect rows to match output**:

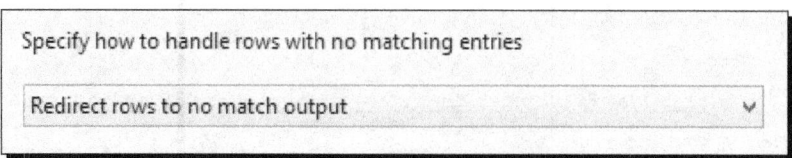

18. Go to the **Connections** tab, verify the **OLE DB** connection manager to be set in the Packtpub_BI_2014 connection, and in the **Use a table or view** drop-down list, choose **[dbo].[Customer]**. You can also preview the existing data. Note that the table is currently empty, so there will be no data rows in the preview.

19. Go to the **Columns** tab; you will see two columns set: the first column is incoming columns and the second one is lookup table columns; connect the **CustomerKey** of both columns set by dragging-and-dropping **Available Input Columns** to **Available Lookup Columns**.

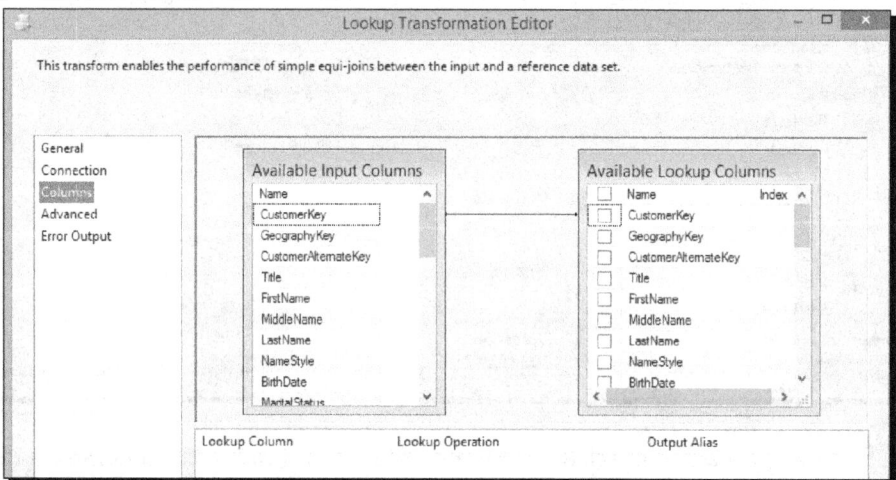

20. Click on **OK** and close the lookup transform.

21. Now, add an OLE DB destination after you close the lookup transform, and connect the data path from a lookup transform to an OLE DB destination. You will see an **Input Output Selection** dialog box that asks if it can select the input data path for the OLE DB destination. This data path appears because the lookup transform, by default, has two data path outputs: one for rows that matched and another for rows that don't match. In this example, we want to insert only new records that are not matched with the lookup table. Choose **Lookup No Match Output** and then click on **OK**.

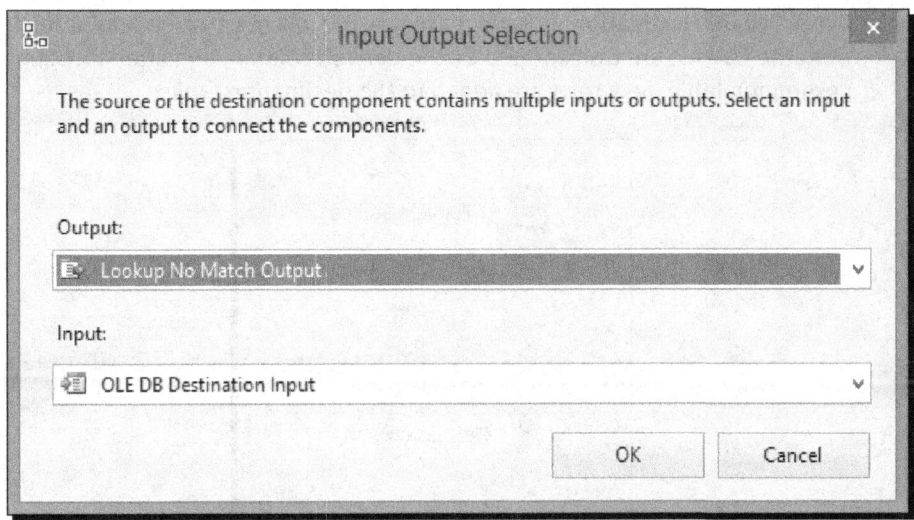

22. Double-click on **OLE DB Destination**. In **OLE DB Destination**, verify the **OLE DB Connection** to be set with the `Packtpub_BI_2014` connection manager.

23. Leave **Data Access Mode** as **Table or view - fast load** and choose the **Customer** table from the drop-down list. Uncheck the **Table Lock** option:

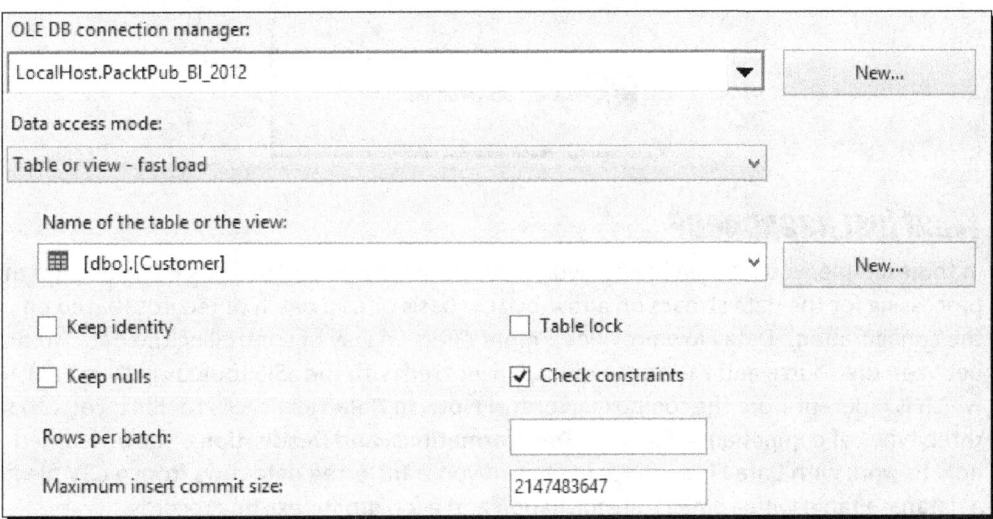

24. Go to the **Columns** tab and verify all the columns to be mapped to each other, from **Input Columns** to **Destination Columns**. The column names in the dataset are similar to the destination table's columns as the mapping is applied automatically.

25. Close **OLE DB Destination**. Run the package. You will see that data rows fetched from the CSV file are transformed by the derived column, and after a lookup on the destination table, new rows are added to the destination table:

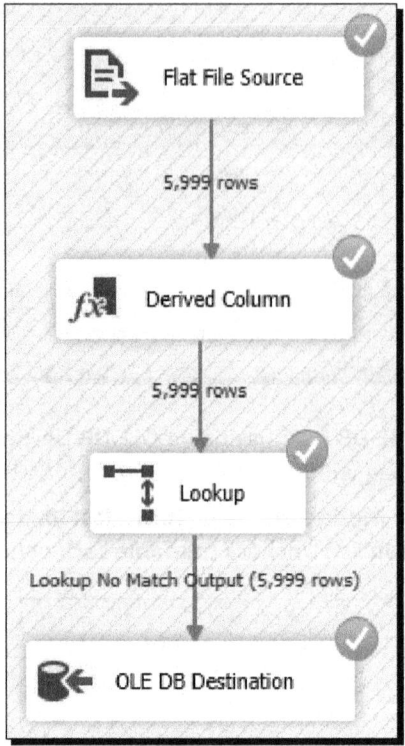

What just happened?

In this example, you learned how to work with **Data Flow Task**. The Data Flow tasks do the processing for the data stream on a row-by-row basis or as a batch of records (based on the configuration). Data Flow provides a more effective way of controlling the data stream between the source and the destination. You worked with the SSIS toolbox in Data Flow, which is different from the toolbox in **Control Flow**. In Data Flow's SSIS toolbox, you can see three types of components: **Sources**, **Transformations**, and **Destinations**. You've learned how to work with Data Flow components and you transferred data rows from a CSV file into a database table with a small transformation and a lookup for existing records.

In step 3, we created a Data Flow task. The Data Flow task, as you've seen in this example, utilizes a specific tab in the package designer with a specific SSIS toolbox that shows Data Flow components.

The Data Flow components

The Data Flow components are of three types: **Source**, **Transformation**, and **Destination**. Source components only have outputs. They might have more than one output based on the source type; for example, an XML Source may have more than one output. Transformations have at least one input and one output; they might have more than one input, such as Union All Transform, or more than one output, such as Multicast. Destination components accept input; they usually don't have a default output.

There is a data path used to connect the **Data Flow** components. As you've seen in step 11, a data path contains data rows. So, the difference between a data path in Data Flow and a precedence constraint in a control flow is that the data path contains data rows, but a precedence constraint defines the order of execution. A blue data path means correct data rows and a red data path means failed or erroneous data rows.

The Source component

In step 4, we created a flat file source to get data from a CSV file. There are different source components in a Data Flow that can fetch data from different data sources, such as databases, excel files, and flat files. The following table shows a list of Source components in an SSIS Data Flow:

Source component	Type of data source that can be used
OLE DB Source	SQL Server, Oracle, and any data source that provides an OLE DB connection provider
ADO.NET Source	SQL Server, Oracle, and any data source that provides an ADO.NET connection provider
ODBC Source	MySQL, DB2, and any data source that provides an ODBC connection provider
CDC Source	Changed data from Change Data Capture in the SQL Server DB
Flat File Source	Text or CSV files that can be delimited or have a fixed width
Excel Source	Microsoft Excel files and spreadsheets
Raw File Source	An internal binary file structure that passes data between Data Flows
XML Source	XML content loaded from a variable or a file connection

Flat File Connection Manager

In step 6, we created a flat file connection manager. The **Flat file Connection Manager** menu connects to text files and has the ability to fetch data rows by delimiters or by a fixed width. There are three different formats that are recognizable for the flat file connection manager: delimited, fixed width, and ragged right. The delimited type, used in this example, is for the text files of which the columns and rows are delimited by one or more characters. In this example, the CSV files that are delimited by a single comma for columns and rows are delimited by a carriage return. Fixed width is useful when columns have a fixed length. Ragged right determines the last column with a row delimiter, which is a little different than fixed length, because fixed length determines the last column with fixed length as well.

We also set the **Text Qualifier** field as "(double quotes) because all data values in the text file are surrounded by double quotes. Since the first row of the text file contains column headers, we checked the **Column** names in the first data row option. We can also choose the number of rows that we want to skip from the first row of the file. This option is useful when there are some header rows for the flat file that doesn't contain data rows.

In the **Columns** tab (step 7) of the **Flat File Connection Manager**, you can change the row delimiter and column delimiter and reset columns to see how columns will be picked with the new setting. The **Advanced** tab (step 8) provides detailed information about each column; you can change properties such as data type, length, and delimiter for each column in this tab.

By default, null values in the flat file will be picked as empty string values. To change this behavior, you can check the **Retain null values from the source** option as null values under the **Data Flow** option in the **Flat File Source Editor** as we did in step 9.

Derived Column transformation

We used a **Derived Column** transformation in this example to calculate a customer's age from the birth year. **Derived Column** is one of the most useful components in the **Data Flow** task because it uses expression language in SSIS, which contains some built-in functions and operations; it can use functions and operations on parameters, variables, and also input columns. As you've seen in steps 13 and 14, we used a simple expression to calculate the customer's age.

The **Derived Column** transform can generate more than one column using expressions, and the generated column can be used to replace the existing columns or acts as a new column in the data stream.

Expression language

The Expression language is a simple functional language for SSIS, and its structure looks similar to C# expressions; there are many built-in functions that can be used. Functions in the expression language are categorized into five main categories: string functions, mathematical functions, date functions, type cast, and null functions. There are operators for conditional statements such as AND and OR as well. More description about SSIS expressions can be found in the MSDN website, `http://technet.microsoft.com/en-us/library/ms137547.aspx`.

Lookup transformation

We used a Lookup Transformation to look up through a reference table (in this example, the customer table) and find the matching or nonmatching records (step 16). Lookup transformation only works with two types of connection managers: the OLE DB connection manager and Cache connection manager. So, as a result, if you want to look up through a reference table that you cannot connect to, with an OLE DB connection, you can use another Data Flow task and load the content of that table into a Cache transform, and then use a Cache connection manager to the Cache transform object in lookup transform.

Lookup components can also use three options for **Cache Mode**: **Full Cache** (default), **Partial Cache**, and **No Cache**. **Full Cache** will load all data rows from the reference table into the memory, so if the reference table is huge or memory of the server is low, you may need to choose other cache modes.

In step 17, we redirected rows that do not match with the transform to find out new records that do not exist in the reference table. In step 18, we set the reference table, and in step 19, we mapped input columns to reference columns. For this example, we find out the existence of a customer by checking the **CustomerKey**. We can also pick any of the reference columns to be fetched as the output (in match output).

As you've learned, Lookup transform has two outputs; when we connect the data path out of this component, we should choose the one that we want to work with (step 21).

Data Flow Transformations

There are many useful transformations in SSIS **Data Flow**. You can perform many data transformations without the need to write scripts. The following table shows the most useful transformations with their usages (not all the transformations are listed in the table):

Transformation	Functionality
Derived Column	Creates new columns with expressions
Data Conversion	Converts data types
Aggregate	Applies aggregation on one or more columns in the data stream

Transformation	Functionality
Conditional Split	Splits the data rows based on one or more expressions
Lookup	Looks up existing values in the reference table
Merge Join	Joins two data streams from different data sources (left or inner join)
Multicast	Creates copies of the existing data stream
OLE DB Command	Executes a SQL statement on an OLE DB connection (with or without parameters)
Row Count	Counts the number of rows and insert the result into a variable
Script Component	Executes a .NET written script on the data stream; this component can be used as a source, transform, or destination
Slowly Changing Dimension	To load data into a data warehouse dimension, you can choose the type of SCD to apply, such as 0 (fixed), 1 (changing), and 2 (historical)
Sort	Sorts a data stream based on one or more columns
Union All	Unites a data stream from all sources
Pivot	Changes values in rows to columns
Unpivot	To change columns to rows
Audit	Adds audit columns in the data stream
Fuzzy Lookup	Applies a fuzzy lookup with threshold on a reference table
Term Lookup	Applies text mining to find terms in an existing string in the data stream

Transformations can be categorized in different aspects. One type of categorization is that it can be based on blocking and non-blocking. For example, Derived Column is a non-blocking transformation because each record will be processed and sent to the output, and then the next record will be processed. Sort transformation is a blocking transformation; all data rows will be loaded first into the memory and then sorted out and sent to the output. It is always the best practice to avoid blocking transformations as they reduce the performance of a package and ETL.

OLE DB Destination

We used the OLE DB destination in step 21 to load data into a SQL Server database table. This kind of destination can be used for all databases in which we can create an OLE DB connection. Usually, you can find the OLE DB connection provider of a database vendor in its website. The OLE DB destination can load data into a database table with the fast load or regular option. The fast load option inserts multiple rows in one batch, which has a good performance. You can also set the batch size and other options (as you saw in step 23).

Input data stream columns were mapped to the destination columns in step 24, and finally in step 25, you saw an execution sample of this Data Flow.

Destination Component

There are different destinations to be used when loading data for example, a flat file, Excel, database table, and others. The following table shows a list of destinations and their usage (all the destinations are not listed):

Destination component	Type of destination that can be used
OLE DB destination	SQL Server, Oracle, and any databases that allow an OLE DB connection
ADO.NET destination	SQL Server, Oracle, and any databases that allow an ADO.NET connection
ODBC destination	MySQL and any databases that allow an ODBC connection
Flat File destination	A flat text file (having a delimited or fixed width)
Excel destination	A Microsoft Excel spreadsheet file
Raw File destination	Internal binary file for moving data between Data Flows
Recordset destination	Object type variable
SQL Server destination	Only works with a local instance of SQL Server

Containers and dynamic packages

You've learned about connection managers and control flow tasks in SSIS, but so far, all you've seen are static connections. There is a vital requirement for tasks and connections to be dynamically set at runtime, for example, when you get the name of the source database servers from an Excel spreadsheet. As another example, server names would be changed for development, testing, and production purposes. In this section, we will learn more about containers to learn how to loop through items of a collection, and then how to set the connection managers dynamically.

Time for action – looping through CSV files in a directory and loading them into a database table

In this example, we will use the `Foreach Loop` container to loop through files in a directory, and then we will set the connection manager of the source file dynamically in the flat file source, and load the content of the source file into the destination database table. Then, we will write a log entry into the database with the name of the file and load date time. For this example, we use packages and tasks that we developed in the last two examples:

1. Create a new SSIS package and name it `Master Package`. Drag-and-drop a Foreach Loop container in **Control Flow**.

2. Create a variable with a string type and name it `FilePath`.

3. Double-click on the **Foreach Loop Container**. In the **Foreach Loop Container Editor**, set **Enumerator** as **Foreach File Enumerator**.

4. In the **Enumerator** configuration, set the source directory to the path of the directory that contains Customers CSV files. Leave other settings as they are:

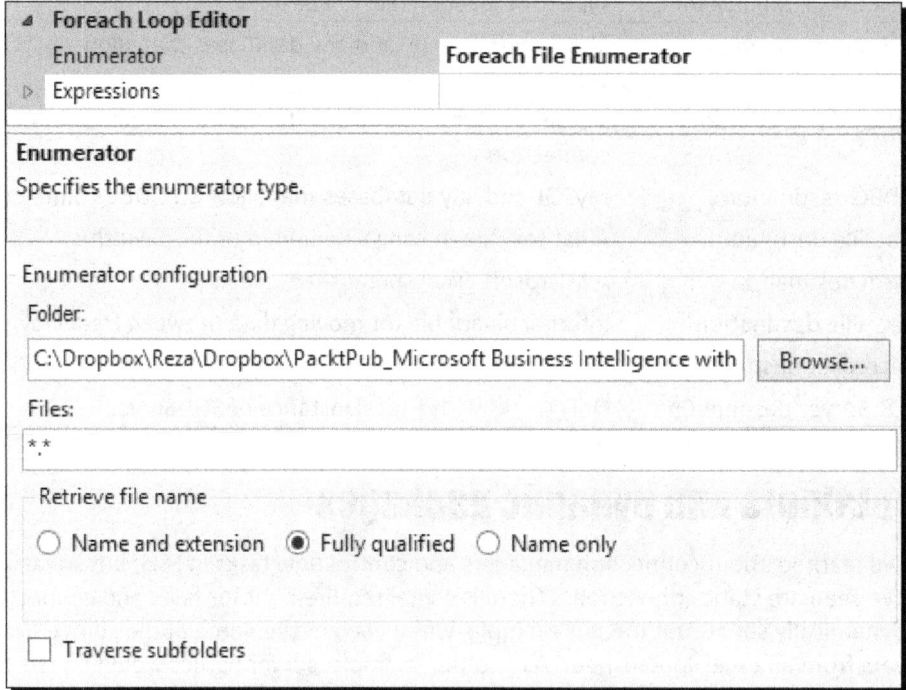

5. Go to the **Variable mappings** tab and choose the **User::FilePath** variable in the **Variable** column; the index automatically will be set to **0**.

6. Close the **Foreach Loop Container Editor**.

7. Go to the **Transfer Customer Data** package (from the previous example), right-click on the **Flat File Connection Manager** and choose **Parameterize**. In the **Parameterize** window, set **Property** as **ConnectionString**. Choose **Create a new parameter** and name it `FlatFileConnectionManager_ConnectionString`. Leave other configurations as they are. Click on **OK**:

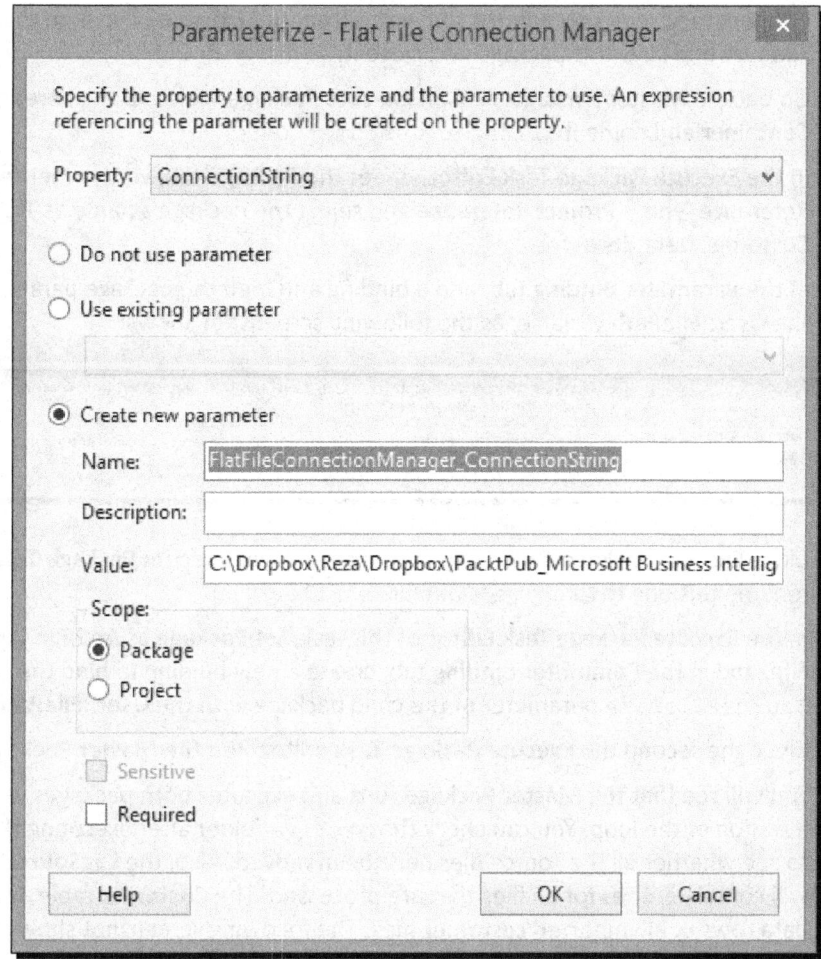

8.   You will see that a small fx icon will appear beside the **Flat File Connection Manager** icon. This fx icon shows that one of the properties of this object will be resolved by an expression at run time, in this case, the ConnectionString will be set by the parameter. Save this package and close it.

9.   Go to the **Archive Customer File** package, and then go to the **Parameters** tab.

10. Create a new parameter and name it SourceFilePath. Set the data type of this parameter as **string**.

11. Drag-and-drop an **Expression** task into the package designer and rename it to assign the parameter value to Variable. Write the following expression in **Expression Task Editor**:

```
@[User::FilePath] = @[$Package::SourceFilePath]
```

12. Connect the green precedence constraint from the **Expression** task to the **Archive File** task and save this package and close it.

13. Go back to **Master Package**. Add an **Execute Package Task** into the **Foreach Loop Container** and name it `Transfer Customer Data`.

14. In the **Execute Package Task Editor**, under the **Package** tab, verify whether **ReferenceType** is **Project Reference** and select the package's name as **Transfer Customer Data.dtsx**.

15. In the **Parameter Binding** tab, add a binding and bind the package parameter with the **User::FilePath** variable, as the following screenshot shows:

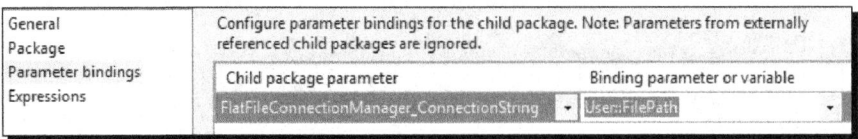

16. Close **Execute Package Task**. Drag-and-drop another **Execute Package Task**, and rename this one to `Archive Customer File`.

17. In the **Execute Package Task Editor** of this task, set **Package** as **Archive Customer File**, and in the **Parameter Binding** tab, create a new binding to bind the `SourceFilePath` parameter of the child package with the **User::FilePath** variable.

18. Close the second the **Execute Package Task** editor. Run the **Master Package**.

19. You will see that the **Master Package** runs and executes both packages within each iteration of the loop. You can check the `Archive` folder after executing the package to see whether all the source files have been moved. Also, the **LogSourceFile** table will contain entries for all files that are processed. The **Customer** table also contains data rows of all imported customer files. The following screenshot shows the result of execution:

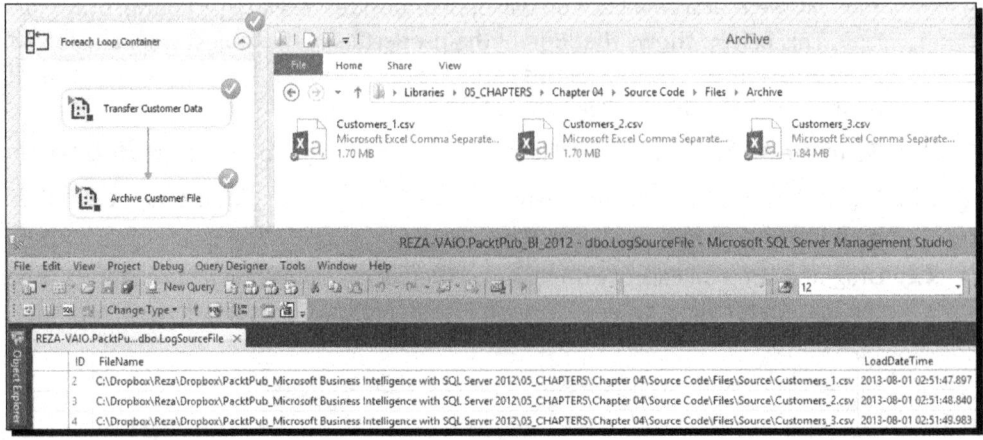

What just happened?

In this example, you learned how to work with a Foreach Loop container and create a dynamic connection using parameters and expressions. You also used **Execute Package Task** to execute other packages. Working with connections dynamically within a loop structure is one of the most common scenarios in data transfer.

The Foreach Loop container

SSIS utilizes three containers: Sequence, For Loop, and Foreach Loop. For Loop is a simple loop structure that uses initialization, conditions for evaluation, and assignment. Foreach Loop is used for looping through items of an object collection, array, files, XML content's node and attributes, SQL Server objects, and so on. There are seven types of enumerators in the Foreach Loop container. Each enumerator type works with a specific kind of object collections.

In this example, we used the Foreach Loop container in step 3, and we used **File Enumerator** in step 4 to loop through files in the source directory. An enumerator configuration for the **File** enumerator allows you to traverse subfolders. You can also use file masks to filter only those files that follow a template; for example, `Customers*.csv` will only pick those files with `Customers` at the beginning of the filename and `.csv` as the extension. You can specify whether you want to pick the full path of the file or just the filename (with or without the extension).

In step 5, we specified a **FilePath Variable** to be loaded with the fully qualified path fetched in each iteration of the loop. The index **0** indicates the first column in the looping dataset. As the file enumerator only has one column, the index **0** will only pick the output column, which is a fully qualified name in this case.

Parameterize

In step 7, we used parameters to set the flat file connection string dynamically. As you've seen, the **Parameterize** GUI helps to create the connection string dynamically. It assigns the value of the specified property with the selected (or created) parameter. The **Parameterize** GUI utilizes the `expression` property in the code behind; in other words, if you check the `Expression` property of the connection string, you will see that an expression sets the connection string property's value with the parameter's value.

In step 9, we created a `package` parameter. This parameter is used as an incoming argument to the package and is good for package-level abstraction. We created the `SourceFilePath` parameter. Then, with an **Expression Task**, we write the parameter's value into the package variable (step 11). The best practice is to always use parameters as an input gate and variables for interaction between tasks inside the package. This will end up with the package having a good level of abstraction.

In the expression language, variables will be identified with the `@[<user or system>::<variable name>]` signature. However, parameters have a slightly different signature as `@[$<package or project level>::<parameter name>]`. You've seen an example of this expression signature in step 11.

Execute Package Task

Calling other packages is one of the vital requirements in an ETL scenario. Using **Execute Package Task**, you can execute other packages, and as a result, you can fortify the design of data transfer in such a way that each package performs a main task. As you can see, in the previous example, we used one package to transfer data between CSV files and database tables, and another package to archive a file and write a log entry. Then, we used two execute package tasks (steps 13 to 17) to run each package.

Execute Package Task is a simple task that asks for the child package to be run. If the child package is protected with a password, you can enter the password in the **General** tab of **Execute Package Task**. The **Parameter Bindings** tab (step 15) will be used for passing the package variable's value to the child package's parameter.

Using **Execute Package Task**, you can utilize a master package and run other packages in the master package. So, logging and troubleshooting of packages will be much easier, and the maintenance cost will be much lower because each package will be responsible only for a specific task.

Deploying and executing

SSIS packages should be deployed in the production environment. SSIS 2012 introduced a new database as a repository for deployed SSIS projects and packages; this database is called SSIS catalog. SSIS catalog can be accessed through SSMS, which is handy for database administrators. SSIS catalog stores projects, packages, relationships of variables, execution log, and many other types of deployment and execution-related information that is useful in production environments.

Usually, there is no SSDT or development tool in the production environment. So, SSIS packages should be executed using the DTEXEC utility, either through SSIS catalog or from a SQL Server Agent Job. Calling SSIS projects from SQL Server Agent Job is one of the most popular methods in real-world scenarios because an ETL process usually needs to run on a scheduled basis.

Time for action – deploying an SSIS project

In this example, we will first create the SSIS Catalog. Then, we will deploy the SSIS project that we created in the previous examples. For this example, you need to have SSIS 2012 or higher versions installed, because SSIS Catalog is not available for earlier versions of SSIS. Perform the following steps to deploy an SSIS project:

1. Open **SQL Server Management Studio** (**SSMS**) and connect to the database engine.

2. In the object explorer, expand the server name and then right-click on the **Integration Services Catalogs** and then click on **Create Catalog**. In the **Create Catalog** dialog box, just set a password and click on **OK**.

3. SSISDB catalog will be added under the **Integration Services Catalogs** node in SSMS. The SSISDB name cannot be changed for this version as well as the earlier versions of SSIS.

4. Go to SSDT and right-click on the **Project** file in **Solution Explorer** and select **Deploy**.

5. Now, the **Integration Services Deployment Wizard** will appear. In the **Select Source** step, leave the configurations as is (in which the project deployment file is present) and then go to the next step.

6. In the **Select Destination** step, browse the database engine instance under which you've created the SSISDB catalog. Then, select **Path** and create a new folder for `Packtpub_BI_2014` as the following screenshot shows:

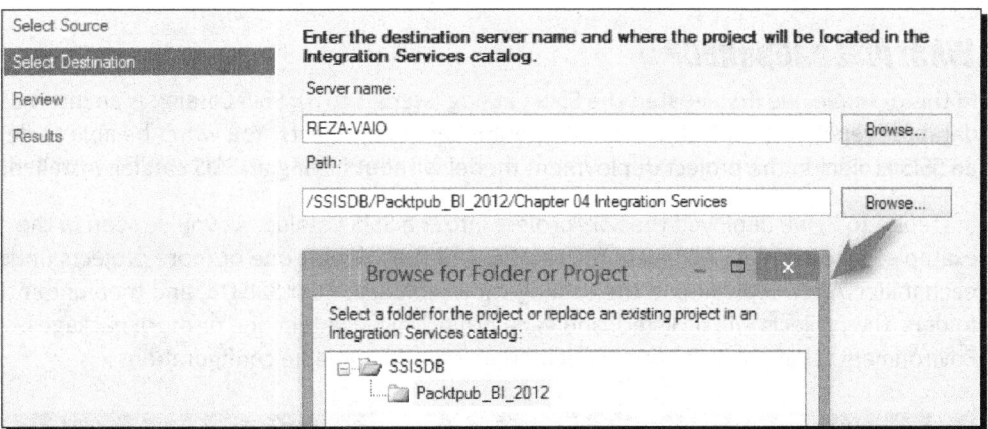

7. Continue the wizard and deploy the project. After successful deployment, go back to SSMS and refresh the **Integration Services Catalogs** node. Now, you will see the new project deployed under the `Packtpub_BI_2014` folder as the following screenshot shows:

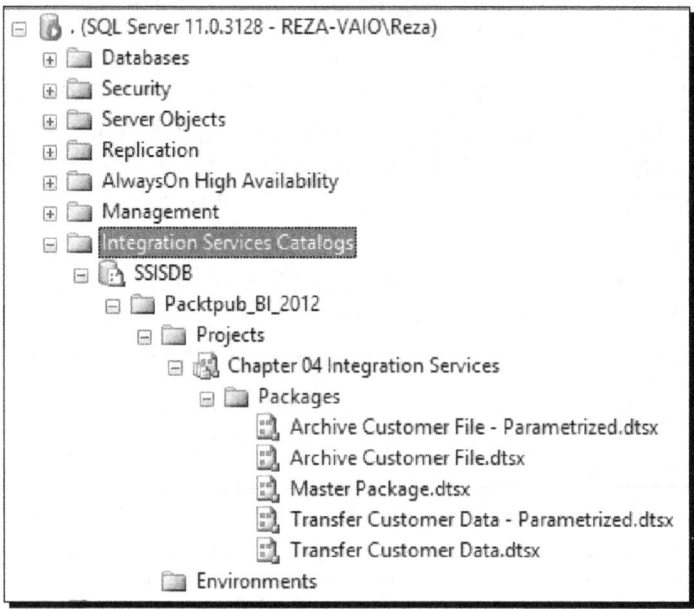

What just happened?

In this example, we first created the SSIS Catalog (steps 1 to 3). SSIS Catalog is an internal database repository for SQL Server Integration Services projects. You won't be able to deploy an SSIS project in the project deployment model without having an SSIS catalog installed.

In steps 4 to 7, we deployed the SSIS project into the SSIS Catalog. As you've seen in the example, we can create folders in the catalog and then deploy one or more projects under each folder. After deployment, the catalog shows folders under SSISDB, and then under these folders, the projects will be listed, and each project may contain one or more packages. Environments that are listed under each project are for variable configurations.

Time for action – executing an SSIS package from a catalog

After deploying the project, we can execute the **Master Package**. Before executing the **Master Package**, revert all the changes, which means move customer CSV files from the `Archive` folder back to the source folder, and truncate the customer and log database tables. To get this sample working, you will need to have the project deployed to SSIS Catalog, as illustrated in the previous sample, and perform the following steps:

1. In the SSMS, under **Integration Services Catalogs**, under **SSISDB**, expand the `Packtpub_BI_2014` folder and then expand the packages under the **Chapter 04 Integration Services** project. Then, right-click on the **Master Package** and click on **Execute**.

2. In the **Execute Package** window, go to the **Connection Managers** tab. You will see all the connection managers here and you will be able to change the properties of the connection managers from this GUI tool. Just leave the configuration as is.

3. Go to the **Advanced** tab and change the **Logging level** to **Verbose** (each logging level provides logging facilities different events. Verbose is the most detailed logging level):

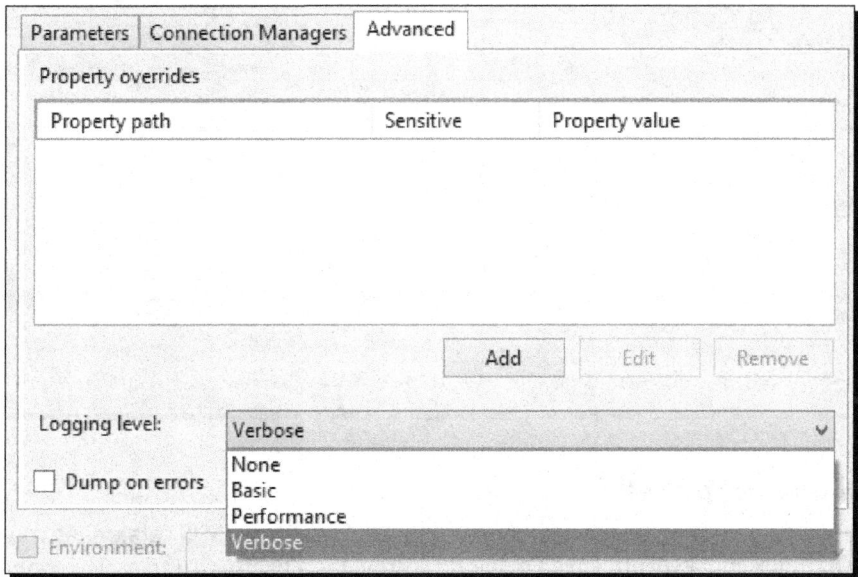

4. Now, click on **OK** to execute the package. You will see that the execution starts. A dialog box appears that asks you to open **Overview Report**. Click on **No**.

5. Right-click on the **SSISDB** node, and from the pop-up menu, choose **Reports** and then **Standard Reports**, and then click on **Integration Services Dashboards**.

6. You will see that the SSRS dashboard shows the execution summary of packages. You can also drill down to the execution details of each package and check the information and error messages for each package at the task level. The following screenshot shows the **Integrated Services Dashboard** window:

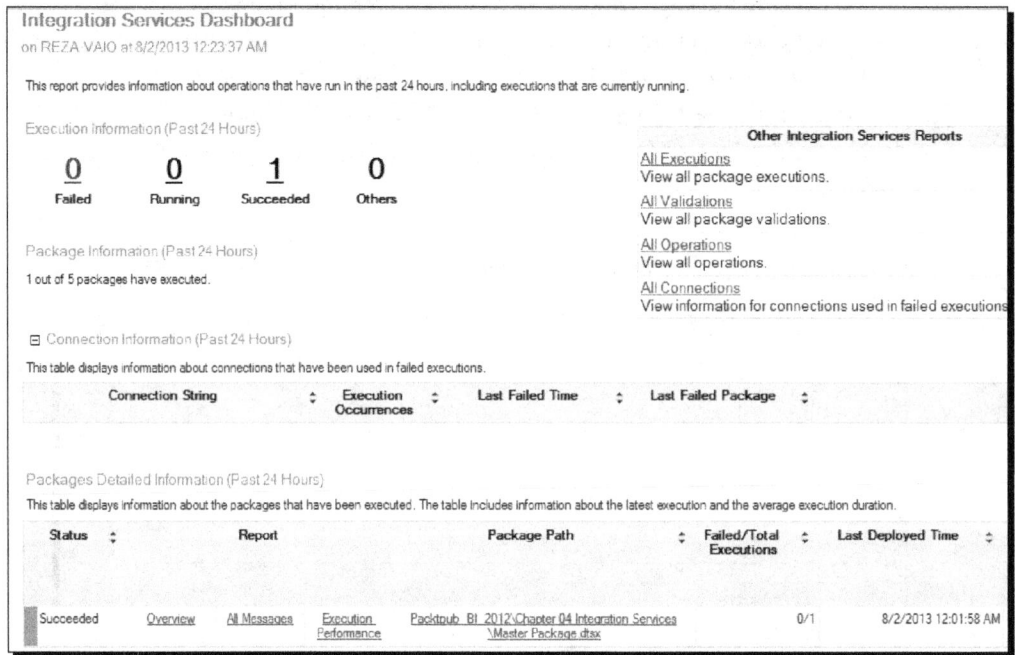

What just happened?

You've seen a very simple example of executing packages from SSIS catalog. As you've seen in this example, the **Execute Package** window provides a useful GUI to assign connection managers and configure log settings before executing the package.

You've also seen that SSIS catalog provides extensive logging as a part of the execution. There are also some SSRS reports that show a summary of high-level information about packages and detailed information about each task and error messages (if there is any).

Summary

SQL Server Integration Services is a data consolidation and ETL tool. SSIS provides many built-in tasks and components that help you to create the data transfer scenarios. An SSIS project contains one or more packages. Each SSIS package has a control flow design area that contains multiple tasks with their order of execution. There is also a Data Flow task that is the main part of ETL development; you can use the sources, transformations, and destination components to a great extent with different data providers and apply complex transformations. SSIS projects can be deployed to SSIS catalog, which is a central repository for Integration Services projects, and provides extensive logging and execution options.

SSIS is a vast topic that cannot be covered in a single chapter. If you want to read more about this technology, you can view SSIS tutorial videos at `http://www.radacad.com/CoursePlan.aspx?course=1`, or read the SSIS book, *Microsoft SQL Server 2012 Integration Services*, which is an expert cookbook published by Packt Publishing.

5

Master Data Management

*Having one version of the truth in a data warehouse and even in database systems is an important step. In this chapter, you will learn why we need **Master Data Management (MDM)** in the BI solution, and you will learn about the structure of Master Data Services as a Microsoft service for implementing MDM solutions. You will also learn how to create models and entities with Master Data Services, how to work with WebUI and Microsoft Excel Add-in, and how to create business rules and secure information.*

Understanding Master Data Management

Assume that some transactional systems and databases such as CRM exist, a retail sales system, and other systems that keep customer information in the form of one or more tables inside their own databases. There might be multiple ways of inserting customer information, such as importing from files or data entry. And each of those systems might keep only part of the customer information that is required for that system.

This is shown in the following diagram:

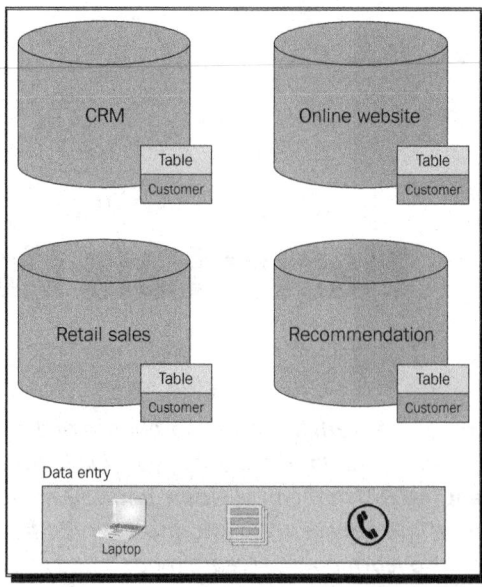

As you can see in the previous diagram, customer information is stored in an inconsistent manner. There might be some customer information in the retail system that is outdated while some part of the customer information might even be missed, for example, in CRM. This is an example of customer information as reference data, because all other systems and databases require this data to work (to insert data into it or get data out of it). For this purpose, we'll keep the reference data (customer information, in this example) in a central repository. Then we enable other systems to import and export data to and from this central repository.

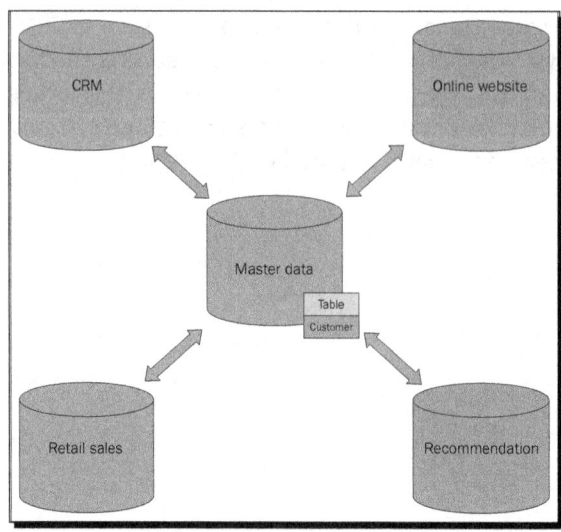

The central repository in the previous example helps to keep the reference data consistent. Now it is time to talk about Master Data Management. MDM is a set of policies, processes, and technologies that store master or reference data in a central repository. Policies define who owns the data and metadata. Process is about how to import and export master data, and technologies help implement the MDM solution. Three major benefits of MDM are: having a single version of the truth, enabling business users instead of IT manage the master data, and ensuring the integrity of the information.

Master Data Services

Microsoft introduced a solution for Master Data Management for the first time in SQL Server 2008 R2; this solution is called **Master Data Services (MDS)**. MDS improved in SQL Server 2012. In this chapter, we will walk through MDS capabilities and you will learn how to implement an MDM solution with Microsoft MDS.

MDS consists of the features shown in the following diagram. It provides domain management with models, entities, attributes, and hierarchies. The ability to create business rules and apply them for data validation is also provided. MDS can work with other systems to import data and also export master data information to them. It can be integrated with **Data Quality Services (DQS)** to apply matching logic on master data as well as data cleanup before inserting data into MDS.

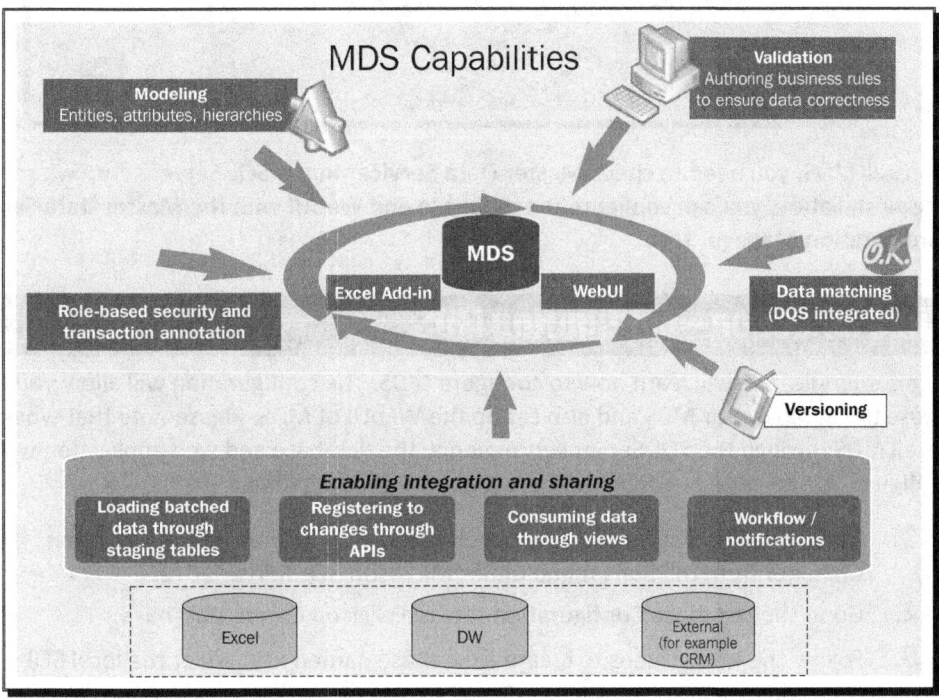

MDS consists of multiple components. The first component is a SQL Server database for storing data and metadata. There is an MDS engine that will read and write information to that database through two graphical user interfaces: WebUI and Excel Add-ins. MDS uses subscription views to export information from MDS to other systems, such as operational and data warehouses. It also uses a staging mechanism to import data from other systems, which is called entity-based staging. The following diagram shows the MDS architecture:

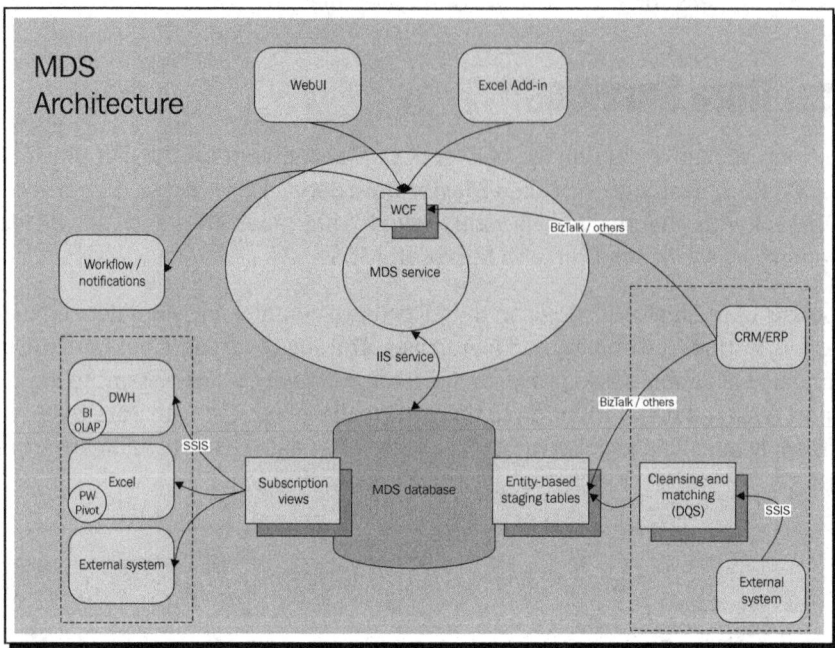

To install MDS, you need to check **Master Data Services** in the SQL Server setup wizard steps. After installation, you can configure the database and WebUI with the **Master Data Services Configuration Manager** tool.

Time for action – configuring MDS

In this example, you will learn how to configure MDS. The configuration will allow you to create the database for MDS and also set up the WebUI of MDS. Please note that when you install MDS through the SQL Server setup media, the database and web application will not configure, so you need to configure them manually the first time.

1. After installing SQL Server 2012, open **Master Data Services Configuration Manager** from the **Start** menu under Microsoft SQL Server 2012.

2. Go to the **Database Configuration** tab and click on **Create Database**.

3. Follow the wizard steps to create a database named MDS under the local SQL Server instance.

4. Go to **Web Configuration** and choose a default website from the drop-down list.

5. Create an application and name it MDS.

 Note that you should have **Internet Information Services (IIS)** installed. If you don't have IIS installed or configured properly, you will get a message in **Master Data Services Configuration Manager** that mentions the configuration that needs to be done.

6. Select the MDS database created in step 3 to associate with the application.

7. Navigate to the URL http://localhost/MDS.

What just happened?

In this example, you've seen that after installing SQL Server, you need to configure MDS manually. **Master Data Services Configuration Manager** is where you can change the database and web configuration of MDS.

In step 3, we created a database for MDS. You can also use an existing database and select it at this stage (this is useful for recovering MDS or for transferring the MDS server). We also created a web application for MDS in steps 4 and 5 and connected that application to the database.

Comparing WebUI with the Excel Add-in

There are two editors for MDS: WebUI and Excel Add-in. When you install and configure Master Data Services, the WebUI will be configured and ready to use (you've seen how to configure MDS and WebUI in the previous example). The Excel Add-in needs to be installed separately from the newly generated WebUI link.

Both WebUI and the Excel Add-in have the ability to do many of the basic tasks in MDS, such as creating and inserting values in entities, browsing entity values, editing values, and other tasks. However, some tasks are only available in one of these editors; for example, permissions can be configured only from the WebUI, and hierarchies can be edited and viewed only in the WebUI. On the other hand, some activities, such as integration with DQS (will be covered in next chapter), are only possible with the Excel Add-in.

From an end user's perspective, the Excel Add-in is more comfortable. However, from the administration's point of view, the WebUI plays an important role. In some of the samples in this chapter, you will see both editors being used simultaneously, such as when working with entities in the very next section. However, in some examples you will see only one editor, and that mainly is because the other editor doesn't support that feature.

Time for action – installing Excel Add-in

In this example, you will learn how to install the Excel Add-in. The important step to take before this is to have the MDS WebUI up and running (which is explained in the previous example).

1. Go to `http://localhost/MDS` and open the MDS WebUI.

2. Click on **Install Master Data Services Add-in for Microsoft Excel**, which is shown in the following screenshot:

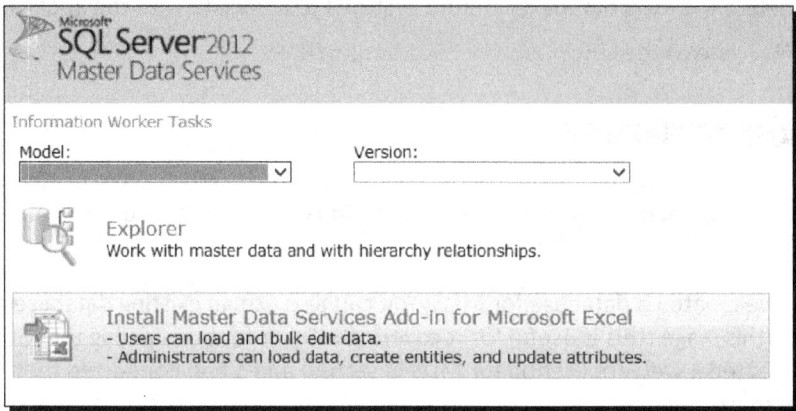

3. You will be redirected to another URL. Pick the download link that meets the 32- or 64-bit version of Office installed on your machine. Install the Add-in after downloading it.

4. Open an Excel spreadsheet. You will see a new tab named **Master Data,** as shown in the following screenshot. Under that tab, you will see the icon set tools for Master Data Services.

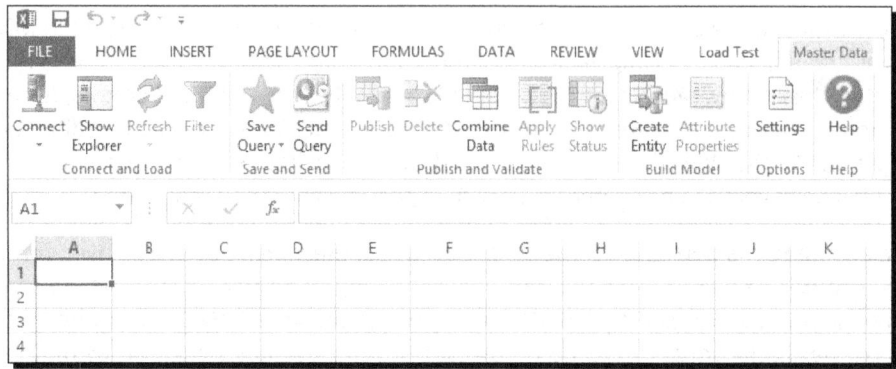

5. Click on the **Connect** icon and create a new connection. Enter a description; then set the MDS Server address as `http://localhost/MDS`.

6. Test the connection, and connect. You will see an explorer pane on the right-hand side of the Excel window, named **Master Data Explorer**. This explorer lists models, and after choosing a model, you will see its entities.

What just happened?

You've learned how to install the MDS Excel Add-in in steps 1 through 4. Then you created a connection to Master Data Services through steps 5 and 6. In the coming examples, you will see how to use the Excel Add-in for MDS tasks.

Creating models and entities

MDS will store data in entities; multiple entities of the same subject can be stored in a model. A model is a container of some entities and can have a specific permission assigned to it. A model in MDS is similar to a schema in a database, because it contains some objects (entities), which has permissions on it related to groups or users. An entity is a data object that is similar to a table in a database. Each entity has two mandatory and default columns (`Name` and `Code`) and the ability to add as many as columns for covering the requirement. Entity members are equal to rows in the table, and entity attributes are columns.

Time for action – creating a model and an entity

In this example, we will create a model and then create an entity using WebUI. We will learn how to configure an entity configuration using WebUI.

1. Go to `http://localhost/mds` in Internet Explorer (IE).

2. Click on **System Administration**; in the dropdown that appears, hover on **Manage** and select **Models**.

3. Click on the **Add** button.

4. In the **Add Model** window, uncheck **Create entity with same name as model**. After unchecking this item, the other two items will be unchecked as well.

5. Enter the model name as `PacktPub_BI_Model`. Save the model using the **Save** button located at top-left hand side under the **Main** menu.

6. Hover on the **Manage** menu again and select **Entities**.

7. In the **Entity Maintenance** window, choose **PacktPub_BI_Model** from the drop-down list.

8. In the **Add Entity** window, enter the entity name as `Product`.

9. Leave the staging table name empty, and check **Create code values automatically**. Set **enable explicit hierarchies and collections** as **no** and save.

10. You will be redirected to a list of entities. Select **Product Entity** and then click on the **Edit** button (second icon from the left-hand side under **Entity Maintenance**).

11. At the bottom section of the **Edit Entity** window, you will see the **Leaf member** attributes.

12. Click on the **add** attribute in the **Add Attribute** window, set the name of the attribute as `Size`, and set **data type** as `text`. Leave the other options as default and save.

13. You will see that a new attribute is listed under `Name` and `Code` in the **Product Entity** attribute list.

14. Go back to the **Entity Maintenance** window and delete **Product Entity** (we will create it again using the Excel Add-in in the very next example).

What just happened?

In this example, we explored the model-entity structure. We've created an entity for the product. The product entity is created under a model. As you can see, creating models and entities can be easily done using WebUI, and you can add attributes to the entities and set their data types.

There were some configurations in this example that we passed without change; we will go through some of them in the next example when we load an MDS entity with data from the Excel Add-in.

Time for action – creating an entity with data from the Excel Add-in

MDS entities can be created with data from the Excel Add-in. In this example, we will load data from a database table into an Excel sheet and then create an MDS entity using the structure and data taken from the Excel sheet.

1. Open an empty workbook in Excel and go to the **Data** tab.

2. Click on the **From Other Sources** option (in the **Get External Data** section) and select **From SQL Server**.

3. Enter `localhost` as the **SQL server** name, then select **AdventureWorksDW2012** as **database**, and select **DimProductCategory**. Click on **Continue** to finish. You will see the product categories listed in the Excel sheet.

4. Go to the **Master Data** tab. Connect to the MDS connection that you created in first example of this chapter.

5. Select the cells of the Excel sheet that contain the data of the product category. Then click on the **Create Entity** icon in the **Master Data** tab under the **Build Entity** section.

6. Choose **PacktPub_BI_Model** as model, leave the version as is, and enter Product Category as the name of the entity.

7. Set productCategoryKey as the Code column and EnglishProductName as the Name column.

8. Click on **OK**. You will see that a new entity is created and records are inserted into that entity. After the insertion of records, the entity with the records will be shown in a new Excel sheet. The following screenshot shows how entity records are shown in the Excel sheet:

MDS Connection: local MDS(http://reza-vaio/mds)		Model: PacktPub_BI_Model	Version: VERSION_1	Entity: Product Category
Name	Code	ProductCategoryAlternateKey	SpanishProductCategoryName	FrenchProductCategoryName
Bikes	1		1 Bicicleta	Vélo
Components	2		2 Componente	Composant
Clothing	3		3 Prenda	Vêtements
Accessories	4		4 Accesorio	Accessoire
my sample	5		5 my sample	my sample

What just happened?

In this example, you've learned how to work with the Excel Add-in for MDM. We used the **Data** tab in Excel to load data from **Adventure Works DW** into the Excel sheet (step 1 to step 3). The Excel Add-in provides the ability to import data into the MDS entity easily with the **Create Entity** option (step 5); you can define the destination entity model and its version (step 6) and specify the Name and Code columns as well (step 7).

The Excel Add-in provides useful functionalities for the data steward (a person from the business who is responsible for the master data, and would apply master data changes) to work with master data. Users can easily filter data with the Excel filter features and all the other useful functionalities to apply changes.

Time for action – change tracking

Change tracking is one of the useful features of MDS. Changes in any attribute values will be logged in the MDS database and are viewable using the Excel Add-in or WebUI. Users or a data steward may also insert comments on every change that occurs on the master data to make the tracking of changes even easier. In this example, we make some changes in an attribute value and then track the history of changes.

1. Add a new member (record) at the end of the **Product Category** entity in the Excel Add-in.

2. A new record will appear in a different color. You need to publish changes to save them back to MDS. You can insert comments when you publish it. After publishing, the color will change back.

3. Change the `Name` column of the new record to something else, and then publish (you can leave comments as well).

4. Perform step 3 again with new names.

5. Right-click on `value` in the `Name` column of the new record (the cell that you've made changes to in step 3 and 4), and then click on **View Transactions**.

You will see a list of changes in each attribute, old and new values, the name of the user who made that change, date and time of change, and annotations related to that change, as shown in the following screenshot:

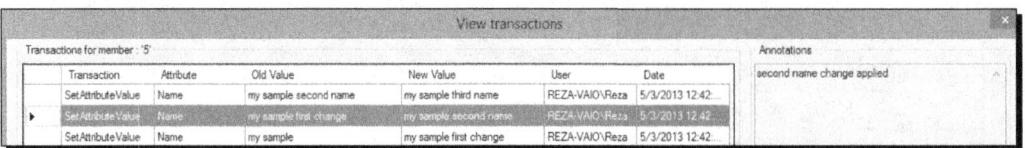

You can view the same transaction history in WebUI as shown in the following steps.

6. Open **MDS WebUI**, select **PacktPub_BI_Model**, and then go to **Explorer**.

7. Select the new record and then select **View Transactions** from the icons at the top. You will see a list of transactions (you may need to install Silverlight to get the WebUI explorer working).

8. You can also make changes through WebUI. Changes can be applied within the **Details** pane on the right-hand side of the entity explorer. The following screenshot shows the WebUI entity explorer and the **Details** pane:

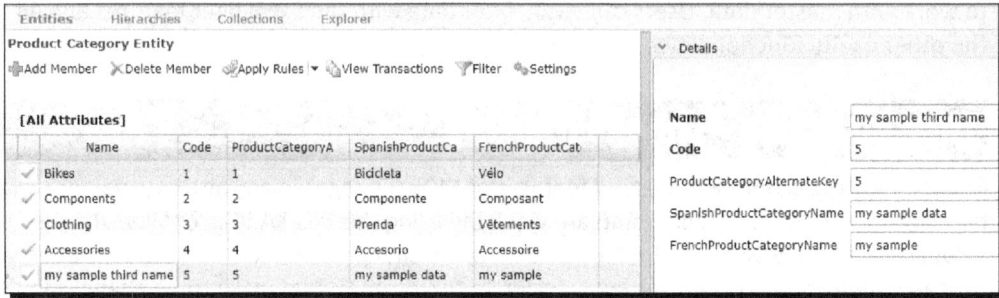

What just happened?

The previous example illustrated how to make changes through the Excel Add-in (from step 1 to 6) and WebUI (step 12). After each change in the Excel Add-in, you need to publish it (as you've seen in step 5); you can also leave comments before publishing the change. All changes through the WebUI will be published automatically after you click on the **OK** button on the **Details** pane.

MDS keeps track of every change in each attribute of the entities. As you've seen in the **View Transaction** windows, all changes with related information are visible and traceable in terms of when a change was made and who made what change on what attribute. Both the WebUI and the Excel Add-in provide full feature abilities to apply changes on entity members and view transactions.

The entity relationship

Entities in MDS can be related to each other, just like database tables, which can be connected to each other with FK-PK relationships. Entity relationships are helpful for a data steward to enter values by selecting from a list of names rather than working with codes and keys.

Time for action – creating a domain-based relationship

In this example, we will create two other entities for the product and its subcategory. We will then create a relationship between these entities with Excel Add-in.

1. Create **Product Sub Category Entity** in the same way we created the product category entity in previous examples. Set **Name** as `English Product Sub Category Name` and **Code** as `ProductSubCategoryKey`. Use `DimProductSubCategory` as the source table in AdventureWorksDW2012.

2. Create a **Product** entity from **DimProduct** and set **Name** as `Name column` and **Code** as `ProductID`.

3. Open the **ProductSubcategory** entity in Excel Add-in. Note that there is a column in this entity named `ProductCategoryKey`. This column does not make sense for a data steward, so we want to change it to point to an equivalent record in the **Product Category** entity; this will help the data steward to manage data easily.

4. Select the `ProductCategoryKey` column and rename it to `Product Category`.

5. Select the `Product Category` column and click on the **Attribute Properties** icon in the **Build Model** section. Change the **Attribute Type** to **Constrained list (Domain-based)**. Then, from the drop-down list of **Populate the attribute with values from**, choose the **Product Category** entity.

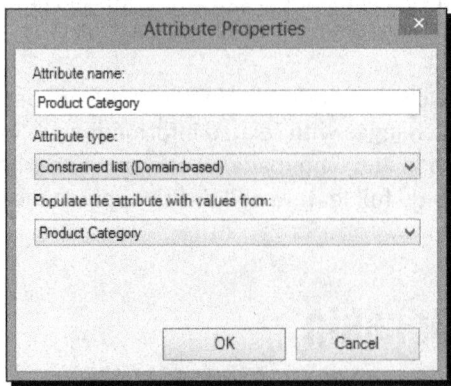

6. After clicking on **OK**, you will see that the column behavior changes; it shows the name value of each product category in a bracket near the code value as well, which is very handy for users to work with. The following screenshot shows how a user will see domain-based columns and can make changes easily.

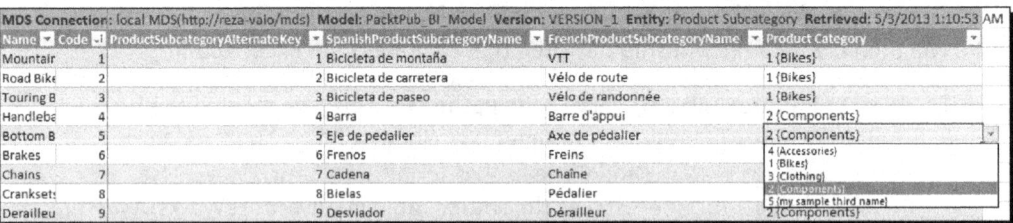

7. Create another relationship between the **Product** entity's `ProductSubCategoryKey` column and the **Product Subcategory** entity.

8. You can even create a new entity from a list of unique values in a column, for example, the `Color` column in the **Product** entity can be fetched out into a new entity. This will cause better consistency for users to work with. To do this, select the `Color` column and then change attributes properties to **Constrained list (Domain-based)**, but choose **the selected column** in the **Populate the attribute with values from** box and type in the name of the new entity in the box below as `Color`.

What just happened?

The previous example showed how you can create a relationship between two entities by configuring the attribute's properties to **Constrained list (Domain-based)**. Step 5 shows an illustration of that configuration. Also, step 8 shows how you can create a new entity from unique values in a single column, such as `color`, and fetch an entity based on those values.

Business rules

Every data structure requires the functionality to define business rules and constraints. Business rules will help business users keep data consistent, reliable, and in the scope of the business. MDS, as a master data management solution, provides an extensive business rules model to write down business logic into expressions for better data management.

Multiple business rules can be created for each entity. Each business rule has a **conditional clause** and a **then clause**. The condition clause defines the situation in which the business logic needs to be applied, and then defines what needs to be done as a business requirement in that situation.

Examples of business rules are: preventing a user from making specific changes (for example, age needs to be a numeric value between 0 and 150), creating calculated attributes (such as a full name, which is concatenated of the first and the last name), or even checking a condition and then starting a workflow.

Time for action – creating a simple business rule

In this example, we will create a business rule for standard cost, which cannot be less than zero. This will help the master data be more reliable and protected from data entry faults.

1. Open the WebUI for MDS. Go to **System Administration**.

2. From the **Manage** menu, click on **Business Rules**. Choose the **Product** entity and add a new business rule.

3. Double-click on the new record's name value and change it to **StandardCost greater than zero**. Then click on the **Edit Selected Business Rules** button on the top of the grid.

4. You will be redirected to the **Edit Business Rule** window, which is the expression designer for business rules.

5. From the **Components** area, under **Actions and Validation**, drag-and-drop **must be greater than** into the **Expression Then** area on Actions.

6. Select **must be greater than** in the actions window of the **Then** area, and then from the **Attributes** area, drag-and-drop the **StandardCost** window to the **Edit Action** area right before **must be greater than**, as shown in the following screenshot. Then set **Attribute value** as 0 and save.

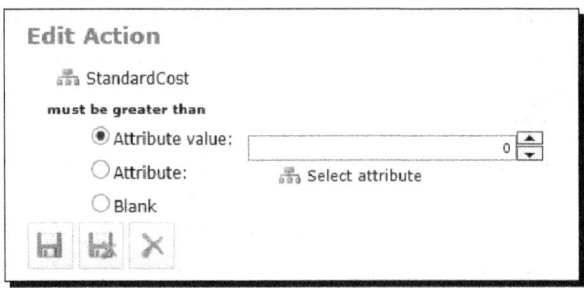

7. After saving the change, the action will change to **StandardCost**, which must be greater than 0.0. Go back to the business rule window and publish the business rule (select the business rule and then click on the **Publish Business Rule** icon at the top of the grid).

8. After successfully publishing it, you would see the status **Active** for that business rule.

9. Go to the Excel Add-in or WebUI and change **StandardCost** of a member in the **Product** entity to -12. You will see an error message that says **StandardCost must be greater than 0.0000** (please note that rules would apply only after publishing if you make changes through the Excel Add-in), as shown in the following screenshot:

MDS Connection: local MDS(http://reza-v:40:21 PM					
$ValidationStatus$	$InputStatus$	Name	Code	ReorderPoint	StandardCost
Waiting for revalidation		StandardCost must be greater than 0.0000		750	0.0000
Validation failed	U			750	-21.0000
Waiting for revalidation	Unchanged	BB Ball Bearing	3	600	0.0000

What just happened?

In this example, we created a very simple example of a business rule to validate the value of an attribute. You learned how to create business rules for entities (steps 2 and 3), create expressions for business rules (step 4 to 7), and publish the rule (step 8). After publishing the rule, the business rule would be applied on any data member in that entity. If its condition is met (in the previous example, there was no condition), then the action will be applied.

As you've probably noticed, there are many kinds of expressions for conditions and also for actions in the business rule editor. Also, we can specify "and/or" logic in expressions. We can create business rules for a combination of attributes as well. All of these mean that we can create complex expressions to meet business requirements.

There are two buttons in the Excel Add-in under the **Publish** and **Validate** section: **Apply Rules** and **Show Status**. The **Apply Rules** button will apply business rules on data and **Show Status** will show or hide two metadata columns named `ValidationStatus` and `InputStatus`. The previous screenshot shows the validation status of invalid data as failed, and the input status shows whether this value is changed or not.

Working with hierarchies

Hierarchies play an important role in information management systems. Hierarchies in MDS provide an easier frontend view for end users, who can then apply changes in hierarchies much more easily.

Hierarchies in MDS come in different types: explicit and derived hierarchies. Explicit hierarchies are kind of ragged hierarchies that are created from a single entity. Derived hierarchies are created from multiple entities based on the relationship between the entities. Explicit hierarchies can be ragged, but derived hierarchies always contain a static number of levels. The following screenshot illustrates examples of derived and explicit hierarchies:

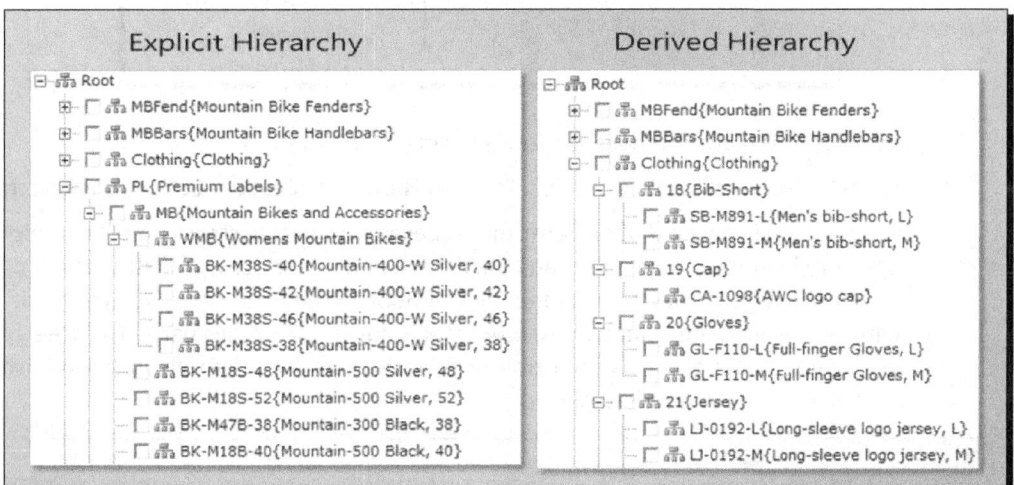

Time for action – creating a derived hierarchy

In this example, we will create a derived hierarchy from a product category, subcategory, and product. You will learn how to create a hierarchy in WebUI. You will also see how easy it is for an end user to make changes to hierarchies. This will be explored in the following steps:

1. Open MDS WebUI, and then go to **System Administration**.

2. Under the **Manage** menu, select **Derived Hierarchies**.

3. Select **PacktPub_BI_Model** and add a hierarchy.

4. Name the hierarchy `Product Hierarchy` and save it.

5. In the **Edit Derived Hierarchy** window, drag-and-drop entities from the **Available entities** pane into the **Current Levels** pane in the following order: **Product**, **Product Subcategory**, and **Product Hierarchy**.

6. After each drag-and-drop action, you will see a preview of results in the **Preview** pane. The following screenshot shows what the product category hierarchy looks like:

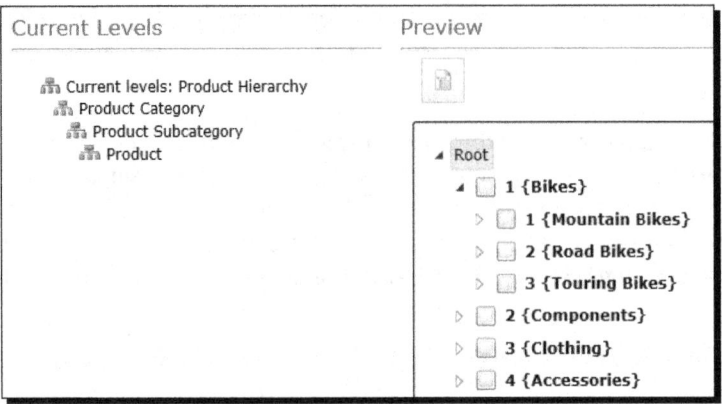

7. Go back to the WebUI main window and select **Explorer**.

8. From the **Hierarchies** menu, select **Derived Hierarchy: Product Category Hierarchy**.

   You will see a new kind of explorer that is based on the tree structure of the product category hierarchy. You can expand each node in the hierarchy, and after selecting each node, you will see the children of that node in the main pane; you can also change the attribute values of each selected node in the details pane. This tree explorer provides a much easier frontend for the end user. The following screenshot shows an example of this explorer:

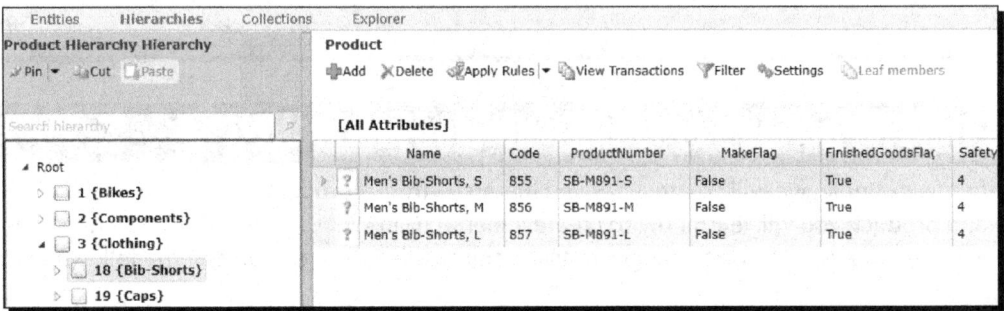

9. Expand **Clothing**, and under that, **Gloves**; you will see different gloves under that subcategory. Now drag-and-drop **Gloves** into the **Components** node.

You will see that the **Gloves** node, with all descendants' nodes, is removed from the **Clothing** category and added under the **Components** node. This kind of change is one of the main benefits of hierarchies for an end user, because they can change the parent node of multiple entries at the same time.

10. Bring **Gloves** back to the **Clothing** category with another drag-and-drop action.

What just happened?

The previous example shows how derived hierarchies can be created. Derived hierarchies, as you've seen in the example, consist of multiple levels, and each level comes from a different entity. The relationship between entities provides the ability to create that hierarchy.

Hierarchies provide a very easy-to-use frontend tool for an end user. A business user can simply find a node in the levels of hierarchy (step 9). Also, a user can change the parent node of multiple items with a simple drag-and-drop of nodes onto each other (steps 10 to 12). Creating and browsing hierarchies is only available through the WebUI in this version of MDS.

Security and permission

MDS provides security and permission based on active directory users and groups. Each user/group can be defined to have access to different functions of WebUI, such as system administration and explorer. A user/group can be defined to have read-only, update, or deny access for different models and even entities. Access to hierarchies can be defined too.

Time for action – permission walkthrough

In this example, we will go through the permission and security options and explore the options that are provided to the security administrator to apply security to the desired model.

1. Open the WebUI of MDS. Go to **User and Group Permissions**.

2. Click on the **Add** button and then enter the name of a user in the **add user** window (the user needs to be a Windows / Active Directory user; you might need to add a Windows user to run this example). You can also add an Active Directory group from the **Manage Groups** menu.

3. Then, go to the **Edit** window. In the **Functions** tab, you can set which functions in the main WebUI menu are accessible for users (functions such as explorer and version management).

4. To change permissions, you need to first click on the **Edit** icon on the top of the window, then make changes, and finally save it.

5. You can define access and permissions to models and entities in the **Models** tab. To make changes, you need to go to the edit mode first (by clicking on the **Edit** icon). You can right-click on each model and choose access rights from options, such as **Read-Only**, **Update**, and **Deny**, as shown in the following screenshot. Access can be set for models, entities, and even attributes.

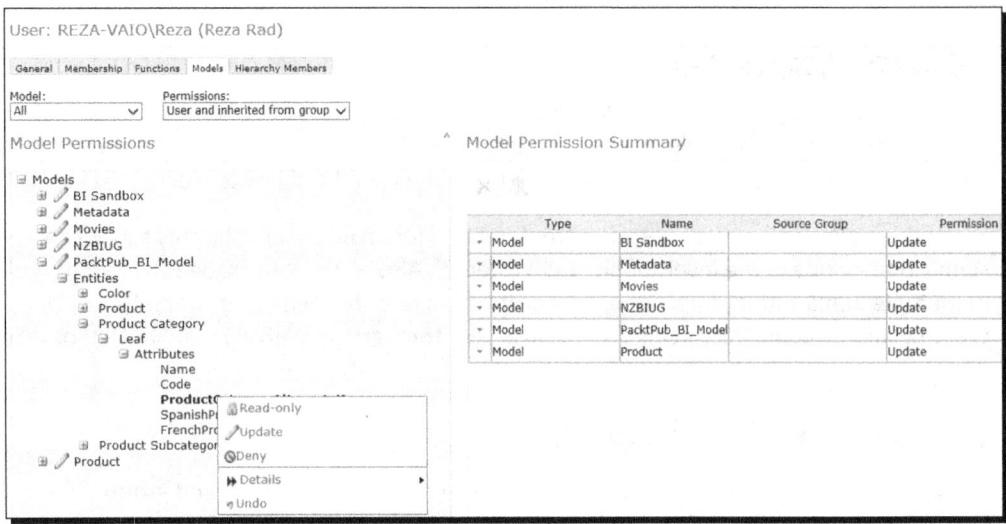

Access to hierarchy members can be defined in the **Hierarchy Members** tab. The permission can be defined in the row level.

What just happened?

In this example, you learned how we can configure the security and permission for Windows and Active Directory users and groups. The permission can be defined for models and entities, even at their attribute levels. Also, row-level security can be applied for hierarchy members.

Integration management

MDS, as a master data management system, provides the functionality to import data into MDS from external applications or export information from MDS to external applications. In MDS, this functionality is called integration management. In this section, which is the last of this chapter, you will learn how to import data into MDS and export data from it.

SSIS plays an important role for integration management in MDS. SSIS, as you've seen in *Chapter 4, ETL with Integration Services*, is a Microsoft integration tool and is very powerful. We are able to create subscription views from entities and hierarchies to export data from MDS. We can even use the user subscription views in SSIS as a source of data.

The procedure for importing information into MDS is a little different. MDS creates a staging table for each entity. We need to insert new information into these staging tables and then call the stored procedure to run a batch job and transfer those new records from the staging tables into the entity tables. All of these tasks can be performed through SSIS tasks and transformations. The method of using staging tables and batch commands to import data into MDS is called **Entity Based Staging** (**EBS**).

Time for action – a subscription view

In this example, we will export product entity records into the SQL Server database table. We will create a subscription view for the product entity and use SSIS to export data rows.

1. Open the MDS WebUI and go to **Integration Management**.

2. Go to the **Create Views** menu item and click on the **Add** button.

3. Set the subscription view name as `VwProduct`, then choose **PacktPub_BI_Model** as the model, and choose **Version_1** as the version. Choose the **Product** entity and set the format as **Leaf members**. Click on the **Save** icon to save the changes made in the **Create Subscription View** window, as shown in the following screenshot:

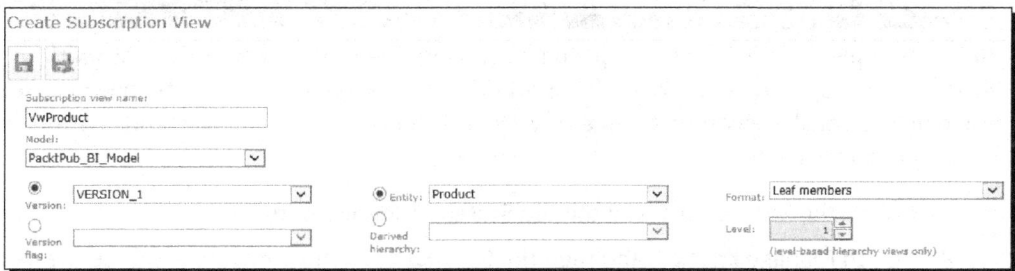

4. Open SSDT and create an SSIS project; name it `Subscription View`.

5. Create a Data Flow task. Inside the Data Flow task, create an OLE DB source.

6. Create a connection to the MDS database from the OLE DB source.

7. In the OLE DB source, set the data access mode as **Table** or **View**. Choose **mdm. VwProduct** as the name of the view. Preview the data rows and then click on **OK**.

8. Add an **OLE DB Destination** path after the source. Connect the data path (blue arrow) from **Source** to **Destination**. Set the connection of the destination to a sample database.

9. Leave the data-access mode as **Table** or **view – fast load**. Then click on the **New** button; in the script for a new table, rename the table to `ProductEntityExported`. Hit **OK**, go to mapping, and then click on **OK**.

10. Run the package. You will see that the records are successfully transferred from the MDS entity into the `ProductEntityExported` table. If you query the table data, you will find some extra metadata columns, which you can get rid of if you don't require that information in the destination table.

What just happened?

Subscription views are a way to export data from MDS to other databases. In this example, you saw how easy it is to create subscription views (step 3). You can also create a subscription view from a hierarchy and choose the number of levels to export. Then you can simply query that subscription view in the MDS database, or use SSIS to select data from the subscription view (step 6 and 7) and load it into any destination, as shown in steps 8 and 9.

Please note that if you change the entity structure, then you will need to recreate subscription views for that entity. To recreate the subscription views, you will only need to edit and save them.

Subscription views in MDS will always be generated under the MDM schema.

Time for action – entity-based staging

In this example, we will import sample data rows into the Product Category entity with the entity-based staging method. We will import data into a staging table first, then we will run the batch to transfer records into an entity. We will import the product categories from an existing Excel file named `Product Categories.xlsx`.

1. Go to the MDS WebUI, and then to **System Administration**.

2. Go to **Manage Entities**, and then the **Product Category** entity. You will see the name of the staging table for this entity is **Product_Category**. This means that the staging table name is `stg.Product_Category_Leaf` (you can check if this table exists by going to SSMS.)

3. Create a new SSIS project and name it `Entity Based Staging`.

4. Create a variable named `BatchTag` of `String` type in the package scope.

5. Add an expression task and name it `Set Batch Tag`.

6. Enter the following expression in the expression task:

```
@[User::BatchTag] ="Product Category_"+
  (DT_WSTR, 4) DATEPART("yy", GETDATE()  )+
RIGHT( "0"+(DT_WSTR, 4) DATEPART("mm", GETDATE()  ),2)+
RIGHT("0"+ (DT_WSTR, 4) DATEPART("dd", GETDATE()  ),2)
```

7. Create a Data Flow task and name it `Import Data into Stage Table`. Connect the precedence constraint (arrow) from the expression task to this task.

8. Then add an Excel source. Create a new connection to the `Product Categories.xlsx` file and check if the first row has column names. Select `Sheet1$` as the table name, preview the records, and then click on **OK**.

9. Add **Derived Column Transformation** and connect the data path from the Excel source to it.

10. Create two derived columns with the following expressions, as shown in the following screenshot:

Derived Column Name	Derived Column	Expression	Data Type	Length
BatchTag	<add as new column>	(DT_WSTR,20)@[User::BatchTag]	Unicode string [DT_WSTR]	20
ImportType	<add as new column>	0	four-byte signed integer [DT_I4]	

11. Add an OLE DB destination after the derived column and connect the data path from the derived column transformation to this destination.

12. In the OLE DB destination, create a connection to the MDS database and choose **stg.Product_Category_Leaf**; then check the mapping. The map columns are shown in the following table:

Input Columns	Destination Columns
BatchTag	BatchTag
ImportType	ImportType
Product Category name	Name
Product Category ID	Code

13. Go back to **Control Flow** and add an Execute SQL task after the Data Flow task.

14. Connect the precedence constraint from the Data Flow task to this task. Name this task `Run Batch`.

15. Set **Connection** to **MDS database**. Then go to the **Expression** tab, select **Property** as **SqlStatementSource**, and write the following expression there:

```
"Exec [stg].[udp_Product_Category_Leaf]
  @VersionName=N'Version_1',@LogFlag=1,@BatchTag=N'"+@
  [User::BatchTag]+"'"
```

16. Run the SSIS package. Then, go to **explorer** and check the product category members. You will see two new members added to this entity. The following diagram shown an overview of the preceding steps:

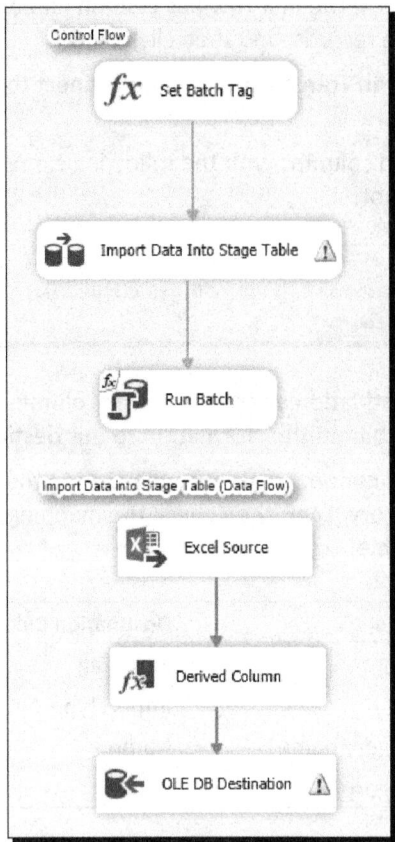

What just happened?

Entity-based staging seems like a bit more work than the subscription view. However, it is quite easy to use. In this example, we first found the name of the staging table (step 2). Then we created a batch tag (steps 4 to 6); this batch tag is a name identifier for each batch (set of records inserted into the MDS entity). This batch tag is required when we want to run a batch and transfer data from the staging table to the entity table. For the sake of traceability, we created the batch tag with the date-stamped string. So, the batch tag of this example would be generated as `Product Category_20130505`.

Then, we imported data from the Excel file into the stage table (steps 7 to 12) through a Data Flow task. The important step during this process is the `Derived` column that creates the two columns (step 10), `Batch Tag` and `Import Type`. The `Batch Tag` column is created based on the `BatchTag` variable from step 9. The `Import Type` column defines what MDS should do with this record. The following table shows the different import types:

Import ID	Name	Description
0 or blank	Merge Optimistic	All populated record information will loaded into the Entity when either the member does not exist or the member exists. Nulls will be ignored.
1	Insert	Only new member records and their attributes will be loaded into the MDS entity all existing records will be flagged as member code already exists. No attributes on pre-existing records will be updated.
2	Merge Overwrite	All populated record information will loaded into the Entity when either the member does not exist or the member exists any blank element in the EBS table will overwrite values within the MDS entity.
3	Delete	Only the member code will be evaluated and these records will be soft deleted from the MDS entity
4	Purge	Only the member code will be evaluated and these records will be removed from the MDS entity version that these records are staged into.
5	Delete Override	Only the member code will be evaluated and these records will be soft deleted from the MDS entity. This will set any Domain Based Attribute references to Null to complete the operation.
6	Purge Override	Only the member code will be evaluated and these records will be removed from the MDS entity version that these records are staged into. This will set any Domain Based Attribute references to Null to complete the operation.

The last two steps (steps 14 and 15) use an Execute SQL Task to run a batch. To run a batch command, you need to call a stored procedure, which has a name that is very similar to its staging table; for example, the batch procedure name for this example is `stg.udp_Product_Category_leaf`. You need to pass the batch tag, version name, and the log flag (1 means log transactions and 0 means do not log transactions) to this procedure.

After running the SSIS package, you can see the two new members added to the entity. You can check the batch run in the MDS WebUI under the **Integration Management** menu and also in the **Import Data** menu.

Summary

In this chapter, you've learned how to use Master Data Services to keep one version of the truth. You've seen that MDS provides an extensible modeling mechanism. You can create entities with attributes, a relationship between entities, and also explicit or derived hierarchies based on the existing entities and their relationships. As a master data management service, we can import data into MDS with entity-based staging, and export data out of MDS with subscription views. The next chapter will be about data cleansing with data quality services.

6
Data Quality and Data Cleansing

Data quality is one of the common challenges in every database system, especially when data comes from different kinds of sources. Assume that some customer data comes in the form of a SQL Server database table, and the table is filled with data from a website's customer application forms. On the other hand, some data comes in the form of Excel files and there are some data files that come from a DB2 database. The incoming data might contain multiple copies of a single customer's information that differ slightly; for example, Mike might be written as Maike somewhere or a company might be written as MSFT somewhere and Microsoft on another location. This chapter will dig into the concept of data quality through a new Microsoft engine for data cleansing named Data Quality Services.

By the end of this chapter, you will have some understanding of the most common challenges in data quality and you will also learn how to design and implement a solution with Data Quality Services to overcome these challenges and provide better data quality for the data warehouse.

Understanding data quality

Data quality is about which data is good for business. Data quality can be different based on source systems, reliability of incoming data, data entry, and so on. Data quality is important because bad data would cause bad business. Bad data quality is one of the barriers of Business Intelligence systems. In other words, one of the building blocks of a robust Business Intelligence system is ensuring the data quality is high.

Data quality issues can be divided into the following categories:

◆ Uniqueness

◆ Validity

◆ Accuracy

◆ Standardization

◆ Completeness

Uniqueness is about multiple copies of the same data, such as Bill Gates and Bill Geates. In this sample, both names seem to be the same. Validity is about different kinds of validation for data, for example, range validity of age is something between 0 and 150 (if there is someone who will live that long). Accuracy is about the correctness of data, for example, the wrong opening date for a store will be considered bad data and needs to be fixed. Standardization is about formatting and coding standards for data, for example, both M and Male give the same information, but it is better to be consistent. Completeness checks whether enough data has been provided, for example, book titles and author names in a book library store might be missing in some of the records. The following diagram shows samples of data quality issues (sourced from Microsoft):

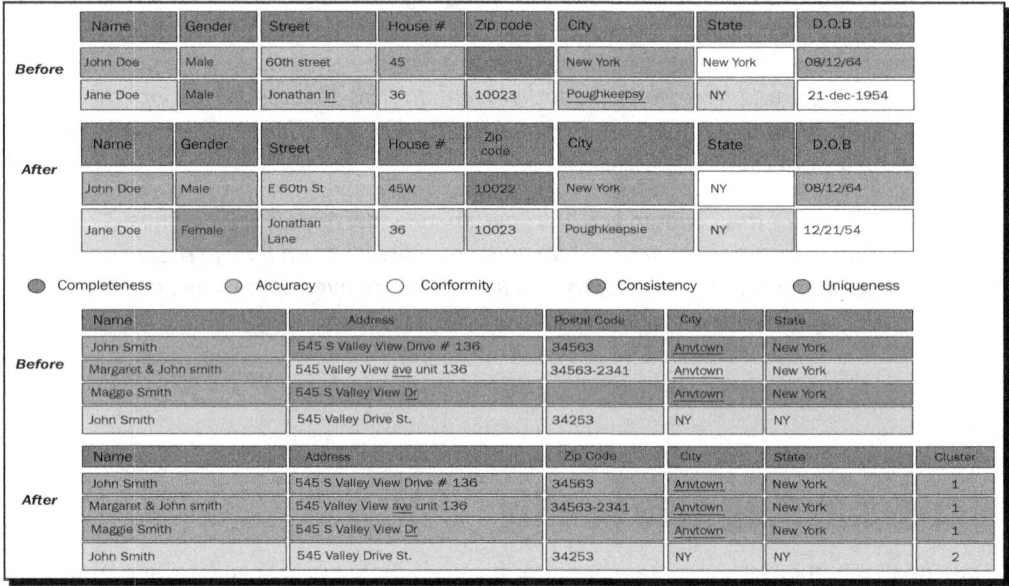

The data quality issues just explained are very critical for a Business Intelligence system, and thus for business. A Business Intelligence system requires data to be valid, accurate, standard, and complete. In this chapter, you will learn how to fix data quality issues with Microsoft solutions to deliver a better BI system for businesses.

Data Quality Services

Microsoft's solution for data quality, introduced in SQL Server 2012 and named **Data Quality Services** (**DQS**), is a service-based application that works based on knowledge-base-driven data quality. Knowledge-base-driven data quality works with Knowledge Bases that consist of domains. Knowledge Bases will be maintained with the business user named data steward. A data steward is someone who knows the domains of the business and can maintain the best quality Knowledge Base for that business. DQS also comes with a functionality to create data-matching rules and apply these rules on the data. The following diagram shows the Data Quality Services process (sourced from Microsoft):

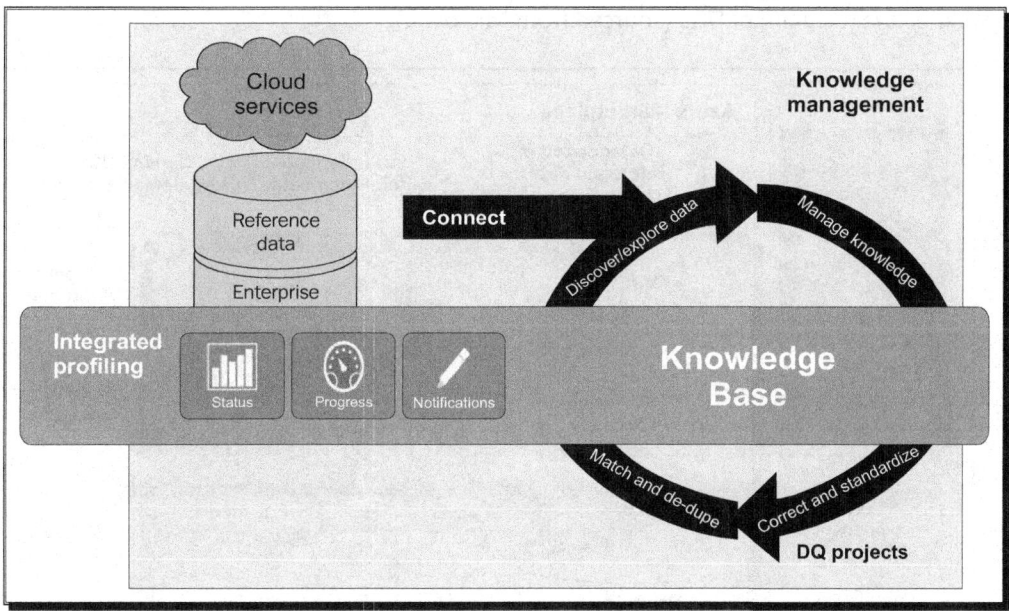

The Knowledge Base can get data from cloud services such as Windows Azure Marketplace, which is called reference data, or it can be created and maintained by a data steward. The process of knowledge discovery, managing knowledge, correction, and matching is like a cycle, and will enhance the Knowledge Base with time. There are some profiling features in DQS that work as utility during this process to help in knowledge discovery.

DQS requires you to move data from your source to DQS, where it is modified. Then you must move and integrate the modified data back into your source or another destination. DQS has the ability to interact with other Microsoft services through SSIS. SSIS can apply Knowledge Base rules on a data stream with a DQS cleansing component and then get cleansed data with metadata information columns from DQS. Matching rules can also be applied through the MDS Excel Add-In before importing data into MDS.

There are four main components in DQS based on the functionality: cleansing, matching, monitoring, and profiling. Cleansing is about cleaning data based on a Knowledge Base and domains. Matching would match data based on the similarity rules and threshold defined in a Knowledge Base. Monitoring will show the status of records during the cleansing and matching projects. And profiling will help in creating business rules or changing the domain rules and Knowledge Base from what the existing data profiling results are.

Data Quality Services contains a service that is the engine of the data quality. It can be a DQ Studio or Data Quality Client, DQS backend databases, monitoring and profiling tools in data quality client, or components to work with SSIS and MDS. The following diagram shows an architectural diagram of DQS (sourced from Microsoft):

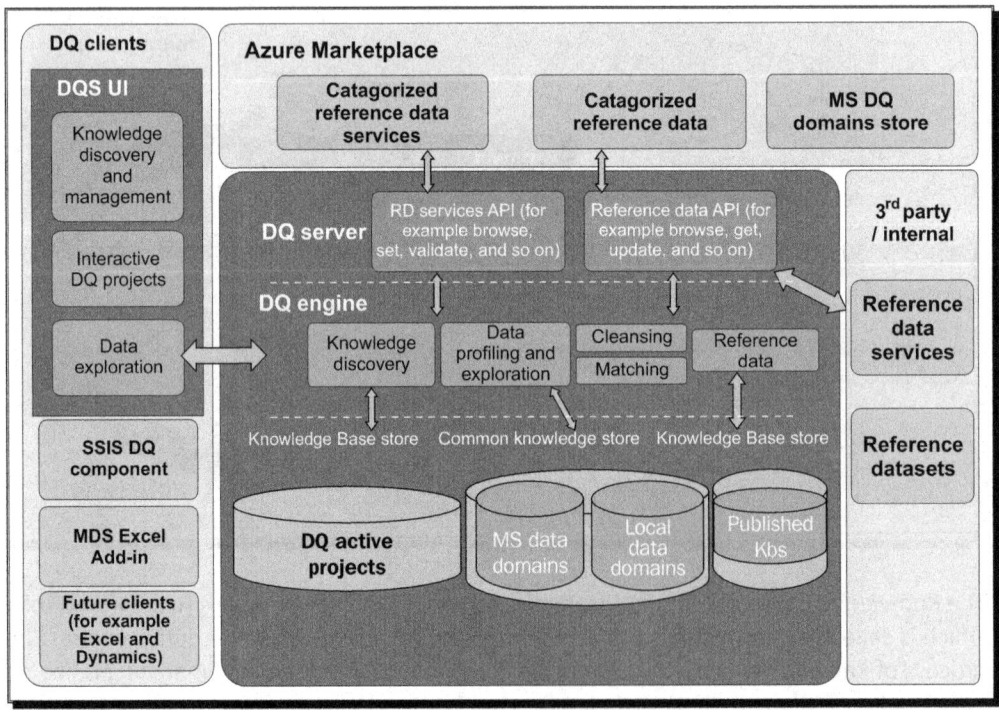

Time for action – installing Data Quality Services

To install Data Quality Services, you need to choose data quality options in the setup wizard steps, but it is not enough. There is another step after that—you need to run `DQSInstaller.exe` to get DQS fully installed on your machine. Let's see how to do it with the help of the following steps:

1. After installing a SQL Server setup media by choosing data quality options, go to **Start | All programs**. Then, under **Microsoft SQL Server 2014** (open the `Microsoft SQL Server 2014` folder) and open **Data Quality Server Installer**.

2. You will see a command prompt installer start. Follow the instructions and continue to complete the installation.

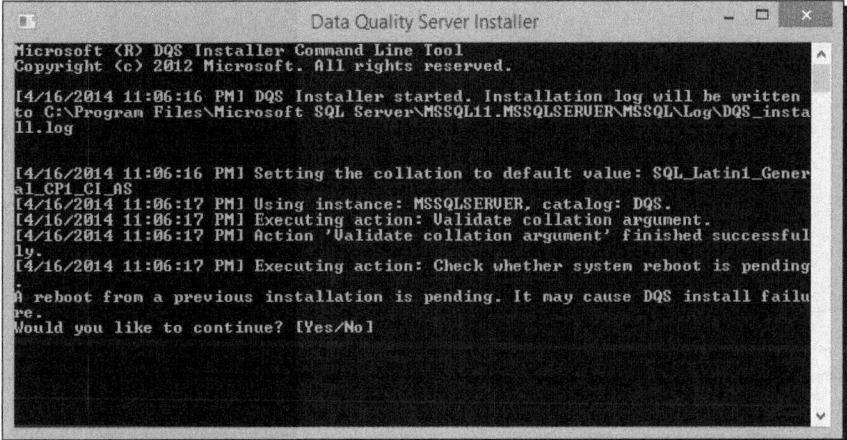

3. After successful installation, open **Data Quality Client** under **Start | All Programs** in **Microsoft SQL Server 2014**.

4. In the **Connect to Server** dialogbox, type in (`LOCAL`) or . as the server name and connect.

5. You will see the data quality client connected to the DQS and show you the development and let you monitor the GUI, as shown in the following screenshot:

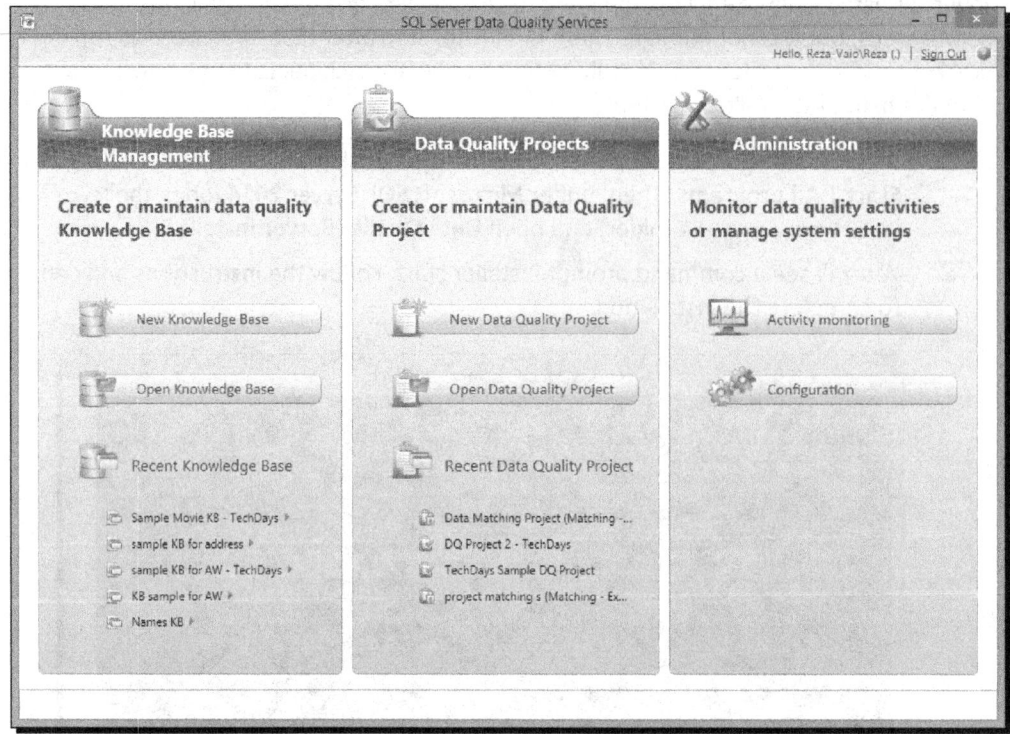

What just happened?

In this exercise, you learned how to install DQS and you had your first experience with the **Data Quality Client** (**DQC**). DQC has the following three main parts:

- Knowledge Base Management
- Data quality projects
- Administration

Knowledge Base Management is where you can create and manage Knowledge Base, domains, and domain rules. Data quality projects can also be maintained through the second section of the data quality client; these projects apply the Knowledge Base and matching rules on an existing dataset and provide results. Monitoring and administration are the last important part of the GUI; configuration and administration tasks can be performed here.

Knowledge Base Management

The main building block for DQS is the Knowledge Base. Knowledge Bases can be created on business scope basis, and there might be one or more domains under each Knowledge Base. Some of these domains might be related to each other and be considered as a composite domain. For example, a Knowledge Base can be set as address data, and domains can be country, city, and address line. And a composite domain named full address might contain all of those domains. In this section, you will see how to create and manage Knowledge Bases, domains, and composite domains.

Time for action – creating a Knowledge Base

In this example, we will create a Knowledge Base for address information, and we will create domains for country, city, and address line. And finally, we will create a composite domain for the full address. Perform the following steps:

1. Open **Data Quality Client** and connect to the server.

2. Under **Knowledge Base Management**, click on **New Knowledge Base**.

3. Name the Knowledge Base `Address KB`, leave **activity** as **Domain Management**, and click on **Next**.

4. In the **Domain Management** window, create domains by clicking on the **Create a Domain** icon on the top-left-hand side.

5. In the **Create Domain** window, name domain as `Country`, leave the other settings as they are, and click on **OK**.

6. Add these domains: **State**, **City**, and **Address Line**.

7. Click on **Create Composite Domain** and name it `Full Address`. Add domains in the following order to this composite domain: **Country**, **State**, **City**, and **Address Line**.

8. Click on **Finish**. A message box will appear, asking if the domain is ready for publishing or not. Choose **Publish**.

What just happened?

In this example, we created a Knowledge Base from scratch. Each Knowledge Base can contain one or more domains. As you see in the example, we created domains for country, city, state, and so on. Each domain has properties such as data type. We can also specify how DQS standardizes the format; for example, for strings it can be standardized to lowercase, uppercase, capitalize, or none. The language can also be defined, which helps the spellchecker work for values of this domain. There are four data types for domains: String, Integer, Decimal, and Date. The String format will show how values of this domain will be shown in each data type. We will discuss the **Use leading Values** option later in this chapter. Take a look at the following screenshot:

You have now seen how to create composite domains—those created from multiple domains, such as full address and full name. **Composite domains (CDs)** are very helpful for creating relation rules between multiple domains. In this example, a composite domain was created for the full address that contained all the domains listed earlier. Later in this chapter, we will discuss how to create composite domain rules.

Knowledge discovery

The process of getting a dataset and applying a Knowledge Base on it and using a result set to enhance domain values in that Knowledge Base is called knowledge discovery. Knowledge discovery is an important process, especially when you are not using reference data, because the Knowledge Base will empower you with more domain values, and it is one of the main methods for adding domain values into the Knowledge Base.

Time for action – knowledge discovery

In this example, we will use an existing Excel file with data rows to enhance the **Address KB** Knowledge Base from the previous example. We will load new values for the **Country**, **State**, and **City** domains. This example will help you to understand process of knowledge discovery. Perform the following steps:

1. Open **Data Quality Client** and then connect to the server.

2. Under **Recent Knowledge Base**, click on **Address KB**. A pop-up menu will open; select **Knowledge Discovery**.

3. The first step of knowledge discovery is mapping source data. Choose **Excel File** as **Data Source**. Choose the `AdventureWorksSampleData.xls` file as the source. Check the box **Use first row as header**.

4. In the mapping section, map the input columns to the Knowledge Base domain as shown in the following screenshot:

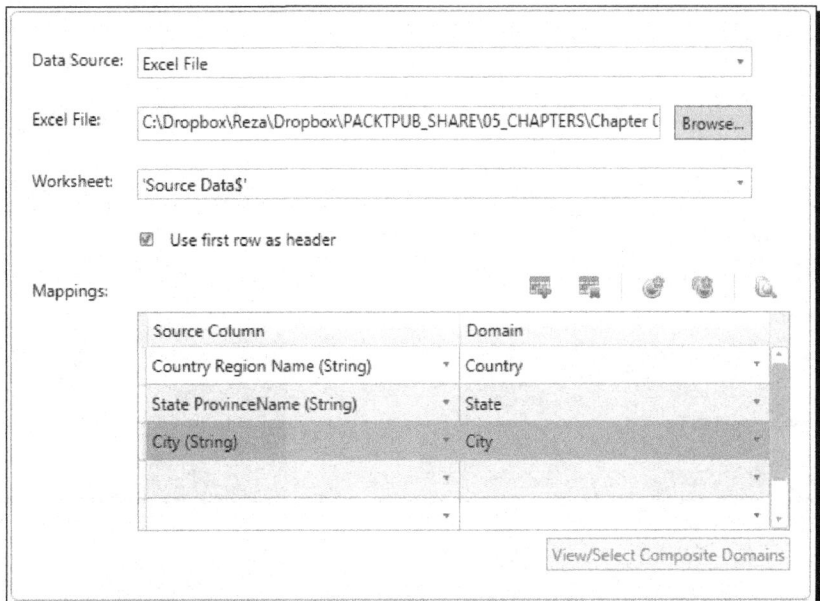

5. In the **Discover** step of knowledge discovery, click on the **Start** button to start discovery. You can also see profiling results in the **Profiler** section of this window. After completing this step, click on **Next**.

6. The final step is managing the domain values. In this step, all fetched domain values can be seen under each domain. For example, if you click on the **Country** domain on the left-hand side pane, you will see six new domain values detected in this knowledge discovery process. Leave everything as is and click on **Finish** to complete the knowledge discovery process and also publish the updated Knowledge Base.

What just happened?

This sample was a simple example of knowledge discovery. Knowledge discovery will enrich the Knowledge Base. This process will usually be done by the data steward. It's worth mentioning again that the data steward is someone involved with the business who understands the Knowledge Base and domains and can distinguish correct or incorrect values and is also able to set rules for each domain. In the process of knowledge discovery, the data steward can use a source data stream (from SQL Server or an Excel file) and map data columns to Knowledge Base domains (steps 3 and 4).

The discovery step shows some useful information, such as the number of records, number of unique values, and new values for each domain, which is very useful profiling information (step 5). The following screenshot shows a sample profiling result for our example in the fifth step:

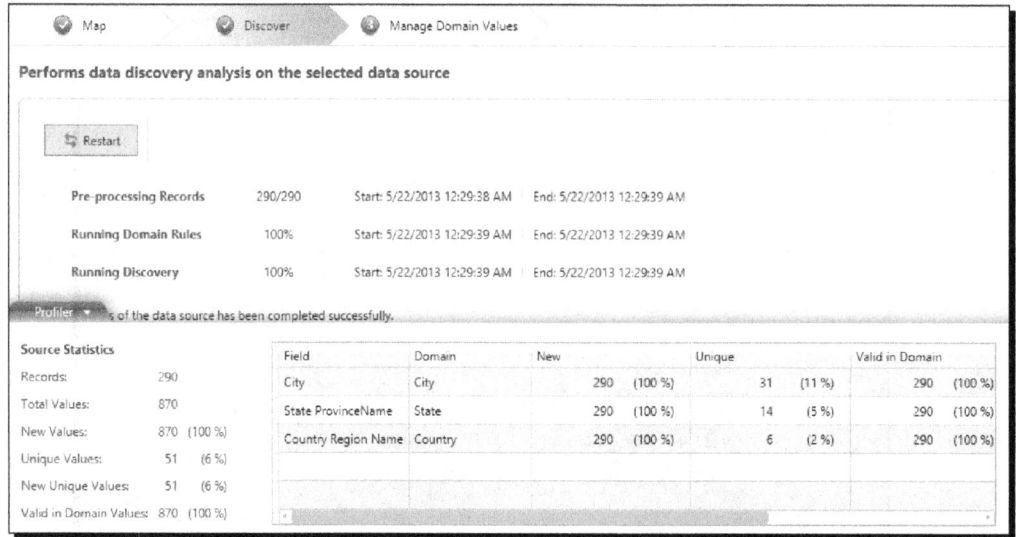

In the final step, the discovered domain values will be shown to the data steward. The data steward can remove incorrect values and mark error values or they can leave correct values (step 6). The **Correct to** column is for defining the correct values for each incoming value (which might be wrong). After the review, it can publish new values and the enriched Knowledge Base into the DQS server. And DQS will consider these values in the data-cleansing projects. The following screenshot shows the Manage Domain Values menu:

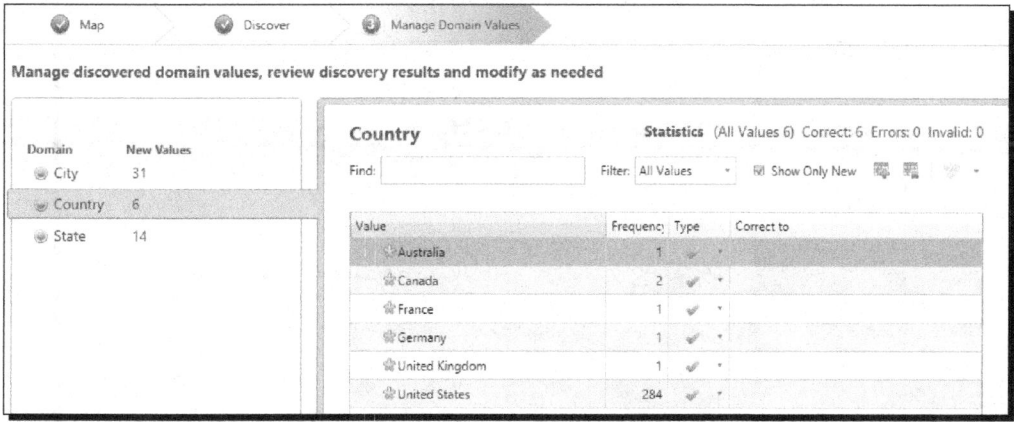

Data cleansing with Data Quality Projects

Knowledge Bases are created for one main reason—cleaning data. **Data Quality Projects** (**DQPs**) are created for the same reason. Each DQP works with one Knowledge Base. It gets data from a source file or SQL Server database and applies the Knowledge Base on it. Then, the result of DQP can be exported to the database tables or files.

In this section, you will see how to create data quality projects to cleanse data. There is also another type of DQP for data matching, which will be discussed later in this chapter.

Time for action – using Data Quality Project for cleansing

In this example, we will use the **Address KB** Knowledge Base to clean the incoming data from an Excel file. There is a point to be noted here; the incoming data has one file for the address—the composite domain named **Full Address**. So we have to map the incoming address column to this **Full Address** domain. And then the Knowledge Base will perform the composite domain parsing. There are three types of composite domain parsing: reference data, in-order, and Knowledge Base parsing. In this example, we will use Knowledge Base parsing, which works based on delimiters and Knowledge Base domain values and rules.

We will export the result of the data cleansing to a file at the end. Perform the following steps:

1. Click on **Address KB** in the list of recent Knowledge Bases and open it in **Domain Management** mode.

2. Click on the **Full Address** composite domain and then in the composite domain's **Properties** tab, at the bottom of domains list, click on **Advanced**.

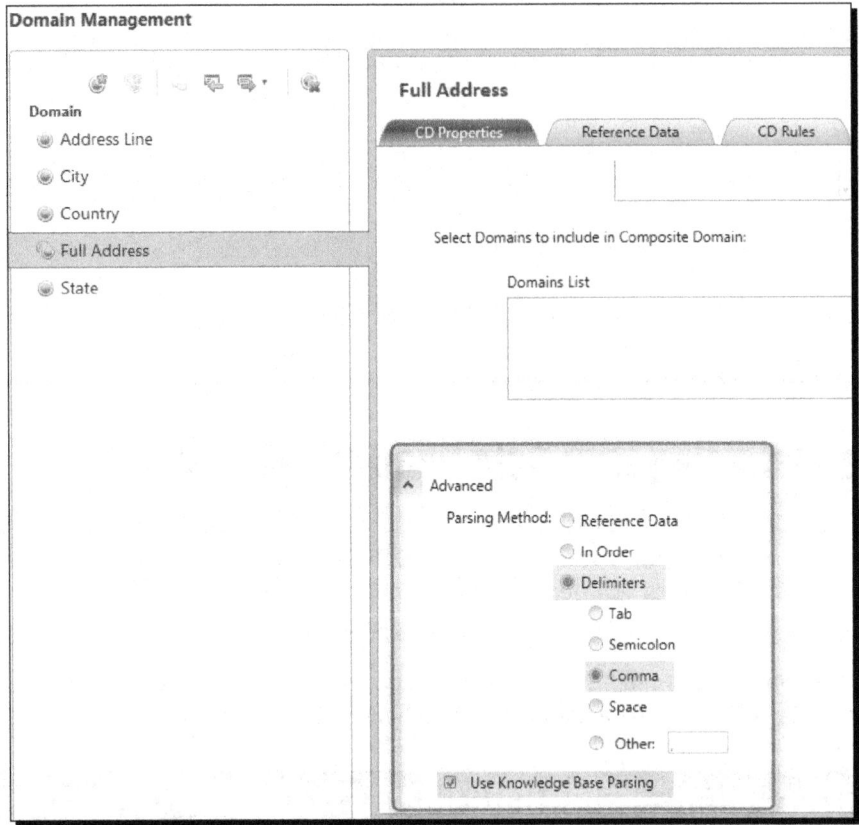

3. Set the parsing method to **Delimiters** and choose **Comma** as the delimiter. Then check **Use Knowledge Base Parsing**.

4. Click on **Finish** and then publish the Knowledge Base.

5. In the data quality client's main window, under **Data Quality Projects**, click on **Create New Data Quality Project**. Name the project Address Cleansing Project. In the **Use Knowledge Base** drop-down list, choose **Address KB**. Leave activity as **Cleansing** and click on **Next**.

6. In the **Map** step, choose **Data Source** as **Excel File** and select the KB `Parsing.xlsx` file. Leave worksheet as is and check the **Use first row as header** checkbox option. In the mapping grid, just map the **Address** column from source to the **Full Address** domain from the Knowledge Base. You will also be able to view the Knowledge Base details on the right-hand side pane, which shows the composite domain, consisting of four domains: **Country**, **State**, **City**, and **Address Line**.

7. Click on **Next**, and in the **Cleanse** tab, start the process. You will see some profiling results that show the status, number of records, and some other information regarding this cleansing process. Click on **Next** after that.

8. In the **Manage and View Results** tab, you will see the list of values on each domain or composite domain. In this example, you will see **Full Address** on the left-hand side pane with seven values, because the Excel file had only seven rows.

9. In the main pane, you will see the tabs **Suggested, Invalid, Corrected, Correct,** and **New**. In this example, all of these records were new for the Knowledge Base. So you will see all of them listed under **New**. In the grid under the tab, you can see the value and the reason cleansing is needed. For this example, you will see that all records mentioned with a reason: **New Value** in domain **Address Line**. As you've seen in prior examples of this chapter, we did the knowledge discovery for **Country**, **State**, and **City**. So, for this reason, the incoming data has nothing new for those domains, but it had new values for **Address Line**. This is one of the advantages of Knowledge Base parsing in composite domains—it will find out the best location for data in the existing domain list based on Knowledge Base domain values and rules.

10. You can approve or reject new values; if you approve them, they will be listed under the **Correct** tab, and if you reject them, they will be listed under the **Invalid** tab. For this example, approve all of them and click on **Next**. The following screenshot shows the **Correct** tab after approving all new values:

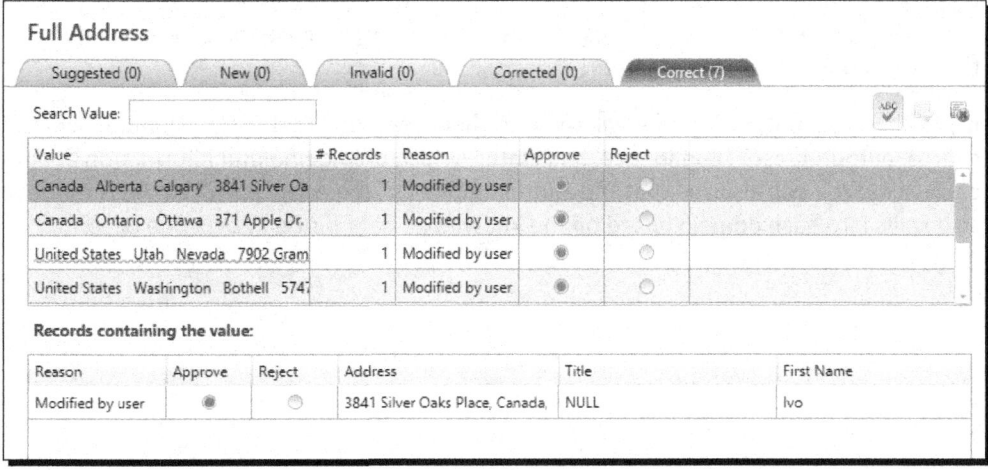

11. In the last step, that is, the **Export** step, you can export results. Choose **Excel File** as **Destination type** and set the output file's name as `Address Cleansing Result.xls`. Leave the other options as is, that is, check **Standardize output** and set **Output format** to **Data and cleansing info**. Then click on **Export**. Now you can view the output file and check the cleansing result.

12. Finish the project.

What just happened?

In this example, you experienced two main parts: setting the method for composite domain parsing and data quality projects for cleansing. In the first steps of the example, we've changed the default composite domain parsing method for **Full Address** (steps 1 to 4). There are differences between parsing methods: reference data works with cloud and is good when you have domain values coming from the cloud and the Windows Azure Marketplace. In-order will only parse the composite domain in the exact order of domains. For example, this method is very good when incoming data has this order: **Country**, **State**, **City**, and **Address**. But this method is not good when incoming data is not ordered. And finally, the Knowledge Base parsing method is using domain values in the Knowledge Base by considering a delimiter. In this example, we used the KB parsing method because the incoming data was not ordered; also, the Knowledge Base was rich (because of previous knowledge discovery), and a rich Knowledge Base will result in good data cleansing with KB parsing.

Then we created a data quality projects for cleansing and assigned a Knowledge Base to this project (step 5). In the **Map** step, we mapped the incoming column to the composite domain directly; this is one of the advantages of having composite domains, because when data is not separated into multiple columns, the composite domain can distinguish it (steps 5 and 6). After the cleansing process, the data steward can go to the **Manage and View Results** tab and look for suggestions such as **New**, **Correct**, or **Invalid** values. They can simply approve or reject any changes (steps 8 to 10). Finally, the result of the cleansing can be exported to the database table or CSV and Excel files. You can also specify to have the cleansing info besides the data in the output format (step 11).

If you check the output file, you will see that there are some metadata columns such as source, output, reason, confidence, and status, which provide helpful information about each value. You will also see that the address input column exists in **Full Address** mode and also splits into each domain based on the knowledge data inside Knowledge Base.

Domain and composite domain rules

In addition to domain values, there is a need to add business rules to each domain or combination of domains. DQS supports the adding of domain rules. The rule can be something like checking if the value is greater than something or matching with a regular expression and so on. Rules can also be applied on multiple domains in a composite domain; CD rules are helpful when providing business rules for the relationship between multiple domains, for example, a female or male title based on their marital status.

Time for action – composite domain rules

In this example, we will create a Knowledge Base with a composite domain for title enrichment. The title enrichment CD has three domains: `Title`, `Gender`, and `Marital Status`. Then we will create a CD rule to fetch the correct title based on gender and marital status with the following steps:

1. Create a new Knowledge Base and name it `Customer KB`.

2. Create three domains of string data type named `Title`, `Gender`, and `Marital Status`.

3. Select the **Gender** domain in the **Domain Values** tab and add two values: `F` and `M`.

4. Add two values for the **Marital Status** domain: `S` and `M`. And add three values for the **Title** domain: `Mr.`, `Mrs.`, and `Ms.`.

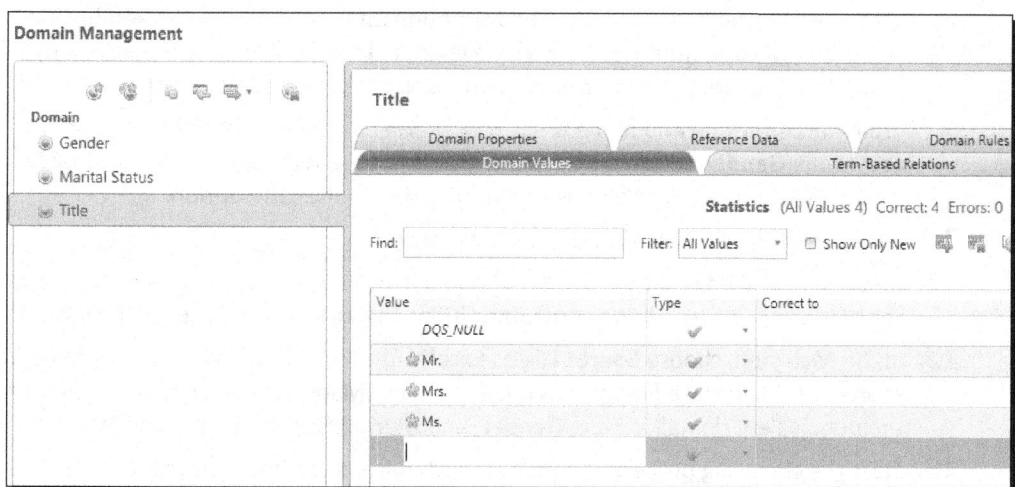

5. Create a composite domain containing all three domains mentioned earlier and name it `Title Enrichment`.

6. Select the **Title Enrichment** domain and then go to the **CD Rules** tab, add a new domain rule, and name it `Male Title`. In the **Build a Rule: Male Title** pane, choose **Gender** in the drop-down list and then choose **Value is equal to** in the rule drop-down menu and type in `M` in the textbox in front of it.

7. Choose **Title** in the **Then** section and then choose **Value is equal to** in the action drop-down menu and type in `Mr.` in the textbox in front of it. The following screenshot shows how this rule is created:

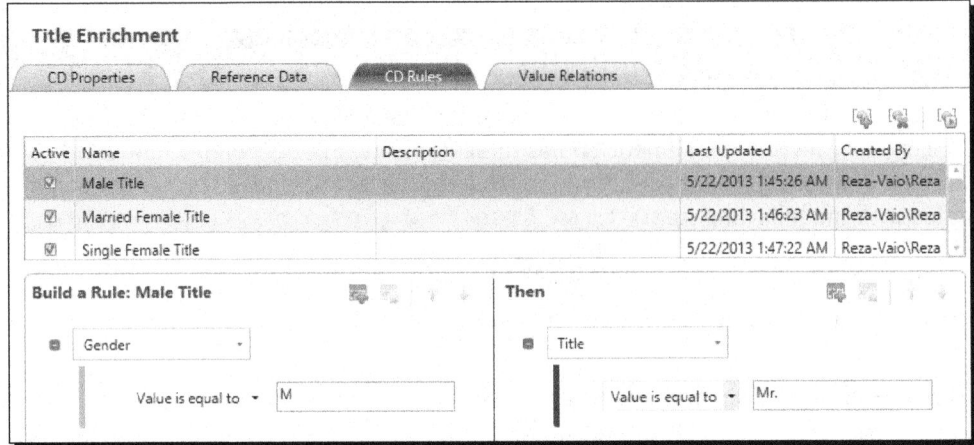

8. Create another rule and name it `Married Female Title`. In the condition part, set **Value is equal to** as `F` in the **Gender** option and then click on the add button to insert an AND operator. Next, set **Value is equal to** as `M` in the **Marital Status** option. In the **Then** section, set **Value is equal to** as `Mrs.` in the **Title** option.

9. Create another rule and name it `Single Female Title`. Set **Value is equal to** as `F` in the **Gender** option and **Value is equal** to as `S` in the **Marital Status** option. In the **Then** section, set **Value is equal to** as `Ms.` in the **Title** option.

10. Click on **Finish** and publish the Knowledge Base.

11. Create a new data quality project and name it `Title Cleansing Project` and set it as `cleansing`. Choose **Customer KB** as the Knowledge Base. Click on **Next**.

12. In the **Map** step, choose **Source File** as **Excel** and select the `CD Rules.xls` file as the source. Check the **Use first row as header** option. Map the three incoming columns to their equivalent domains: **Title**, **Gender**, and **Marital Status**, and click on **Next**.

13. Start the cleansing process and go to the **Manage and View results** tab.

14. You will see five values listed under **Correct** and two values listed as **Corrected**. You can see a record with **F** as **Gender** and **M** as **Marital Status**, mentioned with **Ms.** as **Title**, which is wrong. Fortunately, DQS cleansed that and gave it the correct title, which is **Mrs.**, based on composite domain rules, as shown in the following screenshot:

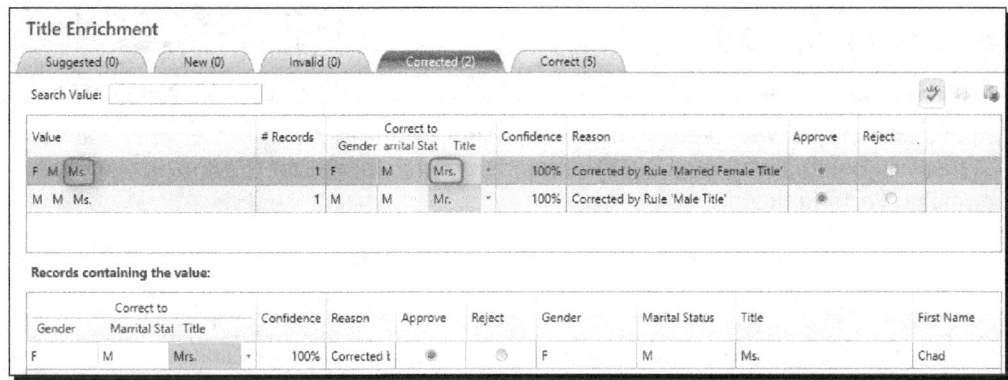

15. Go to the **Export** step and export the results into an Excel file for review. Finish the project.

What just happened?

In this example, you've seen how to create composite domain rules. CD rules are very helpful for creating rules based on the relationship of multiple domains. For this example, we created a rule for title enrichment to fetch out the correct title based on gender and marital status. As you can see in the rule editor, there are a variety of operations that can be done, and a variety of checking that can be applied; for example, you can apply a regular expression to a string, you can check if the date value is before or after something, and so on. You can also add AND/OR operators between conditions, which makes it possible to create complex and rich rules for domains and composite domains.

Synonyms and standardization

There might be different formats to show a value; for example, a date can be shown as 5/23/2013 or it can be shown as 23rd of May 2013. Knowledge Base has the ability to standardize this format based on a predefined format string. This format string can be defined in the domain properties. There are different format strings for the **String**, **Date**, **Integer**, and **Decimal** data types.

A word or sentence might have some synonyms that have the same meaning in terms of business understanding but they just appear to be different. DQS has the ability to understand synonyms based on the knowledge that the data steward has provided. For example, MSFT and Microsoft are synonyms, so in this case it would be helpful if the data steward set these values as synonyms and chose one of these as the heading value (which means that this value will be used for standardization consistency).

Time for action – creating synonyms and setting standardization

In this example, we will create some synonyms for countries, for instance, USA, United States, and US. And we will also set the standardization format for the Knowledge Base domains. Perform the following steps:

1. Open **Address KB** in the **Domain Management** mode.

2. Select the **Country** domain and then go to the **Domain Values** tab.

3. Add two new domain values: USA and US.

4. Select these three values: United States, USA, and US. Then click on **Set selected domain values as synonyms**, which is the fourth icon from the left on the top-right-hand side icons' list.

5. You will see that a hierarchical list will be created under **United States**, with **US** and **USA** as the second levels. This means that the heading value is **United States** and this value has two other synonyms: **US** and **USA**. The following screenshot shows the hierarchical list:

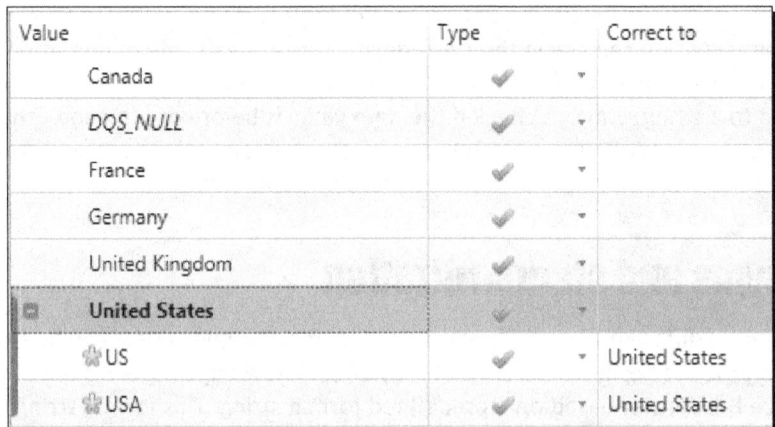

Value	Type		Correct to
Canada	✔	▾	
DQS_NULL	✔	▾	
France	✔	▾	
Germany	✔	▾	
United Kingdom	✔	▾	
United States	✔	▾	
✿US	✔	▾	United States
✿USA	✔	▾	United States

6. Go to the **Domain Properties** tab of the **Country** domain. Make sure you have the **Use Leading Values** checkbox checked. And also format output to **Capitalize**.

7. Click on **Finish** and publish the project.

8. Create a new data quality project for cleansing based on **Address KB** and name it Synonyms Cleansing Project.

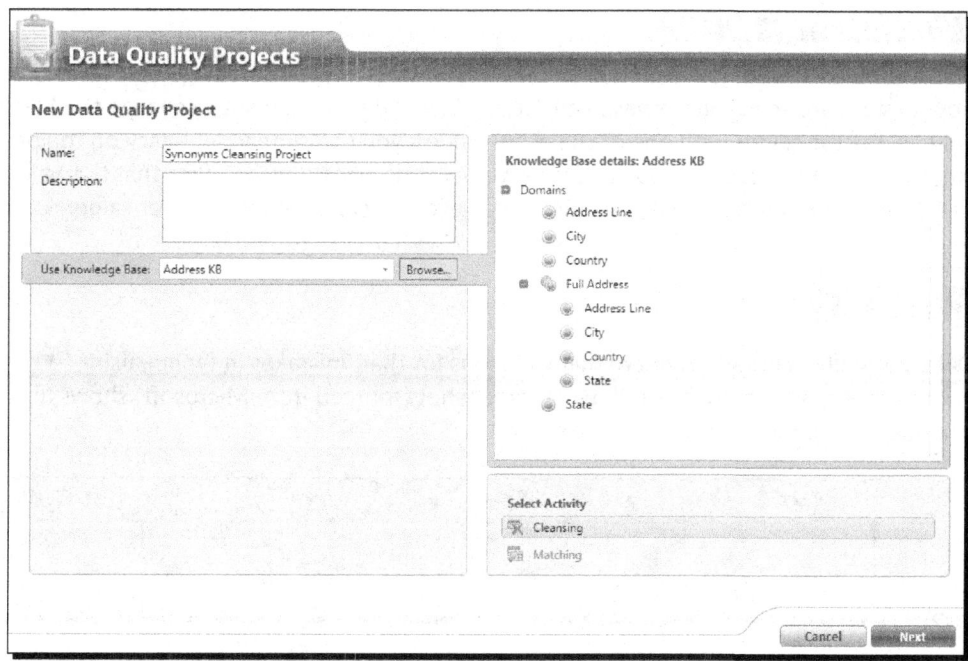

9. Choose `Synonyms.xlsx` as the source Excel file, map the address column to the **Full Address** composite domain, and start the cleansing process.

10. In the **Manage and View results** tab, under **Corrected**, you will see some values that had **US** or **USA** as the country name, and they are corrected to the leading value, which is **United States**, as shown in the following screenshot:

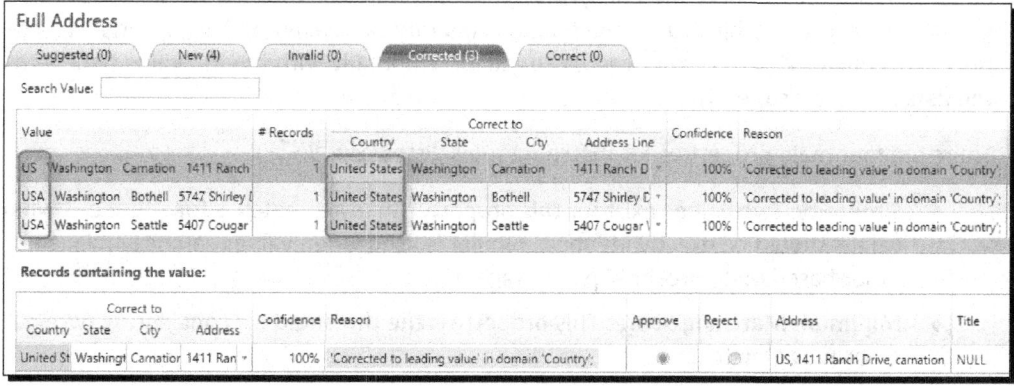

11. Complete the cleansing project, export the output, and finish the project.

What just happened?

This example showed how easy it is to define synonyms in the knowledge base in DQS and how to standardize output to have consistent clean data. If you want to change the leading value in the synonyms with one of the other values, you can simply right-click on the other value and set it as **Leading**. You can also set a value as error, which means that this value will be considered as an erroneous one, and it can even be corrected to another value.

Matching

Data, naturally, is fuzzy. There are many reasons for that; mistakes in typing, using abbreviations, and so on. The following screenshot (sourced from Microsoft) shows an example of two records for the same person:

First Name	Middle Name	Last Name	Gender	Street	City	State	Country	Phone
Kimberly	B	Zimmerman	Female	6040 S. Justine	CHICAGO	IL	USA	123-555-0167
Kim	B	Zimmerman	F	S. Justine	CHICAGO	IL	United States	(123) 555-0167

From the human point of view, both the records shown in the preceding screenshot are for the same person; it just has some abbreviations and different string formats. But from the computer's point of view, these records are different; or, in the other words, they are not exactly similar.

The data matching component of DQS works with a similarity threshold between domain values. The data steward can create matching policies in the Knowledge Base. Each matching policy contains one or more matching rules. Matching rules define how records will match each other. In the matching rules, the type of similarity can be defined as prerequisite, exact match, or similar. Matching rules can be tuned incrementally with the incoming data with the data steward's supervision.

There are four main properties for matching rules, listed as follows:

♦ **Similarity**: Two values exist for this property. An exact match is for situations when values should be exactly identical. Similar is used when values can be similar to each other based on a threshold percentage.

♦ **Minimum Matching Score**: This property is the threshold for considering two records as a match.

♦ **Weight**: This property defines the contribution of each domain in the whole matching rule to find two records as matched or unmatched.

◆ **Prerequisite**: This property categorizes data records based on the defined domain. In the other words, records will be checked to be 100 percent similar based on prerequisite domain value.

Time for action – matching policy

In this example, we will create a Knowledge Base for movies with two domains: director and title of the movie. Then we will create a matching policy based on these two domains to find duplicate records in an Excel file that contains movie information. Perform the following steps to create a matching policy:

1. In the DQ client, create a new Knowledge Base and name it `PacktPub_Movies_KB`. Create two domains in this Knowledge Base: `Director` and `Title`. Both of them will have their string types as the default configuration. Click on **Finish** and publish the Knowledge Base.

2. Now, in the DQ client, under recent Knowledge Bases, click on **PacktPub_Movies_KB**, and from the pop-up menu, choose **Matching Policy**.

3. In the **Map** step, set the source file type as **Excel**, choose `MoviesSampleData.xlsx`, and check **Use first row as header**. Map **Title** and **Director** from the input columns to the Knowledge Base domains and click on **Next**.

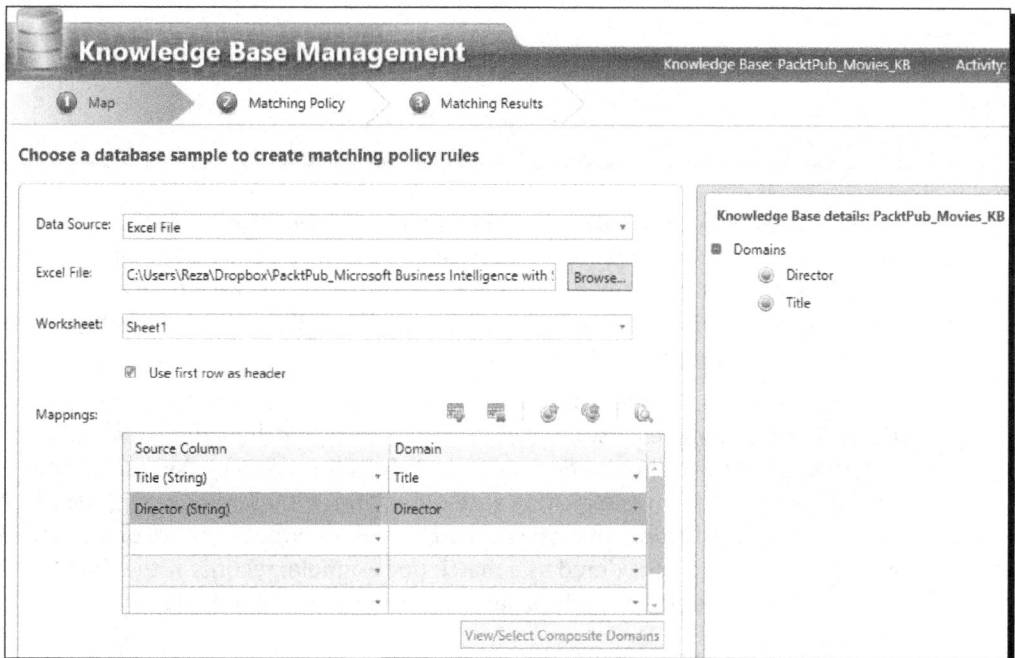

4. In the **Matching Policy** tab, create a matching rule. Name it `De-Dup Matching Rule`. Leave the minimum matching score as **80%**.

5. In the **Rule Editor** section, add a new domain element.

6. Set domain as **Director** and check the **Prerequisite** checkbox.

7. Add a new domain element, set domain as **Title**, leave the similarity column as **Similar**, and set weight as **100%**.

8. In **the Matching Results** pane, click on **Start** to check the matching rule against the sample data.

9. After applying the rule on the sample data, you will see a result similar to the following screenshot:

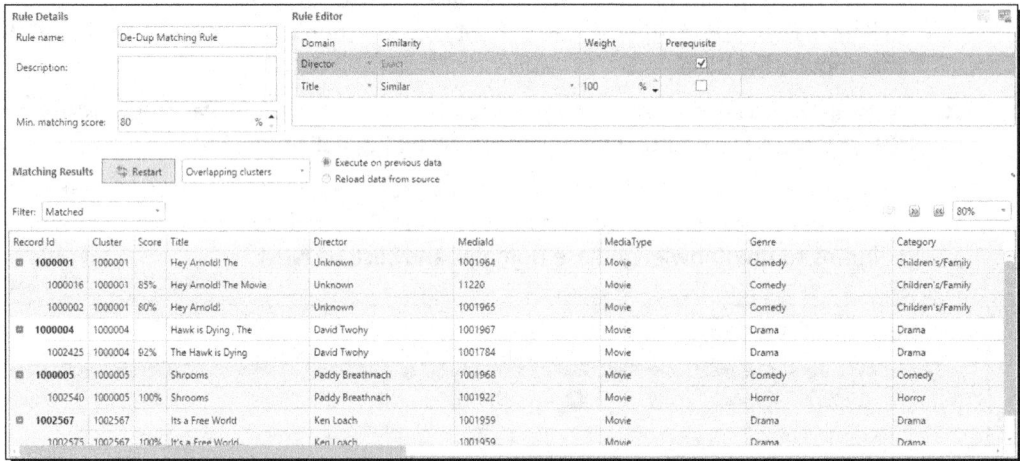

10. In the results, notice the categorization based on the **Director** domain (which is the prerequisite) and the **Similarity** score based on the **Title** domain. The first record in each category is considered as the pivot record with bold **Record Id** and other similar records, which has similarity score more than 80 percent (minimum matching score), listed under the pivot record.

11. Test two scenarios. Firstly, change the minimum matching score to 50 percent and restart the matching results. You will see more items matched under each category. Secondly, delete the **Director** domain from **Rule Editor** and test the results again; you will see more records matching each other, and if you scroll down in the results, you will see some records that do not match each other but because of a similarity in the title, they are considered as a match (for example, records with different directors but similar titles, such as parts two and three of a movie).

12. Roll back the changes that you've made in step 11 (that was just for better understanding of the matching rules). Then click on **Next**.

13. In the **Matching Results** tab, you will see a list of matched records (you can also view unmatched data) in the incoming dataset. Click on Finish and publish the Knowledge Base.

What just happened?

In this example, you learned how to create a matching policy. The most important part of this example was working with matching rules. You've seen that the minimum matching score shows the overall score of similarity of the two records; we've set the minimum matching score in this example to 80 percent (step 4). The **Director** domain plays as prerequisite for this example, and this means that data will be categorized based on this domain (step 6). We've set the **Title** domain as **similar**. **Weight** is set as **100%** because the title is the only domain with a similar status. If we had more than one domain with similar status in a similarity column, then we should set **Weight** for each domain (step 7). In steps 8 to 10, you saw how to check the results for matching rules. You also learned how to play with matching rules and results to get the best tuned rule for the incoming data (step 11).

Time for action – matching projects

Matching projects applies the matching policy in the Knowledge Base to an existing dataset and provides output that can be exported in different formats. In this example, we will create a matching project to apply the matching policy of the previous example to a dataset and we will see the options for exporting data. Perform the following steps:

1. Create a new data quality project and name it `Sample Matching Project` for `PacktPub_Movies`. Use the `PacktPub_Movies_KB` Knowledge Base for this. Select activity as **Matching** and click on **Next**.

2. In the **Map** step, select **source** as **Excel**, **file** as `MoviesSampleData.xlsx`, and map **Director** and **Title** from the input columns to the Knowledge Base domains.

3. In the **Matching** step, click on **Start** to apply matching policy on the dataset. You will see a view of matched and unmatched data rows; click on **Next**.

4. In the **Export** tab, set destination type as Excel, export the results of matching and survivorship to different Excel files, and export the results.

What just happened?

In this example, you learned how to create a matching project and apply the matching policy of a Knowledge Base on the existing dataset and export the results. There are two result sets for matching projects. The matching results lists all matched and unmatched data rows with metadata information about the matching rule applied, similarity score, pivot record, and so on. The Survivorship results lists only records that remained in the list after removing the duplicate records. There are different rules for survivorship; these rules can be set in the **Export** tab. The rules are as follows:

- **Pivot record**: This is the pivot record will be chosen randomly from DQS. Pivot record is the record that showed in the matching result with the pivot ID. This is a default option.

- **Most complete record**: This is the record with the most number of populated fields. A populated field is a column that contains at least one value. Note that even columns that don't participate in the **Map** window of matching will be considered.

- **Longest record**: This is the longest record between matched records. The record with the most length will be picked. Their length will be calculated from total fields, and even those fields that don't participate in the **Map** window of matching will be considered.

- **Most complete and longest record**: This record has the properties of all the other records.

Integrating with MDS and SSIS

DQS has the ability to interact with other data movement components: SSIS and **Master Data Services** (**MDS**). There is a DQS cleansing component in SSIS that provides a connection to a knowledge base. This component will create a cleansing project for the incoming data stream and will apply the Knowledge Base in the DQ server to the data stream and generate the result. There is also a functionality to apply matching rules on the data in an Excel spreadsheet before loading that data into MDS. In this section, we will explore how to use the interaction of DQS with MDS and SSIS.

Time for action – the DQS cleansing component in SSIS

In this example, we will create an SSIS project and get some customer information from an Excel file and apply the **Address KB** rules on the information with the DQS cleansing component and check the result. For this example, we only show results in a data viewer in SSIS, but in real-world scenarios, you might need to export the results into a destination or use them as the source of another transformation. Perform the following steps to create a cleansing component:

1. Open SSDT, create a new Integration Service project, and name it `Chapter 05 Data Quality Services`.

2. Create a Data Flow task and then go to the **Data Flow** tab.

3. Create an Excel source, connect it to the `KB Parsing.xlsx` file, set the first row as header, preview data, and close this component.

4. Drag-and-drop a DQS cleansing component from the SSIS toolbox under the Excel source and connect the data path from the Excel source to this component.

5. In the **DQS Cleansing Transformation** editor, in the connection manager's tab, create a new connection to the DQ server and set the server name as `local`.

6. Choose **Address KB** as the Knowledge Base. You will see a list of domains in this Knowledge Base under available domains.

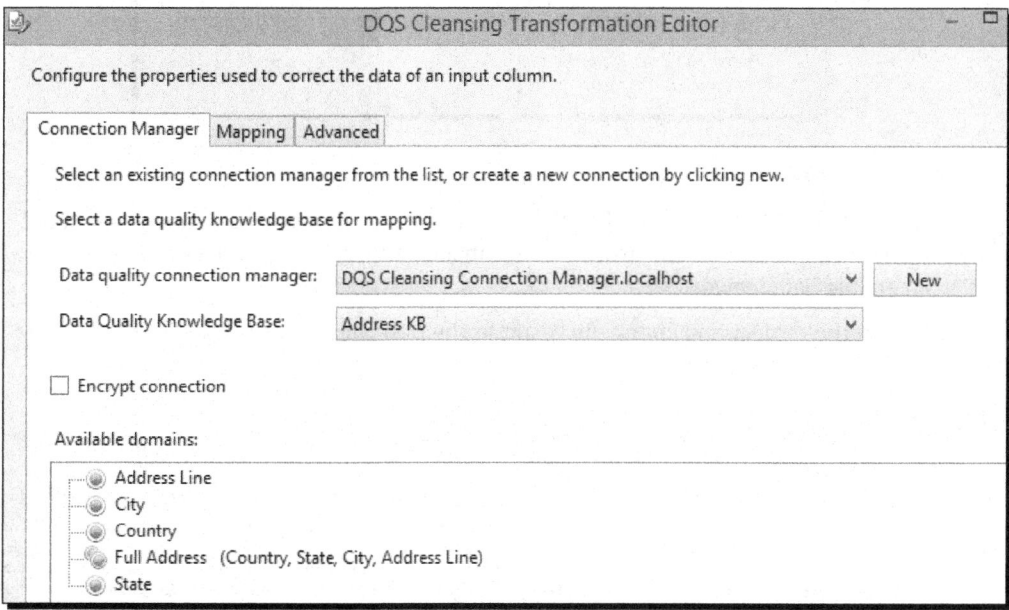

7. In the **Mapping** tab, check the **Address** column and map it to the **Full Address** domain.

8. In the **Advanced** tab, verify that the **Standardize** output option is checked. Check the confidence and reason options under enable field level columns.

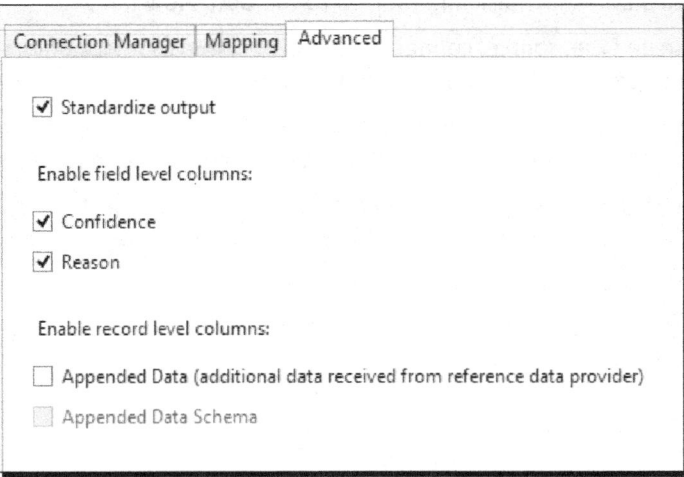

9. Close the DQS cleansing component editor.

10. Add **Union all transform** after the DQS cleansing component, connect the data path to this component from DQS cleansing, and right-click on data path and enable data viewer.

11. Run the project and check the result in the data viewer, as shown in the following screenshot:

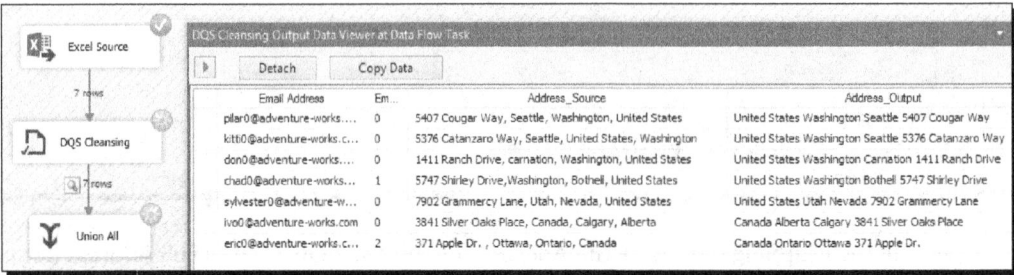

What just happened?

The DQS cleansing component connects to a knowledge base in the DQ server and sends a data quality request, creates a data quality project, applies the Knowledge Base domain rules, and generates results. Then, the results are passed to the SSIS component again and exported as the output of the component. In this example, you've seen a sample of how this component works. The following screenshot (sourced from Microsoft) is a high-level overview of the DQS cleansing component:

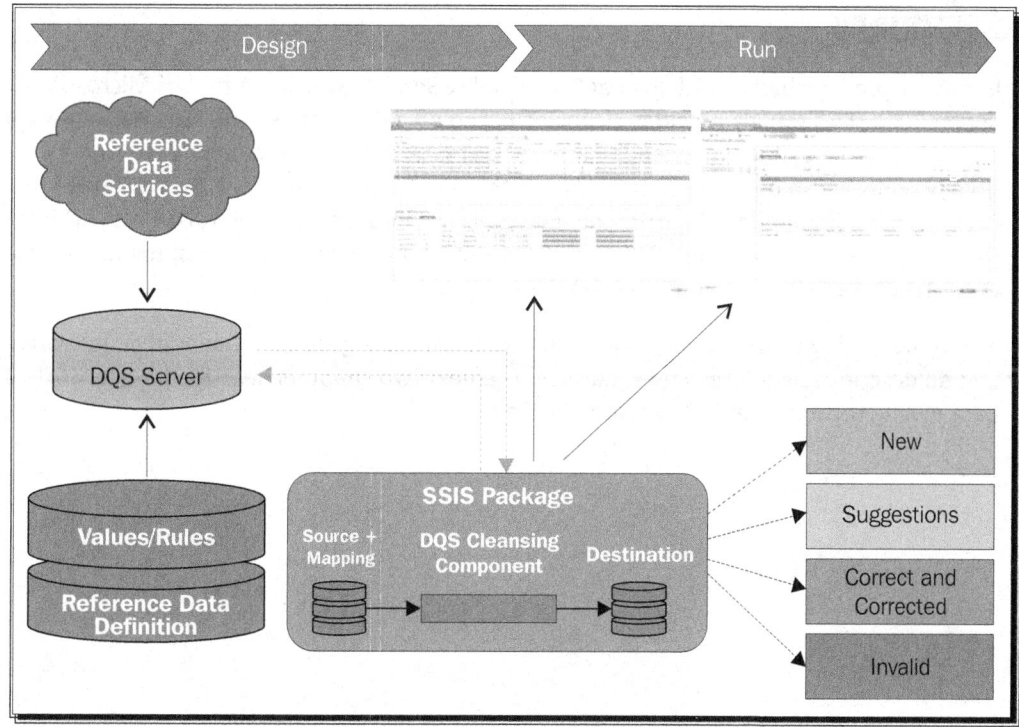

DQS integration with MDS

The DQS components for integration with MDS exist in Excel's **Master Data** tab. The point of using this component is to cleanse data before loading it into MDS. Take a look at the following screenshot:

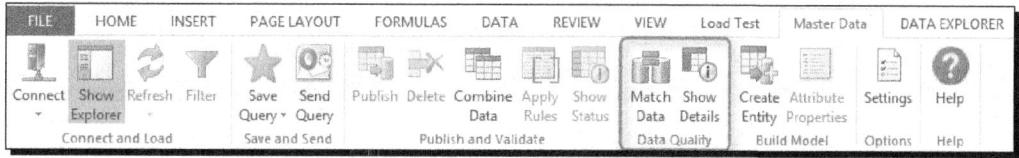

The **Match Data** option will apply a matching project with a matching policy in a Knowledge Base in the DQ server. **Show Details** will explore the metadata columns in the result set of matching with DQS option.

Summary

In this chapter, we had a quick look at Data Quality Service, which is a part of Microsoft SQL Server 2014. This service provides cleansing based on a Knowledge Base. The data steward can define and maintain Knowledge Bases, and create and modify matching policies. Data quality projects can be created directly from the data quality client tool, from SSIS with the DQS cleansing component, or from the data quality components in the MDS Excel Add-In. DQS is a powerful tool to clean data before loading it into data warehouses, to ensure data consistency, and clean different datasets.

When the quality of data is high, we can use data mining algorithms to identify data patterns and do descriptive and predictive analyses. The next two chapters describe how to work with data mining technologies in Microsoft SQL Server.

7

Data Mining – Descriptive Models in SSAS

So far, you've learned about three main components of a BI system, namely data visualization, consolidation, and modeling. There is another important component in a BI system: data mining. Data mining can be performed in two ways; analysis of the existing data and predictions based on a model fetched from an existing dataset. The concept of analyzing an existing dataset is called the **descriptive model***. In this chapter, we will discuss the descriptive model. The very next chapter is about prediction with data mining.*

Microsoft uses Analysis Services as an engine for data mining models. Each Analysis Services database can contain one or more data mining models. The result of data mining models can be checked with a wide set of diagrams. In this chapter, you will learn about the data mining cycle, data preparation, and descriptive mining models such as the association rule. You will also learn how to solve real-world problems with descriptive models. An example is the analysis of products that are sold together, which is called market-basket analysis.

An introduction to data mining

Data mining is the process of finding the problem, thinking about the solution, testing data mining models on a test dataset, and deploying one or more mining models in a live environment. The data mining process does not conclude at any of these steps; it is a circular process that continues to improve data analysis with time.

The following diagram shows the data mining process with Microsoft tools (sourced from Microsoft, `http://technet.microsoft.com/en-us/library/ms174949.aspx`):

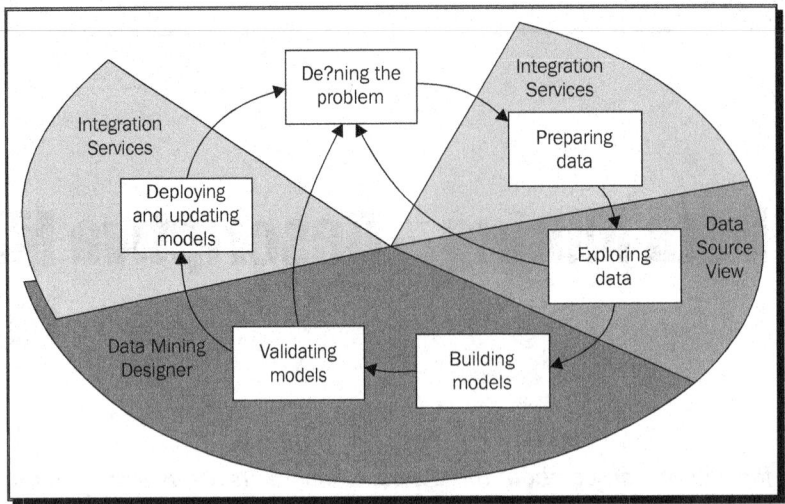

The set of data on which mining algorithms will be applied are called training and test case. There are many data mining algorithms designed and introduced in academic research. Microsoft implemented nine of the most common data mining algorithms as part of the SQL Server product. The following is a list of data mining algorithms and a few lines of information about their usage in solving real-world problems:

- **Decision tree**: This algorithm creates a tree based on the attribute values that play an important role in segmentation.

- **Association rule**: This algorithm identifies the association between attributes. One of the most common usages of this is to perform a market-basket analysis.

- **Clustering**: This algorithm categorizes items in groups with similar attribute values.

- **Naïve Bayes**: This algorithm uses the Bayesian technique for categorization of elements. It is useful for finding attributes that affect the generation of results; for example, finding the prospective buyers of a product.

- **Linear regression**: This algorithm is a part of the decision tree that finds linear relationships between variables. This algorithm is a good option for figuring out the trend between continuous variables, for example, marketing costs and sales.

- **Neural network**: This algorithm works with the state of the input and the predictable variables and generates the possibility of the state's relationships. This algorithm can be a good candidate to answer text mining questions.

- **Logistic regression**: This algorithm is implemented as a version of the neural network algorithm; it calculates the effect of input variables on outputs and generates weights based on calculations. This algorithm can be used to find the weight factor of different inputs to generate the result.

- **Sequence clustering**: This is a clustering algorithm that identifies the sequence of variables. It can be used to answer the work order or the clicking path on a website.

- **Time Series**: This is a useful data mining algorithm for time-based analysis, for example, predicting sales for the next couple of months.

Data mining algorithms require data as the main input, and they perform the analysis based on the variety of the data records; in a nutshell, the more the data provided, the better the data mining results. As a data mining developer, your main job is to apply different algorithms on the dataset and analyze the result. If the purpose of data mining is not prediction and just description and analysis, then you can use data mining viewers to check the result. But if you want to get prediction results based on the current data rows, then you should check the data mining viewers' results, check the Lift Charts and Profit Charts, and finally use data mining queries to generate prediction out of the most compatible mining models.

Data mining algorithms are categorized, on the basis of their functionality, into the following five types:

- **Classification**: This category includes predicting discrete variables such as color. Algorithms in this category are decision tree, naïve Bayes, neural network, and clustering. Examples of use cases with these algorithms include predicting customers who would buy a special product in the future and finding the attributes of customers who deal most with a specific insurance plan.

- **Regression**: This category includes algorithms whose main functionality is to predict continuous variables. The algorithms in this category are linear regression, logistic regression, and time series. Decision trees can also be used with continuous variables. Please note that not all algorithms work with continuous and discrete variables. Examples of use cases with this category of algorithms include getting an estimate sales prediction for the next year and predicting the number of visitors on a website.

- **Association**: The relationship between attributes in data rows will be analyzed with this category of algorithm. The algorithms in this category are association rules and sequence clustering. An example of a use case with these algorithms is finding products that are purchased along with each other in a single purchase basket (market-basket analysis).

- **Sequence Analysis**: The order of happening attributes will be analyzed with this category. The only algorithm in this category is sequence clustering. This algorithm's use cases include finding the order of buying items or the analysis of a work order.

◆ **Segmentation**: This category includes algorithms that cluster data into different segments or clusters. Sequence clustering and clustering are the algorithms in this category. These algorithms' example use case could be finding a fraudulent bank transaction by categorizing banking transaction in patterns.

In this and the next chapter, we will focus on data mining algorithms, and we will go through some real-world scenarios that data mining algorithms help with while problem solving. This chapter is about descriptive models that analyze existing data and provide useful analysis information, such as market-basket analysis. *Chapter 8, Identify Data Patterns – Predictive Models in SSAS*, is about predictive models that help in future predictions, for example, predicting sales over the next few months.

 To run the examples in this and the next chapter, you will need SQL Server Analysis Services installed as part of the Microsoft SQL Server, and the AdventureWorksDW2012 database should also exist. For more information on installing this database, follow the instruction guide in the *Preface* of this book.

The Microsoft Decision Tree algorithm

The decision tree is one of the most common algorithms in decision making. The algorithm identifies nodes and builds the tree based on those nodes. Each node will be a decision made on a selection of attributes, for example, customers who are under 40 years of age or over 40. The next node will be another decision, and a sequence of decisions made on each tree level will end up with a subset of data. In this section, we will use the decision tree algorithm to find out what the attribute values were that led someone to buy a bicycle. In the next chapter, we will use the result of this algorithm to perform some prediction.

Time for action – creating a data mining solution with the Microsoft Decision Tree algorithm

In this example, we will create our first data mining solution with the Microsoft decision tree algorithm. The `AdventureWorksDW` database contains information about bike buyers. We want to use that information as input variables to the decision tree algorithm and find out what drives someone to buy a bike.

1. Open SSDT and create an **Analysis Service Multidimensional and Data Mining** project. Name the project `Chapter 07 Data Mining Descriptive Models`.

2. Right-click on the `data source` folder and create a new data source for `AdventureWorksDW2012`. Choose the impersonation information with the account that has enough privilege, then accept the default name as **Adventure Works DW2012** and complete the wizard.

3. Create a data source view with the Adventure Works DW2012 data source. In the **Select Table and Views** menu, select only **vTargetMail** and add it to the included object's list in the box to the right. Click on **Continue** in the wizard and accept the default name for the data source view.

4. In DSV designer, right-click on the `vTargetMail` table and click on **Explore Data**. You will see the customers' information plus an additional field for the bike buyer. The `BikeBuyer` field is populated with the existing sales record in the `sales` table.

5. Right-click on the **Mining Structures** tab and create a new mining structure.

6. In the **Data Mining** wizard, the first step is to select the definition method. Choose from the existing relational databases or data warehouse.

7. In the **Create the Data Mining Structure** window, click on the **Create mining structure with a mining model** radio button and choose **Microsoft** from the list of algorithms in the **Which data mining technique do you want to use?** dropdown and continue, as shown in the following screenshot:

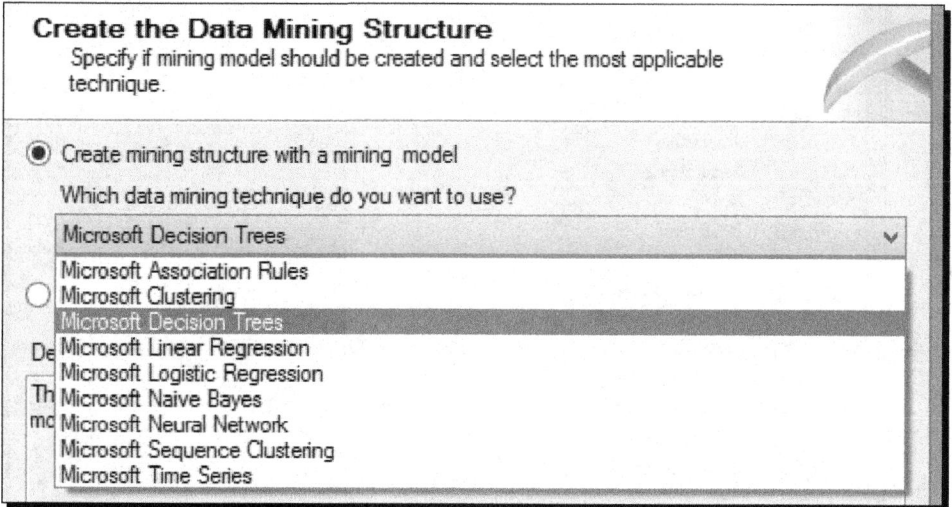

8. In the **Select Data Source View** menu, choose the **Adventure Works DW2012** data source view and go to the next step.

9. In the **Specify Table Types** window, verify that the `vTargetMail` table is selected as the `Case` table, as shown in the following screenshot:

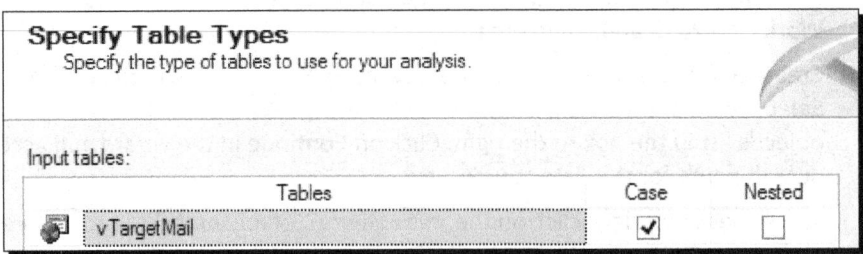

10. In the **Specify the Training Data** window, choose `CustomerKey` as the `Key` column. Select these columns as input: **Age, BikeBuyer, CommuteDistance, CustomerKey, EnglishEducation, EnglishOccupation, Gender, HouseOwnerFlag, MaritalStatus, NumberCarsOwned, NumberChildrenAtHome, Region, TotalChildren**, and **YearlyIncome**. Finally, set **BikeBuyer** as **Predictable**. The following screenshot shows this configuration (note that not all columns are shown in this screenshot):

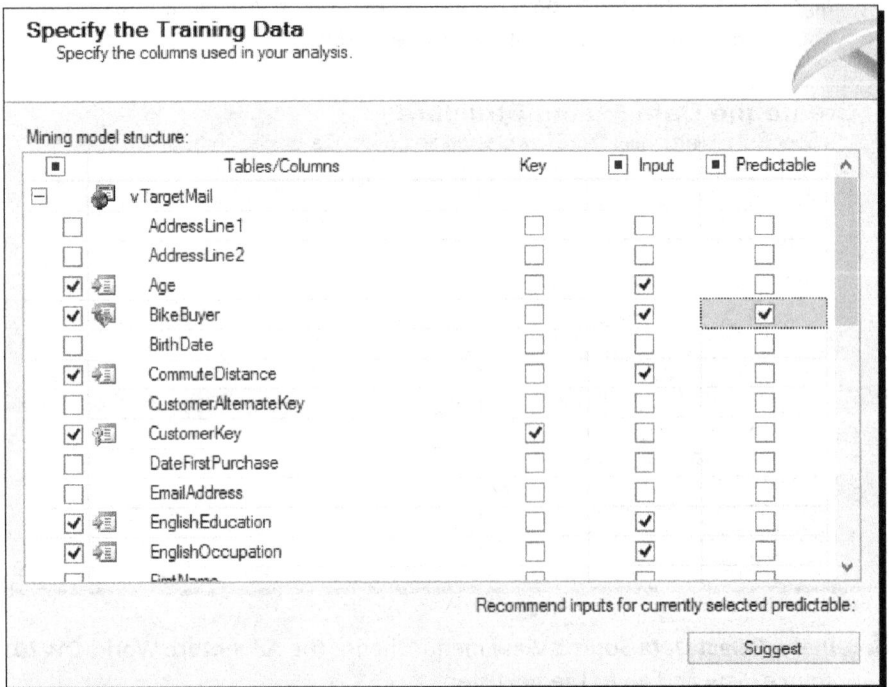

11. In the **Specify Column's Content and Data Type** window, you will see the **Content Type** and **Data Type** of the column fetched based on the metadata of the underlying data source view. Click on **Detect** to adjust the content type based on existing values for each column. As a result, you will see that some columns, such as `BikeBuyer` and `CommuteDistance`, have the content type `Discrete`. This is shown in the following screenshot:

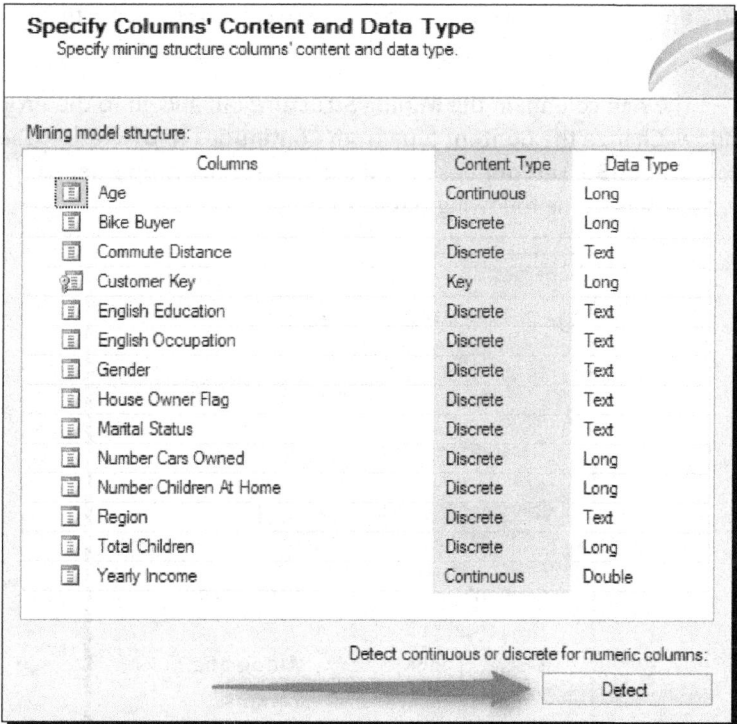

12. In the **Create Testing Set** window, enter `30%` for the percentage of data for testing. Leave the other option as it is and go to the next step.

13. In the **Create Testing Set** window, enter the name of **Mining Structure** as `Target Mail Mining Structure` and rename **Mining Model** to `Target Mail Mining Structure`.

14. After completing the wizard, you will see the **Mining Structure** designer window, and you will see `vTargetMail` as the only case table with a yellow header in the designer.

 Before analyzing the result of the decision tree algorithm, we need to change the input variable with a continuous content type to discrete. The reason for doing this is explained in the *What just happened?* section with full details.

15. Select the **Age** column in the **Mining Structure** tab and go to the **Properties** window. Change the **Content** type from **Continuous** to **Discretized**, set **DiscretizationBucketCount** as 5, and leave the other properties as they are, as shown in the following screenshot:

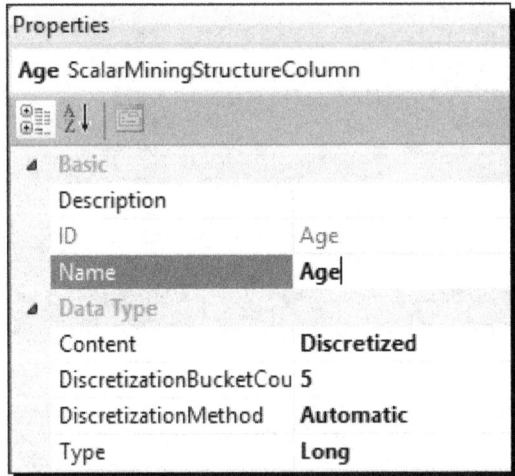

16. Perform the same discretization configuration for the `YearlyIncome` column.

17. In the solution explorer, right-click on **Target Mail Mining Structure** and process it.

18. Go to the **Mining Model Viewer** tab. You will see the **Microsoft Tree Viewer** as the default viewer, which shows that the decision tree structure is fetched based on the mining model configuration and the underlying database.

19. In the **Decision Tree** tab, set the background color as 1. This means that the tree node's background color will be set such that the `BikeBuyer` variable will be 1. As a result, the node with more possibility of bike buyers in its subset will be shaded with a background color of dark blue. This is shown in the following screenshot:

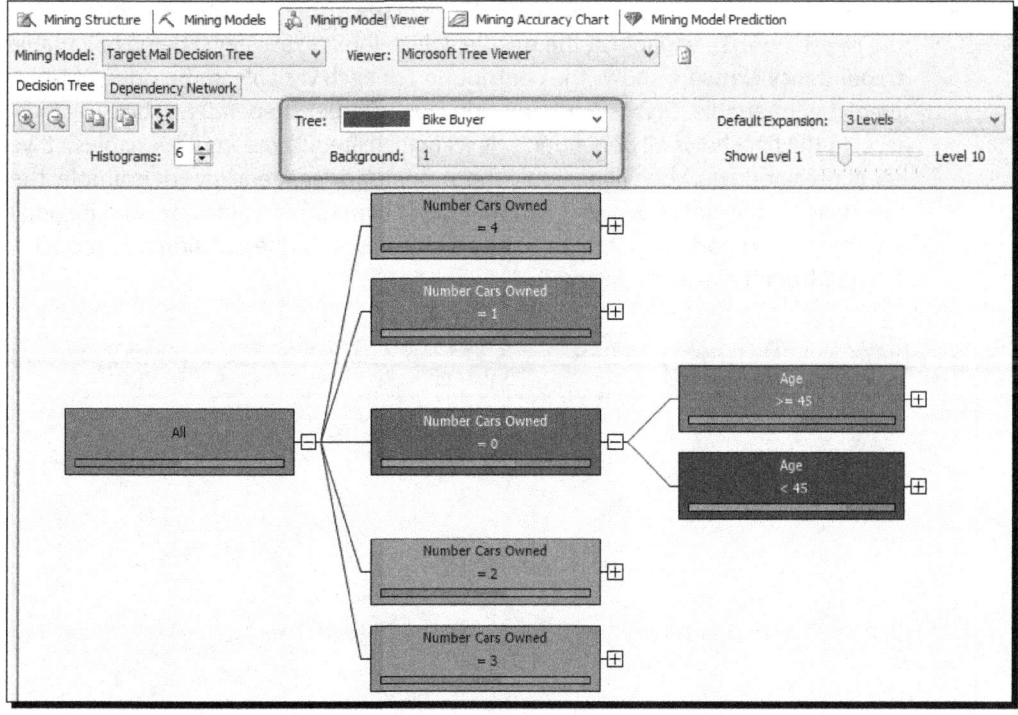

As you can see in the previous screenshot, you can change the level of a decision tree node to explore the decision path that defines input variables with their values that played the most important role to lead most of the customers to buy that product.

The first decision tree level made in the preceding screenshot is the number of cars owned. As you can see, people with no cars have a greater tendency to buy a bike. Then, if you expand the tree, you will see that among the people who don't own cars, those who are younger than 45 are the subset of customers who bought bikes the most. If you continue the decision path, you will find nodes with very high possibility of bike buyers. While hovering on each node, you can see the number of records in that subset, and whether those subsets are bike buyers or not. The following screenshot shows a sample decision path:

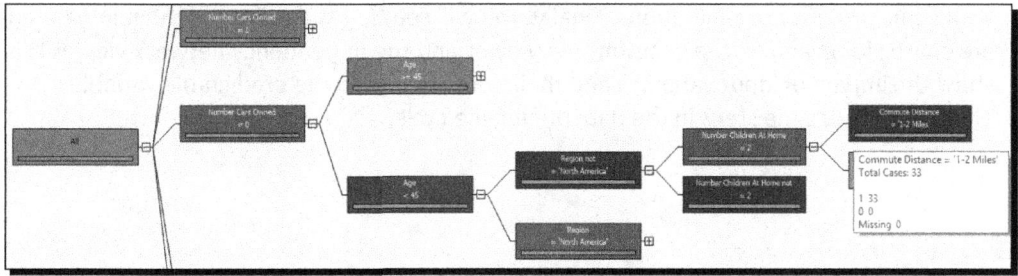

20. Click on the **Dependency Network** tab. You will see a chart of input variables with the `predictable` variable at the middle, which looks like a star schema of variables. **Dependency Network** shows the contribution of each variable in the value of the predictable variable. On the left-hand side, you will see a dependency bar. The highest level in the bar shows all dependency links (which literally means all variables). If you scroll the bar down, you will see only the strongest dependencies. For example, the following screenshot shows that **Number Cars Owned**, **Yearly Income**, and **Region** are the most important directives to buy a bike based on the decision tree model fetched from the existing dataset:

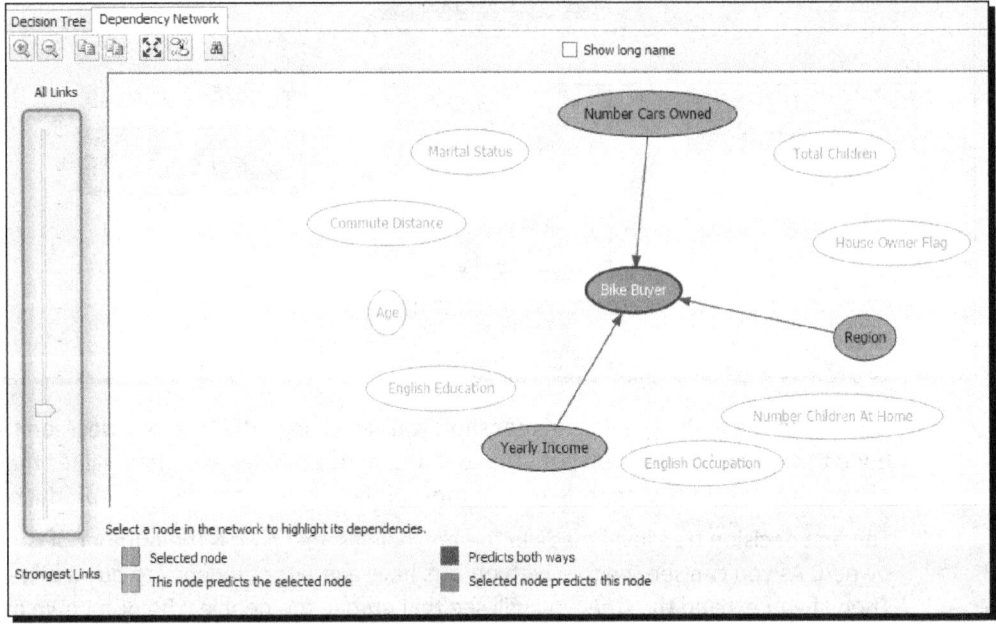

What just happened?

Congratulations! You built your first data mining model in this example. Building data mining models, as you've seen in this example, is easy. You don't need to worry and think about how the data mining algorithm works. You can simply use it with the data mining wizard, and also with some property configurations. Finally, you will see that the results of the mining model are charts; for example, the decision tree viewer and the dependency network viewer that show the impact of input variables and their contribution to the predictable variable.
The following are the steps in the data mining life cycle.

Problem definition

The very first step of each data mining solution is the problem definition. The problem in this example was to find prospective bike buyers. In other words, assume this scenario: the AdventureWorks company wants to build a new bike model, and the company would like to know who would buy this product. They want to use data mining algorithms to focus on customers that might want to buy the new bike, not all of them. There are many reasons why a company would want to focus only on high-probability bike buyers; for example, advertising costs will be much lower and effective if it targets only those customers.

Data preparation

The data preparation step starts after defining the problem. Data preparation is the process of understanding the existing data and finding variables in the existing data. For example, the database view that was used in this sample (vTargetMail) contains customer information such as age, income, number of children, and commute distance. On the other hand, existing customers may or may not have bought a bike from this company previously, so the BikeBuyer field can be gathered based on previous sales data records. The vTargetMail database contains both information, that is, customer fields and the BikeBuyer column.

Data preparation can be done not only with SQL Server and database query tools, but also with Excel. Excel is a very good tool to identify columns that play the most important roles in the result set. For example, the commute distance is an important variable in the decision to buy a bike, but the last name of the customer or the address line is not. In *Chapter 11, Power BI*, you will learn how Excel can be used in data analysis.

After data preparation, the next step is to assign input variables from the existing dataset to data mining algorithms and build models. Microsoft's data mining solution is located in the Analysis Services multidimensional project template. This doesn't mean that you need to build a cube to create a mining model. The SSAS project is just a container for the data mining structure. As you've seen in step 1 of the *Time for action – creating a data mining solution with the Microsoft Decision Tree* algorithm section, the project template that is used in this example is the Analysis Service multidimensional and data mining project.

The data mining structure requires a data source and data source views. So, we simply created a data source and a DSV for the vTargetMail view in steps 2 and 3. Step 4 shows you a view of the existing dataset, which we will use to feed into the mining model.

The mining structure

Microsoft uses the mining structure based on the data mining variables and their data structure for the metadata that was built, for example, data types and content types. In steps 5 and 6, we started to create the mining structure. As you've seen in step 6, the mining structure accepts the dataset from both the relational database and from an Analysis Services cube. In step 7, we can choose to create the mining model beside the mining structure, or not.

The mining model

The mining model contains a data mining algorithm and a set of variables, for example, **input**, **key**, and **predictable**. The mining algorithm will be applied on the existing dataset by considering the variable configuration, and finally the mining model will contain the result of the data analysis. A mining structure may contain one or more mining models. In a data mining solution, you would need to apply multiple mining models on a same mining structure to find the best algorithm that satisfies the test result set. As you've seen in step 7, there are nine data mining algorithms that can be used in mining models.

Steps 8 and 9 show how to set the existing data in `vTargetMail` as an input for the mining structure. In step 9, we selected **vTargetMail** as the **Case** table. The `Case` table is the main input of the mining structure and algorithm. Sometimes, the `Case` table cannot be as simple as one table, and you might need to provide a many-to-one relationship in it. In those scenarios, you should choose the second table as `nested` and the first one as `case`.

Data mining variables

Step 10 is an important step in configuring the mining model. There are three types of variables in mining algorithms: key, input, and predictable. The key variable, as its name suggests, is the variable that defines the key field in the dataset to be analyzed. The **Key** column in our previous example is **CustomerKey**. Input variables are columns whose effects we want to see on the result set. As you've seen, we have chosen columns such as **Age**, **Education**, and **Occupation** as input. The reason is that we want to analyze the effect of the values of these variables on the `predictable` variable. You can find out which columns are most useful to be set as input variables based on the analysis done in the data preparation step and also in the problem definition step.

The content type

In step 11, we used the **Detect** button to detect the content type of the input variables. The content type means that the data type is fetched based on the existing values for that column in the provided dataset. There are nine content types, but the most common are discrete, continuous, discretized, cyclical, and ordered. Short notes on these are presented in the following list:

- **Discrete**: Data values that are separate, for example, the red, yellow, and blue color values
- **Continuous**: Data values that change continuously, for example, age or salary
- **Cyclical**: Data values that are in a cyclical order, for example, the days of a week
- **Ordered**: Data values that are in a sequential order, for example, the days of a month
- **Discretized**: Data values that are continuous but bucketed into categories, and as a result behave discretely

In step 11, you saw that age and yearly income are continuous, while other input variables are discrete. Data mining algorithms work with different content types; for example, Time Series have better results with ordered and cyclical content types, decision trees perform well with discrete values, while regression algorithms have better results with continuous and discrete variables.

The training and test set

When we apply a dataset to the data mining algorithm, a part of the data acts like the training set and the other as the test set. The training set is a subset of the data on which the mining algorithm will be applied; this subset participates directly in generating the mining model. When the mining model is ready, another subset of data will be used to test the model to check the mining model result; this subset is named test set. When you work with prediction algorithms, it is important to set a part of the dataset as the test set, because if you use all of the dataset as a training set, then you have no way to identify the mining model that generates the result correctly (or almost correctly). In this example, we used 70 percent of the data as a training set while the remaining 30 percent was used as a test set (step 12). Defining a test set is only important when you want to perform prediction. For data analysis without the prediction functionality, you won't require a test set.

In steps 15 to 17, we changed the content type of the **Age** and **Yearly Income** columns to **Discretized**. Since the content is continuous, we need to bucket values. The data mining algorithm applies bucketing methods based on the `DiscretizationMethod` and `DiscretizationBucketCount` properties. We set `DiscretizationBucketCount` as `16`, which means age will be categorized in five categories (buckets). In order to apply the data mining algorithm on the training set, the mining structure should be processed (step 18).

Data mining viewers

Each data mining algorithm has a different set of mining viewers. Data mining viewers are visualization tools that show the structure of data based on the training dataset. In this example, you've seen two types of mining viewers: decision tree viewer and dependency network viewer.

The decision tree viewer that you've seen from steps 20 to 22 shows the decision tree built over the training dataset. Each node shows a decision, and nodes can be colored based on the predictable column value (step 20). You've learned how to follow a decision path and analyze the result.

The dependency network viewer shows the dependency of the `predictable` variable to all input variables. You can see the strongest links by changing the dependency bar in this viewer.

Microsoft association rules

Association rules is a data mining algorithm that identifies relationships between different variables in an existing dataset; this algorithm literally finds rules existing on the association relationships of variables. One of the most common scenarios that can be solved with this algorithm is the market-basket analysis. In the following example, you will learn about the association rule algorithm and how to analyze the results of this algorithm.

Time for action – the Microsoft association rule

Assume this scenario as an example: the AdventureWorks company wants to identify a set of products that are usually purchased together. The company can use this information to put these products beside each other or add similar items next to each other in a store to achieve higher sales. This is known as market-basket analysis because it relates to the analysis of products in a single basket in each purchase. In this example, we will use the AdventureWorksDW2012 database.

1. Open the AdventureWorksDW2012 data source view from the previous example.

2. Right-click on an empty area in the data source view and select **Add/Remove Tables**.

3. In the **Add/Remove Tables** window, add **vAssocSeqOrders** and **vAssocSeqLineItems** to the DSV.

4. After adding these views, create a relationship between the two views in this manner: drag-and-drop the **Order Number** column from **vAssocSeqLineItems** to **vAssocSeqOrders** as shown in the following screenshot:

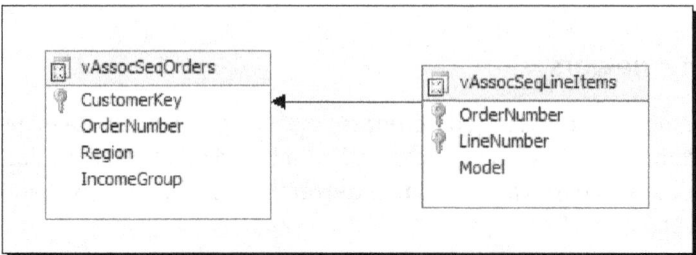

5. Create a new mining structure by right-clicking on the `mining structure` folder in **Solution Explorer**. Choose a definition method from an existing relational database or data warehouse.

6. In the **Create the Data Mining Structure** window, select **Create Mining Structure** as the mining model and then choose the **Microsoft Association Rules** algorithm from the drop-down list.

7. Choose the data source view as **Adventure Works DW2012**.

8. In the **Specify Table Types** window, set **vAssocSeqLineItems** as **Nested** and **vAssocSeqOrders** as **Case** as shown in the following screenshot:

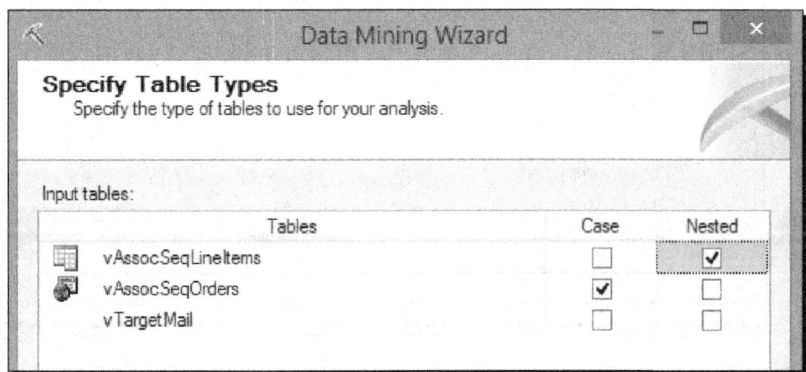

9. In the **Specify the Training Data** window, set **OrderNumber** as **Key** and **Model** as **Key**, **Input**, and **Predictable**. The following screenshot shows this configuration:

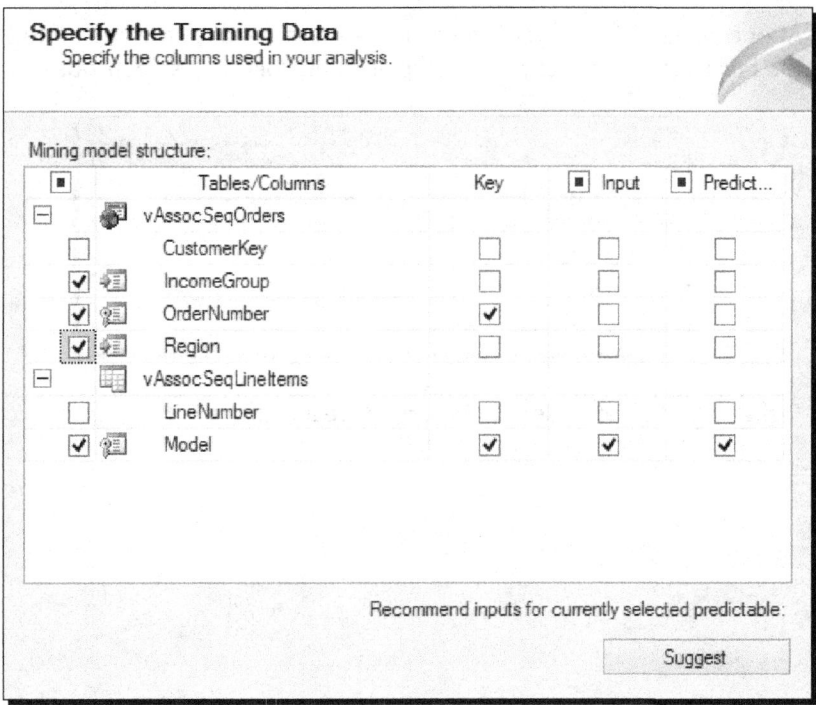

10. In the **Specify Column's Content and Data Type** window that appears next, as shown in the following screenshot, click on **Detect**:

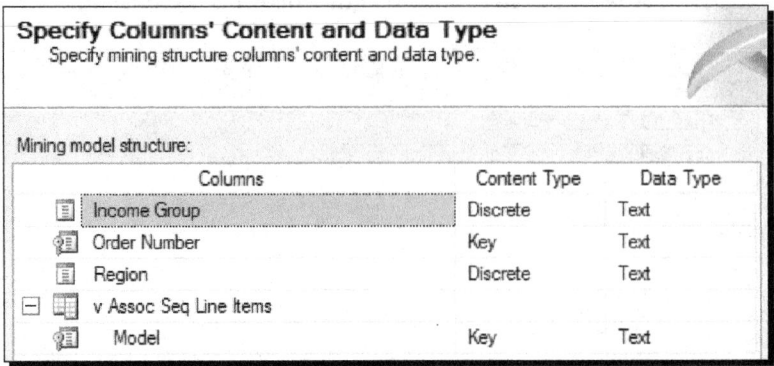

11. In the **Create Testing Set** window, change the percentage of data for testing to 0.

12. Rename **mining structure** to Sales Order Mining Structure and **mining model** to Sales Order Association Rules. Check the option for **Allow drill through** and click on **Finish**.

13. After completing the wizard, you will see a diagram of a case and nested table in the mining structure designer, as shown in the following screenshot:

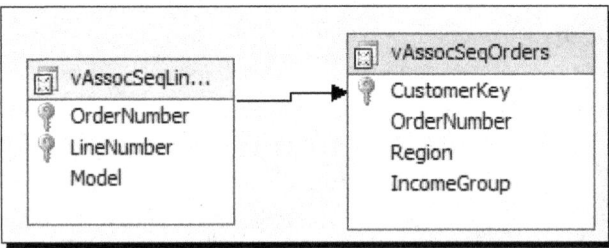

14. Right-click on **Sales Order Mining Structure** and process it.

15. Go to the **Mining Model Viewer** tab.

16. The default viewer is **Microsoft Association Rule Viewer**. In the **Rules** tab, you can see a list of rules fetched by this algorithm applied on the existing dataset.

17. Change the **Show** option to **Show attribute name only** by choosing it from the drop-down list. Change the order of columns to sort by **Importance** or **Probability** (that is descending) and investigate the result set. As you can see in the following screenshot, there are some rules; for example, you wanted to buy Road-250 and Road Tire Tube but you ended up buying HL Road Tire:

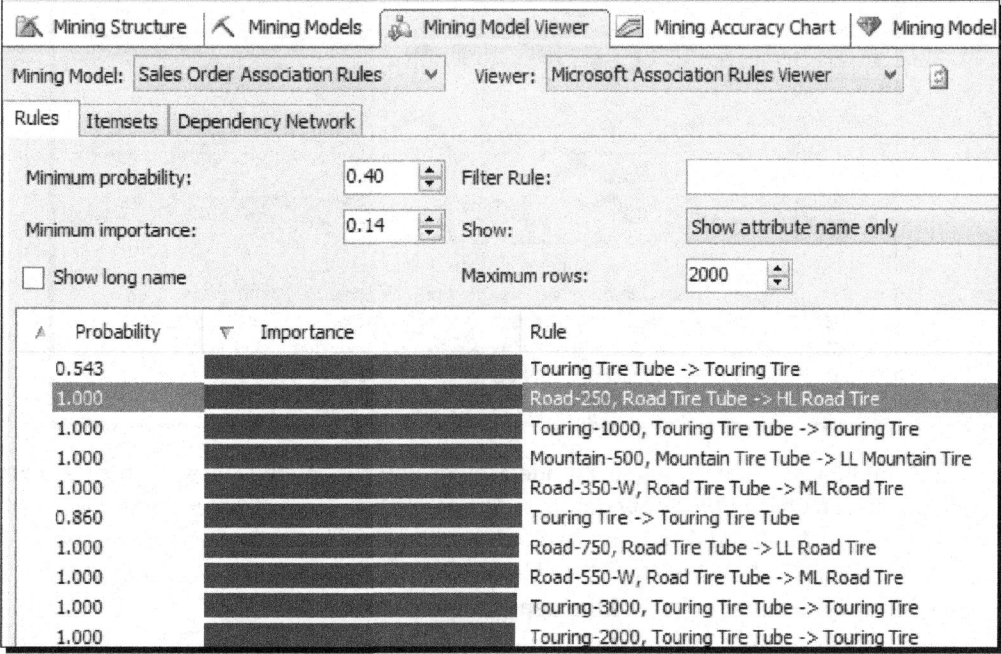

18. To view a list of records from a rule set, right-click on that record and select one of the drill-through options.

19. Go to the **Itemsets** tab. In this tab, you will see a set of items based on the set of items fetched with the association rule algorithm. Change the **Show** drop-down list to **Show attribute name only**, change the size of the set to 3, and change the order of the result set to the descending order of the **Support** column. For example, the first itemset in the following screenshot shows that, in the provided dataset, **589** sale order transactions had the **Mountain Bottle Cage, Mountain-200, Water Bottle** option in the same basket:

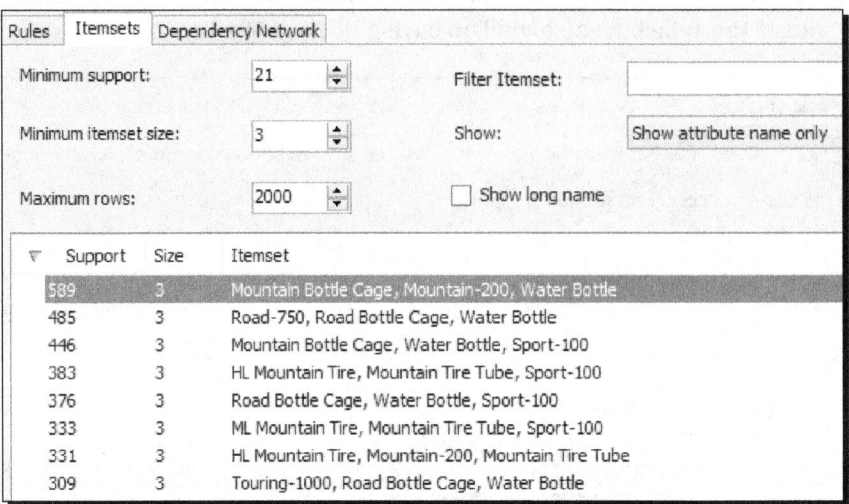

20. In the last tab of this mining model viewer, you will see the **Dependency Network** viewer. Change the **Show** option to **Show attribute name only** by choosing it in the drop-down list and shift the **Dependency Network** bar to **lower**. You will see the relationship between items in a basket and rules fetched. The following screenshot shows a magnified part of the dependency network:

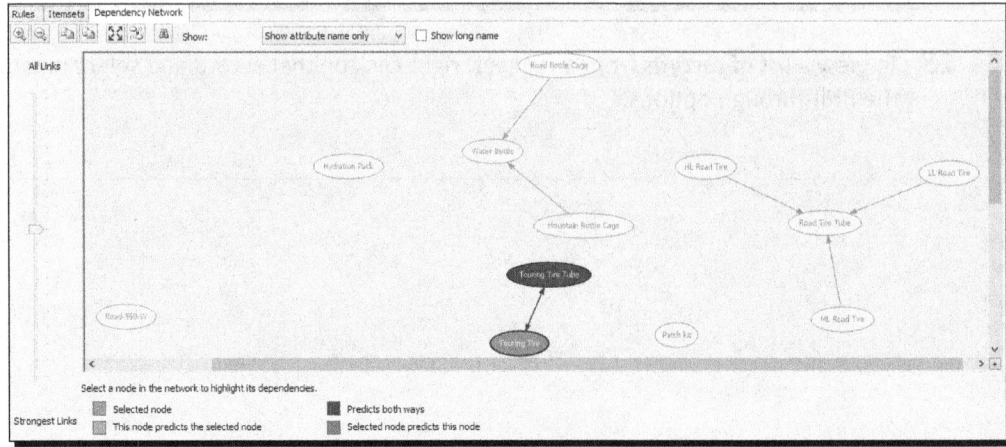

What just happened?

In this example, you've learned how to use the Microsoft association rules algorithm to solve the market-basket analysis scenario. The AdventureWorksDW2012 database contains two views for sales order transactions, that is, vAssocSeqOrders and vAssocSeqLineItems. The vAssocSeqOrders view contains one record per sales order and vAssocSeqLineItems contains one record per item in each sales order. The combination of these two tables provides a list of items bought in each sales order. We used this dataset to train the Microsoft association rules algorithm in this example. Steps 2 to 4 show how to add these tables and create a relationship between them in the data source view. The relationship generated is based on the order number.

We used the Microsoft association rules algorithm (step 6) in this example because it identifies rules between variables existing in a dataset and provides a set of items that are associated with each other. In step 8, we set the vAssocSeqOrders table as a **Case** table because this table contains header records of sales orders. We've set vAssocSeqLineItems as a **Nested** table as it contains detailed item sales records.

Step 9 is an important step because we set variable types in this step. **Order Number** and **Model** is used as a key because **Order Number** itself cannot identify a record. Moreover, we used **Model** as an input as well because we want to see the effect of buying a model based on another model. We also choose the model to be predictable. The configuration of a variable and a column's type is one of the most important steps in data mining solutions.

We've set the entire dataset to act as a training set, so we've changed the test set (step 11) to 0 because, in this example, we didn't want to predict. The main purpose of this scenario is descriptive data analysis.

In step 13, you can see that the case table is shown with a yellow header and nested tables with grey headers in the mining structure designer. After processing the mining structure and the mining model in step 14, you can view the result in the **Mining Model Viewer** tab of the **Mining Structure Designer** window.

The Microsoft association rule viewer contains three types of viewers, namely rules, itemsets, and the dependency network. In step 17, you can see a sample screenshot of the **Rules** tab. The association rules algorithm is applied on the existing dataset and, as a result, it generates rules that are based on the input and predictable variables. As a result, in this viewer, you can see a list of rules that you can filter using some parameters. First of all, rules show attribute names and values by default (which we've changed to **Show attribute name only** in step 17).

Algorithm parameters

You can filter the required options in the minimum probability or the minimum importance tools. Probability, importance, and support are the main parameters in the association rules algorithm. Support shows the occurrence of an item or itemset; it is also called frequency. Probability is a value calculated by Analysis Services that shows the confidence of the prediction of a predictable value based on the items of input values. The importance parameter is calculated based on the likelihood of the condition *if X, then Y* resulting in *Y*. The importance parameter is also called lift. A detailed description of these algorithm parameters is out of the scope of this book. You can read more about them with a brief description in MSDN books, at `http://technet.microsoft.com/en-us/library/cc280428.aspx`.

In the **Rules** tab, as you've seen in step 17, you can look at rules and filter them on the basis of minimum probability or importance to get rid of rules that are not reliable enough to be considered. Algorithm parameters can also be changed in the **Mining Model** tab by right-clicking on the **mining model** column and choosing **Set Algorithm Parameters...** as shown in the following screenshot:

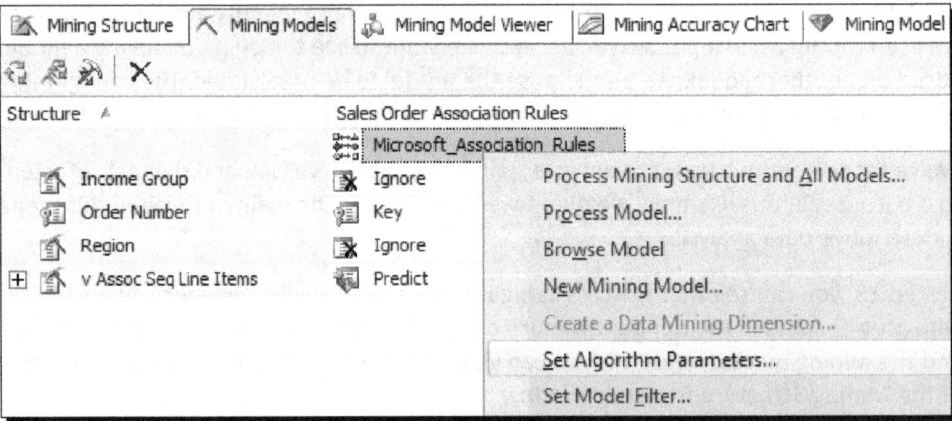

Each data mining algorithm has a different set of parameters. For example, the clustering algorithm can be modified with a number of clusters while association rules can be modified with support, probability, and importance. The following screenshot shows a list of parameters that can be modified when you work with the association rules algorithm:

Step 18 shows how you can use the **drill-through** option in the viewer to see the actual records that cover each rule or itemset. Step 19 shows a different view, which is the itemset viewer. You can change the size of an item set; for example, size 3 will show only those itemsets with at least three items. You can also view the frequency of the itemset in the **Support** column, and you can filter it by changing the minimum support.

Microsoft association rules give us the benefit of seeing the result set in the dependency network viewer. The dependency network viewer, in this mining model, shows how items are dependent on each other based on the market-basket analysis. When you change the dependency bar (step 20), you can see that the lower you go through the dependency bar, you will see more dependent items; this means that those items are bought together most of the times (such as **Touring Tire Tube** and **Touring Tire** shown in the screenshot of step 20).

Summary

In this chapter, you've learned some fundamentals about data mining algorithms. You learned that Microsoft Analysis Services provides nine algorithms for data mining. Data mining algorithms are divided into five categories based on their functionality. You also learned that a data mining solution is not a one-way solution. It is a circular life cycle that starts with problem definition, then data preparation, continues to model design and implementation, followed by testing the results and deployment, and finally finding the next problem.

We went through two common problems that could be solved with descriptive data mining algorithms, namely the analysis of existing bike buyers and market-basket analysis. For the analysis of existing bike buyers, we used the Microsoft Decision Tree algorithm that provided a tree of decisions made based on the value of the variables. You've learned how to analyze the result set of an algorithm in mining model viewers. The market-basket analysis utilized the Microsoft association rules algorithm to identify a set of products or items that were purchased together. You also learned that each data mining algorithm has a different set of parameters, which can be filtered or configured to help get better result out of the mining model.

In this chapter, you've learned about data mining algorithms, also called descriptive models, that analyze existing dataset. In the next chapter, you will learn how to use prediction in these algorithms and also use algorithms such as Time Series to identify patterns over a period of time. You will also learn about DMX, which is the query language for data mining scripts.

8
Identifying Data Patterns – Predictive Models in SSAS

In the previous chapter, you learned how to use data mining for data analysis. In this chapter, we will go one step further to reveal predictions based on an existing pattern. Prediction is one of the most interesting topics of Business Intelligence, because it gives us an estimate of the future behavior of the business.

*The Microsoft SSAS engine understands a specific language for prediction and works with data mining algorithms called **Data Mining Extensions (DMX)**. In this chapter, you will learn how to compare mining models and how to apply prediction on an existing data pattern with DMX. The examples of this chapter will use the scenarios covered in the previous chapter. Also, an example of Microsoft Time Series algorithm usage will be discussed at the end of this chapter.*

Finding the best algorithm

As a data mining developer, you apply different data mining algorithms and models on a dataset. Different mining models will return different patterns and different result sets because each mining algorithm works in a different way. Finding the best mining model is a process that depends on the problem, dataset, and the output of algorithm.

Microsoft provides tools such as Lift Chart and Profit Chart for comparing the result of mining models. As you may recall from the previous chapter, the test set is part of the data that is retained intact to be tested with the recognized pattern of the mining model. Lift Chart and Profit Chart will show how the result of the mining model works compared to actual data in the test set.

Time for action – finding the best mining model with Lift Chart and Profit Chart

In this example, we will add two other data mining algorithms, Naïve Bayes and Clustering, to the Target mail mining Structure example from the previous chapter. Then, we compare Lift Chart and Profit Chart for these algorithms to see which one works better compared to the test set. Perform the following steps to add the algorithms:

1. Open Target mail mining Structure from the first example of the previous chapter.

2. In the mining structure designer, go to the **Mining Models** tab and create a new mining model in one of the following ways:

   ❑ Right-click anywhere on the **Mining Models** tab and choose **New Mining Model**

   ❑ Click on the icon that shows the **Create a related mining model** option on hovering

3. In the **New Mining Model** window, choose **Microsoft Naïve Bayes** as the algorithm and name it `Target Mail Naive Bayes`, as shown in the following screenshot:

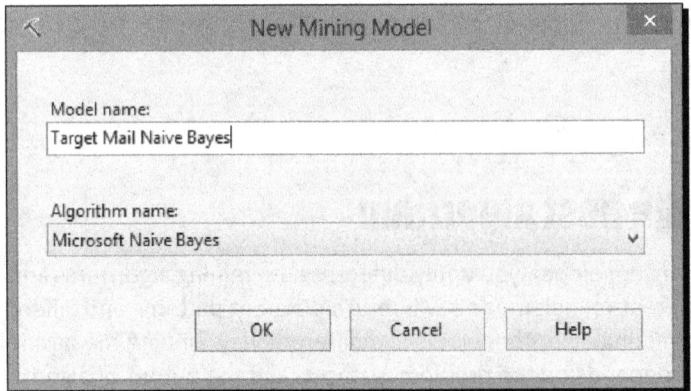

4. Repeat steps 2 and 3 to create a new mining model with the Microsoft Clustering algorithm and name this mining model `Target Mail Clustering`.

5. Deploy and process the SSAS project.

6. Go to the **Mining Model Viewer** tab and choose **Target Mail Clustering** in the mining model drop-down list.

7. You will now see four viewer tabs—**Cluster Diagram**, **Cluster Profiles**, **Cluster Characteristics, and Cluster Discrimination**. The first tab is **Cluster Diagram**. Change the **Shading Variable** option to **Bike Buyer** and change the **State** option to **1**. You will see a list of clusters with links between them. You can change the bar on the left-hand side to show the stronger or weaker links between the clusters. The shading configuration that we created means that the cluster with a darker blue background will be the cluster with more portions of bike buyers. In the following screenshot, **Cluster 1**, **Cluster 9**, and **Cluster 3** have the most density of bike buyers. By hovering the mouse on any of the clusters, you will see the density of the shading variable (which bike buyer is to be numbered as 1) in percentage.

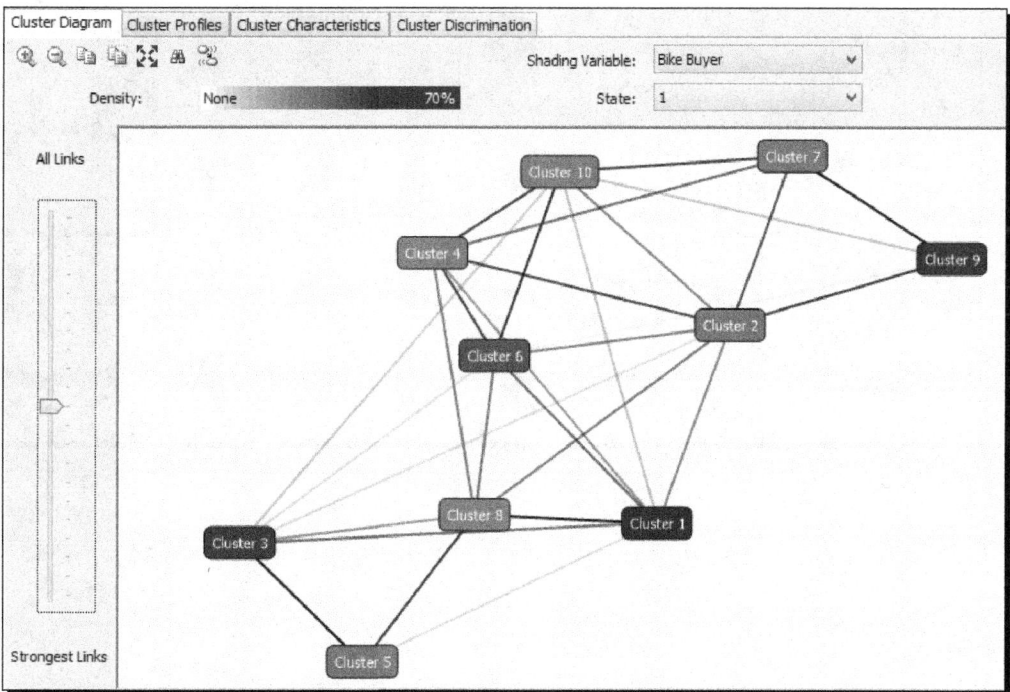

8. Click on the **Cluster Profiles** tab. In this tab, you can see how each cluster is populated. You would see all input variables and the proportion of values for each variable in each cluster. For example, the following screenshot shows that **Cluster 1** contains more bike buyers, and the **English Occupation** tab of this cluster shows that most of them are professionals or skilled manual laborers. You can also see that all customers in **Cluster 2** (which has low density of bike buyers) are in the age group 45 to 54.

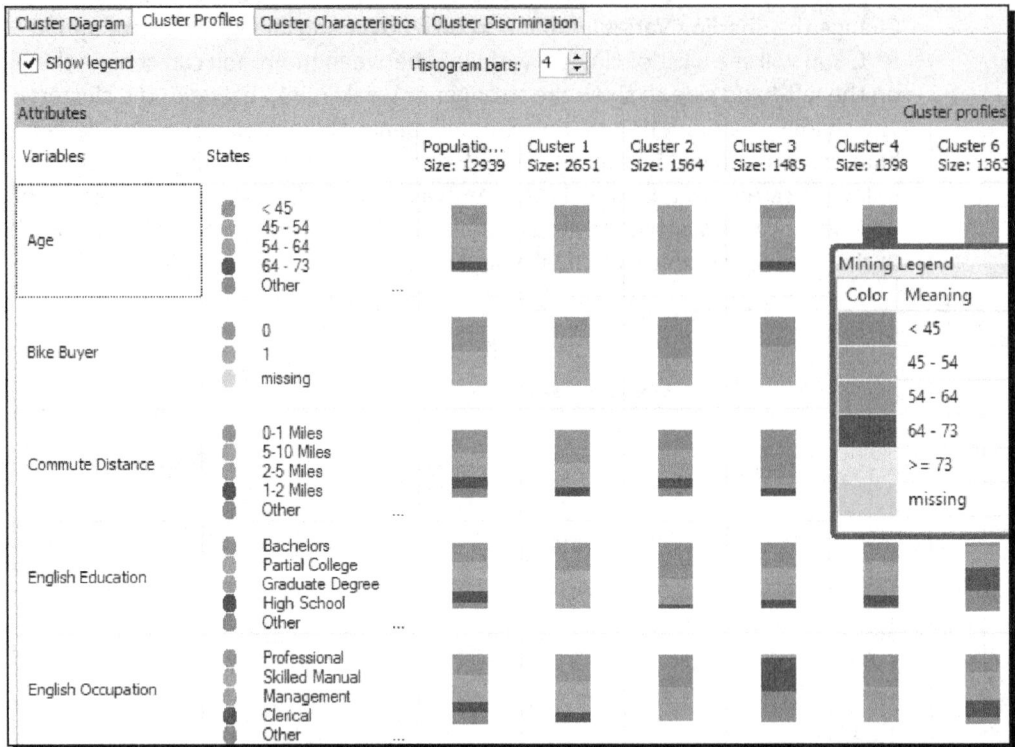

9. The **Cluster Characteristics** tab shows the percentage of each variable value in each cluster. If you choose **Cluster 1** in the cluster's drop-down list, you will see the probability of the variable's values for this cluster. For example, the following screenshot shows that all customers in this cluster are in the yearly income range of 39K to 71K. If you hover your mouse on the **Probability** bar, you will see the percentage of probability. You can choose other clusters to find out the characteristics of those clusters in the diagram. The following screenshot also shows that most of the customers in this cluster have no children at home:

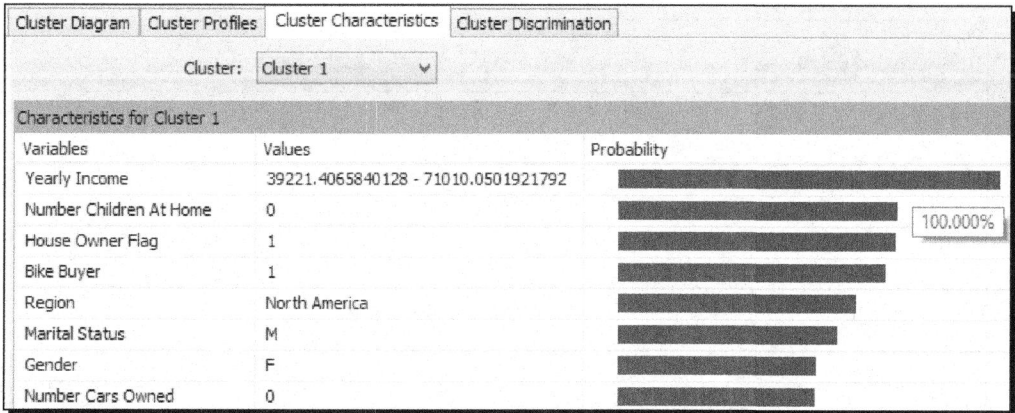

10. Open the **Cluster Discrimination** tab. choose **Cluster 1** and **Cluster 8** sequentially. You will see the distribution of variable values in these two different clusters. The following screenshot shows that **Cluster 8** contains the customers who have two cars at most, but **Cluster 1** contains most of the customers who have no cars:

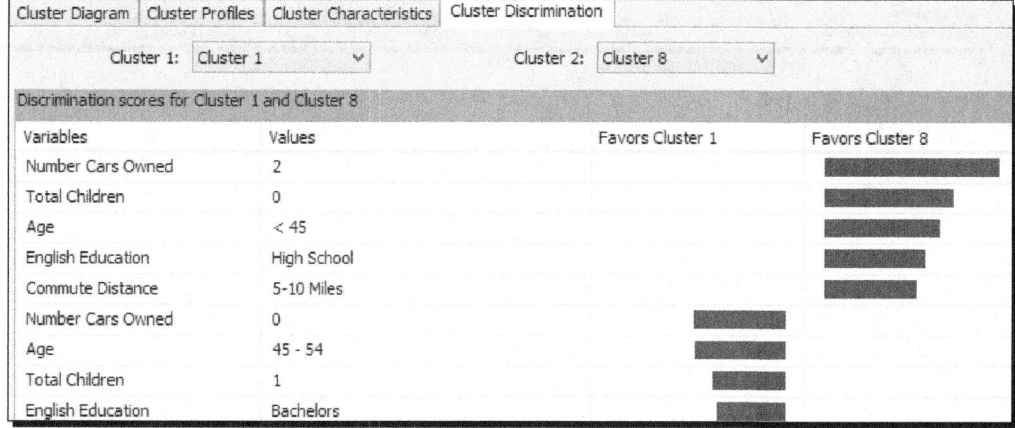

11. Select **Target Mail Naïve Bayes** as **Mining Model** and you will see four different tabs as the mining model viewers.

12. The first tab shows the dependency diagram (which you are familiar with from the previous chapter). As you see in the following screenshot, scrolling the dependency bar down will show only the strongest links. If you compare the results of the **Dependency Network** tab of the Naive Bayes mining model with the dependency network of the decision tree mining model from the previous chapter, then you will find some differences in the strongest links.

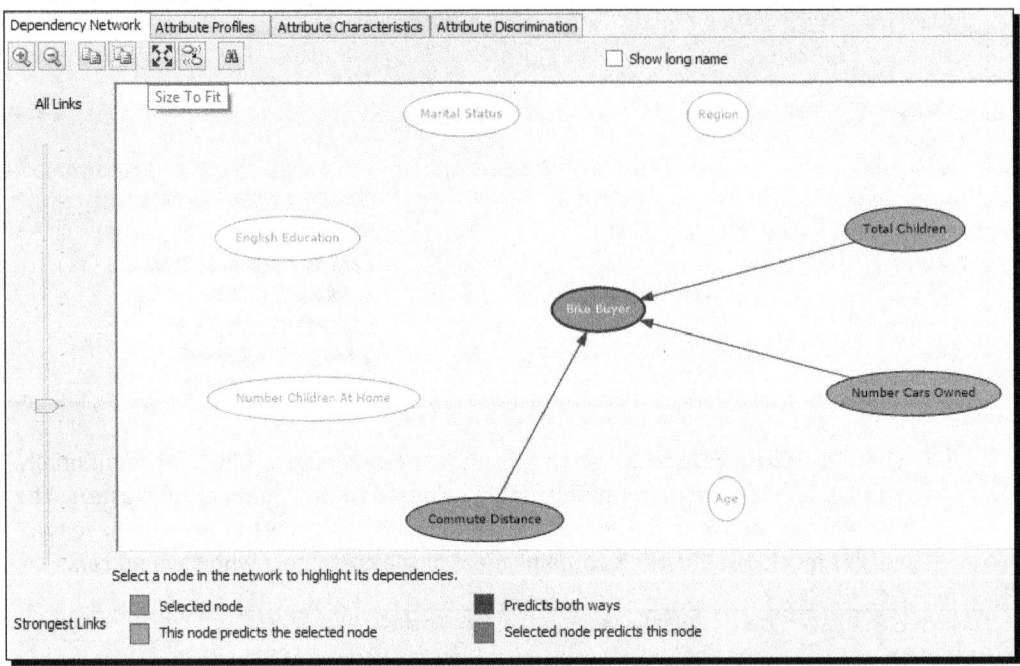

13. The **Attribute Profiles** tab is similar to the **Cluster Profile** tab. It shows the distribution of the attribute values that end up with the value **0** or **1** for the `predictable` variable (**Bike Buyer**).

14. The **Attribute Characteristics** tab shows the probability of attribute values for bike buyers or non-bike buyers. You can configure it by setting the `predictable` variable and its value.

15. The last mining viewer tab is **Attribute Discrimination**. Choose the value **0** and **1** for **Bike Buyer**. And compare the attribute's probability in both sections. You will see that the attribute value **0** for the number of cars owned mostly favors bike buyers, but those who have two cars are less likely to buy a bike.

16. Click on the **Mining Accuracy Chart** tab. In the **Input Selection** tab, change the **Predict Value** of all mining models to **1**. Leave other options as is, as shown in the following screenshot:

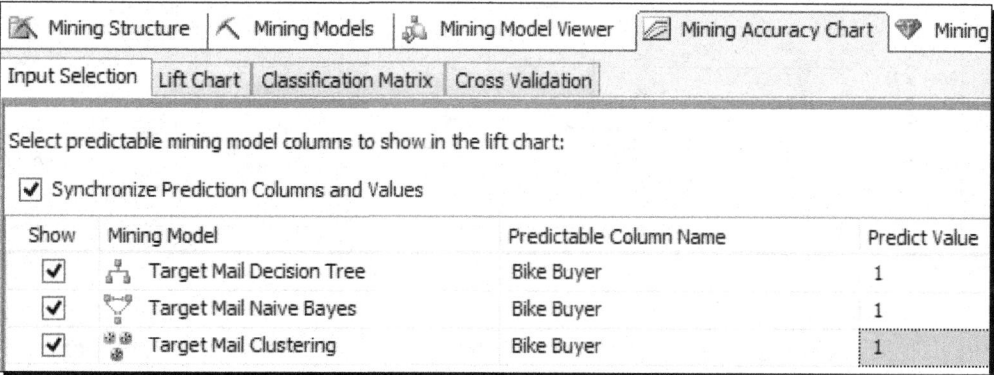

17. Go to the **Lift Chart** tab and you will see a line chart that shows one line per mining model. There are also two other lines: one for random guesses and another for an ideal model. The overall population is listed on the horizontal axis and the vertical axis shows the target population. The mining algorithm that produces most of the target with a lower number of overall population works best. For a more detailed discussion on this diagram, go to the *What just happened?* section. In the following screenshot, you see that the decision Tree mining model is the best algorithm based on this chart:

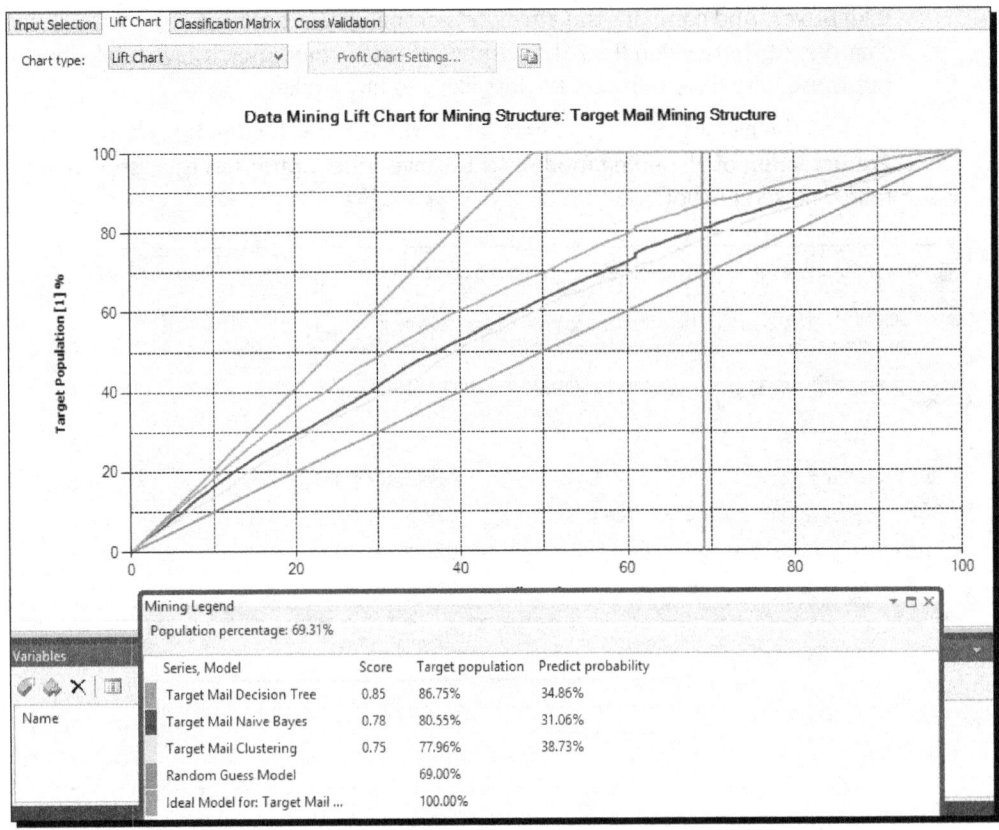

18. Change **Chart type** in the drop-down list to **Profit Chart**, and in the **Profit Chart Settings...** dialog box, accept everything with the default values. When the profit chart is drawn, you will see another line chart that shows one line per mining model. Profit charts show the profit calculated based on the cost of overall population. For example, the profit of using a mining model for sending an e-mail to prospective bike buyers will be calculated based on the cost of sending e-mail to the prospective buyers minus the cost of sending e-mail to those customers who bought a bike. For more information about profit charts, refer to the *What just happened?* section. The following screenshot shows the profit chart for the mining structure:

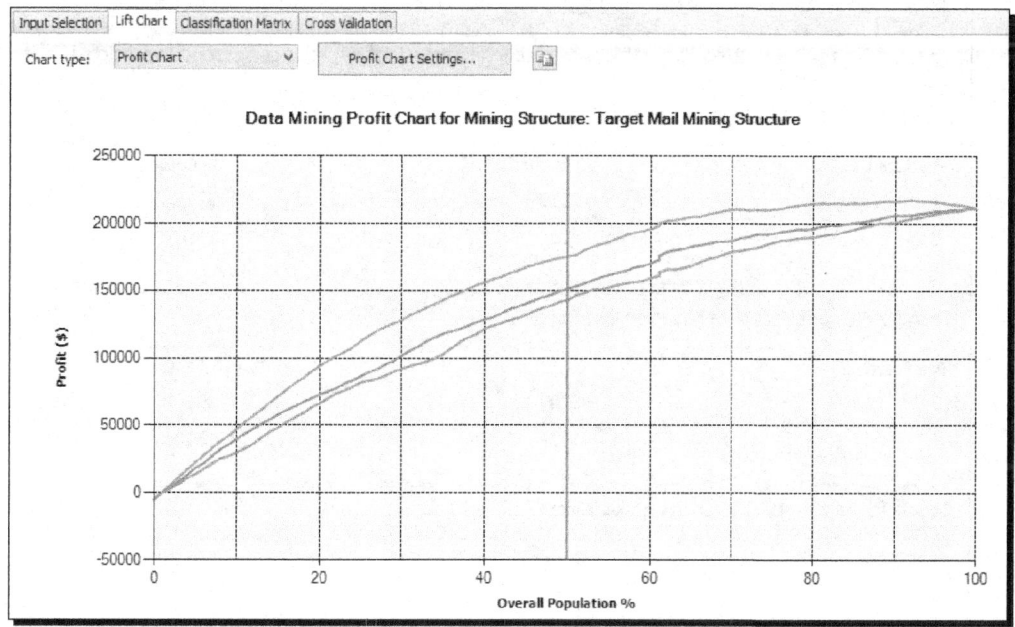

19. Click on the **Classification Matrix** tab. This tab shows one matrix per mining model. In each matrix, you can see the value predicted by actual style matrix. For example, if the value for **Predicted** is **1**, it means that the mining models predicted that this customer would be a bike buyer, but if the value for **Actual** is **0**, it means that the customer actually didn't buy a bike. So the best answer for our prediction would be **1** for **Predicted** and **Actual**. In the following screenshot, you can see that the decision tree generates a better result again by predicting **1788** cases to be the actual bike buyers:

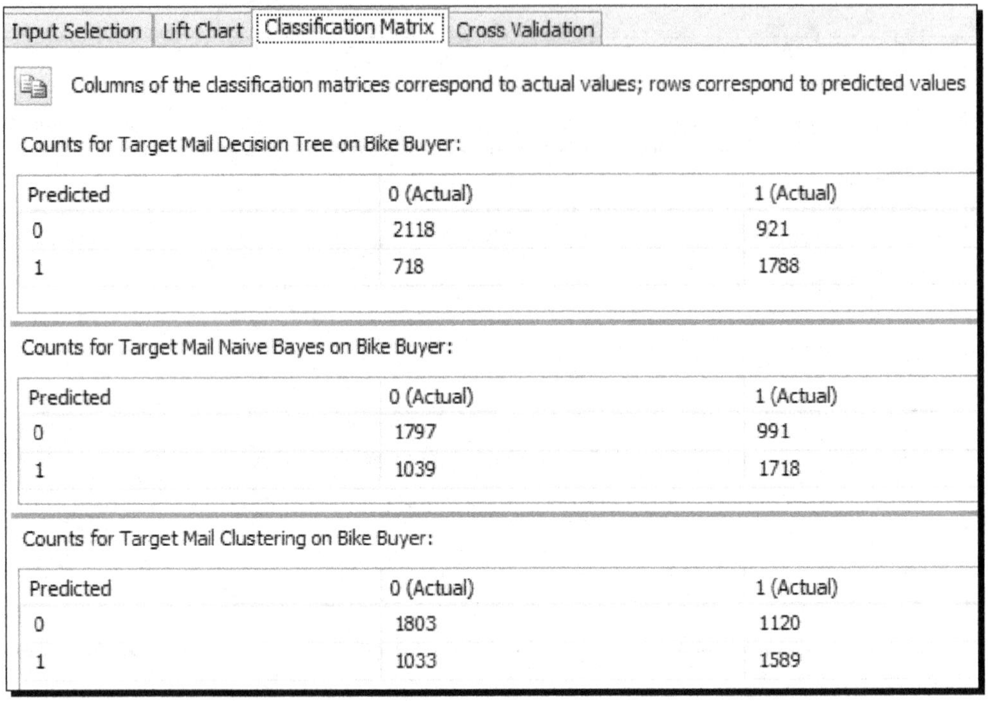

| Input Selection | Lift Chart | Classification Matrix | Cross Validation |

Columns of the classification matrices correspond to actual values; rows correspond to predicted values

Counts for Target Mail Decision Tree on Bike Buyer:

Predicted	0 (Actual)	1 (Actual)
0	2118	921
1	718	1788

Counts for Target Mail Naive Bayes on Bike Buyer:

Predicted	0 (Actual)	1 (Actual)
0	1797	991
1	1039	1718

Counts for Target Mail Clustering on Bike Buyer:

Predicted	0 (Actual)	1 (Actual)
0	1803	1120
1	1033	1589

20. Go to the **Cross Validation** tab, set **Fold Count** to **3**, enter `9000` as **Max Cases**, leave **Target Attribute** as **Bike Buyer**, and set **Target State** as **1**. Next, enter `0.5` as **Target Threshold** and then click on **Get Results**. You will see that 9,000 cases would be divided into three folds. A description of this result set can be found in the *What just happened?* section. The following screenshot shows the settings for the **Cross Validation** tab:

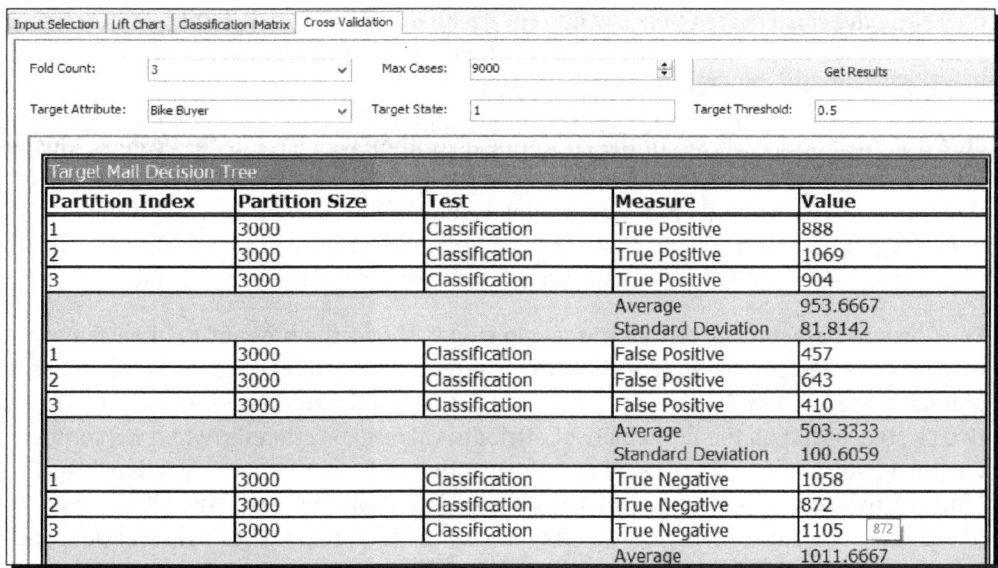

What just happened?

In this example, we've continued the scenario from the previous chapter to find out the best data mining model that generates better results for the problem (which was finding prospective bike buyers for the new product). The best mining model would be the one that generates results that are closest to the test dataset.

As a data mining developer, you are required to train multiple algorithms with the existing dataset. The reason for using multiple algorithms is that different mining algorithms generate patterns differently and give results differently. We will use multiple mining models to find the best results for the defined problem, so we need to find the best algorithm that produces the best results compared to the test dataset. After creating multiple algorithms and training them, you can use a set of mining accuracy charts to figure out which algorithm performs best compared to the real data in the test dataset. In this example, we've added two new mining models to the previous **Target Mail Mining Structure**: clustering and Naïve Bayes (steps 1 to 4).

Microsoft clustering

In step 6, we added the Microsoft clustering algorithm to the mining structure. The clustering algorithm uses methods to categorize cases into clusters. The number of clusters can be changed with changing algorithm parameters. Each cluster will contain a number of cases. In step 7, you saw the first diagram of clustering, which is **Cluster Diagram**; this diagram shows the density of attributes in a cluster and shows the links between clusters, which show how close the clusters are to each other. For example, in step 7, we've shaded clusters after setting the **Bike Buyer** attribute to be **1**, which means the cluster with the darker blue shade has more cases with the **Bike Buyer** property as **1**.

Step 8 shows another viewer of the clustering algorithm, which is **Cluster Profiles**. **Cluster Profiles** shows the distribution of attributes and variables in each cluster compared to other clusters. For each attribute, there is a mining legend in the diagram that shows the definition of colors in the stacked column chart. For example, the screenshot of step 8 shows that most of the cases that **Cluster 3** contains has a commute distance of less than 1 mile.

The **Cluster Characteristic** tab, as you saw in step 9, shows the probability of each attribute's value in the selected cluster. This diagram is useful to understand the specific characteristic of each cluster. In step 10, the screenshot of **Cluster Discrimination** shows a comparison of two clusters based on the probability of attribute values. For example, when we compare **Cluster 1** (which is one of the clusters with customers who are most likely to buy bikes) with **Cluster 8** (which contains cases with a lesser number of bike buyers), you will see that most of the bike buyers do not own cars, and on the other hand most customers without bikes own two cars (as shown in the screenshot of step 10).

Microsoft Naïve Bayes

The Microsoft Naïve Bayes algorithm performs the classification based on the Bayes algorithm. In step 11, we started to review the viewers for the Naïve Bayes mining model. The first viewer of the Naïve Bayes mining model is the **Dependency Network** tab, which we are familiar with from the previous chapter. This diagram shows the relationship of input algorithms and their contribution to leading to the `predictable` variable. In step 12, you can see that this algorithm identifies **Number Cars Owned**, **Total Children**, and **Commute Distance** as the main three variables that derive the bike buyers' prediction. One of the important considerations about mining algorithms is that each mining algorithm may return different results on the same dataset. If you compare the **Dependency Network** of step 12 of this example to the diagram of step 23 in the *Time for action – creating a data mining solution with the Microsoft Decision Tree* algorithm section of *Chapter 7, Data Mining – Descriptive Models in SSAS*, which was the **Dependency Network** of the decision tree algorithm, you will find that in the decision tree algorithm, the three main variables were **Number Cars of Owned**, **Region**, and **Yearly Income**.

Different mining algorithms generate different results because they apply different mathematical calculations and methods on the dataset.

We've explored the **Attribute Profiles** tab in step 13. The **Attribute Profile** tab's diagram is very similar to the **Cluster Profile** tab's diagram. Both of these diagrams show the distribution of attributes in each classification. The only difference is that classifications in **Naïve Bayes Attribute Profile** are one for each value in the predictable variable. In this example, there were two clusters, one for **Bike Buyer** as **1** and another as **0**.

Step 14 shows the **Attribute Characteristics** diagram and step 15 shows the **Attribute Discrimination** diagram, which are similar to the **Cluster Characteristics** and **Cluster Discrimination** diagrams from Microsoft clustering mining viewers.

Microsoft accuracy chart

As you've learned so far, the pattern recognized by each mining model will be different from other mining models, even for the same input dataset. This is the nature of work for a data mining developer. As a mining developer, you need to apply different algorithms on the same dataset and then compare them to find out which algorithm provides the best results. The best results will be based on the pattern recognized by the algorithm (when you trained it with the training set) when applied on the test dataset. Microsoft Accuracy Chart is a set of diagrams and charts to evaluate how each algorithm performs against the test dataset and against other mining models. As a data mining developer, you need to assess the mining models against each other with Microsoft Accuracy Chart and find out the algorithm with the best results. This algorithm can be deployed to the live server for real prediction.

Microsoft Accuracy Chart contains a list of charts and diagrams such as Lift Chart and Profit Chart, Classification Matrix, and Cross Validation. In the **Input Selection** tab (step 16), we've set the predict value of the `predictable` variable (**Bike Buyer**) to **1**. It means that the mining models will predict customers who want to buy a bike. In this step, you can also configure the test dataset. By default, the test dataset would be the percentage of data that you've configured as test set in the mining model (in this case, 30 percent). But there is also an option for you to specify a test dataset in this tab directly.

Lift Charts and Profit Charts

A Lift Chart shows how mining models act on prediction against each other when their patterns are applied on the test dataset. In the Lift Chart that you saw in step 17, there are five lines. There is a line for each mining model: one line for ideal prediction and another for random guesses (worst prediction). Each line in the Lift Chart shows how the overall population led to predict the target population. The best model, as is shown in the ideal mode, is to predict 100 percent of the target with only 50 percent of the overall population. And the worst model is to predict 100 percent of the target with 100 percent of the overall population. So the best mining model would be the one that is closest to the ideal mode. In the screenshot of step 17, you can see that the Target Mail decision tree performs better than the other two models.

The Profit Chart that was shown in step 18 shows the amount of profit calculated based on the usage of any of the mining models on the test dataset. You can configure the Profit Chart settings with changing values of **Population, Fixed Cost, Individual Cost**, and **Revenue per Individual**. The profit in our example can identify the most correct list of prospective buyers because it will reduce the need for sending e-mails to all customers.

Classification Matrix

Classification Matrix shows a matrix of prediction values against actual values for each mining model. In step 19, you saw the **Classification Matrix** tab, which shows the values **0** and **1** as row headers (for **Prediction**) and values **0** and **1** as column headers (for **Actual**). The values inside the matrix cells show the number of cases that were predicted against the actual values. For example, the screenshot of step 19 shows 1,788 cases predicted correctly (the result was predicted to be a bike buyer and he actually bought a bike). However, there are also 718 cases that were predicted to be bike buyers but who didn't actually buy a bike. By comparing the classification matrix of the three mining models, it is obvious that the decision tree performs better than other algorithms.

Cross Validation

The last step of the example shows the **Cross Validation** report (step 20). **Cross Validation** performs mining algorithms on classifications of the input dataset (max cases) with each classification named as a fold (**Fold Count**). You can define the target attribute and its value in that. **Threshold** shows the level of confidence in prediction.

Predicting data with DMX

In this section, we will talk about the most attractive part of data mining, prediction. Microsoft provided a language to query and work with data mining algorithms and perform predictions: DMX. DMX is very similar to T-SQL in terms of the `SELECT`, `FROM`, and `WHERE` clauses. The process of prediction with mining algorithms is that the pattern fetched out of the training from a mining model will be joined to a case table. In other words, prediction is a result of applying this pattern with some DMX functions such as `PredictProbability`.

In this section, you will learn about the DMX language and how to use the **Mining Model Prediction** options to generate a prediction result set out of the mining model and case table.

Time for action – predicting prospective bike buyers

In this example, we will add a case table that contains only a list of new customers with attributes such as yearly income, total children, gender, and so on. Then we will apply DMX queries on the mining model and the case table to find out the list of prospective bike buyers. The prerequisite for running this example is the decision tree example mentioned in the previous chapter. Perform the following steps to predict prospective bike buyers:

1. Open the `Adventure Works DW2012.dsv` designer.

2. Right-click on a blank area in it and click on **Add/Remove Tables**. Select the **ProspectiveBuyer(dbo)** table and add it to the DSV.

3. Right-click on the **ProspectiveBuyer** table in the DSV and explore its data. You will see that most of the input variables of the Target mail mining algorithms are supported as columns of this table.

4. Save the DSV and open **Target Mail Mining Structure** and go to the **Mining Model Prediction** tab.

5. In the **Mining Model** pane, on the top left-hand side of this tab, click on **Select Model** and choose **Target Mail Decision Tree** under the **Target Mail Mining Structure** options.

6. In the **Select Case Table/Select Input** table pane (on the right-hand side), select the **ProspectiveBuyer** table. You will see that joins between the input variables of the mining model and case table will be generated based on the column names. The following screenshot shows the **Mining Model Prediction** tab:

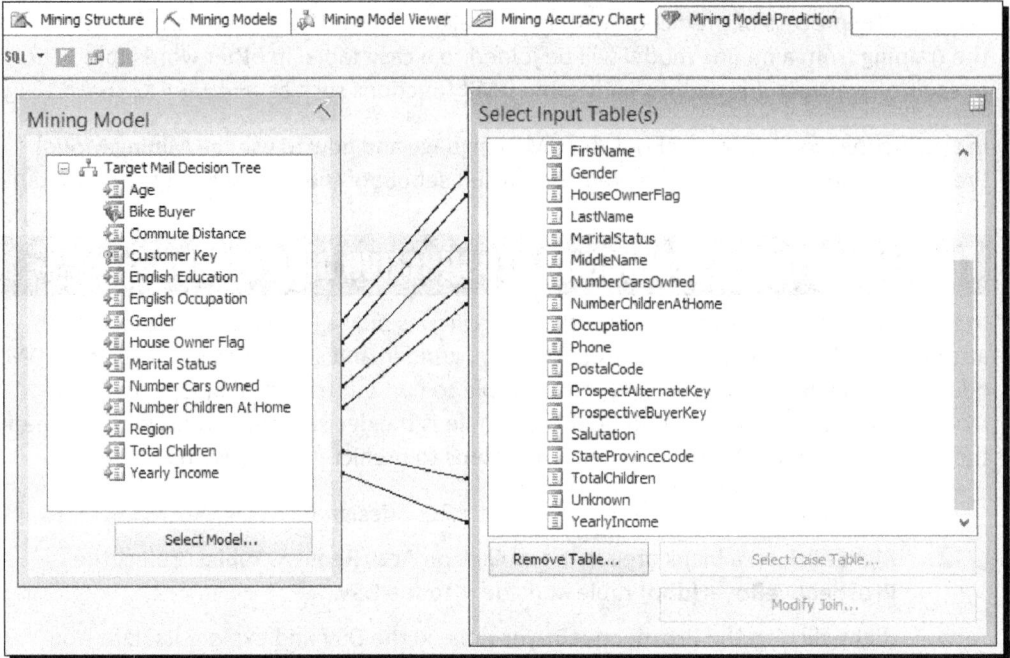

7. Drag-and-drop **FirstName**, **LastName**, **EmailAddress**, **Phone**, and **Salutation** from the case table to the grid under it.

8. In the last record of the grid, add a new row by choosing the **Source** column as **Prediction Function**. Then choose the **PredictProbability** function in the **Field** column. Set **Alias** as **Bike Buyer** and enter the following expression in **Criteria** column (you can also use drag-and-drop to facilitate the writing of the expression):

```
([Target Mail Decision tree].[Bike Buyer],1)
```

Take a look at the screenshot of a record of the grid:

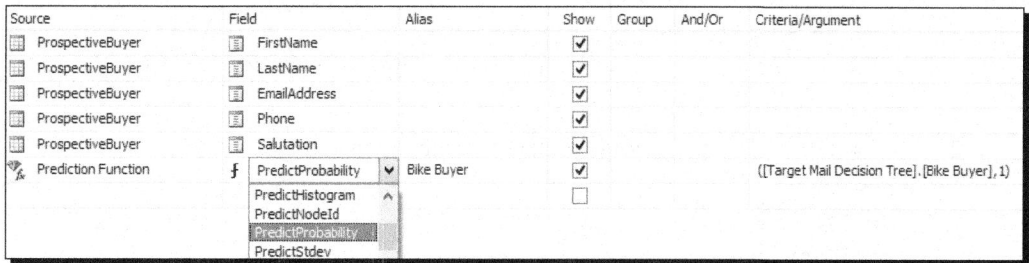

9. Click on the **Mode change** icon. The icon is located on the top left-hand side of the **Mining Model Prediction** tab. Select **Result** in the drop-down menu, as shown in the following screenshot:

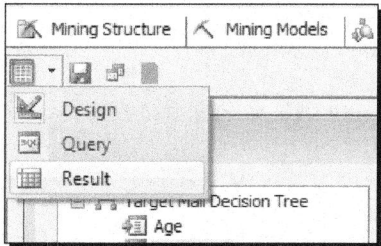

10. You will see the data mining query execution result. The result set shows a list of bike buyers with the probability of buying bikes. The result set is not filtered or ordered. So it shows even customers with less than 0.5 probability of buying a bike, as shown in the following screenshot:

11. Click on the **Mode change** icon and change the mode to **Query**. You will see the SQL-like query. This is the DMX query generated based on the configuration you've performed in the design mode.

12. Add the following expression (where clause and order by) at the end of DMX query:

```
where PredictProbability([Target Mail Decision Tree].
  [Bike Buyer],1)>0.5
order by PredictProbability([Target Mail Decision Tree].
  [Bike Buyer],1) desc
```

13. The whole DMX query should look like the following code:

```
SELECT
  t.[FirstName],
  t.[LastName],
  t.[EmailAddress],
  t.[Phone],
  t.[Salutation],
  (PredictProbability([Target Mail Decision Tree].[Bike Buyer],1))
as [Bike Buyer]
From
  [Target Mail Decision Tree]
PREDICTION JOIN
  OPENQUERY([Adventure Works DW2012],
    'SELECT
      [FirstName],
      [LastName],
      [EmailAddress],
      [Phone],
      [Salutation],
      [MaritalStatus],
      [Gender],
      [YearlyIncome],
      [TotalChildren],
      [NumberChildrenAtHome],
      [HouseOwnerFlag],
      [NumberCarsOwned]
    FROM
      [dbo].[ProspectiveBuyer]
    ') AS t
ON
  [Target Mail Decision Tree].[Marital Status] = t.
  [MaritalStatus] AND
  [Target Mail Decision Tree].[Gender] = t.[Gender] AND
  [Target Mail Decision Tree].[Yearly Income] = t.
  [YearlyIncome] AND
  [Target Mail Decision Tree].[Total Children] = t.
  [TotalChildren] AND
  [Target Mail Decision Tree].[Number Children At Home] = t.
  [NumberChildrenAtHome] AND
```

```
[Target Mail Decision Tree].[House Owner Flag] = t.
[HouseOwnerFlag] AND
[Target Mail Decision Tree].[Number Cars Owned] = t.
[NumberCarsOwned]
```
```
where PredictProbability([Target Mail Decision Tree].[Bike
Buyer],1)>0.5
order by PredictProbability([Target Mail Decision Tree].[Bike
Buyer],1) desc
```

14. Go to the **Result** mode. You will see a list of prospective bike buyers filtered and sorted this time. The higher the value in the bike buyer columns, the higher the probability of that customer buying a bike, as shown in the following screenshot:

FirstName	LastName	EmailAddress	Phone	Salutation	Bike Buyer
Rebekah	Rodriguez	rrodriguez@contoso.com	1 (11) 500 555-0187	Ms.	0.77281077709737
Seth	Martinez	smartinez@blueyonderairlines.com	835-555-0181	Mr.	0.77281077709737
Jesus	Jimenez	jjimenez@lucernepublishing.com	1 (11) 500 555-0121	Mr.	0.77281077709737
Connor	Carter	ccarter@alpineskihouse.com	1 (11) 500 555-0136	Mr.	0.77281077709737
Latoya	Xie	lxie@alpineskihouse.com	913-555-0169	Ms.	0.77281077709737
Abigail	Davis	adavis@fabrikam.com	1 (11) 500 555-0187	Ms.	0.77281077709737
Zachary	Brown	zbrown@fineartschool.net	1 (11) 500 555-0140	Mr.	0.77281077709737
Tony	Goel	tgoel@alpineskihouse.com	277-555-0195	Mr.	0.77281077709737
Alicia	Deng	adeng@cpandl.com	278-555-0139	Ms.	0.637460885113992
Adrian	Rogers	arogers@margiestravel.com	1 (11) 500 555-0121	Mr.	0.637460885113992

15. Click on the **Save** icon on the right-hand side of the **Mode change** icon and save the result set to a new table named `ProspectiveBikeBuyersProbability` under the same data source and data source view, as shown in the following screenshot:

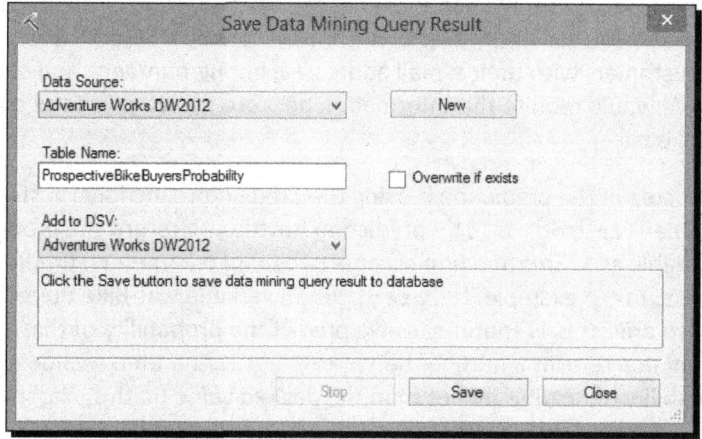

16. If you go back to the DSV designer, you will see the new table created there. You can explore the data of that table and view the result of the data mining query there.

What just happened?

The prediction step is not as difficult as it seems to be. You've seen in this example that once you have your mining model configured, trained, and processed, you can simply build a data mining query (with the data mining query designer or by writing the query) and apply a mining pattern on a dataset and use prediction functions to fetch the predicted result. In this example, we have applied the decision tree mining model's pattern to a dataset and fetched out a list of bike buyers with more than 50 percent probability of buying bikes.

In steps 1 to 3 of this example, we've added a table of new customers, named `ProspectiveBuyer`, to the DSV. This table has columns such as **Gender**, **Marital Status**, **Yearly Income**, and so on. These columns can be joined with the input variables of the mining model to generate the probability of predicting a bike buyer. In step 4, we saw the **Mining Model Prediction** tab. This tab contains the data mining query designer.

Data mining query designer

There is a GUI for designing and building data mining queries. As you saw in step 5, you can choose the mining model that you want to use as the base of the prediction. Step 6 shows how to add a case table. A typical data mining query contains a mining model (in this example, the decision tree mining model) and a case table (in this example, the `ProspectiveBuyer` table). The data mining query will apply the pattern of the mining model to the case table based on joins between the mining model variables and the columns of the case table. In the screenshot of step 6, you saw that joins would be detected automatically if column names and variable names are similar; otherwise, you can simply create the join in the mining query.

In the grid of the data mining query designer, you can add as many columns as you want from the case table to be shown in the result set. This grid is similar to a T-SQL query designer's grid and you can apply alias or criteria on columns. Step 7 shows that we've added the name of customers with their e-mail addresses, phone numbers, and salutation to be fetched out. We would require this information because we want to send an e-mail to each prospective bike buyer.

The important step in the prediction is using the prediction functions. In step 8, you saw that we used the `PredictProbability` prediction function to return the probability of the bike buyer variable as 1. This function accepts two main parameters: prediction variable and prediction value. In our example, the `prediction` variable was **Bike Buyer**, and the value that we want to predict is 1. That means we predict the probability of that customer buying a bike. This function returns a number between 0 and 1. And then a value closer to 1 shows that the probability of result is higher than the desired value (in this example, the value being closer to 1 means that the customer has a higher probability of buying a bike).

In step 9, you learned how to change the mode of the designer. There are three modes: **Designer**, **Query**, and **Result**. The result shown in step 10 is not filtered or sorted by the **Bike Buyer** column. So, in steps 11 and 12, we added the `Where` and `Order by` clause to the DMX query.

DMX query – Data Mining eXtension

Microsoft uses a SQL-like query language to work with mining models and prediction of results based on the patterns out of a mining model. DMX contains **Data Description Language (DDL)** and **Data Manipulation Language (DML)** commands. DDL commands contain commands for creating, modifying, or deleting a mining model or structure. And DML commands are used for selecting and querying results based on the mining models.

The sample DMX query used in this example is a DML command with the following structure:

```
Select <field1>, <field2>,…,<Prediction fuction1>…
From <model>
PREDICTION JOIN
<case table>
<join criteria>
Where <filtering criteria>
Order by <sorting criteria>
```

As you saw in step 13, the DMX query joined the decision tree mining model to the `ProspectiveBuyer` case table. When you write a DMX query, the main source of data is the mining structures and models. Any connection outside of that SSAS project should be handled with external functions. In this example, `OpenQuery` is used to fetch out the `ProspectiveBuyer` table's data rows.

`PREDICTION JOIN` plays an important role in DMX queries. This specific kind of join is used to create a connection between columns of the case table to the input variables of the mining model. Writing join criteria is very similar to T-SQL. `Where` and `order by` clauses in DMX queries are similar to T-SQL. In our example, we've used `Where` clause to fetch out only bike buyers with probability 0.5 and higher. And we sorted the result set in a descending order based on the probability of buying bikes.

Prediction functions are useful functions to fetch out the prediction result. In our example, we've used the `PredictProbability` function. There are some prediction functions in DMX. For a list of all DMX functions used in this book, refer to: `http://technet.microsoft.com/en-us/library/ms131996.aspx`.

The DMX expressions and query language require a more detailed walkthrough and study materials, which doesn't fit the scope of this book. Here, I have just given you an understanding of DMX queries and a use case of it. For detailed understanding of DMX, the best source is the Data Mining eXtension reference on MSDN, available at `http://technet.microsoft.com/en-us/library/ms132058.aspx`.

Microsoft Time Series

In this last section of the data mining discussion, we will reveal the Time Series mining model. The Time Series algorithm is very useful to predict time-based facts such as prediction of future sales of a product based on the information of the last two years, or more.

Time for action – predicting future sales with Microsoft Time Series

In this example, we use a dataset to train a Time Series algorithm with sales information of previous years and then we will see how a Time Series algorithm will help to predict future sales based on the trained pattern.

1. Open `Adventure Works DW2012.dsv` and add a new table to it. Choose **vTimeSeries** from the list of tables.

2. Right-click on the **vTimeSeries** table in DSV and explore the data. You will see that this table contains the sales amount and quantity based on the product model and region and month.

3. In the DSV designer, select both the **TimeIndex** and **ModelRegion** columns from **vTimeSeries** and right-click and choose **Set Logical Primary Key**.

4. Create a new mining structure from the existing relational database and choose **Microsoft Time Series** as the mining model. Set the **vTimeSeries** table as **Case table**.

5. In the **Specify the Training Data** window, set **TimeIndex** and **ModelRegion** as the **Key** columns and set **Amount** and **Quantity** as the **Input** and **Predictable** columns, as shown in the following screenshot:

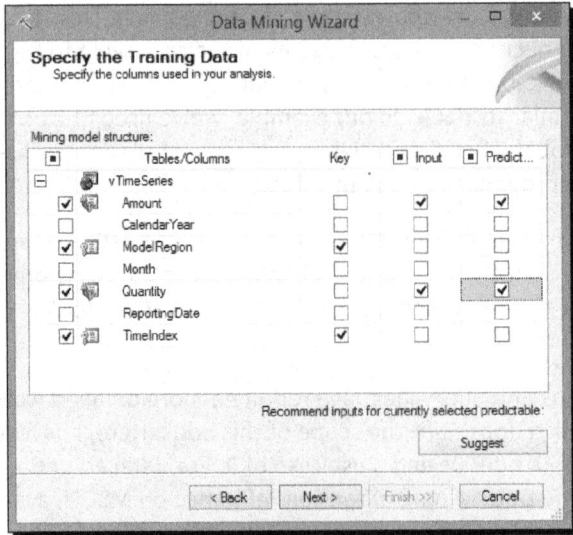

6. Detect the data types in the next step and name the mining structure `Time Series Mining Structure` and the model `Time Series Mining Model`.

7. Deploy and process the mining model.

8. Go to **Mining Model Viewer**. You will see a line chart in the **Charts** tab of **Microsoft Time Series Viewer**. This diagram shows the changing of variables over time. Choose **R 750 North America: Amount** and **R 750 North America: Quantity** from the drop-down list. You can also reduce or increase prediction steps to see how the diagram changes. The following screenshot shows how the R 750 product will sell (amount and quantity) in the next five months:

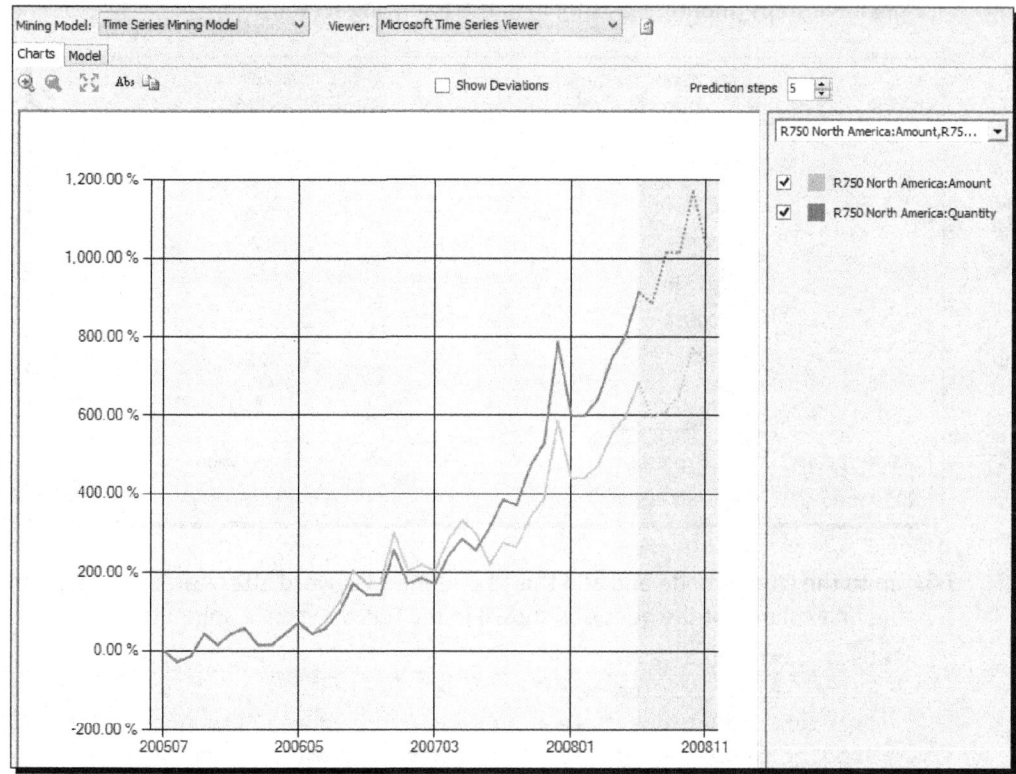

9. Go to the **Mining Model Prediction** tab and verify that the model is **Time Series Mining Model**.

10. Drag-and-drop **ModelRegion** from model to the grid as shown in the next screenshot.

11. Add a **Prediction Function** named **PredictTimeSeries** with the criteria shown in the following line of code:

```
[Time Series Mining Model].[Amount],5
```

12. Add another **PredictTimeSeries** function for **Quantity**. The following screenshot shows how the functions are to be configured:

Source		Field		Alias	Show	Group	And/Or	Criteria/Argument
Time Series Mining ...		Model Region			✓			
Prediction Function		*f*	PredictTimeSeries		✓			[Time Series Mining Model].[Amount],5
Prediction Function		*f*	PredictTimeSeries		✓			[Time Series Mining Model].[Quantity],5

13. Go to the **Result** mode. You will see the result set with two hierarchical columns (one for each prediction result). If you expand the **Expression** columns, you will see a prediction for the **Amount** (second column) and **Quantity** (third column) for the next five steps (months), as shown in the following screenshot:

Model Region	Expression		Expression	
M200 Europe	− Expression		− Expression	
	$TIME	Amount	$TIME	Quantity
	200807	172067.11356...	200807	77
	200808	157879.00458...	200808	64
	200809	152304.00129...	200809	59
	200810	143453.17921...	200810	56
	200811	126490.45833...	200811	56
M200 North Am...	+ Expression		+ Expression	
M200 Pacific	+ Expression		+ Expression	

14. Go to the **Query** mode and add the `flattened` keyword after `SELECT` and before the first column of the query, as shown in the following code snippet:

```
SELECT flattened
   [Time Series Mining Model].[Model Region],
   PredictTimeSeries([Time Series Mining Model].[Amount],5),
   PredictTimeSeries([Time Series Mining Model].[Quantity],5)
From
   [Time Series Mining Model]
```

15. Go to the **Result** mode. This time, you will see that the **Expression** column's values are flattened into columns and rows. This result is more useful when you want to export the result set into a table. The following screenshot shows the results:

Model Region	Expression.$TIME	Expression.Amount	Expression.$TIME	Expression.Quantity
M200 Europe	200807	172067.113565148		
M200 Europe	200808	157879.00458742		
M200 Europe	200809	152304.00129356		
M200 Europe	200810	143453.179211655		
M200 Europe	200811	126490.458337547		
M200 Europe			200807	77
M200 Europe			200808	64
M200 Europe			200809	59
M200 Europe			200810	56
M200 Europe			200811	56
M200 North Am...	200807	363390.688396527		
M200 North Am...	200808	396690.963864866		

What just happened?

In this example, you learned how to apply the Time Series algorithm on a dataset and how to use prediction functions to fetch the desired output of the algorithm. We used the **vTimeSeries** object, which contains information of previous sales and we added that table to the DSV (steps 1 to 3). Then we created a mining structure with **Time Series** as the algorithm (step 4). As **Amount** and **Quantity** are both input and predictable variables, we configured them in step 5.

In step 8, you saw **Microsoft Time Series Chart Viewer**, which shows the predictable variables over the time steps. In our example, the time step is month. It is quite simple to change the prediction steps. The darker background color in the screenshot shown in step 8 illustrates the future sales prediction.

We created the DMX query (steps 9 to 12) and we used the **PredictTimeSeries** prediction function. This function accepts the `prediction` variable and the time steps. In this example, we used this for **Amount** and **Quantity** for five months. This means that the sales of the next five months will be predicted with this function. The default result set of the **PredictTimeSeries** function is a hierarchical model (as you saw in step 13). Using the `FLATTENED` keyword in the DMX query, you can simply flatten the result set into rows and columns, which are more suitable for exporting to a table.

Summary

One of the most important functions of data mining is prediction. In this chapter, you've learned how to find the best mining model for the defined problem and the existing dataset. Microsoft Accuracy Chart provided diagrams such as **Classification Matrix**, **Lift Chart**, and **Cross Validation**, which check the mining model against the test dataset. After finding the best mining model(s), you can use the prediction functionality using the DMX language. You've learned about the DMX query structure and cross-prediction joins with the **Prediction Join** clause. You've applied the mining model pattern on the case table using DMX queries, and you've learned how to use prediction functions such as `PredictProbability` to fetch the probability of a predictable variable.

In the last section of this chapter, you saw an example of the Time Series algorithm. You've also learned how to provide input data with time frames to the algorithm. And after configuring and training the algorithm, you ran a DMX query with the **PredictTimeSeries** function to find out the behavior of variables in future time frames. The next chapter starts with the data visualization part with SQL Server Reporting Services.

9
Reporting Services

Reporting is one of the fundamental components of any Business Intelligence system. Reports help business users see visualized data in a detailed view such as in the form of a grid or in a high-level view such as in the form of a dashboard or chart in the report. Microsoft SQL Server provides a robust Reporting Service component named **SQL Server Reporting Services (SSRS)** *for developing and publishing reports. SSRS has the ability to connect a wide range of data sources such as Oracle, MySQL, DB2, SQL Server Database Engine, and SQL Server Analysis Services. SSRS also provides much functionality and layout configuration in report designing. SSDT will be used as the most common development studio to produce SSRS reports in this chapter.*

In this chapter, we will go through some of the main features and functionalities of SSRS. SSRS reports are not only used for BI reporting, but also widely used for application development on the web and Windows-customized applications.

The Reporting Services architecture

SSRS was first introduced as an add-on for SQL Server 2000, but in SQL Server 2005, it was published as the main component of the SQL Server RTM release. SSRS as a Reporting Service provides web-based reports with charts, grouping, ordering, filtering, and many other features. From SSRS 2005 to the date of writing this book, SSRS improved a lot in terms of features and functionalities.

In the architecture diagram that follows, there are three main components highlighted: **SSRS Databases**, **SSRS Web Applications**, and the **SSRS Report** object itself. Reporting Services installs itself as a part of the Microsoft SQL Server setup media. There are two built-in databases for SSRS: ReportServer DB and ReportServer TempDB. ReportServer DB stores the report definition, snapshot, execution log, and some other information. ReportServer TempDB stores the session and cached information. The following diagram shows the architecture diagram of Reporting Services:

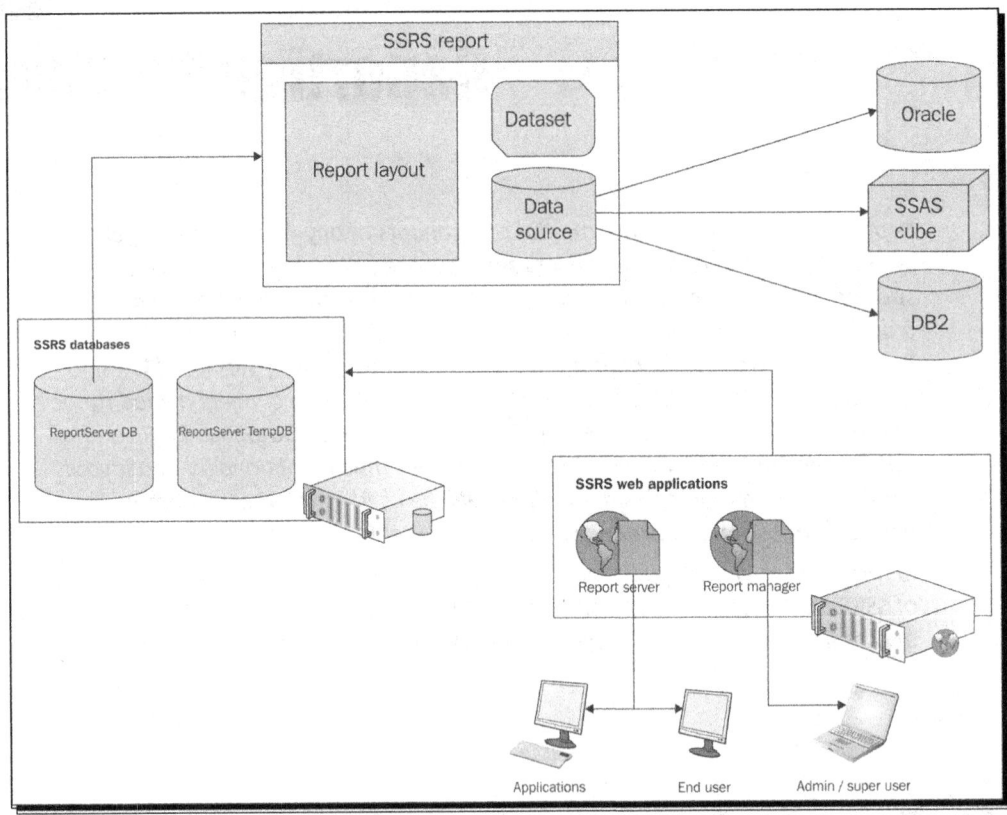

The **SSRS Report** object contains one or more data sources. Each data source can connect to a wide range of databases, such as Oracle, DB2, SQL Server, or even SSAS OLAP cube. The query on the underlying database will be stored as a dataset in the report. Then, the result of the query will be used as report columns and rows.

Reporting Services works with two web applications: **Report Server** and **Report Manager**. The **Report Server** web application controls report definitions. Reports should be deployed to the Report Server URL. Report Manager is a web application for managing folder hierarchy, administration tasks, and security configuration on reports and data sources. Reporting Services uses a tool for configuring all web application and database settings, which is called **Reporting Services Configuration Manager**.

SSRS reports work with a wide range of databases. Thus working with parameters and ordering and grouping based on fields is possible. Charts and KPIs can be added to the report. **Report Layout** can be printer friendly. There are many types of output available for exporting the report result. In this chapter, we will go through some of the main features of Reporting Services. For running the examples in this chapter, you should have Reporting Services 2012, SSDT, and AdventureWorks databases installed. For more information on how to install AdventureWorks databases, follow the instructions in the *Preface* of this book.

Developing a basic report

Designing and developing a basic report in SSRS is as easy as following the steps in a wizard. In this section, we will go through the scenario of creating our first SSRS report with the SSDT report wizard. You will learn about the structure of a Reporting Service project. Data sources will be used to connect to the source database, and then datasets will be explored which contain SQL queries to fetch data from the data source. We will go through the report layout to see how to configure the page and report layout.

Time for action – creating our first report using SSRS

In this example, you will learn how to create a report server project with SSDT. We will use the AdventureWorks2012 database as source. Perform the following steps to create an SSRS report:

1. Open SSDT and create a new project. Under **Business Intelligence project templates**, choose **Report Server Project**. Name the project Chapter 09 SSRS.

2. The new project will be created with three folders: **Shared Data Sources**, **Shared Datasets**, and **Reports**.

3. Right-click on the **Reports** folder and click on the **Add New Report** option from the pop-up menu.

4. Now, the **Report Wizard** will appear. In the **Select Data Source** window, create a connection to the AdventureWorksDW2012 database and name the connection AdventureWorksDW2012. Check the **Make this a Shared Data Source** checkbox option.

 A shared data source can be used in multiple reports and datasets.

The following screenshot shows the **Report Wizard** and its connection properties:

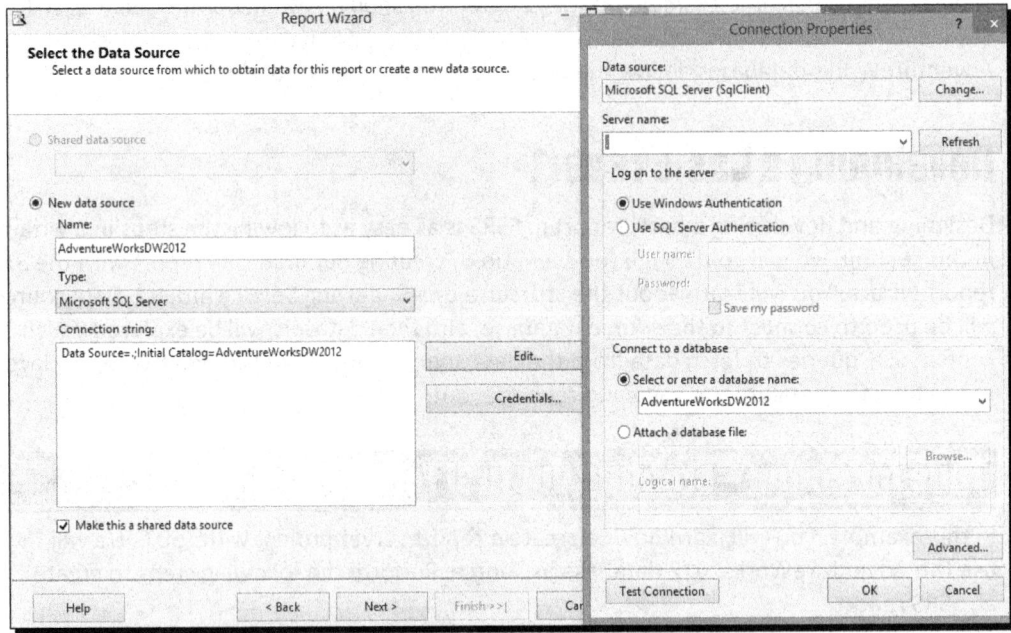

5. In the **Design the Query** window, you can use the **Query Builder** option to build the query. For this example, use the following T-SQL code and paste it in the **Query String** textbox:

```
SELECT DimProductCategory.EnglishProductCategoryName,
    DimProductSubcategory.EnglishProductSubcategoryName,
    DimProduct.EnglishProductName,
                    DimSalesTerritory.SalesTerritoryRegion,
    DimSalesTerritory.SalesTerritoryCountry,
    DimSalesTerritory.SalesTerritoryGroup,
                    FactInternetSales.SalesAmount
```

```
FROM              DimProduct INNER JOIN
                          DimProductSubcategory ON
    DimProduct.ProductSubcategoryKey =
    DimProductSubcategory.ProductSubcategoryKey INNER JOIN
                          DimProductCategory ON
    DimProductSubcategory.ProductCategoryKey =
    DimProductCategory.ProductCategoryKey INNER JOIN
                          FactInternetSales ON
    DimProduct.ProductKey =
    FactInternetSales.ProductKey INNER JOIN
                          DimSalesTerritory ON
    FactInternetSales.SalesTerritoryKey =
    DimSalesTerritory.SalesTerritoryKey
```

6. In the **Select the Report Type** window, choose **Matrix**, as shown in the following screenshot:

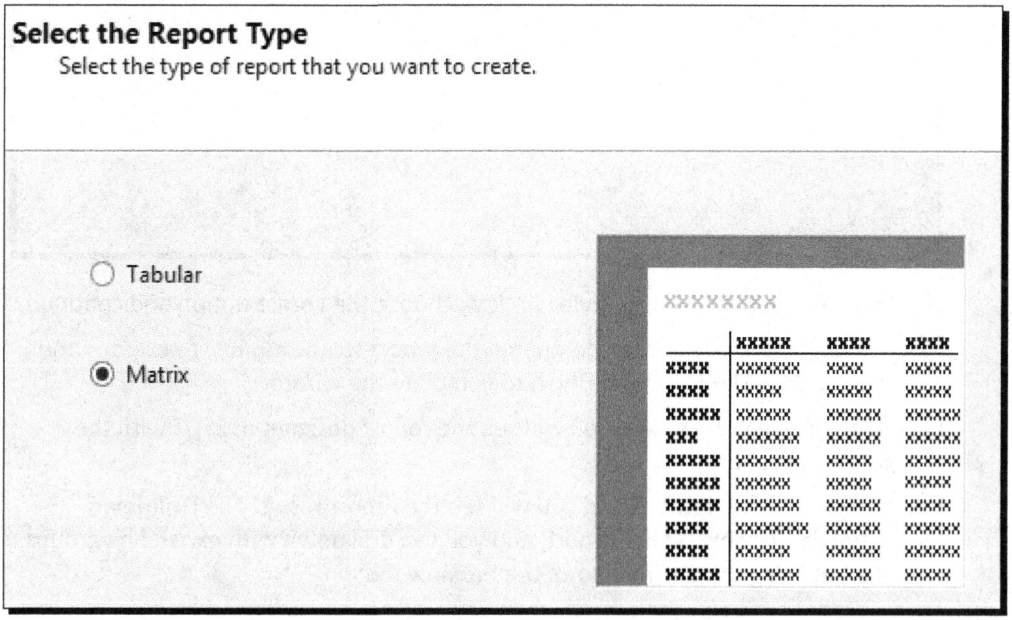

7. In the **Design the Matrix** window, add **EnglishProductCategoryName**, **EnglishProductSubcategoryName**, and **EnglishProductName** sequentially to the **Columns** section. You can add them by simply dragging-and-dropping them to the columns box or by clicking on the **Columns** button once for each item.

8. Add **SalesTerritoryGroup**, **SalesTerritoryCountry**, and **SalesTerritoryRegion** respectively to the **Rows** section.

9. Add **SalesAmount** to the **Details** section. Then, check the **Enable drilldown** option, as shown in the following screenshot:

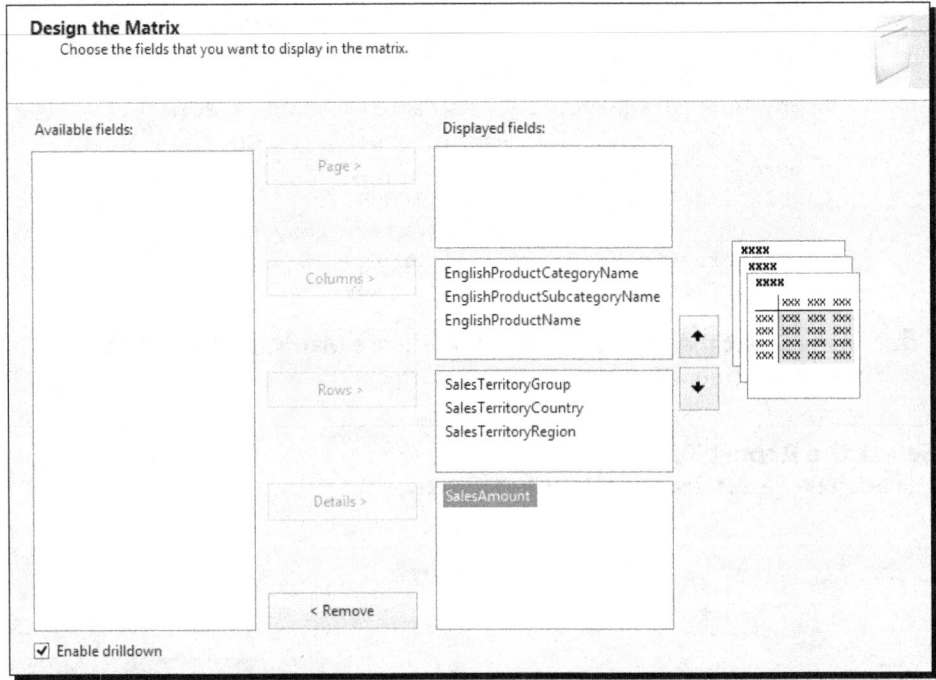

10. In the **Choose the Matrix Style** window, choose the **Forest** option and continue.

11. In the last step of the wizard, rename the report to `Sales by Product and Territory`. Then, click on **Finish** to complete the wizard.

12. After finishing the wizard, you will see the report designer in SSDT with the generated report.

13. Click on the **Preview** tab and you will see the report result. The **Drilldown** option is available on the report, and you can drill down with expanding groups. The following screenshot shows the **Preview** tab:

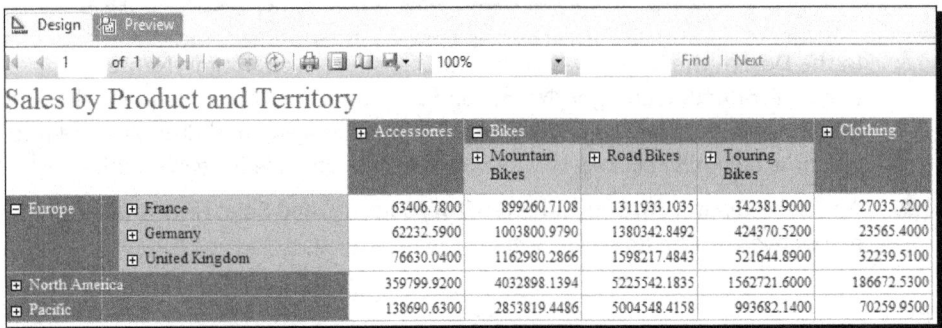

What just happened?

In this example, we used a simple **Add New Report** wizard to create a report using the SQL Server database. We went through the wizard steps, such as creating a data source connection; writing/building a SQL query for the dataset; and choosing a report style, layout, and positioning of the columns in the group.

The **Report Type** field can be chosen as **Tabular** or **Matrix**. The difference can be seen quite simply when you change these options in the small preview window beside it in the **Select the Report Type** window (step 6). The **Tabular** style shows headers only on columns, and data rows will be under it in the form of details. The **Matrix** style shows headers for both columns and rows. Choosing the right style depends on the type of grouping and items you want to show in the report.

After creating the report (step 12), SSDT displays the **Report Designer** menu. In SSDT, this is where report developers spend most of their time developing sophisticated and robust reports. In real-world scenarios, you are always required to develop the report much further than what the basic report wizard generates for you. But the report wizard is a good base for a report, from where you can then enhance it with the designer. The following screenshot shows the SSDT layout for Reporting Services projects:

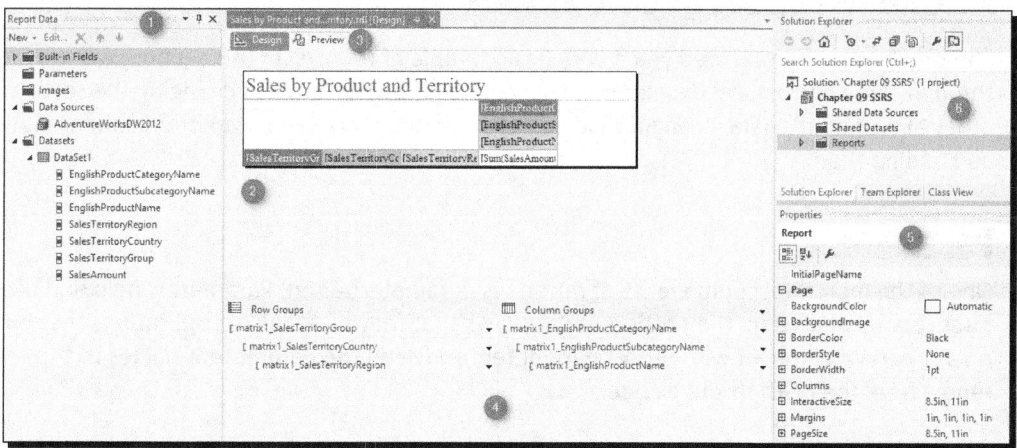

The following are the explanations for each window in SSDT for Reporting Services projects:

- ◆ **Report Data**: This window shows information about data items in the report. Information such as data sources, datasets, query fields, parameters, and built-in fields is shown here.

- ◆ **Report**: This window will be used to change the layout of a report with items from **Toolbox** and data items from **Report Data**.

◆ **Preview**: This is the built-in **Preview** pane that displays a preview of the current report. The SSRS service doesn't need to be up and running to preview the current report.

◆ **Row Groups** and **Column Groups**: The attributes groups will be listed in this pane. You can reorder them here or change the configuration of the existing groups in this pane.

◆ **Properties**: This window shows the properties of the selected object in the report.

◆ **Solution Explorer**: This window shows the Reporting Services project solution structure.

◆ **Toolbox**: This window (not in the previous screenshot) contains report items such as textboxes, graphs, and KPIs that can be added to the report designer.

In this example, you learned how easy it is to generate a report with the drill-down functionality. You can also check the report export options in the **Preview** pane, which are exporting the report to PDF or printing the report. SSRS reports can be made printer friendly with very little effort.

Extended report development

The previous section showed you a very basic sample of reports. In this section, we will go through some customized development scenarios in reports, such as changing the sorting order of a column's data, changing the aggregation functions and parameter configurations, and adding charts.

Parameters

One of the most vital components of reports is parameterization. Parameters help end users filter reports and select the portion of data rows that they want. Also, applications that build on a report can interact with report parameters and send the parameters' values to the report from their GUI through code.

Time for action – adding parameters to a report

In this example, we will add the year and month parameters to the report generated in the previous section. You need to perform the following steps after the execution of the previous example to add parameters to a report:

1. Open the **Sales by Product and Territory** reports that were created in the previous example, and in the **Report Data** pane, right-click on **Dataset** and select **Add Dataset**.

2. In the **Dataset Properties** window, rename the dataset to `Years`.

3. Select the **Use dataset embedded in my report** option. Choose **Data source** as **AdventureWorksDW2012**. Then, in the query box, type in the following query to fetch all years from the **FactInternetSales** table:

```
SELECT      distinct (OrderDateKey/10000) as [Year]
FROM             FactInternetSales
```

The following screenshot shows the **Dataset Properties** window:

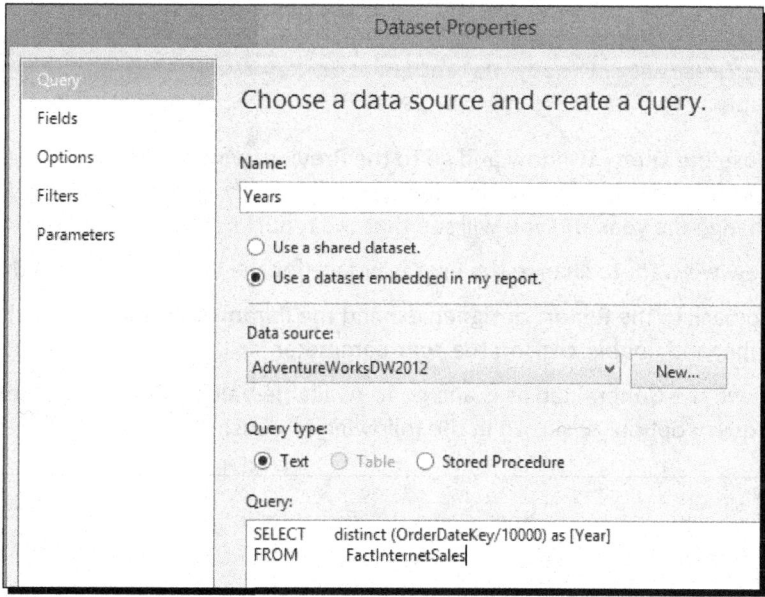

4. Close the **Dataset Properties** window and then right-click on **DataSet1** and select **Query**.

5. In the query designer window, add the following script line at the end of the SELECT query:

```
WHERE        (FactInternetSales.OrderDateKey / 10000 = @Year)
```

6. After adding the preceding line of code, the final query looks like the following code snippet:

```
SELECT         DimProductCategory.EnglishProductCategoryName,
  DimProductSubcategory.EnglishProductSubcategoryName,
  DimProduct.EnglishProductName,
                       DimSalesTerritory.SalesTerritoryRegion,
  DimSalesTerritory.SalesTerritoryCountry,
  DimSalesTerritory.SalesTerritoryGroup,
                       FactInternetSales.SalesAmount
```

```
FROM              DimProduct INNER JOIN
                        DimProductSubcategory ON
   DimProduct.ProductSubcategoryKey =
   DimProductSubcategory.ProductSubcategoryKey INNER JOIN
                        DimProductCategory ON
   DimProductSubcategory.ProductCategoryKey =
   DimProductCategory.ProductCategoryKey INNER JOIN
                        FactInternetSales ON
   DimProduct.ProductKey = FactInternetSales.
   ProductKey INNER JOIN
                        DimSalesTerritory ON
   FactInternetSales.SalesTerritoryKey =
   DimSalesTerritory.SalesTerritoryKey
WHERE             (FactInternetSales.OrderDateKey / 10000 = @Year)
```

7. Close the **Query** window and go to the **Preview** window. You will see that the report asks for the value for **Year** in a textbox. Enter 2007 and click on **View Report**. Change the year and you will see that the report's data will change.

8. Now we want to change the user interface for the **Year** filter to be a drop-down list.

9. Go back to the **Report** designer, expand the **Parameters** folder in the **Report Data** pane, and double-click on the **Year** parameter.

10. Leave the **General** tab as is and go to **Available Values**. Choose the **Get values from a query** option, as shown in the following screenshot:

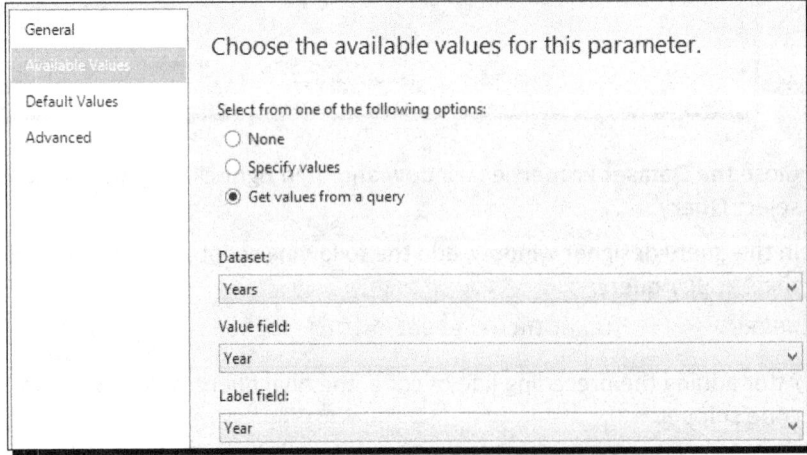

11. Choose **Dataset** as **Years** and select **Year** for both the **Value** and **Data** fields.

12. Close the **Parameter** window and go to the **Preview** pane. You will see that the textbox filter for **Year** changes to a drop-down list and you can see a list of years and can select any of them. The following screenshot shows the **Sales by Product and Territory** report for the year 2008:

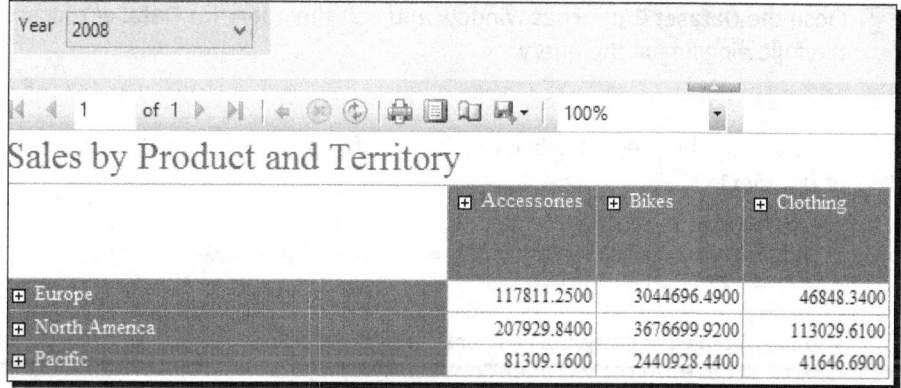

13. Now we want to add the **Month** filter. The month will be selected after the year as a cascade filter.

14. Go back to the report designer and right-click on the **Datasets** folder in the **Report Data** pane and add a new dataset.

15. Rename the new dataset to **Months** and choose the embedded dataset option. Select the data source and write the following query in the **Query** box:

```
SELECT   distinct
DATENAME(MONTH,convert(date,convert(varchar(8),OrderDateKey),
    112)) as [MonthName]
,DATEPART(MONTH,convert(date,convert(varchar(8),OrderDateKey),
    112)) as [MonthKey]
FROM             FactInternetSales
where OrderDateKey/10000=@Year
order by DATEPART(MONTH,convert(date,convert
    (varchar(8),OrderDateKey),
     112))
```

16. Go to the **Parameters** tab of the **Dataset Properties** window and choose the [@ Year] parameter in the **Parameter Value** box, as shown in the following screenshot:

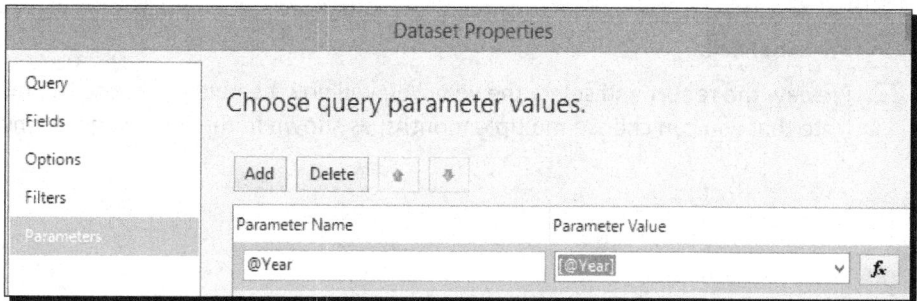

17. Close the **Dataset Properties** window and edit the query for **DataSet1** by adding the following line in the query:

```
AND ((FactInternetSales.OrderDateKey / 100 % 100) IN (@Month))
```

18. After adding the preceding line of code, the following will be the final query of **DataSet1**:

```
SELECT          DimProductCategory.EnglishProductCategoryName,
   DimProductSubcategory.EnglishProductSubcategoryName,
   DimProduct.EnglishProductName,
                         DimSalesTerritory.SalesTerritoryRegion,
   DimSalesTerritory.SalesTerritoryCountry,
   DimSalesTerritory.SalesTerritoryGroup,
                         FactInternetSales.SalesAmount
FROM            DimProduct INNER JOIN
                         DimProductSubcategory ON
   DimProduct.ProductSubcategoryKey =
   DimProductSubcategory.ProductSubcategoryKey INNER JOIN
                         DimProductCategory ON
   DimProductSubcategory.ProductCategoryKey =
   DimProductCategory.ProductCategoryKey INNER JOIN
                         FactInternetSales ON
   DimProduct.ProductKey = FactInternetSales.
   ProductKey INNER JOIN
                         DimSalesTerritory ON
   FactInternetSales.SalesTerritoryKey =
   DimSalesTerritory.SalesTerritoryKey
WHERE           (FactInternetSales.OrderDateKey / 10000 = @Year)
   AND ((FactInternetSales.OrderDateKey / 100 % 100)
   IN (@Month))
```

19. Under the **Parameters** folder in the **Report Data** pane, double-click on the **Month** parameter to edit.

20. In the **General** tab, check the option **Allow multiple values**.

21. In the **Available Values** menu, choose **Get Values from a query**. Next, choose the **Months** dataset, select **MonthKey** as the **Value** field, and select **MonthName** as the **Label** field.

22. Preview the report and select the year. You will now be able to choose the month. Note that you can choose multiple months, as shown in the following screenshot:

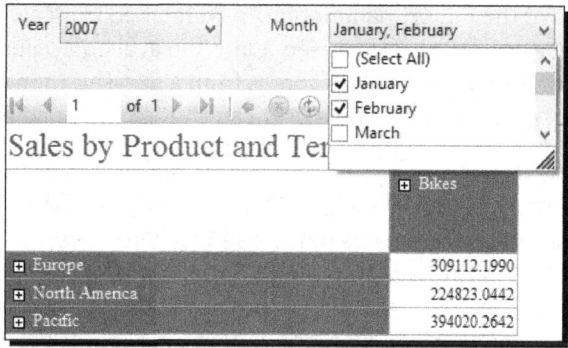

What just happened?

In this example, you learned how to add parameters to a report. Parameters will be added in the report GUI as an interface item and they will also be added to the dataset. Interface or report parameters can be customized in the **Parameter** properties window. You also learned how to cascade parameters in the report. Parameters can be customized to work as a single value, as multiple values, with a default value, and by selecting available values from a dataset.

Steps 1 to 3 show how to add a dataset manually to the report. The datasets created in these steps will be used in the following steps as the source for the available values of the **Year** parameter. The `Distinct` clause in the query will remove duplicate years.

In steps 4 to 6, we added the **Year** parameter to the dataset query of the main dataset. There are two types of parameters in SSRS reports: **Dataset** and **Report**. Dataset parameters will be added to datasets in a similar manner to how we've done so in these steps. To add a Dataset parameter, you only need to add the parameter to the dataset query. For this example, we added the parameter with an @ prefix.

After adding the Dataset parameter, we are able to map the Dataset parameter to a Report parameter. If we don't map the Dataset parameter to a Report parameter, and if there is no Report parameter with the same name in that report, then a new Report parameter will be generated automatically.

Report parameters are interface options on the report that interact with the user. We can specify the data type of a Report parameter as either single value or multivalue. A Report parameter can read the available values from a dataset. As you've seen in step 7, the Report parameter's default interface is a textbox.

The available values of the Report parameter can be fetched from a dataset. You learned how to read the values of a dataset and feed it into the available values of the parameter in steps 9, 10, and 11. When a list of values comes from a dataset, then the Report parameter will be shown as a drop-down list and the user can choose the value from the list (step 12).

You also learned how to add a nested parameter in a report. We used the **Year** parameter as the main parameter, and then we've added the **Month** parameter after that. The **Month** filter, in this example, will be selectable only if the **Year** filter is set. So, we added the **Year** parameter as part of the **Months** dataset query (step 15). We've also picked two columns as the result of a query for this dataset: one for the month number and another for the month name. The **@Year** parameter in the dataset query of the **Months** dataset should be mapped to the **Year** parameter in the report; this mapping will be done in the **Parameters** tab in the **Dataset Properties** window (step 16).

The last part of this example was the configuration of the **Month** report parameter to be multivalue. The first part of the multivalue configuration of a parameter is to write the dataset query that uses this parameter in a way that it can handle multiple values. In step 18, you've seen that we've added the month criteria in a `Where` condition with the `IN` clause. We cannot use the equal operator for this criteria because equal can only be applied on a single value operator. We also changed the **Report** parameter properties to work as multiple value in steps 21 and 22.

Printing and page configuration

Reporting Services reports can be designed in a printer-friendly manner. There are properties in reports that are helpful in the configuration of the page size for printing. In this section, we will go through some page configuration options for the report.

Time for action – changing a page's properties

In this example, we will change the **PageSize** property of the report to reveal how the page size will affect the printing layout of the report. Perform the following steps:

1. Create a new report and use the same data source for it, AdventureWorksDW2012. Then, use the following query as the query string:

```
SELECT          FirstName, LastName, BirthDate, MaritalStatus,
    Gender, TotalChildren, NumberChildrenAtHome,
    EnglishEducation, NumberCarsOwned
FROM            DimCustomer
```

2. Choose **Tabular** as the report type. Next, select all columns to be in the **Details** section in the **Design the Table** window. Rename the report to Customers and complete the wizard.

3. Preview the report. In the **Preview** window, click on the **Export** button and export the report to PDF (as shown in the following screenshot):

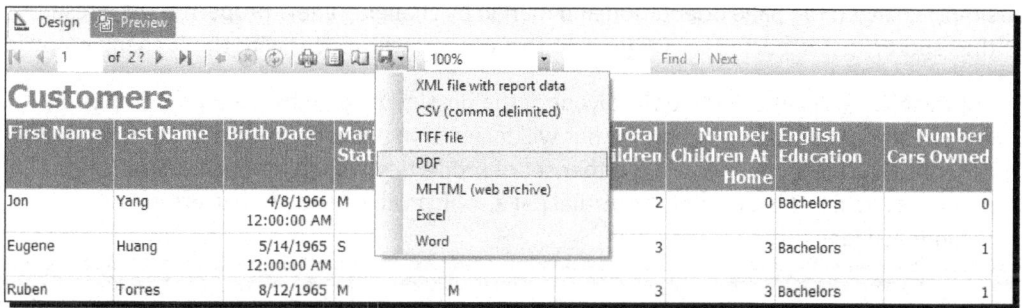

4. Save the PDF file and then open it. You will notice that the number of pages is 1762 by default. Next, the pages exported to the portrait layout caused each report page to split into two PDF pages.

5. Go back to the report designer. In the **Properties** window, select the **Report** object. Then, expand the **PageSize** properties and change **Height** to **8.5in** and **Width** to **11in**. Also, change all margins to **0.5in**, as shown in the following screenshot:

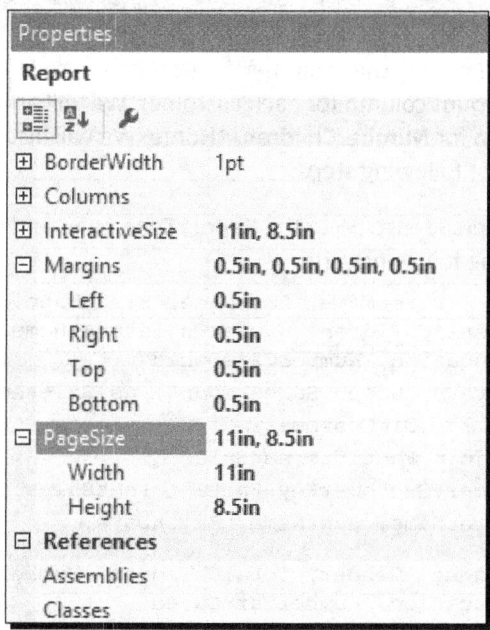

6. Save the changes and preview the report. Export the report to PDF. This time, you will see that the number of pages is 1088. Each report page is exported in landscape in one PDF page.

What just happened?

In this example, you learned an easy way to perform page configuration in the report. We simply changed the page orientation and margin by changing a few properties. As a result, the report pages exported to PDF (or sent to a printer) will appear with those changes applied.

The **PageSize** properties define the layout of the physical page, which is a printer-friendly version of the report, and the properties will take action when the report is exported to PDF or sent to a printer. There is also another set of properties named **InteractiveSize**. These properties define the layout of the virtual page, which will be shown to users in the interactive mode.

Sorting and grouping

Reports show data rows, and one of the main requirements in reporting tools is the ability to order data rows and apply grouping and subtotals on groups. In this section, you will learn how to apply sorting and grouping in the report.

Time for action – applying ordering and grouping on the data rows

In this example, we will modify the customers' report generated in the previous example. We will add a **SalesAmount** column for each customer. We will apply sorting on the report and we will add a group for **NumberChildrenAtHome**. We will also add a subtotal for each group item. Perform the following steps:

1. In the **Customers** report, go to the **Report Data** pane and change the query of **DataSet1** to the following script:

```
SELECT          FirstName, LastName, BirthDate, MaritalStatus,
   Gender, TotalChildren, NumberChildrenAtHome,
   EnglishEducation, NumberCarsOwned
,sum(FactInternetSales.SalesAmount) as SalesAmount
FROM            DimCustomer
left outer join FactInternetSales
on DimCustomer.CustomerKey=FactInternetSales.CustomerKey
group by FirstName, LastName, BirthDate,

   MaritalStatus, Gender, TotalChildren, NumberChildrenAtHome,
   EnglishEducation, NumberCarsOwned
```

2. Now you will see the **SalesAmount** column under **DataSet1**. Drag-and-drop this column to the report designer exactly after the last column in the report.

3. Select the textbox under the **SalesAmount** column in the report designer. Then, in the **Properties** window, change the **Format** property to **#,#.##$**.

4. Select one of the column headers in the table in the report designer. Then, right-click on **Table Header Columns** and choose **Tablix Properties...** from the pop-up menu, as shown in the following screenshot:

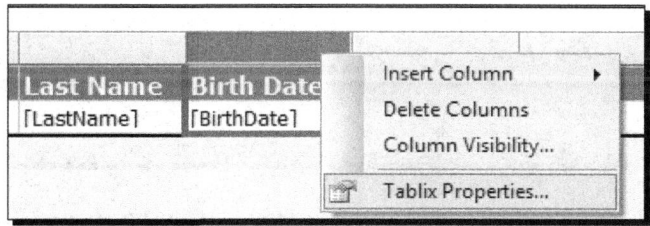

5. In the **Tablix Properties...** window, go to the **Sorting** tab. Then, click on the **Add** button and choose the **SalesAmount** column with descending order (Z to A).

6. Preview the report. You will see that the **SalesAmount** column will be shown with a thousand separator, two decimal points, and a dollar sign. The report is ordered descending by sales amount.

7. Now we want to add interactive reporting to column headers.

8. Click on the **LastName** column header textbox (select the textbox itself – not the text in it) and then right-click on it and choose **Textbox Properties** from the pop-up menu.

9. In the **Textbox Properties** window, go to the **Interactive Sorting** tab, check **Enable interactive sorting on this text box**, and choose the **LastName** column in the **Sort by** section.

10. Preview the report. Now, you can click on the **LastName** column to change the sorting of rows (ascending or descending) based on this column.

11. Go back to the report designer. Click on the second row (the row after the column headers) and then right-click on the header of that row. Then, from the pop-up menu, select **Add Group**. Next, click on **Parent Group**.

12. In the **Tablix group** window, select the **[NumberChildrenAtHome]** column in the **Group by** drop-down list and check the **Add group header** option, as shown in the following screenshot:

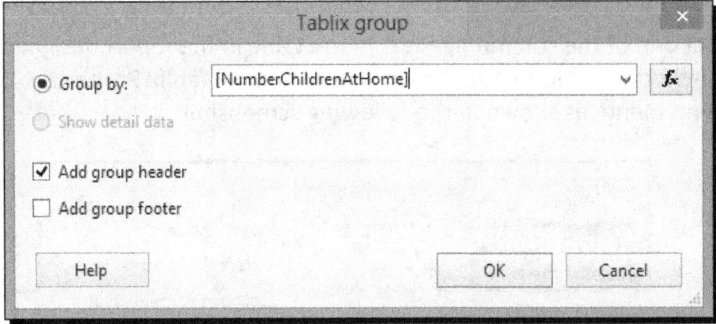

13. You will see that a new row has been added to the **Tablix between header** and **Details** rows. This row is a group header row. Click on the textbox for the **SalesAmount** column in the group header row and then choose the **SalesAmount** expression from the pop-up menu, as shown in the following screenshot:

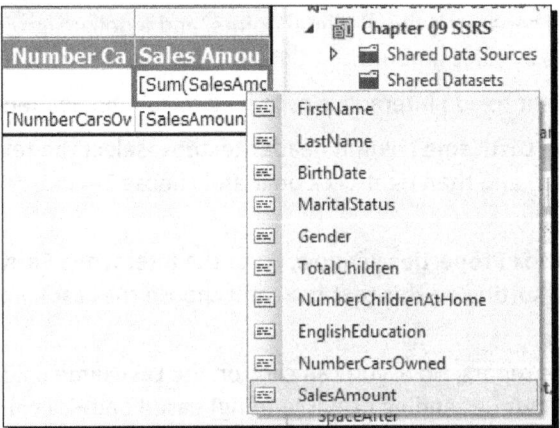

14. In the **Properties** window for this textbox, change the **Format** property to **#,#.##$**.

15. Preview the report. You will see the new group for **NumberOfChildrenAtHome**. The group header row shows the total sales amount for that group.

16. Now, we want to show the average number of cars for each group in the group header.

17. Right-click on the textbox for the **NumberCarsOwned** column in the group header row and select **Expression**.

18. In the **Expression** window, enter the following script:

```
=Avg(Fields!NumberCarsOwned.Value)
```

19. Close the **Expression** window. Change the **Format** property of this textbox to **#**.

20. Preview the report and you will see an average number of cars shown in the group header.

What just happened?

In this example, you learned how to enable interactive sorting for end users. You also saw how to apply a sort on data rows without user interaction. There is part of this example where grouping shows how to add a group on data rows as well as adding total aggregated measure as the group header. You also learned how to apply formatting on a textbox.

In the first two steps of this example, we modified a dataset query for the main report and we added a new data field to the report. Step 3 shows how to change the format string of a textbox to a numeral with a thousand separator and two decimal points. we changed the order of data rows in steps 4 and 5 with the **Sorting** tab of the **Tablix Properties** window. Steps 8 and 9 show how to enable interactive sorting on a column of the table in the report.

Steps 11 and 12 show how to add a group on the **NumberChildrenAtHome** data field for data rows. Groups can be added on either column or rows. There is also a **Grouping** pane in the report designer that shows the hierarchy of groups in rows and columns and provides an easier method to control groups on data fields. In this example, we've added the subtotal record for the group, and in step 13, we used that space to add the total of the sales amount for each group.

Steps 17 and 18 show how to add another textbox in the group header row with an expression. SSRS uses an expression language specific to itself. The expression language uses some built-in functions, and can be combined with data rows from the dataset and also some operators.

Expressions

SSRS expressions play a vital role in creating calculated fields in the report. Expressions are also an important part of dynamism in reports; for example, the background color of text can be changed based on an expression. In this section, we will have a very quick overview of expressions with an example that is based on the previous reporting project.

Time for action – changing the background color of data rows based on expressions

In this example, we want to distinguish records for male and female customers by changing the background colors of the row. For this purpose, we will write an expression and use that in the background color property of the data row using the following steps:

1. Go to the report designer of the **Customer** report from the previous example.

2. Click on the row header for the details record (third row in the Tablix).

3. In the **Properties** window, find the **Background Color** property and click on your desired color from the color picker menu.

4. Choose **Expressions** from the color picker pop up as shown in the following screenshot:

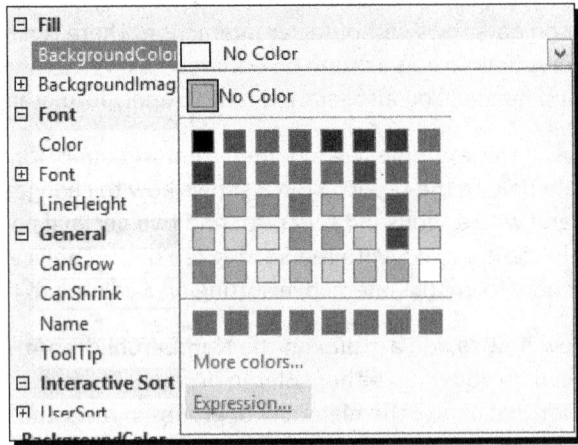

5. In the **Expression** editor window, enter the following script:

```
=iif(Fields!Gender.Value="M","Light Green","Khaki")
```

6. Close the **Expression** window and preview the report. You will see that male and female data rows are now different with regard to background color, as shown in the following screenshot:

Customers

Number Children At Home	First Name	Last Name	Birth Date	Marital Status	Gender	Total Children	Number Children At Home	English Education
0								
	Adriana	Gonzalez	7/18/1946 12:00:00 AM	S	F	5	0	Partial College
	Bonnie	Nath	8/18/1944 12:00:00 AM	M	F	5	0	Bachelors
	Bonnie	Xie	11/15/1968 12:00:00 AM	M	F	0	0	Graduate Degree
	Carmen	Rana	2/23/1967 12:00:00 AM	M	F	0	0	Bachelors
	Cory	Kapoor	4/18/1967 12:00:00 AM	M	M	0	0	Bachelors
	Isabella	Ward	8/13/1963 12:00:00 AM	M	F	1	0	Bachelors

What just happened?

This quick example explained how to change the background color of a set of textboxes (in a data row) with the result of an expression. As you can see in step 4, you can set the value of the background color property with an expression. Fortunately, most of the properties in SSRS report objects can be set with expressions. This feature empowers the dynamism of the report.

Expression is a functional language for writing scripts inside the report for collecting data with report items from dataset fields, or for creating calculated fields or scripts that can be used in the report item's properties (such as this example). Expression generates from a combination of built-in functions, operators, dataset fields, and/or variables. The following screenshot shows the **Expression** editor window and its sections:

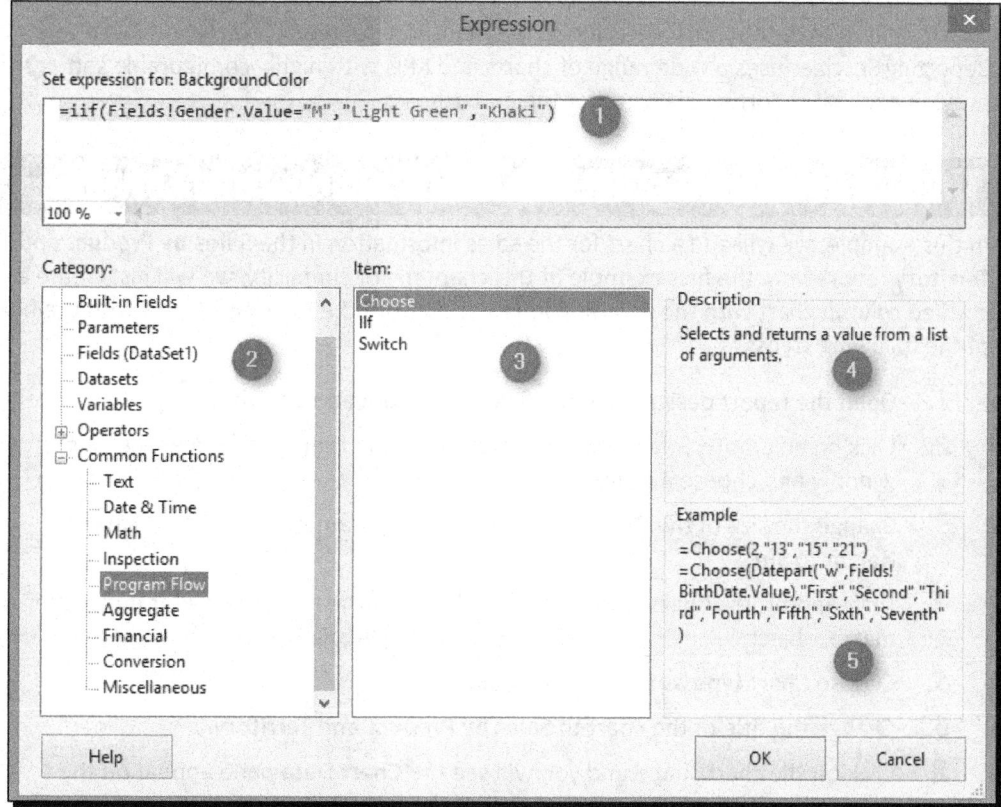

The following is a list of the sections in the **Expression** editor in SSRS:

- Window for the script/text of the expression
- Category of functions / operators / variables

◆ Item list (the example shown in the screenshot is a list of functions under the **Program Flow** category)

◆ Description of the selected item

◆ Example scripts with the selected item

Explaining the full set of the **Expression** functions and operators is beyond the scope of this book. However, you can read any SSRS book to get more details about expressions. Online Microsoft MSDN books can also give you a lot of information on expressions, which can be read at `http://msdn.microsoft.com/en-us/library/dd220516.aspx`.

Adding charts

Charts, KPIs, and dashboards are some of the main components of analytical reporting. Reporting Services uses a wide range of charts and KPIs with highly configurable settings that provide a robust reporting platform for the end user.

Time for action – working with charts in Reporting Services

In this example, we will add a chart for the sales information in the **Sales by Product and Territory** report from the first example of this chapter. For simplicity, we will just create a stacked column chart with the default configuration from the existing dataset with the help of the following steps:

1. Open the report designer for the **Sales by Product and Territory** report.

2. Click on an empty area in the report designer and then go to the **Properties** window and choose a **Body** object.

3. Change the size of the **Body** object with these parameters: **Width** to **5in** and **Height** to **5in**.

4. Drag-and-drop a **Chart** object from **Toolbox** into the report designer under the **matrix** object.

5. Choose **Chart type** as **3-D Stacked Column**.

6. Change the title of the chart to **Sales by Product and Territory**.

7. Click on the chart shape and you will see the **Chart Data** pane appear on the right-hand side of the chart, as shown in the following screenshot:

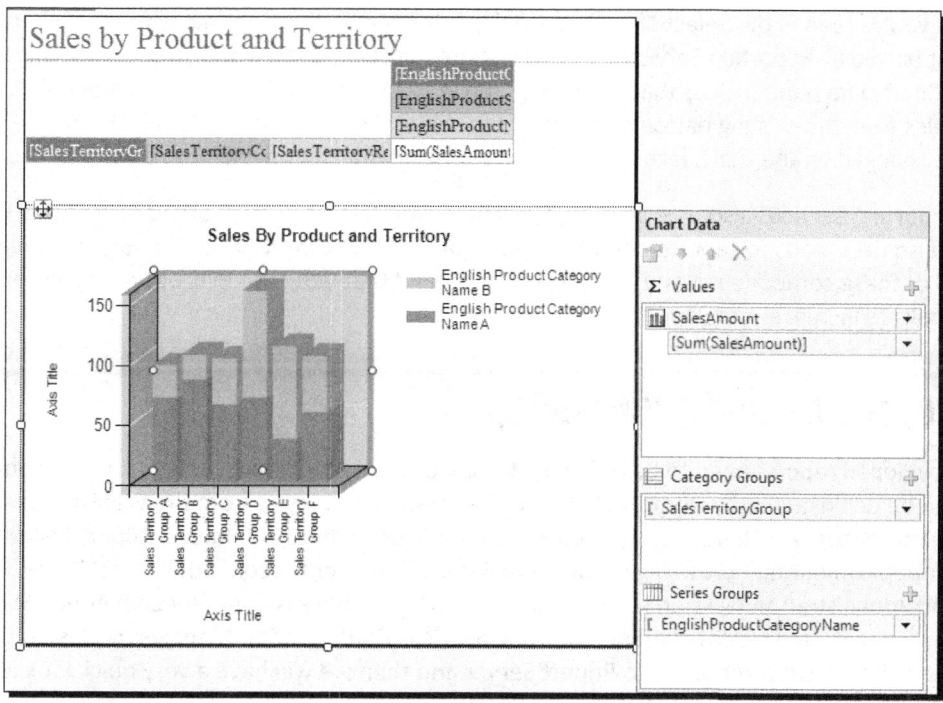

8. From the **Report Data** pane, drag-and-drop **SalesAmount** into the **Values** section of **Chart Data**. Drag-and-drop **SalesTerritoryGroup** from **Report Data** into **Category Groups** of **Chart Data**. And finally, drag-and-drop **EnglishProductCategoryName** into **Series Groups**.

9. Preview the report for all months of the year 2008 and you will see that information in the chart right below the matrix.

What just happened?

This example showed how to work with charts in SSRS reports. In this example, we just used a very simple configuration by changing the **Chart Data** menu to show the functionality of charts in Reporting Services. Real-world charts would require more configurations on the chart properties; legend configurations; axis titles and settings; and color, size, and other configurations for the columns themselves.

As you've seen in the **Select Chart Type** dialog box (step 5), there are many types of charts supported by Reporting Services, such as column, bar, line, scatter, and so on. Every chart has a **Chart Data** pane such as that you configured in steps 7 and 8. **Chart Data** includes all data fields from the existing datasets that build the chart. There are many configurations that can be changed on the chart, legend, and/or axis with a right-click on each component of the chart.

Reporting Services also uses Gauges, Sparkline, and Data Bar, which are very useful as KPIs. It also uses maps to show geographical information. This chapter is not enough to explain all of these components, and I strongly recommend that you read BOL or Reporting Services books to increase your reporting skills with SSRS.

Deploying and configuring

Developed reports need to be deployed to UAT or production environments. SSRS reports can be deployed easily from SSDT. Reports can also be deployed from the WebUI to the **Report Manager**. There are two web applications for Reporting Services: **Report Server** for deployment and browsing reports and Report Manager for configuration, security, and administration tasks on reports and data sources. There is a tool for configuring SSRS components, named SQL Server Reporting Services Configuration Manager. In this section, we will deploy our reports into Report Server and then we will have a very quick look at **Report Manager** and Configuration Manager.

Time for action – deploying a report

In this example, we will first find the report server URL from Reporting Services Configuration Manager, and then we will use that URL to deploy reports from SSDT. Finally, we will browse those reports to see them from the Report Server web application by using the following steps:

1. Go to **Start | Microsoft SQL Server 2014** and expand **Configuration tools**. Then, click on **Reporting Services Configuration Manager**.

2. When **Reporting Services Configuration Manager** opens, it may ask for a connection. Just choose the default instance and connect.

3. You will see the service status that shows information about the SQL Server version, edition, and service status information.

4. Click on **Web Service URL**. The URL of the Report Server web application can be viewed or changed in this option, as shown in the following screenshot:

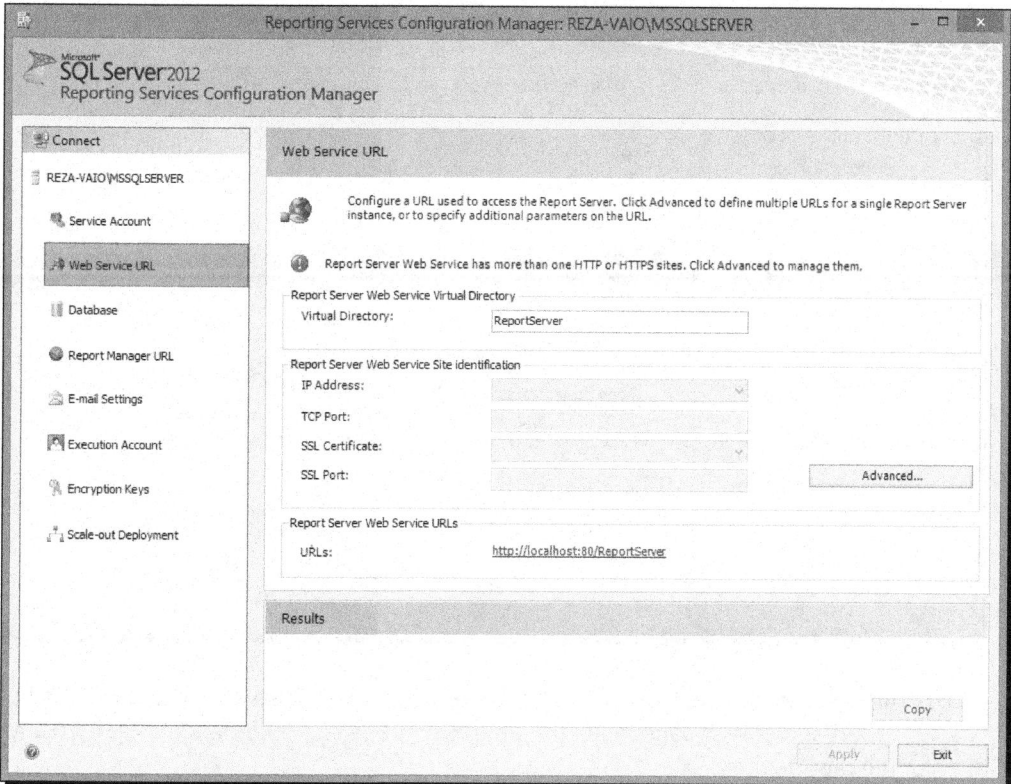

5. Go to **SSDT** and right-click on the Reporting Service project, and then from the pop-up menu, select **Properties**.

6. In the **Project Properties** window, change the **TargetServerURL** option to the URL of the report server that you picked from Reporting Services Configuration Manager. Then, close the **Properties** window.

7. Right-click on the project and click on **Deploy** to deploy the project, as shown in the following screenshot:

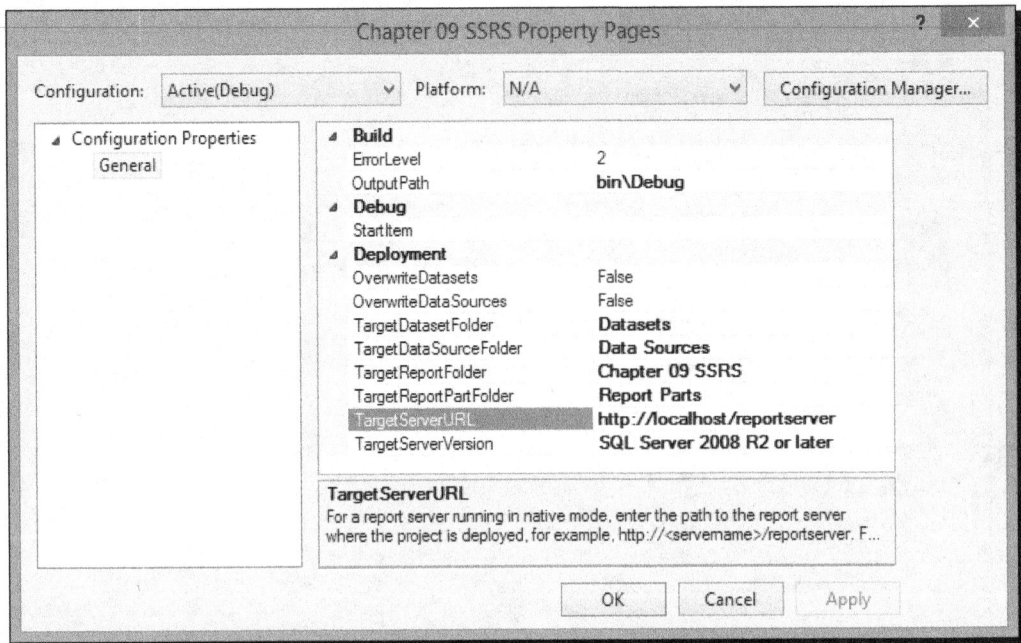

8. After successful deployment, go to the report server URL on Internet Explorer. In the report server web page, open the `Chapter 09 SSRS` folder and navigate to any of the reports there.

What just happened?

You've learned how to work with Reporting Services Configuration Manager. The Reporting Services Configuration Manager is the centralized configuration application for Reporting Services. You can configure web applications, database connections, service accounts, and other settings of Reporting Services with this tool.

We used **Reporting Services Configuration Manager** in this example to find the Report Server URL. The Report Server web application can also be generated or modified in this configuration window. SSDT asks for the Report Server URL of the target Reporting Services server to deploy reports in that server.

Time for action – using Report Manager

Report Manager is the second web application in Reporting Services that provides an administration panel for reports, folder hierarchy of reports, and data sources. Administration tasks such as security configurations, changing data sources, and adding or removing subscription to reports can be performed with this tool. In this example, we will have a very quick look at this tool:

1. Find the Report Manager URL from the **Reporting Services Configuration Manager** window and browse to its URL (the default URL for Report Manager is `http://<server name>/reports`).

2. In Report Manager, go to the `Chapter 09 SSRS` folder. Hover on the **Customers** report and then click on the arrow on the right-hand side of the report icon, as shown in the following screenshot:

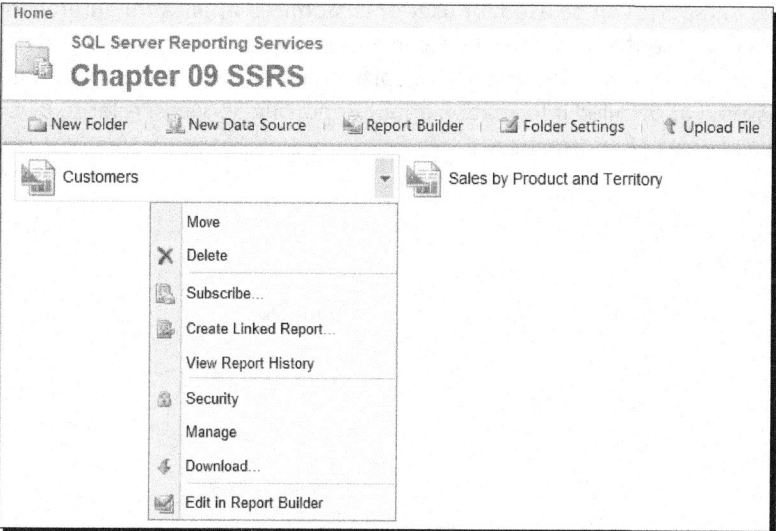

3. In the pop-up menu, click on **Manage**.

4. In the **Manage Report** page, you will see the administration panel on the left-hand side. You can view/change the data source for this report. You can also view/change the subscription information and some other options.

5. The **Security** option is where you can apply permissions on this report. You can choose the user from the **Active directory users** or **Groups list** window and then apply permission roles to it.

What just happened?

In this example, you saw how to work with the **Report Manager** option and you saw how to use it for configuration and security settings.

Summary

Reporting Services is one of the components of SQL Server 2014 for developing robust and powerful reports. SSRS provides a wide range of charts and components such as Gauges and Data Bars to be added to the report. SSRS reports also use expressions, which are a powerful way to add dynamism. They also provide the functionality to add calculated fields or KPIs in reports. A wide range of data sources are supported by Reporting Services. In this chapter, we only showed the SQL Server database engine as the main source for our samples, but SSRS can connect to analysis services cubes and databases and many other data sources as well.

Parameters in reports can be used for user or customized application interaction. Parameters can be added and configured from the **Report Data** pane. In this chapter, you've also learned to apply formatting on visualization items. Sorting and grouping of items in data fields was also discussed. For detailed information about Reporting Services, refer to BOL and MSDN as the main sources of information.

10
Dashboard Design

Data visualization is the only part of the BI system that contains viewable elements for end users, so data visualization will be considered to design the frontend table of BI system (Kimball methodology states that ETL is the kitchen of the restaurant). Data visualization is all about displaying analytical information that is processed in an OLAP cube or a tabular model based on the logical design of data model (there are some scenarios where visualization will be done directly out of a data warehouse, and not the cube or BISM). Analytical information can be presented in many ways: grids, charts, static and dynamic reports, dashboards, or any feature that helps users to understand data and numbers in the best way.

Microsoft released a bunch of tools, such as SSRS, PerformancePoint, Power View, Excel, and Excel Services, for frontend designing. You learned about SSRS in previous chapters, and you already know that SSRS is one of the most powerful tools in reporting. The only downside of it is the development time. In this chapter, you will learn about PerformancePoint, which is a part of the SharePoint product. You will also learn about Power View, which can be part of SharePoint or Excel 2013.

The PerformancePoint service

PerformancePoint is one of the SharePoint services that was released for the first time with SharePoint 2007. It is a dashboard and data visualization tool for Microsoft OLAP cubes. To install PerformancePoint, you need to install SharePoint first. This means that you cannot install PerformancePoint on a nonserver operating system because a SharePoint server can only be installed on a server operating system.

After installation of SharePoint, you will need to configure and enable the PerformancePoint service application. Finally, you can create the Business Intelligence site where you can design dashboards using Dashboard Designer, and deploy them onto the BI site. In the following sections of this chapter, we will go through each of these steps to illustrate how to create and design dashboards using PerformancePoint Dashboard Designer.

For all PerformancePoint examples in this chapter, you will need an operating system server edition to be able to install SharePoint and configure PerformancePoint on it. In this book, we used Windows Server 2012 and SharePoint 2013.

Time for action – configuring PerformancePoint in SharePoint

This example shows the steps to configure PerformancePoint and create a Business Intelligence site. These steps are a prerequisite for other samples in PerformancePoint. For this example, Windows Server 2012 must be installed. Installation of SharePoint is not explained in this book (SharePoint configuration and installation requires another book in itself). We WILL just start from the point when you have SharePoint 2013 installed on your server machine. So, let's get started with the configuration using the following steps:

1. After installing SharePoint 2013, start **SharePoint Central Administration**.

2. Go to **Manage Service Applications** and click on **PerformancePoint Service Application**.

3. Then, go to the **PerformancePoint Service Application Settings** page and use the **Unattended Service Account** option (map it to a domain account on an active directory). Please note that to get this step working, you may first need to configure **Secure Store Service Application**.

4. Next, go back to **Central Administration**.

5. Then go to **Application Management**, and under **Site Collections,** click on Create a **Site Collection**.

6. Set the site title as `PacktPub BI Site` and set the last part of site URL as `PacktPubBI`. In the template selection section, under **Enterprise,** choose **Business Intelligence Center**, as shown in the following screenshot:

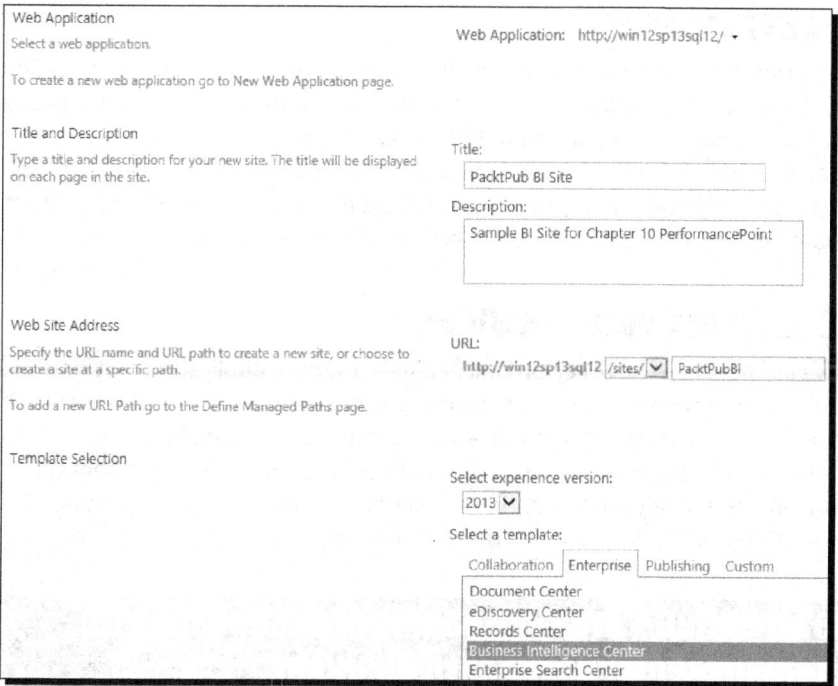

7. Set the **Primary Site Collection Administrator** value and click on **OK** to create the site collection.

8. After creating the site collection, you can browse to it using the SharePoint URL, followed by /sites/PacktPubBI. For example, if the SharePoint URL is http://win12sp13sql12, then the site URL will be http://win12sp13sql12/sites/packtpubbi, as shown in the the following screenshot:

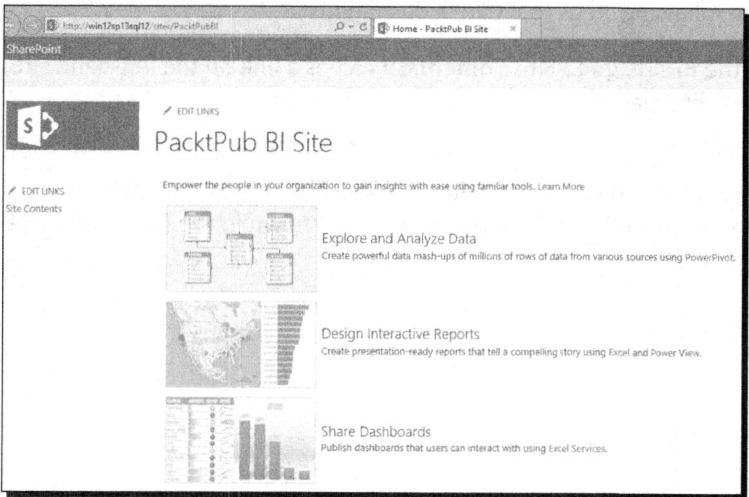

What just happened?

The first three steps of this example explained how to enable the PerformancePoint service application. To use the PerformancePoint service, you must have an active directory account to use as unattended service account. In the next steps, you learned how to create Business Intelligence Center-based site collection. Note that if you want to create PerformancePoint dashboards and deploy them, you need to have a Business Intelligence site collection. In the next examples, we will go through working with Dashboard Designer.

The Dashboard Designer utility

As you've learned up to now, PerformancePoint is a service application that runs under SharePoint. This service provides an engine to create dashboards from SSAS and SQL Server databases. To create and design dashboards, another utility from SharePoint named Dashboard Designer exists. Dashboard Designer is the other compartment of PerformancePoint and is the development studio for dashboards. In this section, you will learn how to work with Dashboard Designer, and you will learn about its main components.

Time for action – creating your first dashboard with PerformancePoint Dashboard Designer

After creating the BI site collection, it is the time to create dashboards with Dashboard Designer. In this example, we will see how we can open Dashboard Designer, which is the designer tool for PerformancePoint. Then, we will connect to an analysis service cube. After that, we will create a very simple dashboard from measures and dimensions.

For this example, you need to have AdventureWorksDW2012MultiDimensional-EE installed. For a description on how to install this SSAS database, refer to the *Preface* of this book. Perform the following steps to create a dashboard:

1. In the BI site, go to **Site Contents**, which is a link on the left-hand site of the BI site's first page.

2. Select the `PerformancePoint Content` folder and then click on **New Item**.

3. An application will be launched (for the first time, it may take longer). You will then see that Dashboard Designer is open, as shown in the following screenshot:

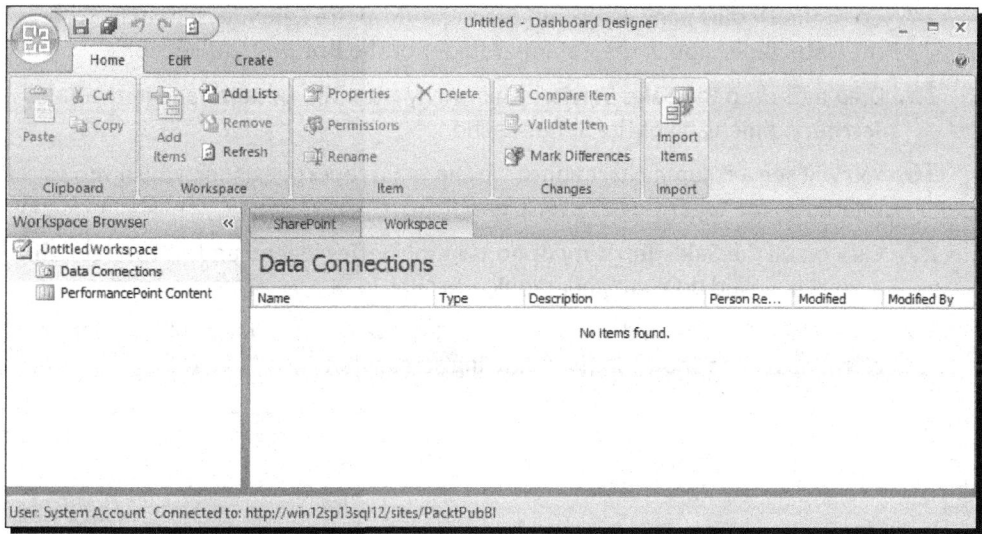

4. Right-click on the **Data Connections** option in the **Workspace Browser** menu and select **Create a New Data Source**.

5. In the **Select a Data Source Template** dialog box, choose **Analysis Services**.

6. The new data source will be created under data connections, and the **Properties** window will be opened in the main pane of Dashboard Designer. Right-click on the data source and rename it to `Sales Summary Cube Connection`.

7. In **Connection Settings Editor** in the main pane, set the server name as `local`, the database name as `AdventureWorksDW2012MultiDimensional-EE`, and **Cube** as `Sales Summary`. Leave the other configurations as default and test the data source.

8. Right-click on **PerformancePoint Content** under **Workspace Browser** and create a new report.

9. In the **Select a Report Template** menu, choose **Analytical Chart**.

10. The **Create an Analytic Chart** dialog box will appear and ask for data source connection; choose **Sales Summary Cube Connection** under the data connections and click on **Finish**.

11. Name the new report `Sales by Territory`.

12. You will see the **Report Designer** option in the main pane. You will also see the list of measures, dimensions, and Named Sets coming from cube in the right-hand side pane of the **Details** pane.

13. In the **Details** pane, under **Measures**, drag-and-drop **Sales Amount** to the report's **Background** section.

14. Go to the **Details** pane again and drag-and-drop the **Calendar** hierarchy under the **Date** dimension in the **Calendar** folder of the **Bottom Axis** section.

15. Drag-and-drop the **Sales Territory** hierarchy from the **Details** pane in the **Sales Territory** dimension of the **Series** section.

16. You will see a column chart appear in the main report designer, which shows the total sales for all territories over a period.

17. Click on all the **Sales Territory** options in the **Series** legend and you will see that a chart is drilled down to geographical groups.

18. Click on **All Periods**, and you will see that the chart will create columns for each calendar year as shown in the following screenshot:

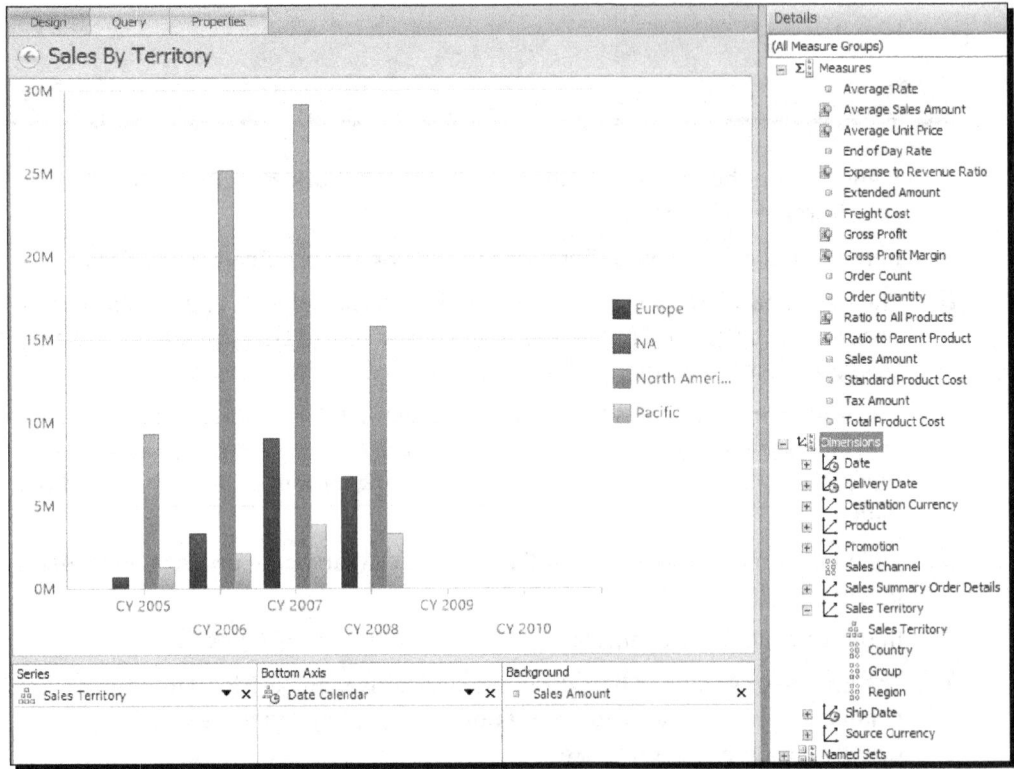

What just happened?

Congratulations! You made your first PerformancePoint dashboard in Dashboard Designer just now. As you saw, it was just as easy as dragging-and-dropping measures and dimensions. Now, let's go through each step and take a closer look at what we did in this example.

Dashboard Designer can be run from the SharePoint website (as you saw in steps 1 to 3). The two main components of a PerformancePoint dashboard are: data sources and PerformancePoint contents. Data sources are connections to Analysis Services, SQL Server databases, Excel files, and/or PerformancePoint contents, which we will discuss in detail in the next sections. They contain charts, grids, dashboard pages, filters, and content related to dashboards.

The first step to creating a dashboard is to create a data source. Data sources in PerformancePoint 2013 are limited to Analysis Services, SQL Server, Excel Services, Import from Excel Workbook, and Share Point List. In this example, we created a connection to Sales Summary Cube in Analysis Services (as shown in the steps 4 to 7). Report is one of the main contents of PerformancePoint, which can visualize data in analytical-chart type (defined in step 9) and grid or other types, which will be discussed later. A report needs a data source to work with (we set a data source for the report in step 10).

The Report designer window is a simple designer that contains data source entities in the **Details** pane on the right-hand side. A report itself is shown in the main pane; this report displays the main components at the bottom (in this case: **Series**, **Bottom Axis**, and **Background**). The default chart type in PerformancePoint is the **Column** chart, which can be changed (we will go through that in the next examples). Steps 12 to 16 showed how simple it is to create a column chart report based on the sales amounts in territories and calendars.

One of the main advantages of PerformancePoint reports is that it is well junctioned with analysis services hierarchies. In this example, in steps 17 and 18, you saw how easy it is to drill down to the first level of each hierarchy with a simple click on the root.

The dashboard pages

In the previous section, you learned about how to create reports in PerformancePoint. In this section, you will learn about dashboard pages. A report or chart is not viewable in SharePoint, since the SharePoint site does not work with web pages. So, you would need to create a web page that contains one or more reports; such web pages are called dashboards in PerformancePoint.

Time for action – creating a dashboard page

In this example, we will create a dashboard page. We will add the report from the previous example to it and then we will deploy the dashboard to the SharePoint site with the help of the following steps:

1. In Dashboard Designer, right-click on **PerformancePoint Content**, and in the left-hand side pane, click on **Create a New Dashboard**.

2. In the **Select a Dashboard Page Template**, choose the first option, which is **1 Zone**, and click on **OK**.

3. Rename the dashboard to `Sales Dashboard`.

4. In the main pane of Dashboard Designer, you will see the name of the web page, which by default is set as **Page 1**; change it to **Sales**.

5. In the right-hand side pane (the **Detail** pane), you will see PerformancePoint's contents, such as **Scorecards**, **Reports**, and **Filters**, listed. Click on **Expand Reports**, expand **PerformancePoint Contents**, and under it you will see the report **Sales by Territory** that was designed in the previous example.

6. Drag-and-drop the **Sales by Territory** report into the **Dashboard Content** pane (this pane is located in the main pane of the bottom section).

7. Right-click on the **Sales Dashboard** option in **Workspace Browser** and choose **Deploy to SharePoint...**, as shown in the following screenshot:

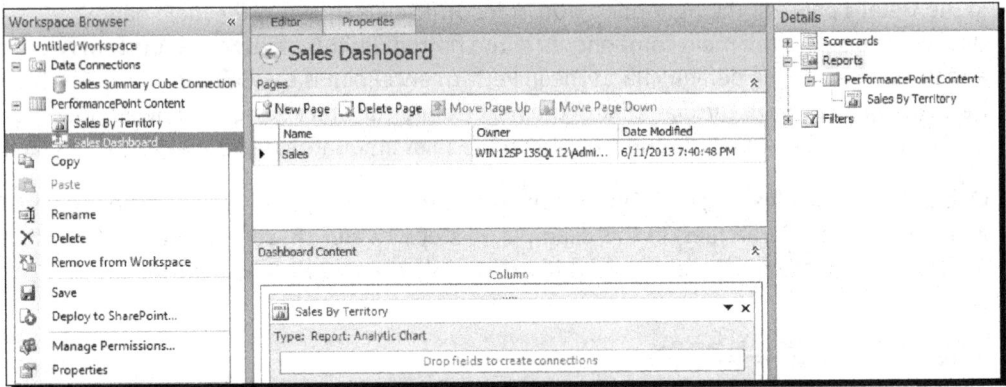

8. In the **Deploy to BI site** dialog box, leave the default configuration as is and deploy it to the `dashboards` folder (as it is by default).

9. A few moments later, you will see the **Dashboard** page deployed to the SharePoint site and showed to you in the browser. The **Dashboard** page contains the **Sales by Territory** report.

10. Now, we want to create a quick link for the **Dashboard** page and copy the URL from the open web browser. The URL is be similar to `http://win12sp13sql12/sites/PacktPubBI/Dashboards/Sales Dashboard/Sale.aspx`.

11. In the left-hand side of the SharePoint page, under the SharePoint icon, you will see an edit icon with the text **EDIT LINKS** beside it. Click on that.

12. Click on the **Add link** button. The **Add a Link** window will be opened. Enter `Sales`, and in the address box, paste the address that you've copied from the web page previously.

13. Save the link.

14. Now, you will see the **Sales** link in the left-hand side of your BI website. This link will be durable through most of the pages in this website; it provides easy and quick access to the **Dashboard** page, as shown in the following screenshot:

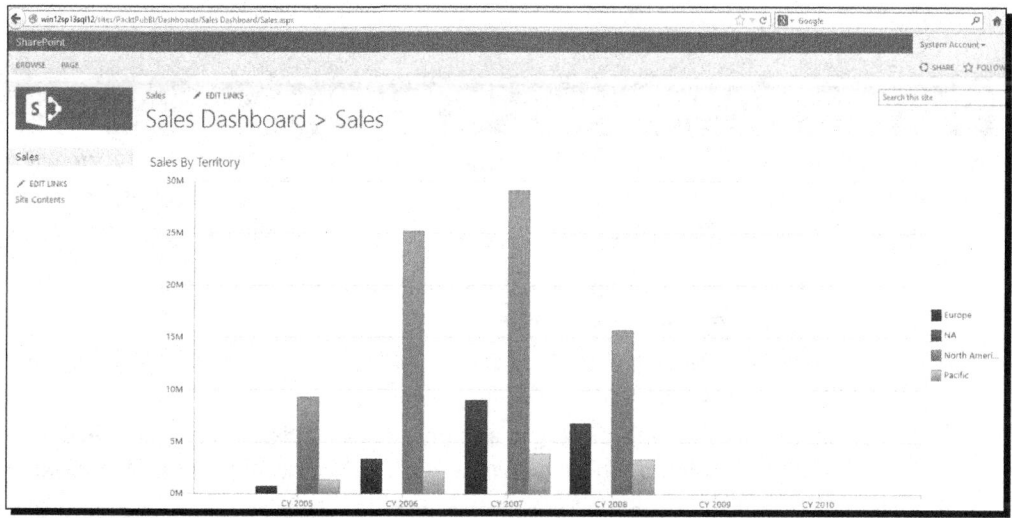

What just happened?

In this section, you learned how to create a dashboard page (steps 1 to 4). Each dashboard can contain one or more pages. The dashboard that we created in this example had just one page. However, you can add more pages to it. Each page contains one or more zones. Zones are containers of PerformancePoint contents. In other words, each dashboard page can contain one or more types of PerformancePoint content (such as report, filter, and scorecard). You can choose the **PAGE** template at the time of creating the dashboard (step 2), or you can change zones in the dashboard content pane after creating the page, by right-clicking on the empty area outside the zone and adding new zones (we will go through a sample of this in the next sections).

You can add reports or other types of PerformancePoint content to each zone with a simple drag-and-drop action from the **Details** pane into the zone (step 6). Step 7 shows how to deploy the dashboard page to the BI website collection. After deployment, the dashboard page will be shown as a page in the SharePoint site (step 9). You also learned how to create a quick navigation link in the SharePoint site to the dashboard page (steps 10 to 14).

PPS dashboard's on-the-fly features

One of the main advantages of **PerformancePoint Services dashboards** (**PPS dashboards**) is on-the-fly features such as filtering, sorting, changing chart layout, drilling down to dimension attributes, drilling up, and adding or modifying measures in the report. On-the-fly features are options that can be changed when a report is running in the web page. As you saw in the previous chapter, SSRS is a very powerful reporting tool. However, to have on-the-fly features such as drilling down/up, you would need to spend some time to develop them in the report. Fortunately, PerformancePoint dashboards and reports are very flexible in terms of on-the-fly features.

Time for action – exploring on-the-fly features

In this example, we will explore on-the-fly features of PerformancePoint reports. We will go through features such as sorting, filtering, drilling down/up, changing measures, and report type with the help of the following steps:

1. Go to the **Sales** dashboard page that we created in the previous example. Open the page in an Internet browser.

2. In the right-hand legend, you will see some geographical groups listed. From that list, click on the **Europe** option.

3. You will see that the report changes and only Europe's data is being displayed. The legend will show countries such as **France**, **Germany**, and **United Kingdom**.

4. Now, right-click on the legend of countries and from pop-up menu, choose **Drill Up**.

5. Now, you will see two calendar years (2009 and 2010) without data in the calendar axis.

6. Right-click on one of the items in the calendar axis, and from the pop-up menu, click on **Filter**, and then choose **Filter Empty Axis Items**, as shown in the following screenshot:

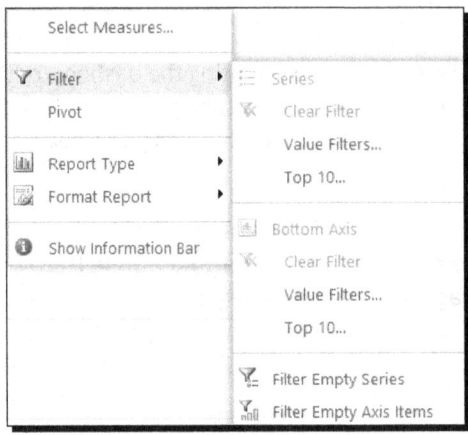

7. You will see that the years 2009 and 2010 have been removed from the chart because they had no data rows.

8. Now, right-click again on the **Sales Territory** legend in the right-hand side, and select **Drill Up**. You will then see the sales for the all **Sales Territory** options.

9. Right-click on all the **Sales Territory** legends. Under **Drill Down To**, select the **Product** option and choose **Product Category**.

10. You will see that instead of sales territory categorization, the chart is now categorized based on the product's category.

11. Right-click on the bland area of the chart and change the **Report Type** option to **Line Chart with Marker**. You will see how easy it is to change the report type on the fly. Take a look at the following screenshot, which shows this step:

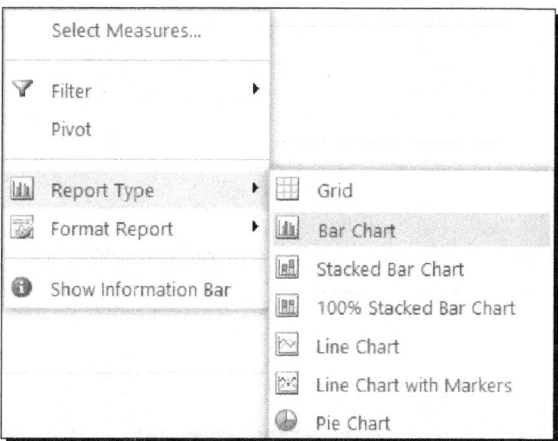

12. Right-click on the chart again and click on **Select Measures**. In the **Select Measures** dialog box, add **Standard Product Cost**. You will see that you can add/modify measures simply in this way.

13. Now, right-click on the **Product Category** legend and drill up to all product categories. Then, right-click again on **Product Category** and drill down to **Sales Territory** and then to **Country**.

14. Then, right-click on **CY 2007** in the calendar axis and drill down to the **Product** option and then again to product. You will see that the x axis will show a large number of products, which is not very effective for visualization in the dashboard.

15. Then, right-click on the x axis, and under **Filter**, choose **Top 10**. In the **Filter** dialog box, accept all defaults. Now, you will see that only the top 10 products that have the highest sales amounts will be displayed.

16. Now, click on the small rectangle icon in the right-hand side of the report, and from the pop-up menu, choose **Reset View**. You will see that the report view resets to the view after publishing.

17. Then, right-click on **Chart** and change the report type to **Grid**.

18. Select **Reset View** again. Then, right-click on one of the columns and choose **Decomposition Tree**.

19. You will see that the **Decomposition Tree: Sales Amount** window will show a hierarchical view of information when you click on each node. You can then drill down to another dimension attribute and follow the hierarchy. The **Decomposition Tree: Sales Amount** window is shown in the following screenshot:

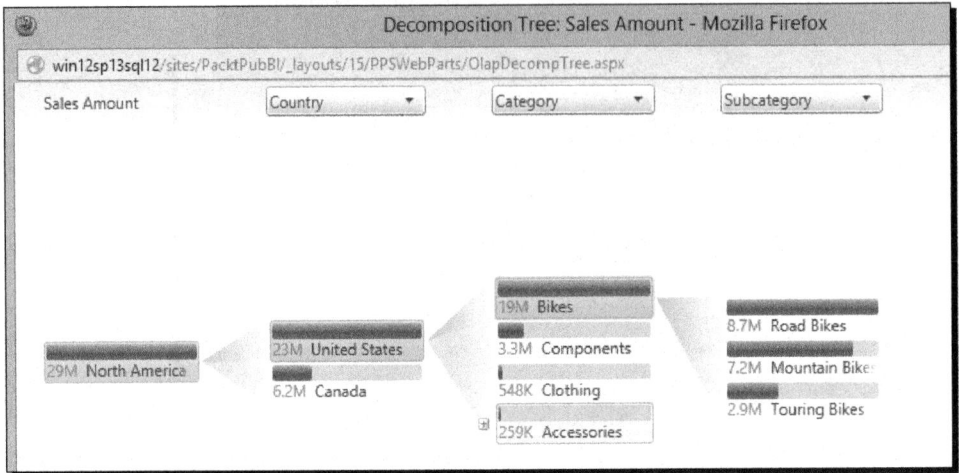

What just happened?

This example revealed the level of flexibility for a user working with PerformancePoint dashboards on the fly. You can check the following options one by one:

- Drilling down and drilling up in a hierarchy (steps 2 to 4)
- Filtering empty values (steps 5 to 7)
- Drilling down to other dimension attributes (steps 9 and 10)
- Changing the report type (step 11)
- Adding/removing measures (step 12)
- Filtering the top 10 items (step 15)
- Resetting the view to its default predefined state (step 16)
- Decomposition Tree (step 19)

As you've seen, it is the high level of dynamism and flexibility that makes the PerformancePoint an outstanding dashboard tool for a user. The Decomposition Tree is specific data visualization based on Microsoft Silverlight, which is only available in PerformancePoint and provides the ability to drill down to related dimension attributes through a tree structure.

Filters

PerformancePoint reports can be empowered with filters. There are different types of filters. For example, a filter can be a list of members in a dimension attribute, or the result of an MDX query can be used as a filter. A SQL Server table or view are also other candidates for filters. Filters will be developed separately from the report, but they can be connected to the report in a dashboard page. Each filter may connect to one or more reports and each report may have one or more filters associated with it.

Time for action – working with filters

In this example, we will create a filter for the product category hierarchy. For this filter, we will use the product category hierarchy in the cube, and then we will associate this filter with the sales category of the territory report. Let's see how to do it by performing the following steps:

1. Go to Dashboard Designer, right-click on the **PerformancePoint Content** in **Workspace Browser,** and add a new filter by clicking on **New Filter**.

2. In the **Select a Filter Template** dialog box, choose **Member Selection**, as shown in the following screenshot:

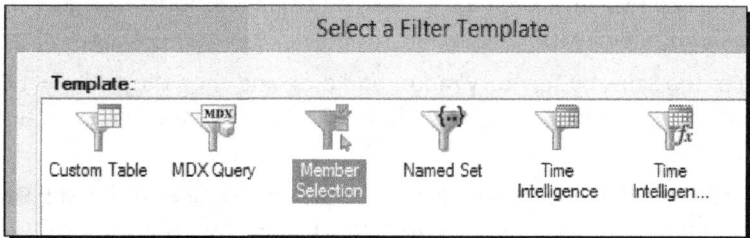

3. Now, the **Create a Filter** wizard will be opened. In the first step, assign **Sales Summary Cube Connection** as the data source and continue.

4. In the **Select Members** window, click on **Select Dimension**.

5. In the **Select Dimension** dialog box, expand the **Product** dimension and choose the **Categories** hierarchy.

6. Click on the **Select Members** button, and in the **Select Members** dialog box, check the default member. Then, right-click on **All Products**, and from the pop-up menu choose **Autoselect Members**, and then click on **Select All Descendants**.

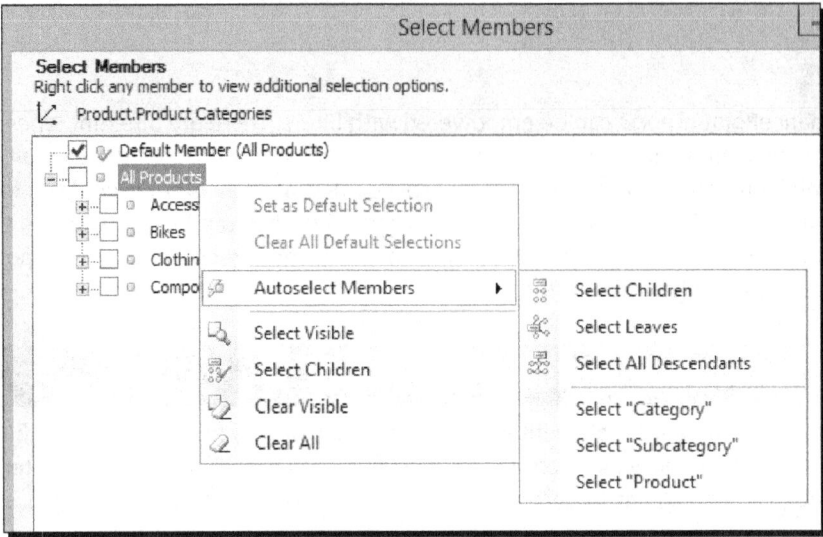

7. Leave the other settings as they are and go to the next step.

8. In the **Select Display Method** menu, choose the third option (**Multi-Select Tree**) and finish the wizard; name the filter **Product Categories Filter**.

9. As the **Sales by Territory** report does not contain **Product Category** hierarchy, we should change it.

10. Go to the **Sales by Territory** report and drag-and-drop the a **Product Categories** hierarchy from the **Detail** pane into the **Background** section of the report. Then, save the report.

11. Go to **Sales Dashboard** and right-click outside the zone area of the **Dashboard Content** option. From the pop-up menu, choose **Add Above**.

12. You will see that a new zone is added on the top of the previous zone.

13. In the **Details** pane, expand **Filters**, and under **PerformancePoint Content**, drag-and-drop **Product Categories Filter** into the new zone.

14. Now, drag-and-drop **Member Unique Name** from the filter in top zone to the report in the lower zone, and in the **Connection** dialog box, connect **Product Categories** to it (as shown in the following screenshot):

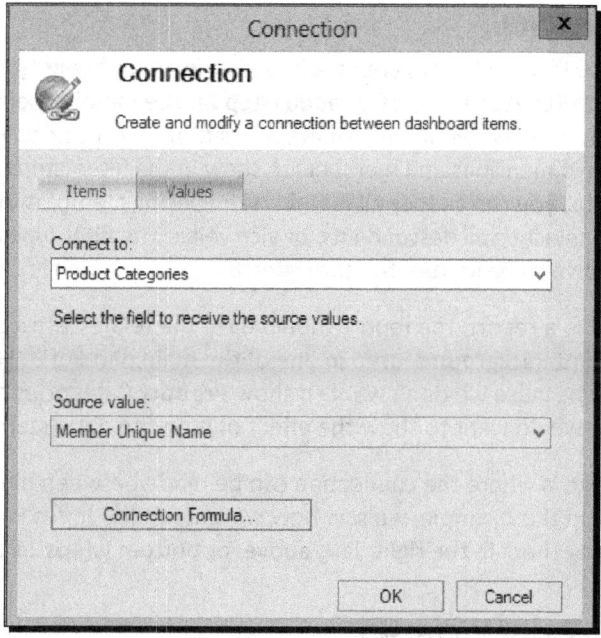

15. Save the dashboard and deploy it to SharePoint.

16. Check the dashboard page after the deployment. You can simply click on the filter and choose **Bikes**, and you will see the effect on the report data after that, as shown in the following diagram:

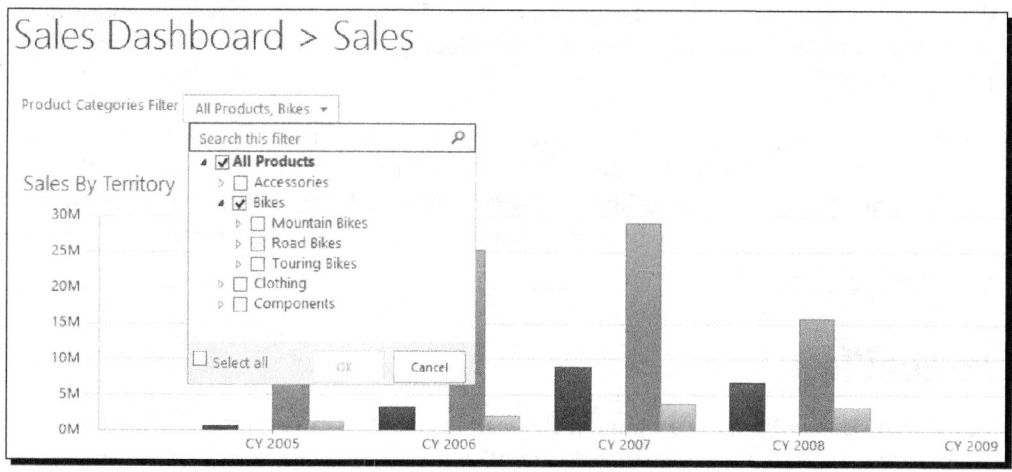

What just happened?

In this example, you learned how to create a filter. There are different types of filters; you choose the type of filter at the time of creation (step 2). The member selection type is good for filters that want to show the number of members from the specific dimension attribute. Then, we chose the dimensions and members to show in the filter (steps 4 to 6). In the **Select Members** dialog box, you can choose all members or specific members by checking them, selecting children, selecting all descendants, or vice versa. The filter type can be single select or multiselect; it can also be in tree structure (step 8).

To connect a filter to a report, the report should have the related attributes, which are **Series**, **Columns**, and **Background**, used in one of the main parts of it. For this example, we used **Background**, because we don't want to show **Product Categories** as a column or data series visually, but we do want to show the effect of it on the data (steps 9 and 10).

The dashboard page is where the connection can be made between filter and report (steps 13 and 14). In this example, we saw how we can modify zones in the dashboard page by adding/removing them in the right, left, above, or bottom (steps 11 and 12) positions.

PerformancePoint Wrap Up

PerformancePoint is a dashboard tool that comes as a service in SharePoint server. The development tool for this service is called PerformancePoint Dashboard Designer. In the dashboard designer, the first step is to create data source connections to databases. Then, **Reports**, **KPIs**, and **Scorecards** can be created based on the data structure in the data source. **Reports** and **Scorecards** can then be added to a web page under the BI site, named dashboard page. Each dashboard may also contain filters and relate filters to reports and scorecards. The dashboard page, finally, can be deployed to SharePoint, and a web link can be created for that.

High levels of on-the-fly flexibility for PerformancePoint dashboards is one of the unique features that make this a great dashboard tool. The other important factor is that the design and implementation time for dashboards with Dashboard Designer is very low because of its simplicity. In the second part of this chapter, we will go through another reporting/dashboard tool called Power View.

Power View

Power View is a dashboard component that can be installed on either Excel 2013 or SharePoint 2010 and higher versions. Power View provides powerful tools with an easy development interface for BI systems. Power View currently works with both the Tabular and Multidimensional models of SSAS.

For the examples in this chapter, we use the SSAS Tabular sample model of Microsoft, named AdventureWorks Tabular Model SQL 2012.

 For instructions on how to install this sample database, read the preface.

In this book, we will only use Power View for Excel 2013 for our examples. This means that you should have Excel 2013 installed on your machine to get the samples of this chapter working.

Time for action – enabling Power View in Excel

Before we start working with Power View, we will go through the simple steps of enabling the Power View add-in for Excel:

1. Open an empty Excel workbook.
2. Go to the **File** menu, then **Option**, and finally to **Add-Ins**.
3. In the **Manage** drop-down list at the bottom of the main pane, select **COM Add-ins**, and then click on **Go**.
4. In the dialog box that appears, select the **Power View** option and click on **OK**.

What Just Happened?

Here is a screenshot that demonstrates adding the add-ins:

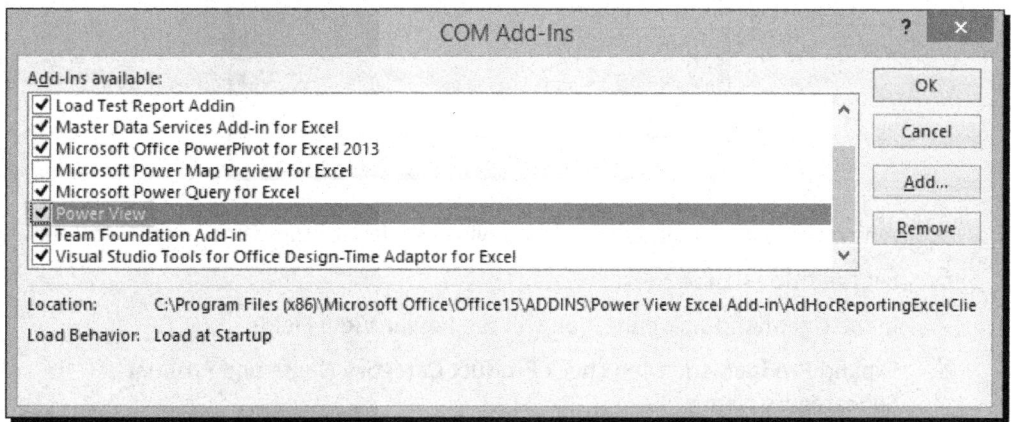

Time for action – creating the first Power View dashboard

In this example, you will face Power View for the first time. You will also learn how to connect to the SSAS Tabular model through Excel, and then use it as a source for Power View data visualization, as explained in the following steps:

1. Open an empty Excel workbook, go to the **Data** tab, and under the **Get External Data** menu section, click on **From Other Sources**, and then choose **From Analysis Services**.

2. The **Data Connection Wizard** will appear in the first step. Enter the server name (such as `local\Tabular`) and click on **Next**.

3. In the **Select Database and Table** tab, choose **AdventureWorks Tabular Model SQL 2012**, and then choose the **Model** cube from the main section.

4. Exit the wizard by clicking on **Finish**. The **Import Data** dialog box will appear. Choose **Power View Report** and click on OK to continue, as shown in the following screenshot:

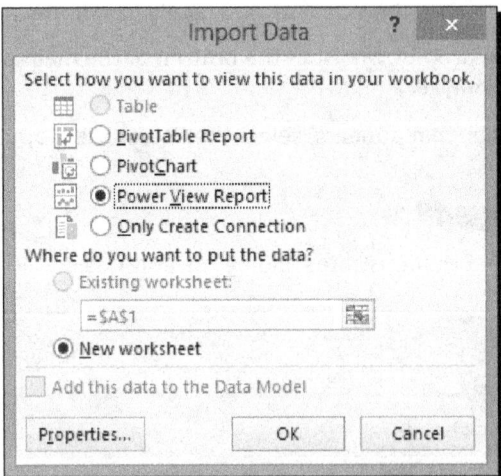

5. A new sheet will be opened and you will see a Power View designer environment.

6. Set the title as `Internet Sales`.

7. In the right-hand side pane, you will see **Power View Fields**.

8. Expand **Product**, and then check **Product Category Name** and **Product Subcategory Name**.

9. Then, expand **Internet Sales** and check **Gross Profit**.

10. You will see that a grid has materialized in the main pane; maximize the grid using mouse pointer on the edge lines of it. Now, you will see that the grid shows a list of product categories and subcategories with their equivalent gross profit.

11. In the **Switch Visualization** menu bar section, choose **Stacked Bar** from **Bar Chart**.

12. You will see that a chart appears instead of grids, with bars and colors. Now, you can also see the **Chart Options** pane in the right-hand side, under **Power View Fields**.

13. Drag-and-drop **Product Category Name** (under the **Product** dimension) from **Power View Fields** into the chart options pane's **Tile By** section, and change the **Axis to Product Subcategory Name** option. Set **Legend** to **Product Category Name** (with a drag-and-drop action).

14. You will see that a bar chart will be modified with a tiled header. Each tile shows a product category name. On selecting each tile, product subcategories related to that category will be listed in a bar chart, as shown in the following screenshot:

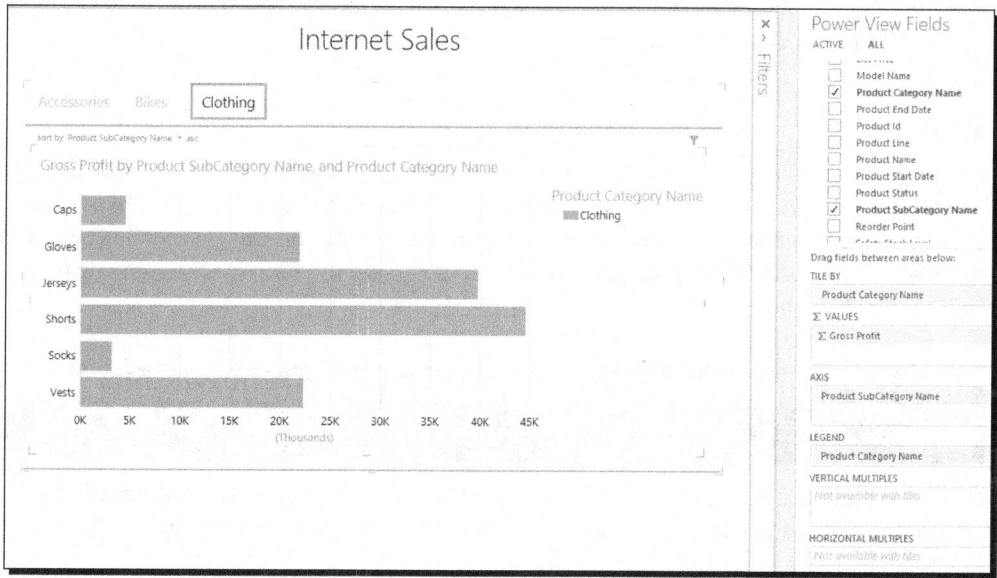

What just happened?

In this example, you created your first dashboard using Power View. The example shows how easy it is to create dashboards for a tabular model by just dragging-and-dropping and changing few configurations. Also, you saw that Power View charts could be made a little bit different using tiles, which is very helpful for data visualization.

In the first three steps (steps 1 to 3), we created a connection to a tabular model. Then, we opened the Power View designer for that data connection (steps 4 and 5). The main parts of the Power View designer as explained are: the main pane or **Report** pane, **Power View Fields** pane, **Chart** pane, **Filter** pane, and menu bar options. In this example, we only dealt with the **Report** pane, **Power View Fields**, **Chart** pane, and menu bar options.

The **Power View Fields** pane lists all attributes and measures in the underlying tabular model, categorized with dimensions and measure groups. To create a report, grid, or chart, you need to check those attributes or measures from the **Power View Fields** pane (steps 8 and 9). Then, you see a grid report in the **Report** pane. The grid view is the default data visualization view in Power View, but you can change it by simply using the **Switch Visualization** menu bar items (step 11).

Each chart, grid, or data visualization item has its own configuration, which will appear under the **Power View Fields** pane. This is the pane that we refer to as the **Chart** pane. Here, you can change chart configurations such as **Axis**, **Legend**, and **Tile** options (steps 12 and 13).

In the next examples of this chapter, we will go through other kinds of data visualization items, features, and also filter configurations. We will also take a look at two specific data visualization items of Power View: **Map** and **Scatter Chart**.

Map

Power View uses Bing maps to create data visualization based on geographical data. This type of visualization is very useful when you have geographical information such as region, country, state, and city name, and you want to show information of the measures sliced-and-diced by these attributes. Using Bing maps provides the ability to get the Bing map search engine and spot the right location.

Time for action – geographical data visualization using Power View

In this example, we will create data visualization based on sales territory information such as country, state, and city, and we will reveal the potentials of the Map visualization item in Power View. To do this, refer to the following steps:

1. Open another **Power View** tab, using the first three steps of the previous example.

2. In the **Power View** tab, replace the title of **Internet Sales** with **Geographical Info**.

3. From the **Power View Fields** pane under **Geography**, check **City**. Under **Internet Sales**, check **Sales Amount**.

4. Click on the grid generated in the report pane. Under the **Switch Visualization** menu bar section, click on **Map**.

5. A map will appear instead of a grid; hover on the right-top-hand side section of the map and click on the small pop-out icon to maximize the map.

6. You will see that the sales amount, according to cities, appears on the Bing map view of the world. The sizes of the circles represent the sales amount in each city.

7. Under the **Product Category** dimension in the **Power View Fields** pane, drag-and-drop **Product Category Name** to the **Colour** section of the **Map** options (below the **Power View Fields** pane).

8. You will see that the **Product Category** legend appears and circles are painted with each product category's color. For example, you will notice that **Bikes** (red color) are sold in many countries, but **Accessories** and **Clothes** (blue and orange color, respectively) are mainly sold in the United States.

9. Since the city itself is not enough to spot the exact location in the map (there might be cities with the same name in different states), we would need to add additional geographical information. Under the **Geography** dimension, drag-and-drop **State Province Code** into the **Map** option's pane, in the **Locations** section at the top of **City**.

10. You will see that the map has changed a little and the number of circles have reduced. This is because of the fact that a map visualizes a circle for each state and when you double-click on each state, it will visualize that state only with a circle for each city.

11. Under the **Geography** dimension, drag-and-drop **Country Region Name** in the **Map** options pane's **Tile By** section. The following screenshot shows what the **Chart** option pane looks like:

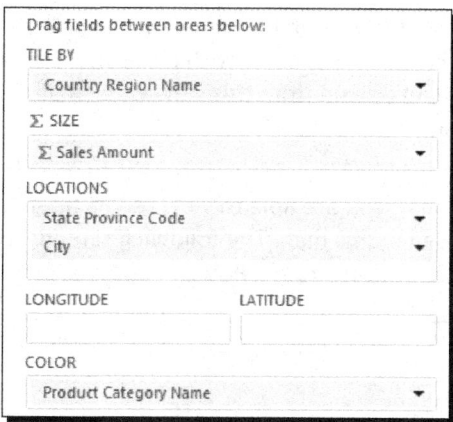

12. Now, you are able to view a tiled map visualization, in which each tile shows a country. When you click on each country, you are able to view states of that country and the sales amount categorized by product category.

13. Go to the United States by clicking on the **Tile** title. Then, click on **Bikes** in the legend; you will see that **Bikes** is highlighted. To go back to the original visualization, just click outside the legend area.

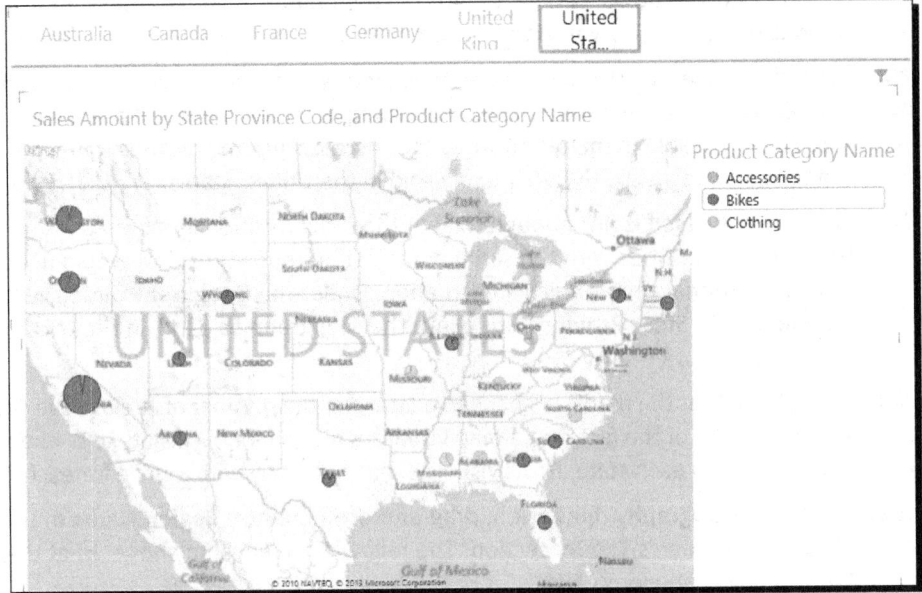

14. Double-click on California's circle. You will see that the map drills down to the state of California and shows cities with circle sizes based on the sales amount in each city. You can drill up from this view with small the **Drill Up** button in the top-right-hand side of the report.

15. There is also a small filter icon in the top-right-hand side of the report. When you click on it, you are able to view report filters based on the attributes and measures used in this map. The following screenshot shows how to access **Drill Up** and **Filter** buttons from a **Power View** chart:

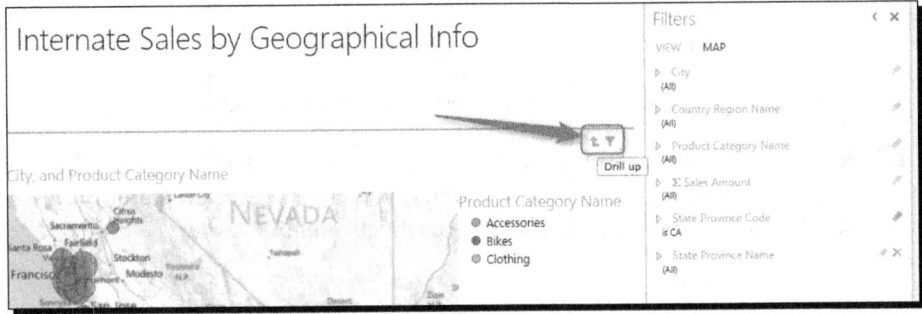

What just happened?

The power of **Map** in **Power View** illustrated in this example. You saw how easy it is to configure a a map is based on geographical data fields. You also saw how maps are helpful for data visualization. They show geographical information based on spots in the Bing map and circle sizes based on the measure (in this example, **Sales Amount**); the categorization can also be applied with coloring based on another attribute (in this example, **Product Category**). The ability to drill down, drill up, and filter provides a good set of utilities to empower this visualization.

Maps can visualize geographical information based on latitude and longitude, or country, state, city, and address that is searchable with the Bing map search engine. Here, you saw an example of using city and states to spot the location in a map.

In this example, you also learned how to use the highlighting feature in the **Power View** reports (step 13). This is a very useful feature to visualize specific categories of items. You can also have multiple charts and grids in each Power View report item. If you highlight an attribute member in one of the charts, you will see that other charts will also be highlighted based on the selected member.

Filtering information is another useful feature of Power View. In steps 14 and 15, you saw how to drill down into cities from states, and then drill up. You also learned how to view the chart filter pane. The **Chart** filter pane is a way of filtering information for only the selected chart. If you want to apply a filter on a set of charts, you should consider creating a report filter.

Scatter chart

There is a big difference between the scatter chart in Power View and other data visualization tools that you've seen. The scatter chart in Power View has the ability to show information based on the ongoing timeframe. In the other words, you can see changes in a measure based on attributes as time passes in years, months, and days. This kind of data visualization will create an animation style chart that provides very useful information based on time. To create such a visualization with other tools, you might need to use a combination of charts and filters together; but here, all these will be created in the scatter chart of Power View.

Time for action – visualizing time-based information with a scatter chart

To use a scatter chart, need require to use more than one measure. In this example, we will use **Order Quantity**, **Product Cost**, and **Gross Profit** all together, to show in the scatter chart. We will also categorize data based on geographical group. Finally, we will add the time factor to see how these factors work against each other over different periods of time.

Let's see how to do it through the following steps:

1. Open a new Power View report.
2. In the **Power View Fields**, under **Sales Territory**, check **Sales Territory Group**.
3. Under **Internet Sales**, choose **Order Quantity**.
4. Under the switch visualization menu section, click on **Other Charts**, and then choose **Scatter**.
5. Maximize the scatter chart, check the **Chart** options pane, and ensure that **Order Quantity** are present in **X Value**, and **Sales Territory Group** in the **Details** section.
6. Now, drag-and-drop **Total Product Cost** from **Power View Fields** into the **Chart** option pane on the **Y Value**.
7. You will see different bobbles in the chart; each bobble visualizes a geographical group and shows the sum or order quantity and sum of total product costs in that group.
8. Now, we can visualize another measure with the size of bobbles. Drag-and-drop **Gross Profit** from **Power View Fields** into the **Size** area of the **Chart** option.
9. You will see that the bobble's size changes, which shows the gross profit, as shown in the following screenshot:

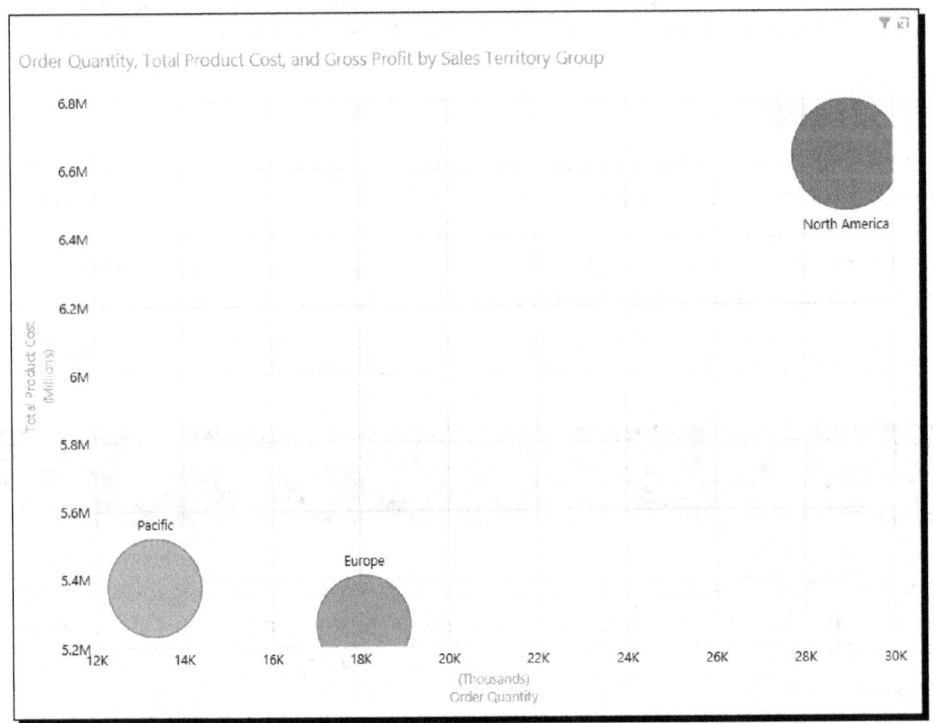

10. Now is a good time to add the time factor to this chart. From **Power View Fields**, under **Internet Sales**, drag-and-drop **Order Date** onto **Play Axis** in the **Chart** option.

11. Verify that the chart option configuration is similar to the following screenshot:

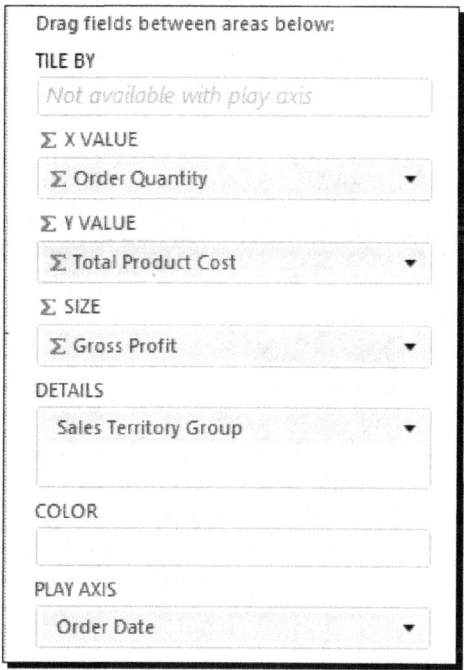

12. You will see a date bar under the scatter chart, which shows the time period from the first order date to the latest. There is also a play button near it.

13. Click on the play button. You will see the changes in all the measures for each geographical group in an animation mode.

14. After completing the animation, you can click on any of the bobbles to highlight changes of that geographical group. For example, the next screenshot shows changes of order quantity, product cost, and gross profit for Pacific by the time.

15. If you hover your mouse over the view of any of the bobbles, as shown in the following screenshot, you will see details of that spot, which is the junction of all factors:

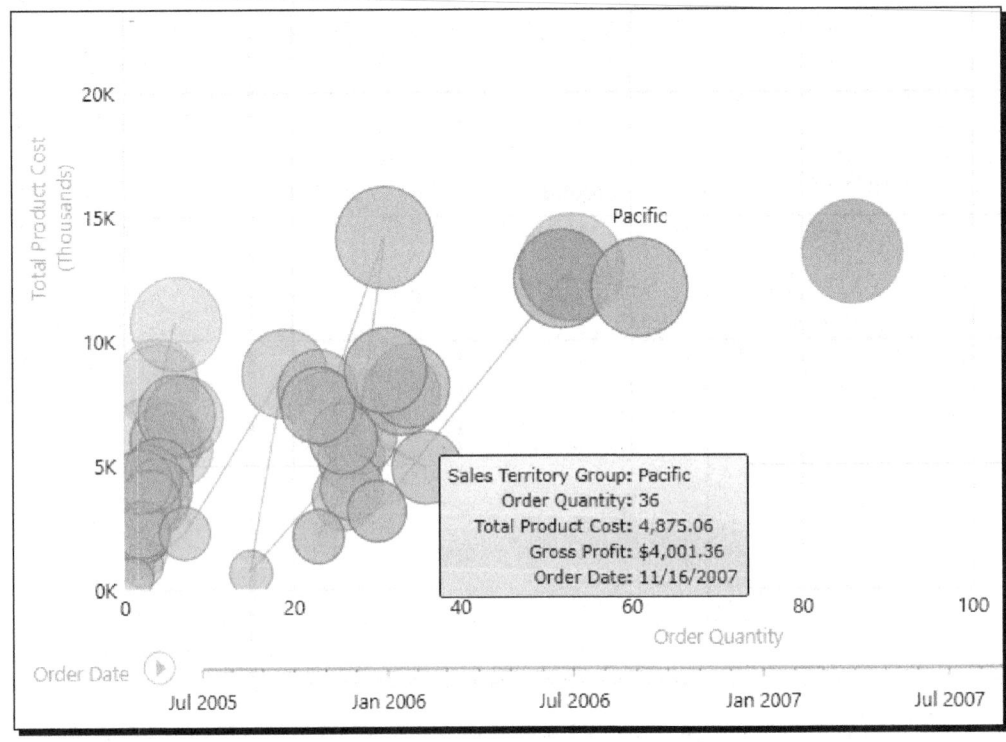

What just happened?

In this example, you saw how powerful and useful the scatter chart in Power View is. The example also showed how you can visualize more than one measure, order quantity, and product cost in different axes. The order quantity was shown in the *x* axis and the product cost was shown in the *y* axis. Data was categorized with different bobbles based on the sales territory group. The size of bobbles shows another measure, which is the gross profit. The scatter chart, till this step, is similar to the scatter chart of many other visualization tools.

By adding the play axis, we added the visualization for another factor, which is **Order Date**. The play axis provides a useful way of showing data with changes to the attribute provided. In this example, the play button shows how other measures change by **Order Date**.

Filtering data

Power View, like many other reporting and dashboard tools, can use the benefits of filtering data. There are two ways of filtering data in Power View: the **Report Filter** and **Chart Filter**. The **Chart Filter** can be simply reached at by clicking on the far-right-top edge of each chart on the filter icon. This will show all the attributes and measures that participated in that chart in the filtering pane, and then each of these measures and attribute values can be changed with different filtering options. **Chart Filter** can be applied only on specific charts; this means that if you have more than one chart in a single Power View report, you might need to apply the same criteria on all chart filters that you want to affect by changes. Here, **Report Filter** comes into play; report filters will be applied on all charts in the Power View report.

Time for action – using Filter in Power View

In this example, you will learn how to create report filters and use them to apply the same criteria on multiple charts, using the following steps:

1. Open a new Power View report, copy and paste the map from your previous samples into this report, and also do the same for the **Bar Chart** from the first example of this chapter.

2. Now, you have a Power View report with two visualization items: **Map** and **Bar Chart**.

3. From the **Power View Fields** menu, under the **Sales Territory Group**, drag-and-drop **Sales Territory Country** into the **Filter** pane.

4. You will see a list of countries in the **Filter** pane. If you choose a country, for example France, you will see only information for that country in the map and bar chart, as shown in the following screenshot:

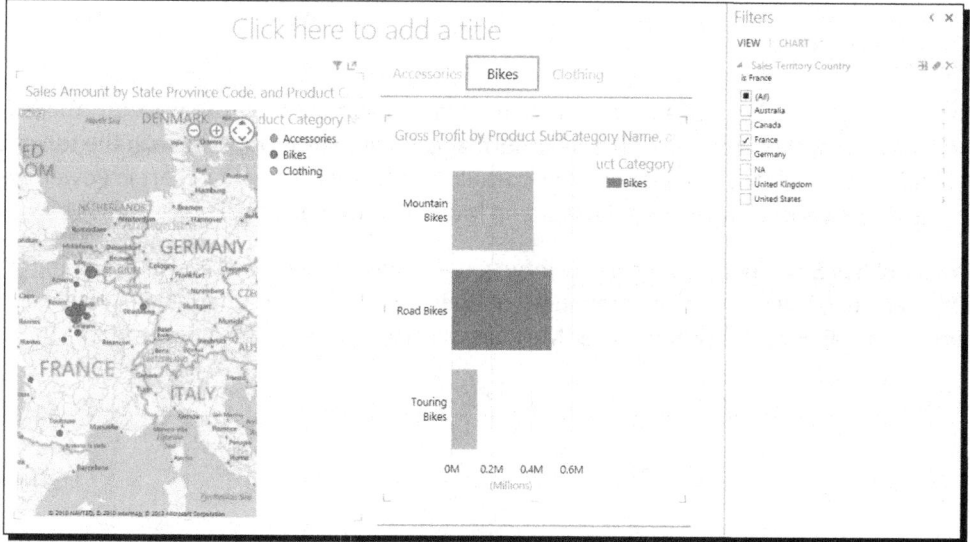

5. Also, you can highlight a specific part of data in any of the charts (for example, Road Bikes in the bar chart), and you will see that the other chart also highlights information for that category. Check the preceding screenshot that shows France's data highlighted for **Road Bikes**.

6. Filters in Power View can be accessed in multiple ways. If you see the **Sales Territory Country** filter in the preceding screenshot, you will see three icons in the top-right-hand side of it; the first icon is **Advanced Filter Mode**. After selecting this icon, you will see other ways of filtering information, which differ based on the data type of attribute in the filter. For example, for string data type, it can be a search filter that has the options **contains** and **starts with**. For date and data types, it can be a range of the start and end period.

Wrapping up Power View

You've learned about another data visualization tool, named Power View, which comes as part of Office 2013 and SharePoint 2010. Power View was first released as a dashboard tool for the SSAS Tabular and PowerPivot Tabular models. However, the current version of it is capable of working with SSAS Multidimensional as well. You learned in this chapter how easy it is to create dashboards with Power View; you also learned about Power View report features, such as highlighting and inter-relationship between charts.

Map is one of the most powerful features of Power View, since it works with Bing maps with geographical information, and is also capable of showing measures and attributes with size and color in bobbles. The other powerful chart in Power View, which makes it as a kind of specific frontend BI tool, is the scatter chart. Scatter charts in Power View, empowered with the play axis, provide the ability to view changes in other measures and attributes by time.

Summary

In this chapter, you learned about a couple of data visualization tools of Microsoft. You learned how to build dashboards and charts in PerformancePoint (which works best on the top of SSAS Multidimensional). You also learned how to build charts, such as scatter chart in Power View. Power View works with both the Tabular and Multidimensional model types of BISM.

Power BI has 5 components; Power Query, Power Pivot, Power View, Power Map, and Power Q&A. Power View is the main component of Power BI. In the next chapter, you will learn more about Power Query and Power Map as two main components of Power BI.

11
Power BI

With a rising number of cloud and on-premises databases on one hand and a high demand for self-service BI on the other hand, Microsoft has come up with a new product named Power BI. Power BI is a self-service BI solution for on-premises databases and cloud data. It is a part of the Office 365 product.

In this chapter, we will go through two main components of Power BI: Power Query and Power Map. Power Query is a self-service ETL tool, and Power Map is a 3D data visualization tool designed especially for geospatial information. Microsoft Power BI includes PowerPivot and Power View as well. PowerPivot is a tabular modeling engine that works like SSAS Tabular, but in an Excel environment. Power View is a data visualization tool, which we discussed in the previous chapter.

Self-service ETL with Power Query

Power Query is a self-service ETL tool for Excel 2013 and Office 365. This tool was previously named Data Explorer. It supports many data sources such as SQL Server, ODBC connections, and most web sources. It has unique features such as fetching data from online searches. There are some data transformation features embedded in this tool that makes ETL very easy to use.

Power Query is not as strong as SSIS; rather, it can be considered as a lighter version of SSIS. Data transformations using this tool are not that mature compared to some SSIS transformations, such as a slowly changing dimension and an OLE DB command. However, it is highly useful for integrating data from sources such as files, database tables, and online data; applying merge or append; creating new columns; or splitting with some other transformations to make the data ready for self-service data analysis.

The result of the data built by Power Query can be used in PowerPivot modeling or directly imported into the Power View or Power Map visualization tools. In this section, we will start working with Power Query and perform data transformation. In the next section of this book, we will take a brief look at Power Map.

To use the samples of this book, you will first need to install Excel 2013 and then download the Power Query Excel Add-in from `http://www.microsoft.com/en-nz/download/details.aspx?id=39379` and install it.

Time for action – self-service ETL with Power Query

In this example, we will retrieve smartphone data from the Web and perform some transformations on it, such as combining, unpivoting, splitting, and adding extra columns by performing the following steps. We will also append data from two different sources:

1. Open a new blank Excel spreadsheet and go to the **POWER QUERY** tab.

 If you cannot find the **POWER QUERY** tab, download and install the Power Query add-in for Excel 2013 from `http://www.microsoft.com/en-nz/download/details.aspx?id=39379`.

2. In the **POWER QUERY** tab, click on the first icon from the left, named **Online Search**, as shown in the following screenshot. This option is a part of getting data from external sources. Also, with **Online Search**, you can extract data from online sources based on the result of a web search.

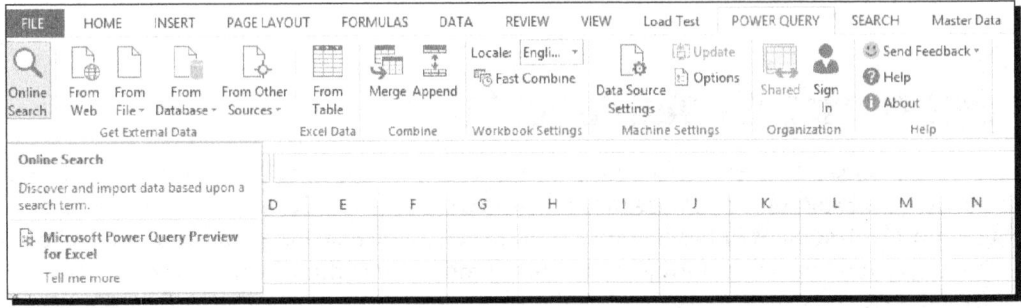

3. You will be redirected to a new tab named **SEARCH**, and in the right-hand pane, you will see a search pane. In the search box, type `smartphones 2013` and press *Enter*. You will see search results displayed under the search box. When you browse any of the items in the search results pane, you will see a preview of the existing data; sometimes, the existing data can even be fetched out as a table.

4. Hover on the **2013 – Hardware and OS – Comparison of smartphones** link, as shown in the following screenshot. You will see a table listing the hardware specifications and the OS of smartphones.

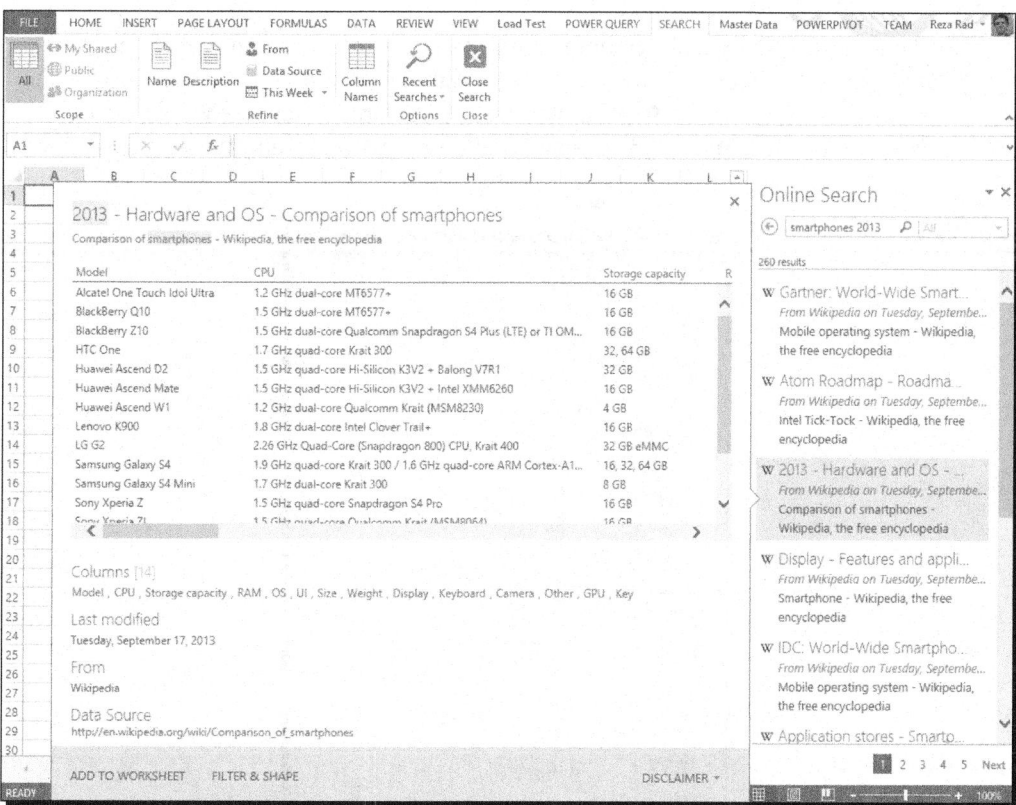

5. As you can see in the previous screenshot, the preview pane shows the same records of the data, a preview of the extraction, a list of columns (when you select a column in **Columns**, that column will be highlighted), and the source information (such as Wikipedia, the last modified date, and a link to the source page). Click on the **ADD TO WORKSHEET** button at the bottom left of the preview pane. After a few seconds (depends on the connection speed of the Internet), data rows will be imported into the spreadsheet.

6. When the data table is imported into the spreadsheet, you can see data columns such as **OS** and the ones for hardware specification. We want to apply transformation on this dataset. So, on the right-hand side pane (which is the query setting pane), click on the **Filter and Shape** button.

The **Query Editor** window will open. In this window, you will see a data table with columns and data rows. If you look at the **Weight** column, you will see that this column is a text column and has a **g** character, which represents grams. We want to change the type of this column to numeric and remove the **g** character.

7. Right-click on the **Weight** column. You will see the menu option that allows you to change the column with some transformations, as shown in the following screenshot. Click on the **Replace Values...** option. In the **Replace Values** dialog box, set **Value** to **find as g** and leave the **Replace with** box empty.

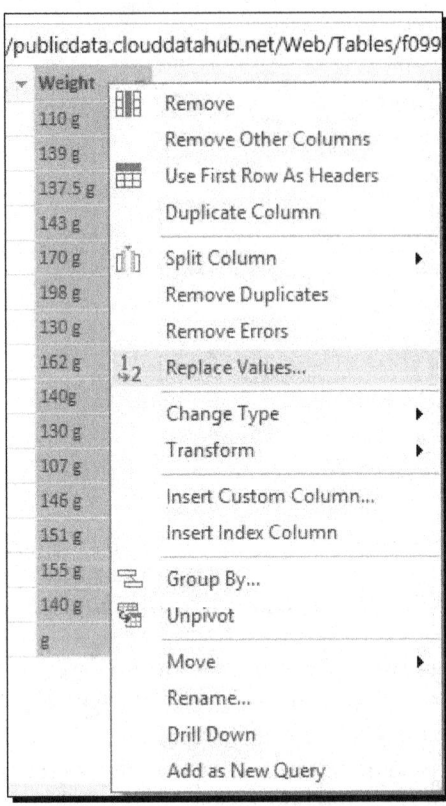

8. After replacing the **g** character, you can right-click on the **Weight** column again (which has only numeric values this time), and under **Change Type**, choose **Number**. We didn't apply the change type before replacing the **g** character because it will cause an error in the type conversion.

Look at the column with the header name **Other**. This column shows a list of accessory hardware, such as Wi-Fi and Bluetooth. This list is separated by commas. Now, we want to split these values into different columns. It is obvious that analysis on data based on separated values is much easier and cost-effective than searching the text.

9. Click on the following columns while holding the *Shift* button down: **Model**, **OS**, **Weight**, **Other**, and **Key**. Then, right-click on one of the column headers and select **Remove Other Columns**.

10. Drag-and-drop the **Key** column from the end to the beginning of the dataset. The dataset will change as shown in the following screenshot:

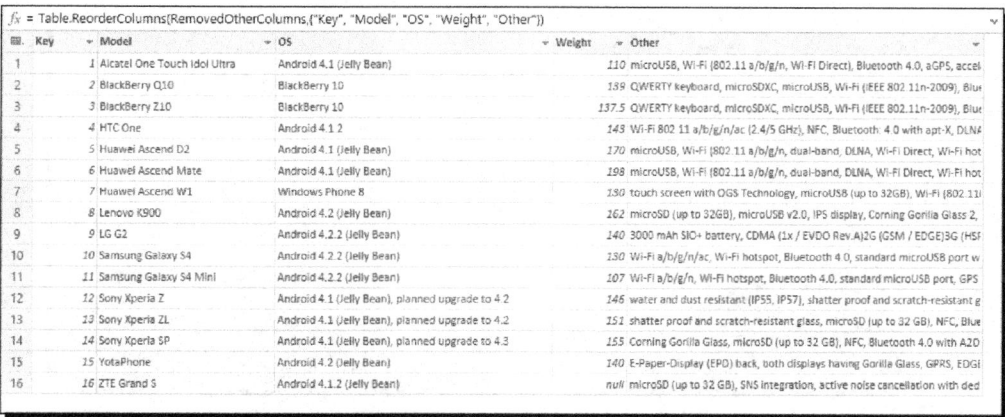

11. Look at the right pane and you will see a list of steps that we've performed on the existing dataset from the first load to the last one, which was reordering columns. You can click on any of the steps and view the dataset after the change in that step. For example, click on **Source** (shown in the right pane in the previous screenshot) and you will see the dataset as it was in the beginning. If you want to undo any change, just click on the small delete icon in the left side of each step (don't do that for this example).

12. Right-click on the **Other** column, and under the **Split Column** option, choose **By Delimiter...**, as shown in the following screenshot. In the **split column by delimiter** dialog box, leave the delimiter as **comma with default options** (in the advanced option, you can also define the number of columns for a split function).

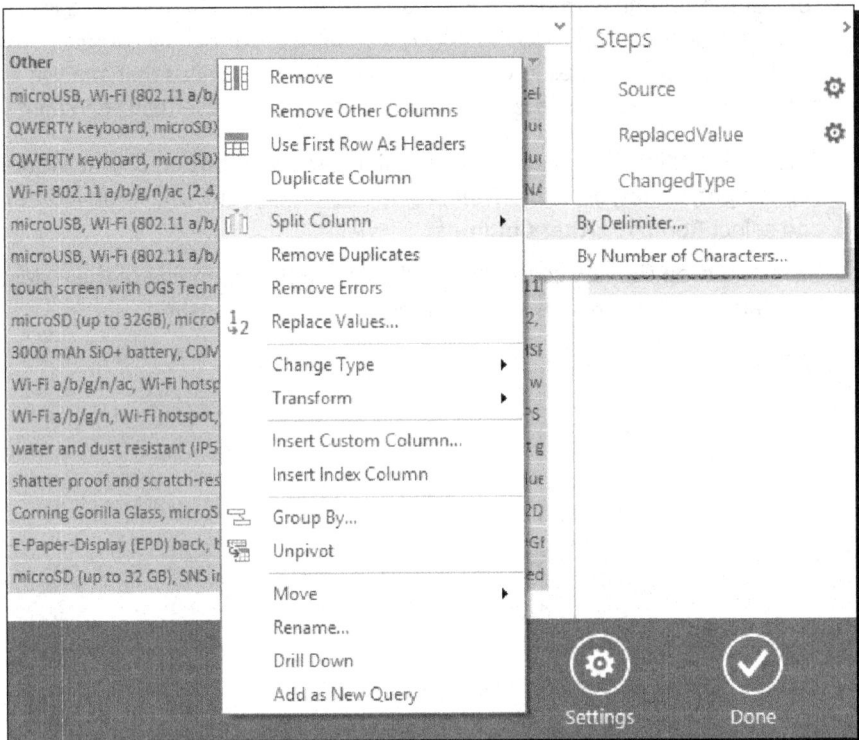

13. After the split, you will see 21 columns with headers such as **Other.1**, **Other.2**, and so on. You will see that the separate columns look like pivoted information. Select all "Other.X" columns together, right-click, and choose **Unpivot** from the pop-up menu (to select all "Other.X" columns together, click on the **Other.1** column, then hold the *Shift* key and select till you reach the **Other.21** column).

14. After **Unpivot**, you will see two columns, namely **Attribute** and **Value**. The **Value** column shows the hardware specifications, but the **Attribute** column is useless. Just right-click on the **Attribute** column and remove it. The dataset will look like the following screenshot after the changes:

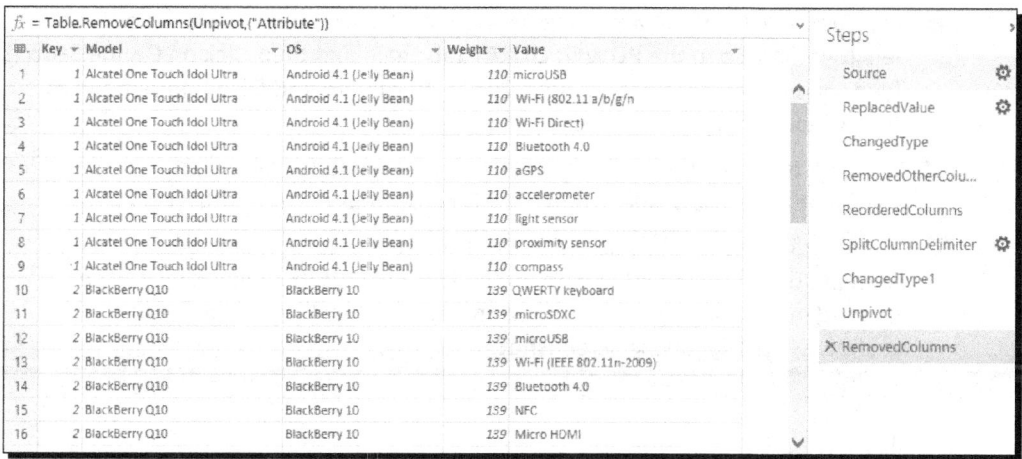

As you can see, so far we have simply transformed the multiple values separated by a comma in a single record by using separated values in different records. In the next step, we want to add a column to show the release year (which is 2013 for all records).

15. Click on the small table icon in the header of the column's header row and then choose **Insert Custom Column...**, as shown in the following screenshot:

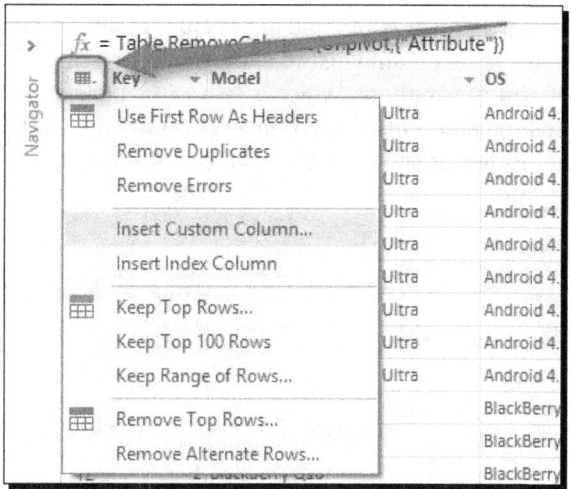

16. In the formula section for the new column, just type 2013 after the = sign and click on **OK**. You will see that the new column has appeared at the end of all the columns. Rename the new column to Release Year.

17. Now, click on the **Done** button to load the dataset back to the Excel spreadsheet.

18. We want to load the smartphone details for 2012 and combine these two result sets together. Go to the **POWER QUERY** tab again and then click on **Online Search**. Type Smartphones 2012, choose **2012 – Hardware and OS – Comparison of Smartphones**, and add it to the worksheet.

19. We want to do the same transformations on this dataset as well, so redo steps 6 to 20 on this dataset; please note that **Release Year** for this dataset is **2012**.

20. After loading the 2012 transformed data into the Excel spreadsheet, we can combine the 2012 and 2013 data. In the **POWER QUERY** menu, click on the **Append** menu and append the 2012 and 2013 datasets with each other, as shown in the following screenshot:

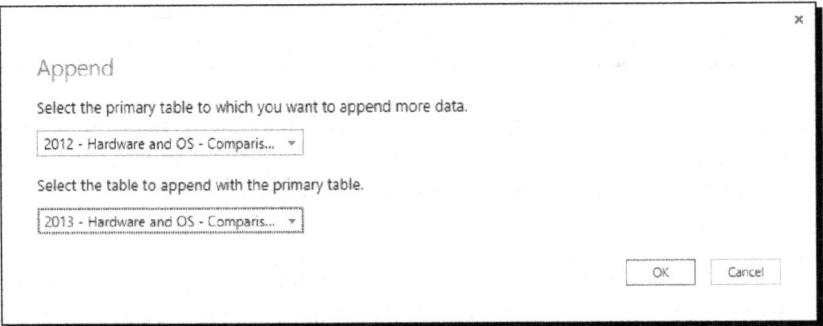

21. You will see two datasets combined in the **Query Editor** window. In this step, we remove the **Value** column just to show one of the other functionalities of Power Query transformations, which is removing duplicates. Right-click on the **Value** column and remove it. Then, click on the table header and then on **Remove Duplicates**, as shown in the following screenshot:

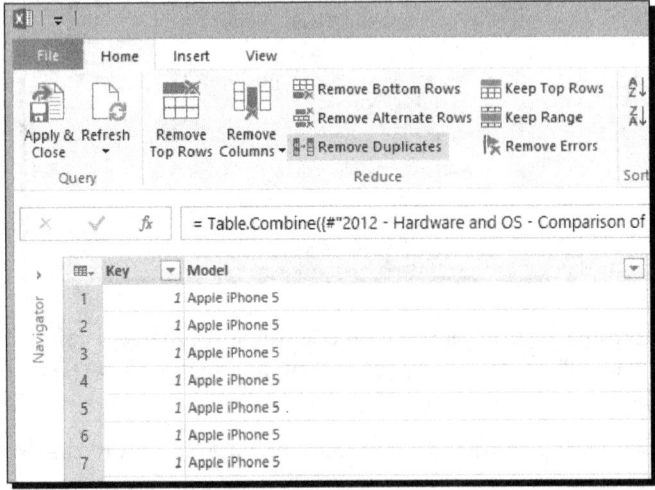

22. The **Remove Duplicates** option will remove records that have the same values in all columns for two separate rows. After removing duplicates, you will have a single record for each smartphone, as shown in the following screenshot:

Append1
Preview downloaded at 1:56 PM.

fx = Table.Distinct(RemovedColumns)

▦.	Key	Model	OS	Weight	Release Year
1	1	Apple iPhone 5	iOS 6.0	112	2012
2	2	HTC One V	Android 4.0.3	115	2012
3	3	HTC One S	Android 4.0.3/4.0.4	119.5	2012
4	4	HTC One X	Android 4.0.3/4.0.4	130	2012
5	5	HTC One X+	Android 4.1.1	135	2012
6	6	Nexus 4	Android 4.3 (Jelly Bean)	139	2012
7	7	Nokia Lumia 900	Windows Phone 7.5	160	2012
8	8	Nokia Lumia 920	Windows Phone 8	185	2012
9	9	Samsung Exhibit II 4G	Android	135	2012
10	10	Samsung Galaxy Note	Android 4.1.1 (Jelly Bean)	180	2012
11	11	Samsung Galaxy S III (	Android 4.04	133	2012
12	12	Samsung Galaxy S III S	Android 4.04	138.5	2012
13	13	Samsung Galaxy S III S	Android 4.04	133	2012
14	14	Samsung Galaxy S III (	Android 4.04	133	2012
15	15	Samsung Galaxy S III r	Android 4.1.2	112	2012
16	16	Sony Xperia V	Android 4.0	120	2012
17	17	Sony Xperia S	Android 2.3 (upgradable to	144	2012
18	18	Sony Xperia Sola	Android 4.0	126	2012
19	19	Samsung ATIV S	Windows Phone 8	135	2012
20	1	Alcatel One Touch Idc	Android 4.1 (Jelly Bean)	110	2013
21	2	BlackBerry Q10	BlackBerry 10	139	2013
22	3	BlackBerry Z10	BlackBerry 10	137.5	2013
23	4	HTC One	Android 4.1.2	143	2013

As you can see in the formula bar of the previous screenshot, the formula uses the **Distinct** function to remove duplicate records.

What just happened?

In this short example, you've learned how to work with Power Query for Excel to load data, transform it, and combine it with other datasets. Power Query uses a formula language, which is known as M. M is the core of Power Query transformations and data mash-ups. There are many Power Query formula (M) functions that can be used for transformations and work with data. A list of all the functions can be found in the PDF guidelines published for free by Microsoft at `http://office.microsoft.com/en-nz/excel-help/ learn-about-power-query-formulas-HA104003958.aspx`.

Power Query also supports a wide range of data sources. The **Online Search** option that we've used in this example was one of the data sources supported by Power Query. You can also load data from most databases such as Oracle, SQL Server, and DB2; on the other hand, you can use Facebook as the source of data or load data rows from Big Data such as Hadoop. The following screenshot shows some of the data sources supported by Power Query:

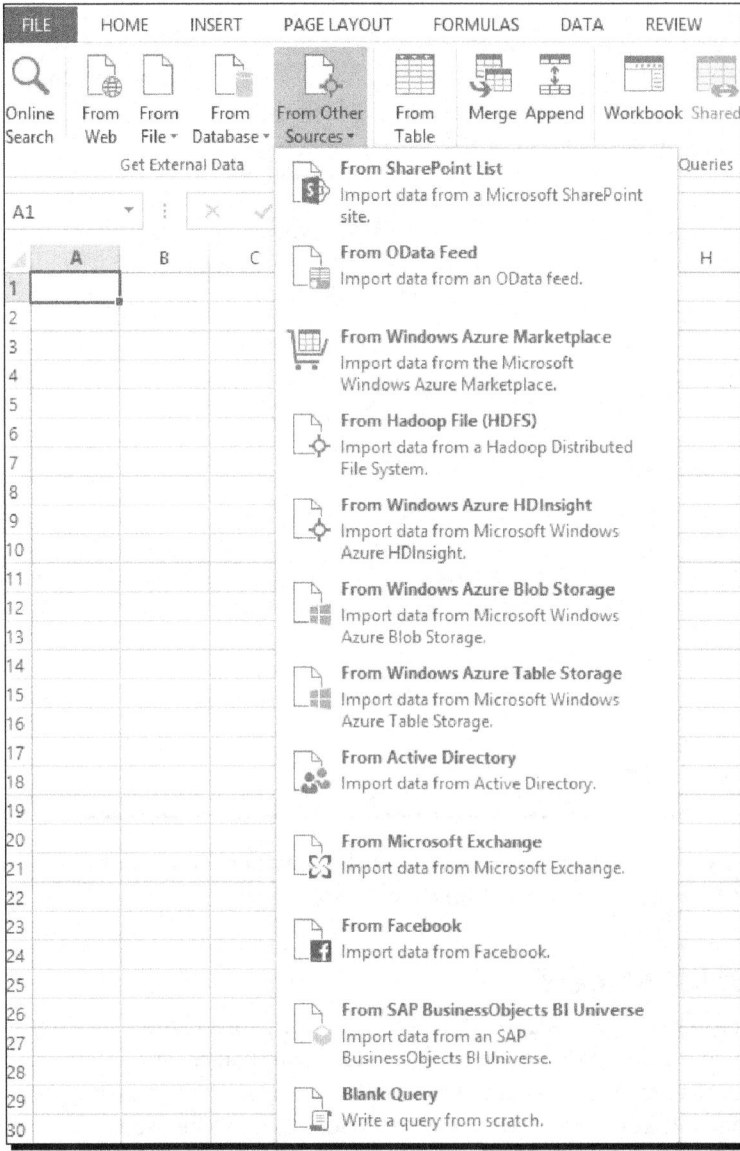

Power Query, as a mature ETL tool, is not as powerful compared to SSIS, but it has many powerful and rich M functions. If you want to learn about Power Query more in depth, the M and Power Query formula reference guides provided by Microsoft are the best references. They can be found at `http://office.microsoft.com/en-nz/excel-help/learn-about-power-query-formulas-HA104003958.aspx`.

Power Map

Microsoft recently released a geospatial 3D visualization tool named Power Map. Power Map, previously named GeoFlow, is a data visualization tool that is very powerful because of the correlation of this component with Microsoft Bing Maps. As a result, this tool can visualize geospatial information on a Bing map using charts and graphs, such as using a column chart as a 3D view of facts.

As you are familiar with Power View maps and charts from the previous chapter, you know that Power View maps do not provide 3D visualization on Bing maps. So, the Power Map tool fills that space and performs great visualizations, especially when you want to compare facts based on geographical information.

For working with the examples in this section, you need to download and install Power Map for Excel 2013 from `http://www.microsoft.com/en-us/download/details.aspx?id=38395`. We also use Excel files with geospatial data samples released by Microsoft. You can download sample files from the code bundle of this book or from `http://office.microsoft.com/en-nz/excel/power-bi-download-add-in-FX104087144.aspx`.

Time for action – data visualization with Power Map

In this example, we will work on a sample data file named `Dallas Utility Demo.xlsx`, which shows information of houses in Dallas, such as the size and year they were built. It also has information such as the KWH power consumed for the house. So, we use this source file to perform visualization of the data based on the year it was built and its power consumption by executing the following steps. You can download the file from the code bundle of this book:

1. Open `Dallas Utility Demo.xlsx` and have a look at the data rows. You will see geospatial information such as **latitude and longitude**, **year built**, **condition**, and **kwh power consumption**.

2. Go to the **Insert** tab in Excel, and under **Map**, select **Launch Power Map**, as shown in the following screenshot (if you cannot see this option, download and install Power Map for Excel 2013 from `http://www.microsoft.com/en-us/ download/details.aspx?id=38395`):

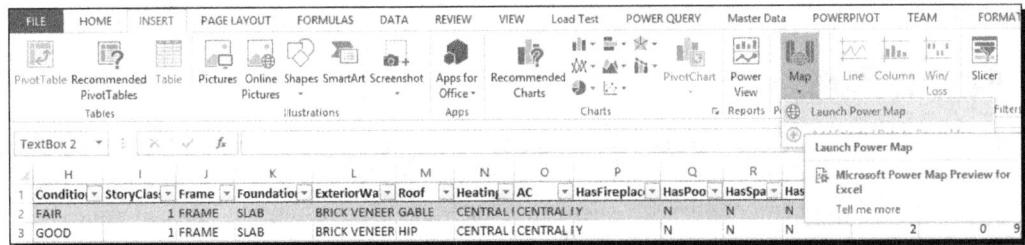

3. In the **Launch Power Map** dialog box in the bottom-left corner, click on **New Tour**.

4. The Power Map editor will open. As you can see in the following screenshot, Power Map contains a list of menu options on the top bar, a tour pane on the left side, the layer pane and its properties on the right side, and the main section, which is a Bing map, at the center:

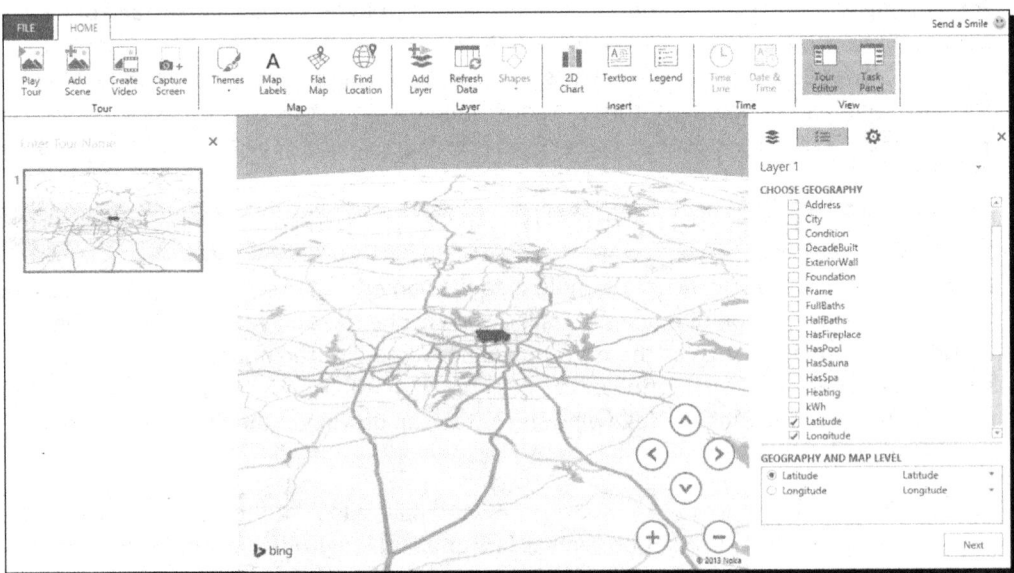

5. In the **Layer 1** section on the right side, only select **Latitude** and **Longitude** as the geography and then click on **Next**. Zoom in with the buttons on the bottom-right section of the map to see the area with blue color markers.

6. From the list of columns, choose **SquareFeet** and drag-and-drop it to the **Height** section in the properties pane under the layers pane. You will see a column chart (this is defined by default in the chart type option) on the geographical points on the map, as shown in the following screenshot:

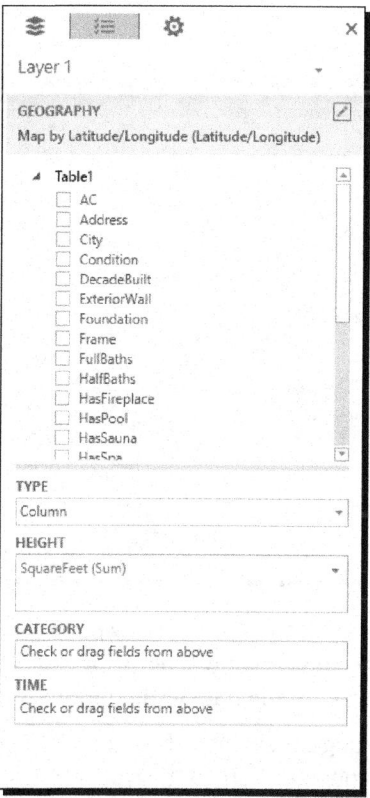

7. The height of the column chart shows the sum of the square feet of houses built in that geographical point, which is addressed by latitude and longitude. You can see that the sum of the square feet in most areas is similar, but at some points, they are much higher. Click on **Add Scene** to save this view point of data visualization.

8. Drag-and-drop the DecadeBuilt field from the fields' list to the **CATEGORY** section of the properties pane. You will see the column chart painted with a color based on the decade the houses were built.

9. Click on the **Legend** icon from the top menu bar under the **Insert** section. You will see a legend that shows the categorization of the decades the houses were built. Adjust the map and the legend in a way that you can see both in the main window, as shown in the following screenshot:

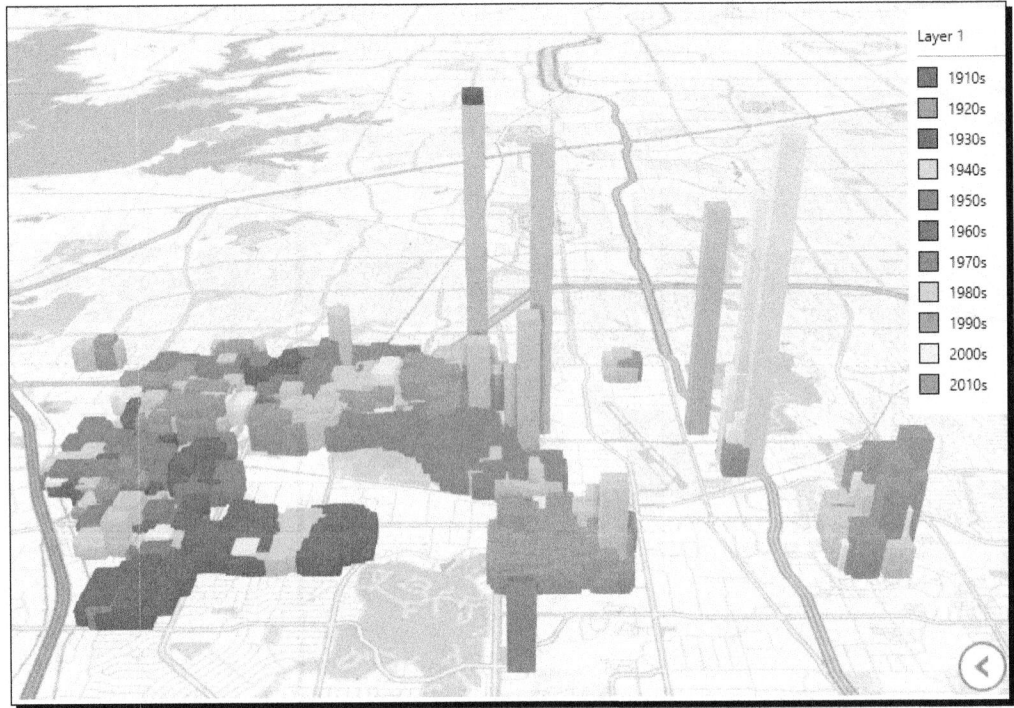

10. Click on **Add Scene** again to save this view point as well. As you can see, each time you add a scene, the view point will be stored in the tour pane, and you can simply click on each scene to see the data visualization of that view point.

11. Now we want to change the width of columns in the column chart; click on the layer in the layer pane and then go to layer settings. In the settings section, change **Thickness** to **20%**. You will see that the thickness of the columns has lowered and you have better visibility of the neighborhood areas now.

12. There is an area around the bottom-left of the map that shows two red areas (houses built in the 1960s) with a light yellow color section in the middle (houses built in the 1980s). Zoom in to that area and create a third scene there, as shown in the following screenshot:

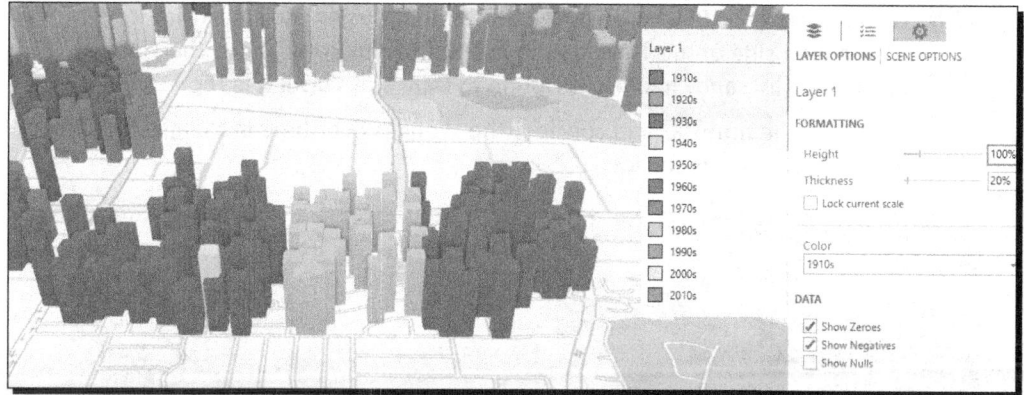

13. Now we want to look at the power consumption of these areas that contain two different sets of houses built in the 1960s and 1980s and compare them. Go to the **Layers** tab and add a new layer. The following screenshot shows how to add a new layer:

14. In the **New Layer** settings, choose only **Latitude** and **Longitude** as the geographical fields and click on **Next**. Change the **TYPE** of the chart to **HeatMap**. Then, drag-and-drop **kWh** from the fields' list into the **VALUE** section of the **HeatMap** properties.

    Now, **HeatMap** shows the power consumption (the sum of power consumption in kilowatts per hour) of those areas. However, this view is not that helpful because you cannot clearly distinguish the difference between areas in terms of power consumption. So, we need to add another dimension to this visualization.

15. Drag-and-drop the **PeriodStart** field into the **TIME** section of the **HeatMap** chart settings. Now you will see a time bar under the map that has a **Play** button. When you click on **Play**, you can see how kWh changes over time.

16. Before clicking on **Play**, change the time settings using the small click icon on the right side of the **TIME** option in chart settings and above the **TIME** drop-down list, and change the option to **Data stays until it is replaced**.

17. Now, play the time bar and consider the changes over time in kWh, as shown in the following screenshot:

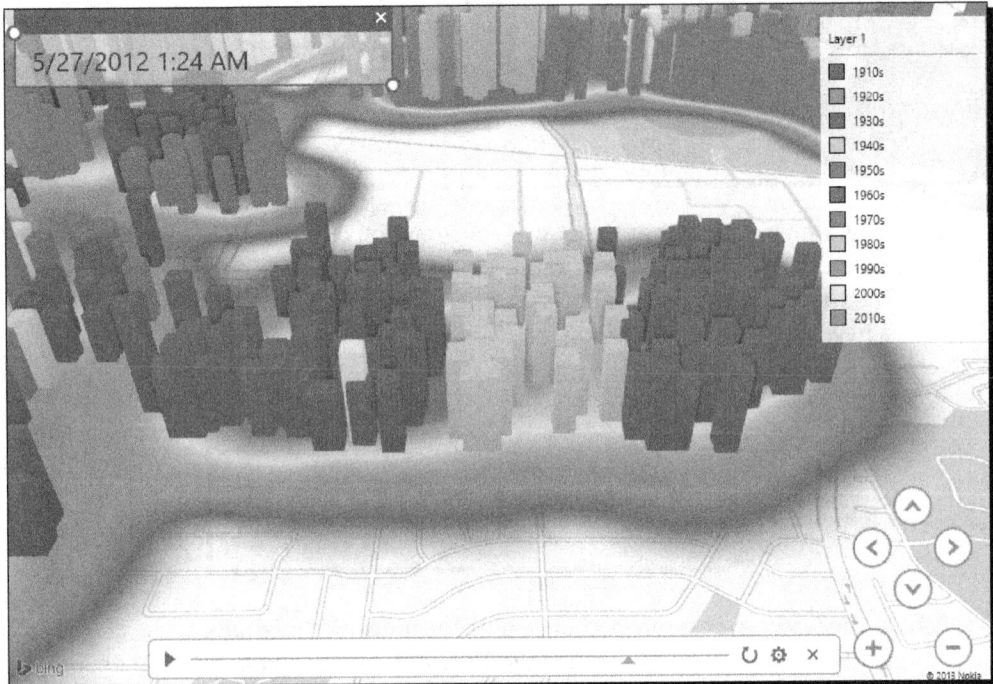

18. You will see that the power consumption of the two areas with houses built in the 1960s is higher than the area with houses built in the 1980s as time goes on. You can also pause the time player anytime you want to have a clearer view of the power consumption in a particular time period. There is also a date and time textbox shown in the top-left corner of the map, which shows the exact date and time.

You can change the speed of the time player with a click on the settings icon in the time bar. This icon will redirect you to the scene setting. In the scene setting, you can set a name for the scene. Define the visual effects for the scene and configure the time settings.

19. Add another scene and zoom out of the map to have a view of all the columns in the map in the window. Then, select the setting icon on the time bar and go to the **Scene options** pane. Change **Effect** to **Circle**, and reduce **Effect Speed** to **very low**.

20. From the menu bar under the **Map** section, click on **Map Labels**. You will see that the map shows the labels of roads and locations.

21. Go back to the first scene and add a **Text** box with the title `SquareFeet by Area`. In the second scene, create a **Text** box with the title `SquareFeet by Year Built and Area`.

22. Click on the **Play Tour** icon in the menu bar. You will see a full screen and a 3D and animated view of each scene, as shown in the following screenshot; wait until you see all four scenes. In the fourth scene, you will see that the camera turns on a circle around the area based on the configuration we made in step 19.

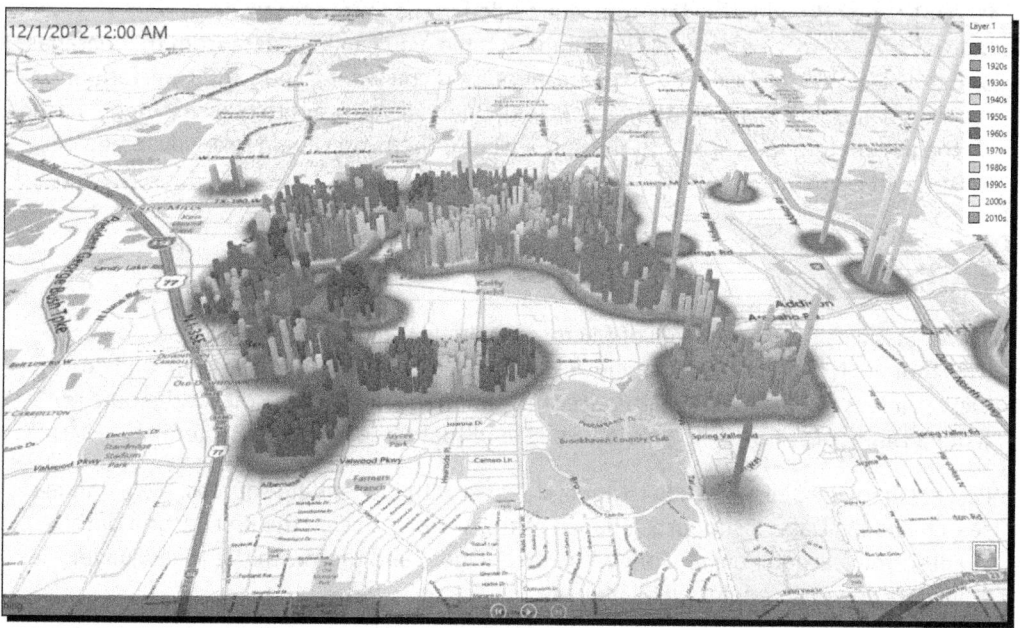

You can also create a video based on the tour. This will provide a visualization even without Excel with just a media player.

 You don't need to save the tour or scene or any part of Power Map. It will automatically keep its last state and configuration. The only thing you need to do is save the Excel file.

What just happened?

In this example, you've learned how to visualize geospatial data based on the latitude and longitude in a 3D view with other facts. There are multiple chart types supported by Power Map, such as **Column**, **Bobble**, and **HeatMap** charts. You can create a scene for each view point. Also, you can create a tour with animated effects from multiple scenes. A combination of different charts together as different layers is a good way to visualize multiple facts in comparison with each other. Similar to the Power View scatter chart, there is a play bar for the time dimension. This type of visualization is pretty good for displaying a behavior of facts based on time changes.

Power Map works with the data source provided in the Excel spreadsheet; so, if you want to use Power Map for a dataset in a database table, you can load data from that database using the **Data** tab of Excel into a spreadsheet, or if you want to perform transformation on the data before loading it, you can use Power Query. If you want to create a model based on the data before loading it into the spreadsheet, then you should take advantage of PowerPivot modeling.

Summary

Power BI is a self-service BI tool of Microsoft, mainly based on Excel services. Power BI uses four main components, namely Power Query, PowerPivot, Power Map, and Power View (there is also a Q and A feature recently announced by Microsoft; at the time of writing this book, there is no preview version of that feature to discuss here).

Power Query is a self-service ETL tool that works with lots of data sources, even online search and Big Data; it supports a bunch of transformations. In the first section of this chapter, you learned how to work with Power Query and then with the M language, which is a Power Query formula language.

PowerPivot is a data modeling tool. In *Chapter 4, ETL with Integration Services*, you learned how to perform tabular modeling. PowerPivot uses the same data modeling engine with a very similar interface. So, if you want to work with PowerPivot or the DAX language, refer to *Chapter 4, ETL with Integration Services*. PowerPivot is embedded in Excel 2013, so you may only need to enable it in the Excel options.

Power Map is a 3D data visualization tool for geospatial data such as latitude and longitude, or even information based on the address, city, and country (since it uses the Bing search engine, it can point to the exact location based on this information). Multiple layers of charts can be added to the display view. Also, the viewpoints can be stored and played as a tour.

Power View, as you learned in *Chapter 10, Dashboard Design*, is the new data visualization tool from Microsoft that is especially used for creating dashboards. Creating charts is very easy with a few drag-and-drops; it doesn't require deep technical knowledge such as SSRS. Because of its simplicity and richness in creating charts and dashboards, it is very useful for developers and also power users.

Power BI with the four components previously described is an outstanding self-service BI tool that plays an important role in the data analysis of many organizations and small to medium-size BI projects. There is also a fifth component in Power BI, which we didn't explore in detail in this book. Power Q&A is a question-and-answering engine for Power BI, which runs on top of the PowerPivot model. The user can ask questions in any natural language and get a response in grid, chart, or other visualization elements. The following blog provides a good introduction to Power Q&A:

```
http://blogs.msdn.com/b/microsoft_business_intelligence1/
archive/2013/07/25/q-amp-a-feature-of-power-bi.aspx
```

Microsoft BI tools work with .NET libraries, which means you can interact with BI components through a .NET application. In the next chapter, you will learn how to write .NET applications that work with BI components.

12

Integrating Reports in Applications

It is not usual to use customized applications as the BI system's frontend table, but sometimes, this requirement is a sensible option for embedding SSRS reports or other data visualization elements inside a customized application. In this chapter, we will walk through the methods of embedding SSRS reports into a .NET application. We will go through different kinds of applications such as a web/Windows application and a Metro style application. We will also explore methods of passing parameters and data sources from code behind the application's interface to the report's parameters.

For the examples of this chapter, you need to have Visual Studio 2012 installed and the code of this chapter is written in C#. A variety of .NET applications such as web-based, Windows-based, and Metro style applications will be revealed. You would also need to install an SSRS report's sample set named AdventureWorks sample reports from the URL available at `http://msftrsprodsamples.codeplex.com/releases/view/72275`. Detailed information will be provided in the first example of this chapter. In this chapter, we shall cover the following topics:

- ◆ Designing .NET applications with reports
- ◆ Developing reports in a web application
- ◆ Developing reports in a Metro application
- ◆ Working with ReportViewer in a local processing mode
- ◆ Passing parameters to a report
- ◆ Using the results of a mining model in an application

Designing .NET applications with reports

Microsoft provides a .NET framework that acts as the programming engine for C# and VB.NET languages. VB.NET and C# have the same set of controls for Windows and web development. In this chapter, we will focus only on the reporting controls. There exists a ReportViewer control as a part of built-in components for web and Windows development. Regardless of Windows or web applications, the .NET framework provides a ReportViewer control for viewing reports of **SQL Server Reporting Services** (**SSRS**). This component will connect to the report in the report server and get the report definition. Then, it will show the report data while the application is running. The .NET application can help in passing parameters from the code behind or from a user interface to the ReportViewer control and through it to the report server. There are many configurations and settings for each report in the report server that can be modified and changed through the .NET application. In this chapter, we will reveal many examples of working with the ReportViewer control in a web or windows application, passing parameters, and changing configurations from code behind or customized UI will be also experimented.

Time for action – installing AdventureWorks SSRS sample reports

For samples in this book, we need to install SSRS sample reports mentioned in this section. For this reason, this section shows the installation steps. Perform the following steps for installation:

1. Download the sample reports from the URL `http://msftrsprodsamples.codeplex.com` and then install reports.

2. After installation, go to **Start**, and under **All Programs**, open **Microsoft SQL Server 2008R2 Community and Samples Code**.

3. Then, go to the folder `AdventureWorks 2008R2 Sample Reports` under `Samples/Reporting Services/Report Samples`.

4. Now, double-click on the `AdventureWorks 2008R2.sln` solution file.

5. The solution will be opened in SSDT, and it will also be upgraded in SSDT 2010 or 2012. So continue by clicking on **Upgrade wizard** and upgrade the project.

6. In the **Solution Explorer** window, under **Shared Data Sources**, open `AdventureWorks2008R2.rds` and click on **Edit** in the **Shared Data Sources Properties** window.

7. In the **Connection Properties** window, change the database name to `AdventureWorks2012`. Click on **OK** and save it.

8. Deploy the solution to `http://localhost/reportserver` (the description on how to deploy an SSRS project can be found in *Chapter 2, SQL Server Analysis Services Multidimensional Cube Development*).

9. After deployment, browse the report server on the address `http://localhost/reportserver`. To verify the successful change, open the `AdventureWorks 2008R2` folder and click on one of the reports.

What just happened?

By performing the previous steps, we installed sample SSRS reports. We will use this sample report set for future examples.

Developing reports in a web application

Web applications are widely used with a high progressive rate of Internet usage. In this section, you will see an ASP.NET application that works with a ReportViewer and shows data of an SSRS report through ASPX web forms.

Time for action – working with reports in web/Windows applications

In this section, we will use ReportViewer to show one of the SSRS reports on the report server (deployed in the previous example). Perform the following steps:

1. Open **Visual Studio 2012** and create a new project.

2. In the **New Project** dialog box, under **Visual C#**, select **Web**. Then, from the templates' list, choose **ASP.NET Empty Web Application**, as shown in the following screenshot:

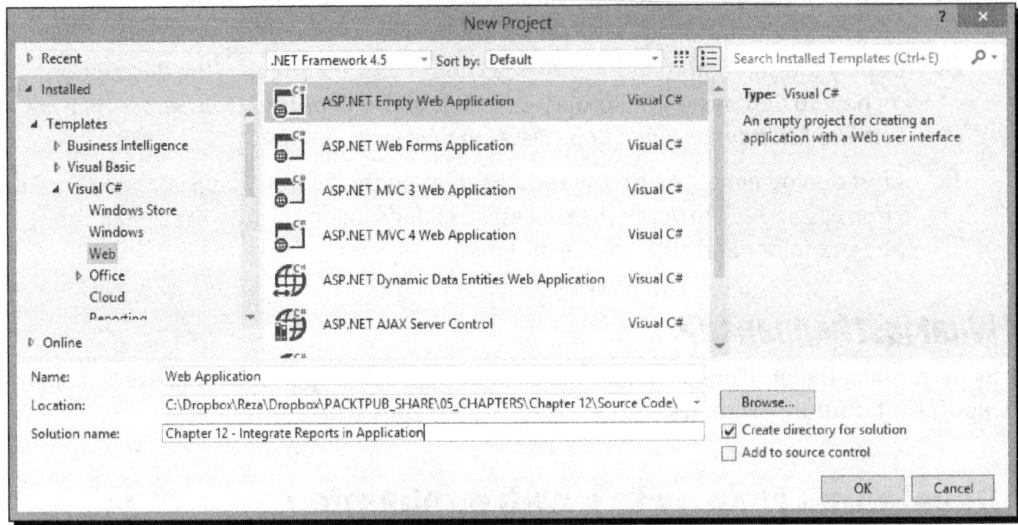

3. When the new project is created, right-click on the project in the solution explorer, and under **Add**, click on **Web Form**. Name it `SampleReportViewerPage`.

4. Open `SampleReportViewerPage.aspx` from the solution explorer.

5. Navigate to **Toolbox | Reporting** and double-click on **ReportViewer**.

6. When the ReportViewer control appears on the web page, click on the small smart tag icon (a smart tag is a visual pane for configuring each component in an easier way; it can be opened by clicking on the top right-hand side of the control with a > icon).

7. In the ReportViewer smart tag, set **Choose Report** as **<Server Report>**, and set **Report Server URL** as `http://localhost/reportserver`. Set **Report Path** as `/AdventureWorks 2008R2/Sales_by_Region_2008R2`.

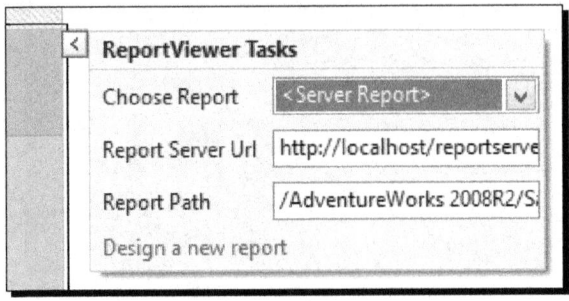

8. Set the width and height of the ReportViewer control in the **Properties** window to **100%**.

9. From the toolbox, under **AJAX** extensions, double-click on **Script Manager**. This control will be added to the page as well. As ReportViewer uses some AJAX functionalities, it requires a script manager.

10. Now, run the project. You will see that the SSRS report will be shown on the ASPX web page as shown in the following screenshot:

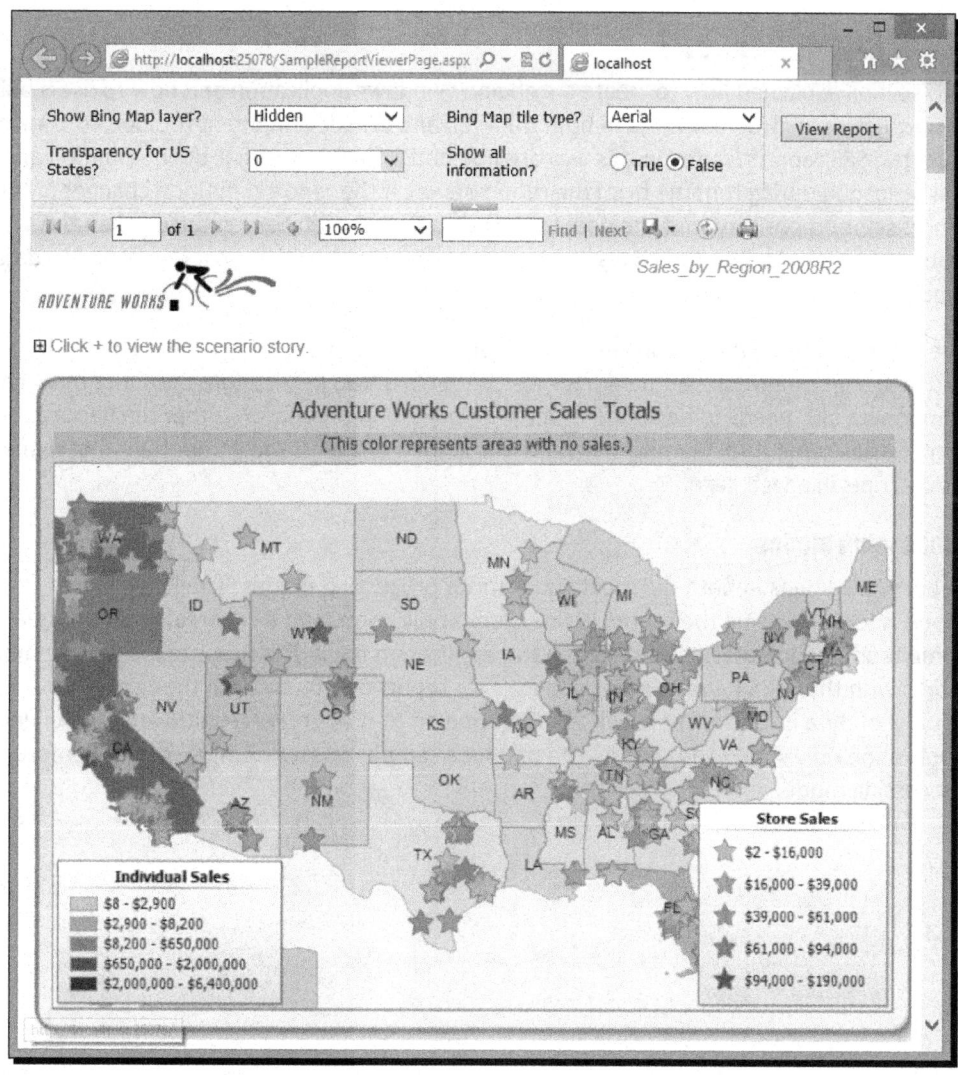

11. Navigate to **File | Add | New Project**, and under **Visual C#**, choose **Windows** and then select **Windows Form Application** and name it `Win Application`.

12. In the form designer for `form1.cs`, drag-and-drop a ReportViewer control from the toolbox, and set the report's configuration similar to what we did in step 7.

13. Go to the **Properties** window and set the **Dock** property of ReportViewer to **Fill**.

14. Right-click on **Win Application**, and set it as a startup project. Run the project, and you will see that the windows form will contain the same SSRS report in the running mode.

What just happened?

This section explained how to create a web and Windows application and how to use a built-in ReportViewer control that exists in both the Web and Win development toolbox, to load SSRS reports. SSRS reports loaded in this way are not static. This means that their definition and data will be loaded during runtime from the report server. If the report definition changes in the report server repository, or if the data from the underlying database changes, then the Win/web application catches that changes automatically and shows the most recent, up-to-date report definition with data.

The process of using the ReportViewer control is simple and almost similar in a Windows and web application. One of the differences is that in a web application, the script manager component also needs to be added to the web page, and the reason is that the ReportViewer control uses some AJAX features in it, and the script manager is the component that manages AJAX scripts in a web page.

Processing modes

ReportViewer acts in both the **local** and **remote** processing modes. The local processing mode is for processing the report in the client application, and it is useful when there are some reports and datasets designed in the application itself. The Remote processing mode works with the SSRS Report server and asks for report definition from the report server; loading of data into the report will also be done on the report server side, and the client application only shows the report. The previous sample was an example of the Remote processing mode.

ReportViewer in Web and Windows

ReportViewer has some equivalent features in both the Web and in Windows, and they are as follows:

- ◆ Viewing the toolbars and filters pane
- ◆ The local and remote processing modes
- ◆ .NET libraries for writing code that deals with reports, parameters, data sources, and other components of the report

There are some differences between the web and Window versions of ReportViewer. These differences are because of the nature of each kind of application; for example, the deployment strategy for a web application requires considering authentication, session states, and so on, or there are some browser-dependent features or limitations in web applications.

The ReportViewer toolbar

The ReportViewer toolbar contains some useful features that are good for navigation, export, and refresh. The following screenshot shows this toolbar. As you can see, there are navigation icons, a document map, a search pane, export and print (which work based on the printer configuration in a Windows application, and activeX printing configuration of a web browser in a web application), and refresh controls that help the user to work with reports easily.

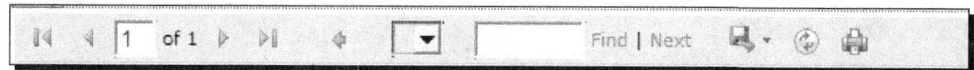

Developing reports in a Metro application

As you've seen in the previous section, loading SSRS reports in Windows and web applications was easy because of the existing ReportViewer control. In Metro applications, there is no ReportViewer control (at the time of writing this book), but this is not a dead end. As SSRS reports are web-based, they can be opened from a component that could connect to web pages. Fortunately, there is a component for web browsing in the Metro development environment, which is named Web View. In this section, we will work with this control to create a Metro application that works with SSRS reports.

Time for action – working with reports in Metro applications

In this section, we will open an SSRS report with the help of the Web View control in a Metro application. In a Metro-style application, you will see an XAML code behind. XAML is a well-structured coding method for building powerful GUI. This coding method isolates C# programming for business logic from the XML-based language for the development of a GUI named XAML. Perform the following steps:

1. Create a new project, and under **Visual C#**, select **Windows Store**. Then, choose **Blank App** and name it App.

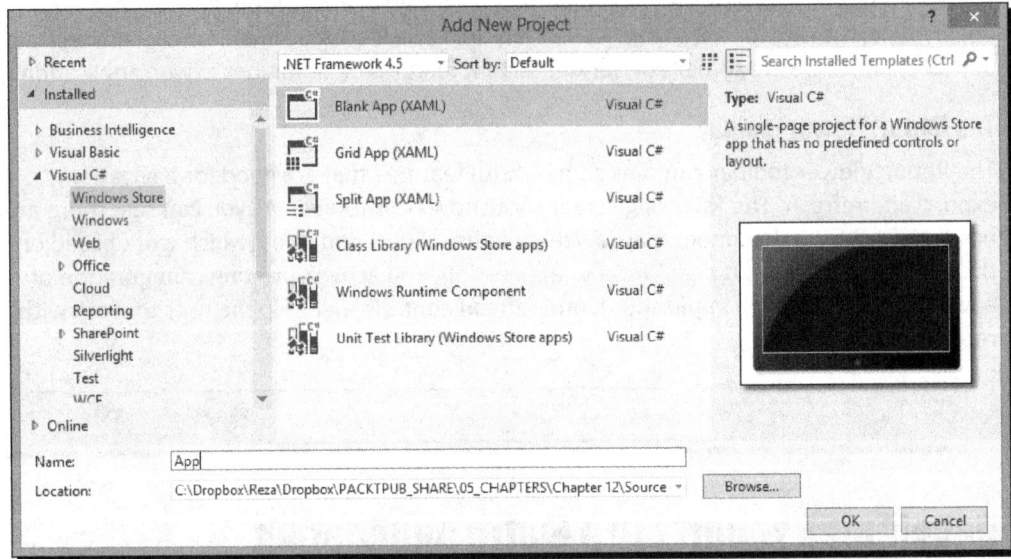

2. Double-click on MainPage.xaml in the solution explorer. You will see that the designer window opens in the main pane, with both the design area and XAML code behind.

3. From the toolbox, under **All XAML Controls**, double-click on the **Web View** control.

4. When the web view appears in the design area, you can change the **Height** and **Width** values of this control from the **Properties** window or even from XAML code (when you select the control, the XAML code lines related to that control will be highlighted). Change **Height** to 600 and **Width** to 800. Also change the horizontal alignment to center.

5. Name the web view control as webViewReport.

6. Now, add the loaded function in the **Page** node in XAML. For adding this event, you can just use the **Properties** window, and then go to the events section and double -click on **Loaded**, or simply type `loaded` in the XAML code in the **Page** element as a new attribute. You will see that IntelliSense will appear, and following it is just simple. The following screenshot shows how changes look in the XAML code:

```
<Page
    x:Class="App.MainPage"
    xmlns="http://schemas.microsoft.com/winfx/2006/xaml/presentation"
    xmlns:x="http://schemas.microsoft.com/winfx/2006/xaml"
    xmlns:local="using:App"
    xmlns:d="http://schemas.microsoft.com/expression/blend/2008"
    xmlns:mc="http://schemas.openxmlformats.org/markup-compatibility/2006"
    mc:Ignorable="d" Loaded="Page_Loaded">

    <Grid Background="{StaticResource ApplicationPageBackgroundThemeBrush}">
        <WebView HorizontalAlignment="Center" Name="webViewReport" Height="600" VerticalAlignment="Top" Width="800"/>

    </Grid>
</Page>
```

7. Now, go to the C# code behind the `Page_Loaded` event handler and write the following code there:

```
Uri targetUri = new
  Uri(@"http://localhost/reportserver/AdventureWorks
    2008R2/Sales_by_Region_2008R2");
            webViewReport.Navigate(targetUri);
```

8. Run the project and you will see that the report appears in the Web View control in the center of the app.

What just happened?

Viewing SSRS reports in an app is possible using the Web View control. This control helps in browsing web pages; in this case, we used this to browse SSRS reports' web pages.

Working with ReportViewer in a local processing mode

Previously, you saw an example of the remote processing mode that is useful for connecting to reports in a report server and loading the report's definition and data to show in the ReportViewer control. In this section, we will discuss about the second processing mode, which is the local processing mode that provides the ability to design and use reports inside the application.

Time for action – designing reports and working with the local processing mode

In this example, we will use the local processing mode feature in the ReportViewer control to design a new report based on the data in the AdventureWorks sample database, and the report data will be shown in the application form. For this sample, we will be using a Windows form application created in the previous examples. Now, perform the following steps:

1. Open SSMS, connect to a local instance of SQL Server in your machine, and run the following script on the AdventureWorksDW2012 database to create a view of the sales information:

```
CREATE VIEW [dbo].[SalesView]
AS
SELECT          dbo.DimProduct.EnglishProductName,
   dbo.DimProductCategory.EnglishProductCategoryName,
     dbo.DimSalesTerritory.SalesTerritoryCountry,
                         dbo.DimSalesTerritory.
SalesTerritoryRegion,
   dbo.DimSalesTerritory.SalesTerritoryGroup,
     dbo.DimProductSubcategory.EnglishProductSubcategoryName,
                         dbo.FactInternetSales.SalesAmount,
   dbo.FactInternetSales.OrderQuantity
FROM            dbo.DimProduct INNER JOIN
                         dbo.DimProductSubcategory ON dbo.
DimProduct.ProductSubcategoryKey = dbo.DimProductSubcategory.
ProductSubcategoryKey INNER JOIN
                         dbo.DimProductCategory ON dbo.
DimProductSubcategory.ProductCategoryKey = dbo.DimProductCategory.
ProductCategoryKey INNER JOIN
                         dbo.FactInternetSales ON dbo.DimProduct.
ProductKey = dbo.FactInternetSales.ProductKey INNER JOIN
                         dbo.DimSalesTerritory ON dbo.
FactInternetSales.SalesTerritoryKey = dbo.DimSalesTerritory.
SalesTerritoryKey
```

2. Open the `Win Application` project, right-click to create a new Windows form, and name it `LocalProcessingMode`.

3. Add a ReportViewer control, and in the smart tag, click on **Design a New Report**.

4. A new report designer will be opened, and immediately, a **Data Source Connection Wizard** comes up and asks if you want to create a new data source.

5. Choose the data source's type as **Database**, and when choosing a database model, select **dataset**.

6. Create a new connection to your local instance of SQL Server, and choose AdventureWorksDW2012 as the database name. Next, the new connection asks to be added in the `app.config` file so that it is configurable in the deployment steps. Check the connection to be added in the configuration file.

7. In step 5, check **SalesView**.

8. In the Report Wizard, in the Dataset properties, just change the dataset's name to `Sales`.

9. In the **Arrange fields** window, insert **OrderQuantity** and **SalesAmount** in the **Values** area, drag-and-drop **EnglishProductCategoryName**, **EnglishSubcategoryName**, and **EnglishProductName** in order to the **Column groups**, and add **SalesTerritoryGroup**, **SalesTerritoryCountry**, and **SalesTerritoryRegion** to the **Row groups**. The following screenshot shows a view of this step's configuration:

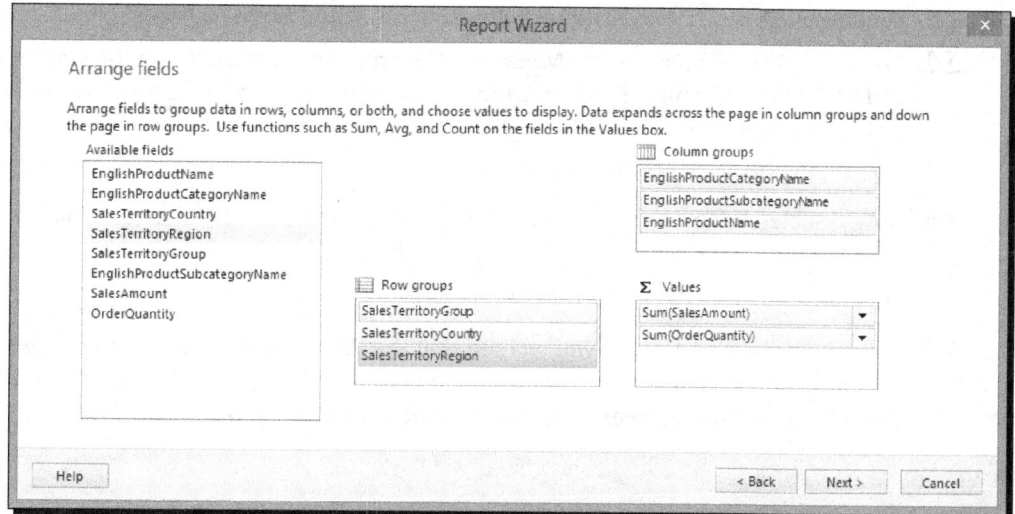

10. In the **Choose the layout** window, just leave everything as default, choose a style in the next step, and close the wizard.

11. Now, you will see the main report's layout, which is very similar to the SSRS report designer. You have the same report data pane on the left-hand side, the groups in the bottom of the main pane, and the report content itself is visible in the main pane.

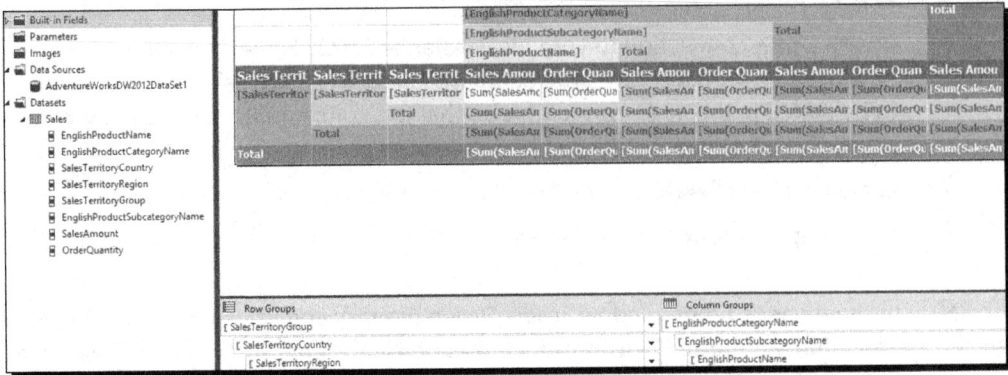

12. In the solution explorer, you will see a `report1.rdlc` file created in the project. The RDLC file is equivalent to RDL files in Reporting Services, with a few differences.

13. Rename `report1.rdlc` to `Sales Report.rdlc` and save the report.

14. Go back to the **LocalProcessingMode** windows form designer, click on the smart tag, and in the ReportViewer Tasks smart tag, choose the report as `Win_Application.`
`Sales Report.rdlc`.

15. Click on the dock control in the container.

16. Now, double-click on `Program.cs` in the solution explorer, and change the last line of code in the `main` method to the following line:

```
Application.Run(new LocalProcessingMode());
```

17. Save the project and run it; you will see that the Windows form opens and shows the loaded report with data. You can expand each column group or row group and view slicing and dicing sales data by the product category and sales territory.

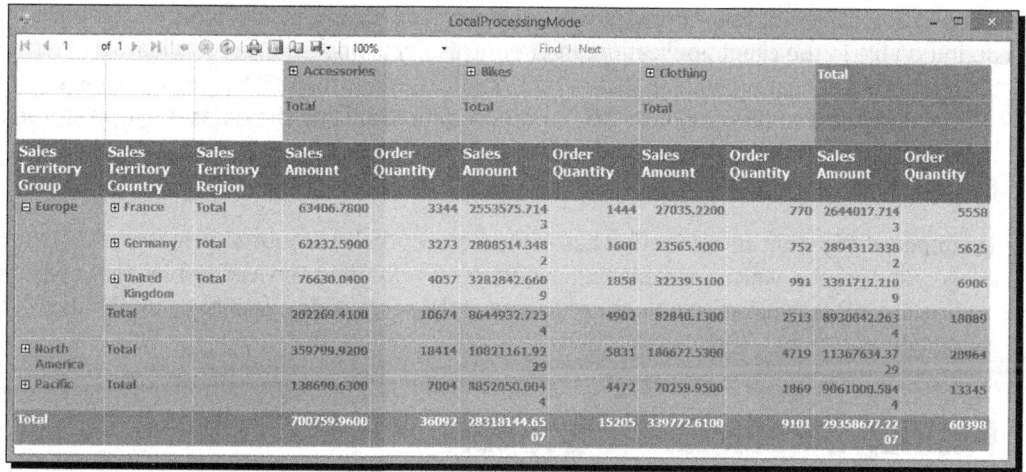

Sales Territory Group	Sales Territory Country	Sales Territory Region	Accessories Total Sales Amount	Order Quantity	Bikes Total Sales Amount	Order Quantity	Clothing Total Sales Amount	Order Quantity	Total Sales Amount	Order Quantity
⊟ Europe	⊞ France	Total	63406.7800	3344	2553575.7143	1444	27035.2200	770	2644017.7143	5558
	⊞ Germany	Total	62232.5900	3273	2808514.3482	1600	23565.4000	752	2894312.3382	5625
	⊞ United Kingdom	Total	76630.0400	4057	3282842.6609	1858	32239.5100	991	3391712.2109	6906
	Total		202269.4100	10674	8644932.7234	4902	82840.1300	2513	8930042.2634	18089
⊞ North America	Total		359799.9200	18414	10821161.9229	5831	186672.5300	4719	11367634.3729	28964
⊞ Pacific	Total		138690.6300	7004	8852050.0044	4472	70259.9500	1869	9061000.5844	13345
Total			700759.9600	36092	28318144.6507	15205	339772.6100	9101	29358677.2207	60398

What just happened?

In this section, you've learned how to create and design reports directly from Visual Studio's Windows application project. The process is the same for a web application because both of these types of projects support ReportViewer in the local processing mode. The Local processing mode, as you've seen, allows you to create the report definition on the application side, and also designs the report as you want; connection to the report will also be set up in the application.

In steps 4 to 6, you learned how to create the data source connection in the project; the connection string of the data source could be stored in the `app.config` or `web.config` file. The benefit of storing the connection string in the configuration file is that each time that database connection requires a change, this can be simply done by changing the XML code lines of the configuration file, which prevents the changing of the C# or VB.NET code within. So, data source connections can be changed without the need to rebuild the project.

Step 7 showed you how to choose database objects, and step 9 showed you how to add each field or attribute in the column groups, row groups, or values section. Step 10 showed you how to change the layout or the grouping configuration such as subtotals in the report. All of these steps are parts of the Report Wizard. To create a report, you can use this wizard, or you can create a dataset and groups individually using the report designer. The Report Wizard is good for creating the basic template, but for more configuration and further development, you should always use the report designer.

As you saw in step 12, the report file will be generated as an RDLC file, which is a report definition file in the client application. In *Chapter 9*, *Reporting Services*, you learned that SSRS reports are created with an RDL extension. RDLC is another extension for reports created in a client application. RDLC is the report definition, and the dataset will be stored in the project with the XSD extension, which is an XML schema based on selected objects from the data source.

The report designer in an application has many features of SSRS reports such as creating charts, gauges, and graphs, which we explained in *Chapter 9*, *Reporting Services*, earlier. However, reports in a client application do not participate in the server-side administration that the report server provides, such as scheduling reports.

Passing parameters to a report

As you've learned so far, ReportViewer is a built-in .NET component for Windows and web applications that work in the remote and local processing modes to show a report from the report server or from a client application to the user. This is not the only feature that ReportViewer provides. This component also provides functions and subclasses to work with the report object and parameters. This means that as a C# or VB.NET developer, you can get parameters from some controls in your application and pass the parameters through the code behind to the ReportViewer, and this will cause the report to be loaded by considering those parameters.

Time for action – changing a report configuration with a ReportViewer Object through code behind

In this section, we will explore some .NET object library functions and properties of the ReportViewer, and we will change the report parameters based on these functions. Perform the following steps:

1. Open `Win Application`, go to the `RemoteProcessingMode.cs` Windows form, and click on the ReportViewer control.

2. In the **Properties** window, change the `reportViewer1` name to `rvwSales`, and change the **Modifier** setting to **Public**. This change is because we want to access this ReportViewer from outside of this page.

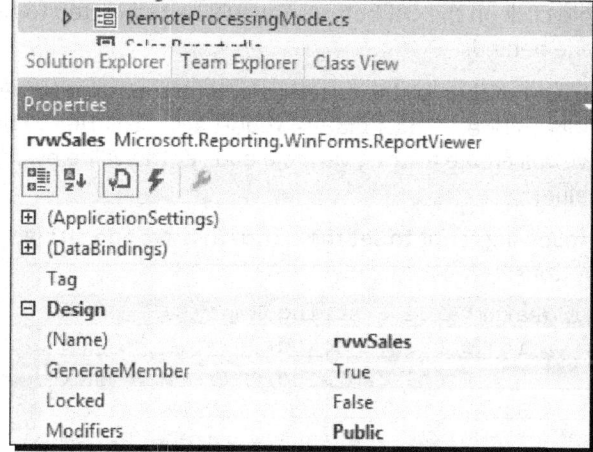

3. Also, in the code behind the form, re-mark the line of code in the form's load event handler with double backslashes, as the following code shows:

```
public RemoteProcessingMode()
        {
                InitializeComponent();
        }


        private void Form1_Load(object sender, EventArgs e)
        {
                //this.rvwSales.RefreshReport();
        }
```

4. Create a new windows form, and name it `Filter Form`.

5. In **FilterForm**, design a Windows form with labels, radio buttons, and an **OK** button, as the following screenshot shows:

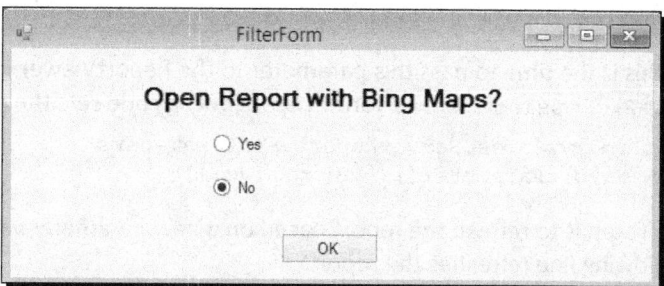

6. In the previous filter form, rename the radio button with the **Yes** label to `rbtYes`, rename the radio button with the **No** label to `rbtNo`, and rename the button with the **OK** text as `btnOK`.

7. Now, double-click on the **OK** button. You will be redirected to the `btnOK` click event handler code behind.

8. Create a string variable to storing the value of the parameter. As the parameter in the `RemoteProcessingMode.cs` report accepts string values of `Visible` or `Hidden`, we will create a string variable and set the value by checking the radio button's values.

9. Write the following script to set the `BingParamValue` string variable that is based on radio buttons:

```
string BingParamValue = string.Empty;
        if (rbtYes.Checked)
            BingParamValue = "Visible";
        else
            BingParamValue = "Hidden";
```

10. Then, instantiate a new instance from the report form (note that `RemoteProcessingMode` is the report form that was generated in the second example of this chapter) using the following code:

```
RemoteProcessingMode reportFrm = new RemoteProcessingMode();
```

11. For the upcoming steps of this sample, we will use classes of a specific namespace of reporting, so we add the following line at the very first line of the `FilterForm.cs` code behind:

```
using Microsoft.Reporting.WinForms;
```

12. Now, we can create the `ReportParameter` object to be used for passing parameters to the ReportViewer. The following code shows how to create a `ReportParameter` object; the first argument is the name of the parameter, and the second is the value (which comes from the `BingParamValue` string variable that was seen in the earlier code):

```
ReportParameter BingParam = new ReportParameter
    ("ShowBingMaps", BingParamValue);
```

13. Now, this is the time to pass this parameter to the ReportViewer in the `RemoteProcessingMode.cs` form. The following code sets the parameter:

```
reportFrm.rvwSales.ServerReport.SetParameters
    (new ReportParameter[] { BingParam });
```

14. The last step is to refresh the report based on a new parameter value; the following line refreshes the report:

```
reportFrm.rvwSales.RefreshReport();
```

15. To show the new form, we use the `Show` method as follows:

```
reportFrm.Show();
```

16. Double-click on `Program.cs`, and change the first form of the application to `RemoteProcessingMode.cs`, shown as follows:

```
[STAThread]
    static void Main()
    {
        Application.EnableVisualStyles();
        Application.SetCompatibleTextRenderingDefault(false);
        Application.Run(new FilterForm());
    }
```

17. Run the project. The filter form shows up and asks you for the parameter. By choosing **Yes** and clicking on **OK**, you will see that the report form appears with the Bing map layout.

18. Now, stop the project from the debug mode, and add the following line before the code used for refreshing the report:

```
reportFrm.rvwSales.ShowParameterPrompts = false;
```

19. Run the project again; this time, you will see that the report form doesn't show the parameter pane at the top of the report because it is disabled in the code behind. The following screenshot shows a sample of running the project with `ShowParameterPromts` set to `false`:

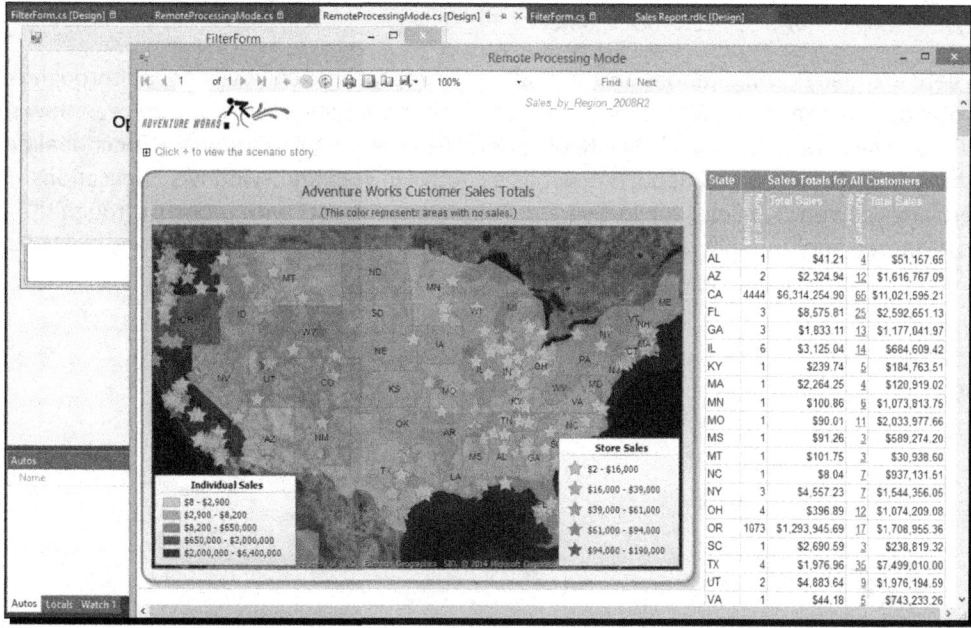

What just happened?

In this section, you learned how to work with the `ReportViewer` object dynamically through the code behind. `ReportViewer` has two main properties: `LocalReport` and `ServerReport`. Based on the processing mode selected for the ReportViewer, the local or server report can be used. `LocalReport` is for the local processing mode, and `ServerReport` is for the remote processing mode. In this sample, we worked with the remote processing mode and the `ServerReport` object, but the procedure and syntax for working with local reports are similar.

In step 2, we changed the access modifier of the `RemoteProcessingMode.cs` Windows form to access the ReportViewer control from other forms. The private or protected access modifiers are restricted to the class itself; this means that the default access modifier of this control doesn't provide the ability to work with this control from other forms and classes. Internal or public classes can be accessed from this project or even external projects.

In steps 4 to 6, we created a new windows form that acts as a filter form and asks the parameter whether Bing maps can be displayed or not. As the parameter in the report is not Boolean (you can see this in SSDT in the report definition of the report file), we used an `if` statement to set the string variable's value based on the value of the radio buttons (steps 8 and 9).

In step 11, we wrote a `using` statement to include the namespace for Reporting to work with objects and classes in this code file. Step 12 shows how to create a `ReportParameter` object and how to set the parameter name and its value. In step 13, you saw that we can assign an array of parameters with the `SetParameters` method, which is a method of the `LocalReport` or `ServerReport` object.

There are many configurations and settings in the report that can be changed through code behind; in this sample, you've only seen how to set parameters. Also, you've seen how to disable the parameter pane in the ReportViewer. However, there are many functionalities that can be changed, and ReportViewer as a control in web and Windows applications provides powerful abilities for software developers to interact with reports through the customized application with a few lines of C# or VB.NET code.

Using the results of a mining model in an application

In the last section of this chapter, we will use a deployed mining model and use DMX queries to apply PREDICTION JOIN on the result set of the mining model to the existing data. Before starting this section, make sure that you've read *Chapter 8, Identifying Data Patterns – Predictive Models in SSAS*, because this section is heavily based on models developed and deployed in that chapter.

Time for action – running DMX queries from a .NET application

In this example, we will deploy the existing predictive data mining model to Analysis Services. Then, we will use a DMX query in the .NET application to create a PREDICTION JOIN between the mining model and the raw data in a database table. As a result, we will have a model applied to the dataset through C#, .NET, and DMX. Perform the following steps to run queries from an application:

1. Open the source code of *Chapter 8, Identifying Data Patterns – Predictive Models in SSAS*, which is Chapter 08 Data Mining Predictive Models.sln in SSDT.

2. Right-click on the project (not the solution) and go to **Properties** in the pop-up menu.

3. In the **Property Page** menu, go to the **Deployment** tab, and change **Database** to **Chapter 08 Data Mining Predictive Models**. Then, click on **OK** and deploy the project, as shown in the following screenshot:

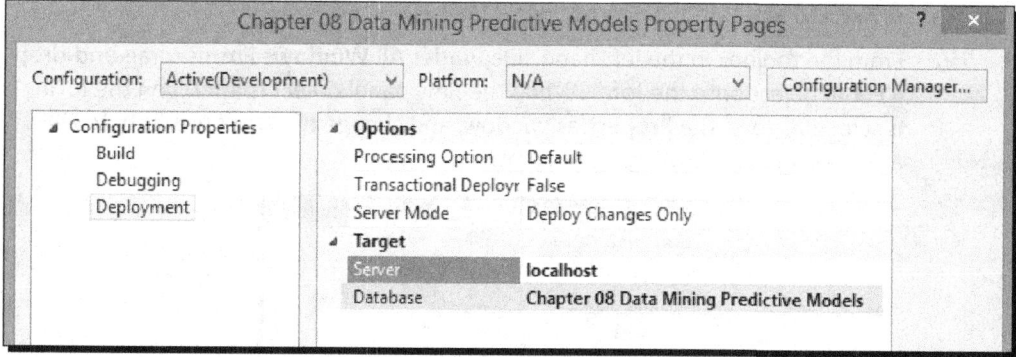

4. After successful deployment of the project, open **SSMS** and connect to your local SSAS Multidimensional engine. In that window, you should be able to view the deployed project, as shown in the following screenshot:

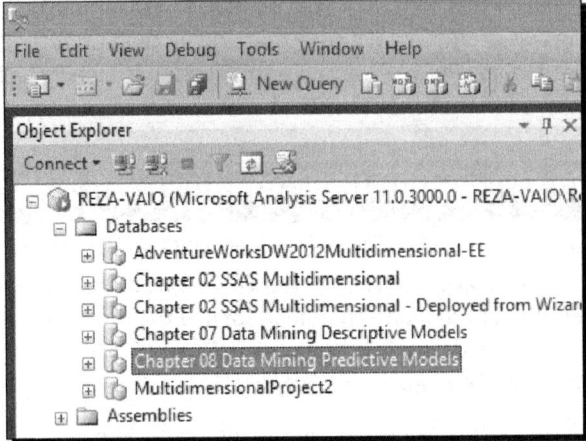

5. Open **Visual Studio** and then create a new project using **Windows Application Project**, and name it `DMX Query through Application`.

6. In the created project in solution explorer, right-click and remove `Form1.cs`.

7. Right-click on the project and create a new Windows form and name it `InputData.cs`.

8. Double-click on `InputData.cs` in the **Solution Explorer** window. You will be redirected to a Windows form's designer.

9. From the toolbox in the left-hand side, under **All Windows Forms**, drag-and-drop a **Panel** object onto the form. While the new panel object (**panel1**) on the form is selected, go to the **Properties** window, and change the **Dock** property to **Fill** as shown in the following screenshot:

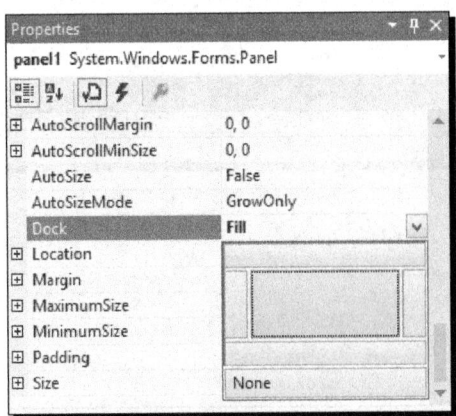

The panel will fill the whole area of the Windows form.

10. Now, drag-and-drop another panel (**panel2**) from the **Control Panel** and change the **Dock** property of the new panel to **Bottom**. You will see that the new panel only covers the bottom area of the main panel and the windows form.

11. Next, drag-and-drop the third panel (**panel3**) on the top of the first panel (**panel1**), and change the **Dock** property of **panel3** to **Fill**.

 The real cause of creating these three panels was to split the design area of the form. This type of splitting works even if the size of the form changes at runtime.

12. Drag-and-drop a button from the toolbar onto **panel2**, and change the text of the button to `Update` and rename the button to `btnUpdate`.

13. Drag-and-drop another button from the toolbar onto **panel2**, which is right after the `btnUpdate` button. Rename the new button to `btnPrediction` and change its **Text** property to **Prediction**.

14. Drag-and-drop a **DataGridView** property from the **Data** section of the toolbox onto **panel2**. Then, change the **Dock** property of this grid to **Fill**.

15. Now, you will have a layout that is similar to the following screenshot (but without column headers, which will be added in the next few steps):

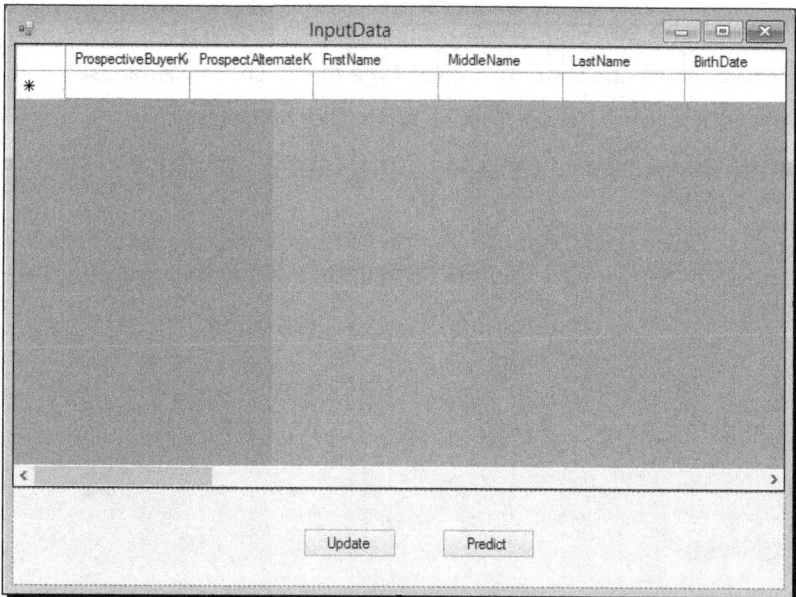

16. Click on **DataGridView**, and on the top right-hand side of the grid, you will see a small arrow pointing to the left. Click on this arrow (which is called a smart tag). After clicking on the smart tag, you will see the **DataGridView Tasks** pop-up menu. Next, click on the drop-down list in front of **Choose Data Source**. Then, click on **Add Project Data Source...**, as shown in the following screenshot:

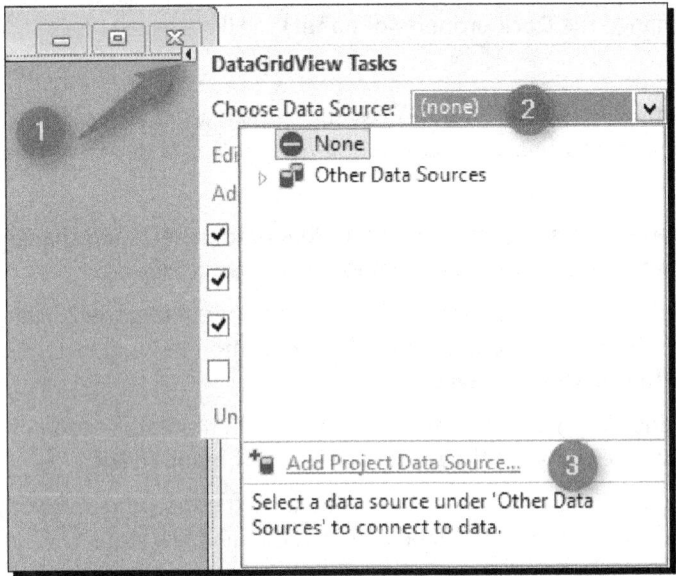

17. By clicking on **Add Project Data Source**, you will see **Data Source Configuration Wizard**. In the **Choose Data Source Type** menu, choose **Database**.

18. In the **Choose a Database Model** menu, click on **Dataset**.

19. In the **Choose a Data Connection** menu, create a connection to AdventureWorks DW 2012.

20. In the **Choose Your Database Objects** window, under the list of tables, select the **ProspectiveBuyer** table, and click on **Finish**.

21. Now, you will see that three new objects are added to the form (**Dataset**, **Binding Source**, and **Table Adapter**). You will also see that the layout of the grid and column names changes to the exact number of columns in the **ProspectiveBuyer** table.

22. Double-click on the **Update** button on the form, and you will be redirected to the code page of the `InputData.cs` form and to the new event handler created for the **Update** button. You will also see that a line of code generated and written in the **Form Load** event handler populates the grid with data from the database.

23. In the **btnUpdate_Click** event handler method, write the following script (this script will update the underlying database table with changes made by the user on the datagrid):

```
this.prospectiveBuyerTableAdapter.Update
    (this.adventureWorksDW2012DataSet.ProspectiveBuyer);
```

24. Now, add another Windows form to the project and name this one as `Prediction.cs`. Drag-and-drop a **DataGridView** property from the toolbar to this form, and change its **Dock** property to **Fill**. Rename the grid view to `grdPredictionResult`.

25. Go back to the `InputData.cs` form and double-click on the **Predict** button. In the **btnPredict_Click** event handler, write the following script (this script will open the `Prediction` form when a user clicks on the **Predict** button of the `InputData` form):

```
Prediction frmPrediction = new Prediction();
        frmPrediction.Show();
```

26. Go back to `Prediction.cs` and double-click on the header of the form in the designer, and you will be redirected to the **Prediction_Load** event handler.

27. Before writing the code for the DMX query execution, you would need to add a reference for AdomdClient of the Analysis Services. This reference is required when you want to work with Analysis Services through the .NET code.

28. Right-click on the `References` folder of the project and choose **Add Reference**. In the **Reference Manager** window, click on **Browse**, and add the `Microsoft.AnalysisServices.AdomdClient.dll` file from the `C:\Program Files\Microsoft.NET\ADOMD.NET\110` location.

29. After adding the reference, add the following line of code to the top of the code lines of the `Prediction.cs` form:

```
using Microsoft.AnalysisServices.AdomdClient;
```

30. Inside the **Prediction_Load** event handler, write the following code to create the connection to Analysis Services, and then create a connection and the command objects:

```
DataSet ds = new DataSet();
        AdomdConnection Conn = new AdomdConnection("Data Sourc
e=localhost;Catalog=Chapter 08 Data Mining Predictive Models");
        AdomdDataAdapter DMXCmd = new AdomdDataAdapter();
        DMXCmd.SelectCommand = new AdomdCommand();
        DMXCmd.SelectCommand.Connection = Conn;
```

31. Write the following code to assign the DMX query to the AdomdCommand object that we built previously:

```
DMXCmd.SelectCommand.CommandText = "SELECT " +
  "t.[FirstName], " +
  "t.[LastName], " +
  "t.[EmailAddress], " +
  "t.[Phone], " +
  "t.[Salutation], " +
  "(PredictProbability([Target Mail Decision Tree].
    [Bike Buyer],1)) as [Bike Buyer] " +
"From " +
  " [Target Mail Decision Tree] " +
"PREDICTION JOIN " +
  " OPENQUERY([Adventure Works DW2012], " +
  "   'SELECT " +
  "      [FirstName], " +
  "      [LastName], " +
  "      [EmailAddress], " +
  "      [Phone], " +
  "      [Salutation], " +
  "      [MaritalStatus], " +
  "      [Gender], " +
  "      [YearlyIncome], " +
  "      [TotalChildren], " +
  "      [NumberChildrenAtHome], " +
  "      [HouseOwnerFlag], " +
  "      [NumberCarsOwned] " +
    "FROM " +
    " [dbo].[ProspectiveBuyer] " +
    "') AS t " +
"ON " +
  " [Target Mail Decision Tree].
    [Marital Status] = t.[MaritalStatus] AND " +
```

```
"   [Target Mail Decision Tree].[Gender] = t.
    [Gender] AND " +
"   [Target Mail Decision Tree].
    [Yearly Income] = t.[YearlyIncome] AND " +
"   [Target Mail Decision Tree].
    [Total Children] = t.[TotalChildren] AND " +
"   [Target Mail Decision Tree].
    [Number Children At Home] = t.
    [NumberChildrenAtHome] AND " +
"   [Target Mail Decision Tree].
    [House Owner Flag] = t.[HouseOwnerFlag] AND " +
"   [Target Mail Decision Tree].
    [Number Cars Owned] = t.[NumberCarsOwned]   " +
"where PredictProbability([Target Mail Decision Tree].
    [Bike Buyer],1)>0.5 " +
"order by PredictProbability([Target Mail Decision Tree].
    [Bike Buyer],1) desc ";
```

> The DMX code of this example is exactly the same as the code that is used in step 13 of the *Predicting data with DMX* section of *Chapter 8, Identifying Data Patterns – Predictive Models in SSAS*. For more information on the function used and the structure of a DMX query of this sample, read the *Predicting data with DMX* section of *Chapter 8, Identifying Data Patterns – Predictive Models in SSAS*.

32. Finally, insert the following lines at the end to open the connection, execute the command, and fill the result set into `grdPredictionResult`:

```
Conn.Open();
        DMXCmd.Fill(ds, "tbl");
        Conn.Close();
        grdPredictionResult.DataSource =
            new DataView(ds.Tables[0]);
```

33. Open the `Program.cs` file and set **InputData** as the startup form of the application with the following lines of code:

```
static void Main()
    {
        Application.EnableVisualStyles();
        Application.SetCompatibleTextRenderingDefault(false);
        Application.Run(new InputData());
    }
```

34. Execute the project, and you will see that the data of prospective buyers appears first in the grid. When you click on the **Predict the Prediction** form, the DMX command will be executed. This will apply the data mining model onto the prospective buyers and it will produce prediction probabilities in the grid for you, as shown in the following screenshot:

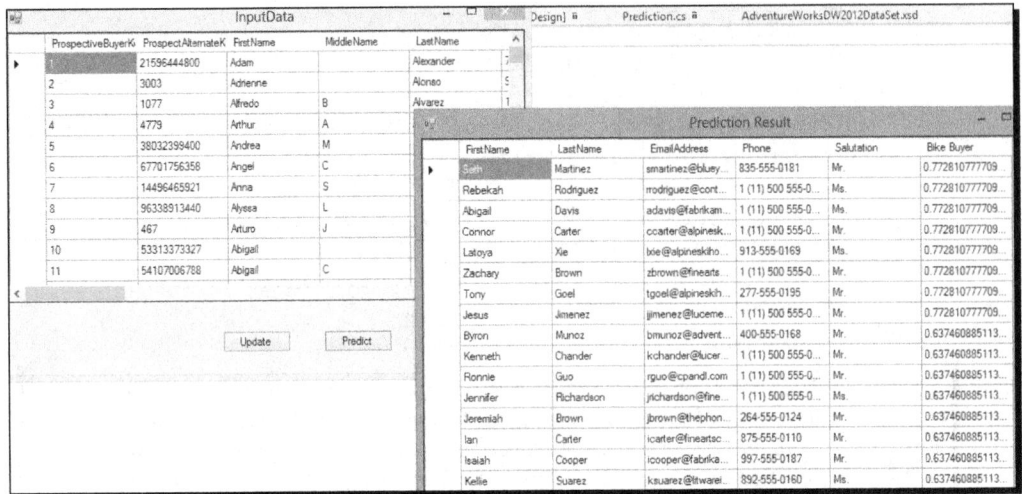

35. Try this scenario; first look at **Alexandria Cooper** (on the bottom of the **Prediction** grid). You will see that the probability of **Bike Buyer** for her is low (**0.52**). Now, close the **Prediction** window. Find **Alexandria** in the **InputData** form. Note that she has no children and she owns **3** cars. Change the number of her total children to **5**, change **NumberChildrenAtHome** to **3**, and change **NumberCarsOwned** from **3** to **0**. Now, click on **Update** to save the changes to the database table. Then, click on **Predict**. In the prediction result grid, search for **Alexandria** again, and you will see that the probability of her buying a bike has changed to a higher value (**0.63**).

What just happened?

In this example, you learned how to work with Analysis Services through the .NET Adomd connection and command objects. We used the exact same data mining model as was used in *Chapter 8, Identifying Data Patterns – Predictive Models in SSAS* for testing DMX queries. As you see in this example, we built a Windows form for a user to create the input dataset (`InputData.cs`) and write that dataset back into the **ProspectiveBuyer** table in the database. Then, we applied the data mining model while running the DMX query from the C# code behind the `Prediction.cs` form on the data of the table.

Step 32 contains a scenario that shows how changes in important variables of the mining model such as **NumberChildrenAtHome**, **TotalChildren**, and **NumberCarsOwned** affect the prediction probability of the DMX query.

Summary

This chapter provided some examples of working with SSRS reports through web, Windows, and even Metro applications. The main component that we discussed in this chapter was ReportViewer. ReportViewer provides the ability to work with SSRS reports that reside in the report server through the remote processing mode. On the other hand, this component provides the ability to design and create reports in the client application with client data sources that connect to databases through a local processing mode. ReportViewer also provides an extensive functionality for working with report objects from C# or VB.NET code behind that helps in creating a customized application with an SSRS frontend for the BI system.

In the final section of this chapter, you learned how to work with data mining models and apply data mining models on existing datasets to produce a prediction result set from the .NET application.

Index

Symbols

.NET application
DMX queries, running from 313-320
.NET applications
designing, with reports 296

A

Accuracy 144
add attribute 126
Add button 135, 137
Add link button 255
Add Related Tables button 34
AdomdCommand object 318
ADO.NET destination 107
ADO.NET Source 103
AdventureWorks SSRS sample reports
installing 296, 297
Aggregate transformation 105
algorithm parameters
about 190, 191
URL 190
Analysis Service Execute DDL Task 94
Analysis Service Processing Task 94
Analysis Services project
creating 31, 32
Apply Rules button 133
Association rule algorithm 172
attribute hierarchy 49
AttributeHierarchyDisplayFolder property 41
AttributeHierarchyEnabled property 41
AttributeHierarchyVisible property 41

attributes 15
Audit transformation 106

B

background color
changing, of data rows 237-239
Background Color property 238
BatchTag variable 141
best algorithm
finding 193
best mining model
finding, with Lift Chart 194-203
finding, with Profit Chart 194-203
Bike Buyer attribute 204
BikeBuyer field 175
Bike Buyer property 204
BI semantic model. *See* BISM
BISM 10, 11, 79
BI system
about 7, 8
architecture and components 9
BISM 10, 11
data quality 12
data visualization 12
data warehouse 9
Extract Transform Load 10
MDM 12
Bridge table. *See* **Factless Fact table**
browser
cube, viewing 37-39
btnUpdate button 315
Bulk Insert Task 94

Business Intelligence. *See* **BI system**
Business Intelligence Development Studio (BIDS) 85
business rule
  about 131
  creating 131-133
  examples 131

C

calculated members 53, 54
Calculate function
  URL 76
catalog
  SSIS package, executing from 114-116
CDC Control Task 94
CDC Source 103
change tracking 127-129
charts
  SSRS, working with 240-242
Classification Matrix 206
cleansing
  Data Quality Project, used for 153-156
cleansing component
  creating, in SSIS 166-168
Clustering algorithm 172
Completeness 144
composite domain rules
  creating 157-159
Composite domains (CDs) 150
Conditional Split transformation 106
connection manager
  URL 94
content type 182, 183
Control Flow tasks
  about 93
  Analysis Service Execute DDL Task 94
  Analysis Service Processing Task 94
  Bulk Insert Task 94
  CDC Control Task 94
  Data Flow Task 93
  Data Profiling Task 94
  Execute Package Task 93
  Execute Process Task 93
  Execute SQL Task 93
  Expression Task 93
  File System Task 93

  FTP Task 93
  Script Task 93
  Send Mail Task 93
  Web Service Task 93
  WMI Data Reader Task 94
  WMI Event Watcher Task 94
  working with 88-95
  XML Task 93
Cross Validation 206
CSV files
  looping through, Foreach Loop container used
    107-110
cube
  viewing, in browser 37-39
cube, creating
  benefits 37
customer dimension 19, 20

D

dashboard
  creating, with Dashboard Designer 250-253
Dashboard Designer
  dashboard, creating with 250-253
dashboard page
  about 253
  creating 253-255
data
  entity, creating with 126, 127
  securing 76
Data Analysis eXpression. *See* **DAX**
database table
  information, loading into 96-102
Data Conversion transformation 105
Data Description Language (DDL) 213
Data Flow components
  Destination component 103
  Source component 103
  Transformation component 103
Data Flow Task 93
DataGridView property 317
Data Manipulation Language (DML) 213
data mining
  about 171-173
  algorithms 173
  content type 182
  data preparation 181

mining model 182
mining structure 181
mining variables 182
problem definition 181
test set 183
training set 183
URL 172
data mining algorithms
Association rule algorithm 172
Clustering algorithm 172
decision tree algorithm 172
functionality 173
Linear regression algorithm 172
Logistic regression algorithm 173
Naïve Bayes algorithm 172
Neural network algorithm 172
Sequence clustering algorithm 173
Time Series algorithm 173
Data Mining Expression
URL 213
Data Mining Extensions. *See* **DMX**
Data mining query designer 212
data mining relationship 49
data mining solution
creating, with Microsoft Decision Tree 174-180
data mining viewers 183
data mining viewers 183
data preparation 181
Data Profiling Task 94
data quality
about 12, 143
Accuracy 144
Completeness 144
Standardization 144
Uniqueness 144
Data Quality Client (DQC) 148
Data Quality Project
used, for cleansing 153-156
Data Quality Services. *See* **DQS**
Data Quality Services integration
with MDS 169
data rows
background color, changing 237-239
data, securing
tabular security 77, 78
Dataset parameter 231

data source
creating 253
Data Source View. *See* **DSV**
Data Transformation Services (DTS) 85
data visualization
about 12
used, with Power Map 285-292
data warehouse
about 9, 13, 14
dimensional modeling 14
dimension types 23, 24
fact types 22
Internet sales example 16, 17
Snow flake schema 16
star schema 16
date dimension
URL 22
DAX
about 73
time intelligence functions, using 73-76
decision tree algorithm 172
degenerate dimension 24
Deployment Wizard
URL 56
Derived Column transformation 104, 105
Derived hierarchy 133-135
descriptive model 171
Destination component
about 107
ADO.NET destination 107
Excel destination 107
Flat File destination 107
ODBC destination 107
OLE DB destination 107
Raw File destination 107
Recordset destination 107
SQL Server destination 107
DimDate 20-22
dimensional modeling
about 14
dimension tables 15
fact 15
Fact table 15
Grain 15
performing 17
dimension designer 39-42

dimensions
Fact relationship, adding 46-49
using 46
dimensions, types
degenerate dimension 24
junk dimension 24
dimension tables 15
DimProduct 22
DimStore 22
DirectQuery mode 79
DirectQuery with In-Memory mode 79
DiscritizationBucketCount property 41
DiscritizationMethod property 41
DMX 207
DMX functions
URL 213
DMX queries
running, from .NET application 313-320
DMX query 213
Dock property 300
domain-based relationship 129, 130
Done button 281
DQS
about 121, 145, 146
installing 147, 148
DSV
Named Calculation, creating 45
Named Query, using 46

E

Edit button 126
Edit Selected Business Rules button 131
entity
creating 125, 126
creating, with data 126, 127
entity-based staging 138-141
entity relationship
domain-based relationship 129, 130
ETL
staging 84, 85
ETL tools
SSIS 85, 86
Excel
Power View, enabling on 263

Excel Add-in
installing 124, 125
WebUI, comparing with 123
Excel destination 107
Excel Source 103
Execute Package Task
about 93
using 112
Execute Process Task 93
Execute SQL Task 93, 95
Explicit hierarchy 133
Expression
about 239
URL 240
Expression language 105
Expression Task 93
Extract process 83
Extract Transform Load 10

F

Factless Fact table 23
Fact relationship
about 49
adding 46-49
fact 15
FactSales 18, 19
Fact table 15
fact types
Factless Fact table 23
snapshot fact 22
Transactional fact 22
File System Task
using 93
Filter and Shape button 277
filters
about 259
used, in Power View 273, 274
working with 259-262
first cube
creating 33-37
developing 31
first report
creating, SSRS used 221-226
flat file connection manager 104

Flat File destination 107
Flat File Source 103
FLATTENED keyword 217
Foreach Loop container
　　about 111
　　used, for looping through CSV files 107-110
FormatString property 44
FTP Task 93
future sales
　　predicting, with Microsoft Time Series 214-217
Fuzzy Lookup transformation 106

G

GeoFlow. *See* **Power Map**
geographical data visualization
　　Power View, used for 266-269
Grain 15
grouping
　　applying, on data rows 234-237

H

hierarchy
　　about 133
　　attribute hierarchy 49
　　creating 50-69
　　creating, from multiple tables 71, 72
　　creating, from single table 70, 71
　　Derived hierarchy 133
　　Explicit hierarchy 133
　　user hierarchy 49

I

information
　　loading, into database table 96-102
In-Memory mode 79
In-Memory with DirectQuery mode 80
Inmon methodology
　　URL 14
input variable 182
integration management
　　subscription view, creating 137, 138
Internet Information Services (IIS) 123
Internet sales example
　　customer dimension 19, 20
　　DimDate 20-22

DimProduct 22
DimStore 22
FactSales 18, 19
IsAggregatable property 41

J

junk dimension 24

K

KeyColumns property 41
Key Performance Indicators (KPIs) 12
key variable 182
Kimball methodology
　　URL 14
Knowledge Base
　　about 149
　　creating 149, 150
knowledge discovery 151, 152

L

Lift Chart
　　about 206
　　best mining model, finding with 194-203
Linear regression algorithm 172
Load process 83
local processing mode
　　working with 304-307
Logistic regression algorithm 173
Lookup transformation 105, 106

M

Many to Many relationship 49
Master Data Management. *See* **MDM**
Master Data Services. *See* **MDS**
matching policy
　　creating 163-165
matching projects
　　creating 165
matching rules
　　properties 162
MDM
　　about 12, 119-121
　　benefits 121

MDS
about 121
components 122
configuring 122
Data Quality Services, integrating with 169
features 121
installing 122
integration management 136
permissions, applying 135, 136
security, applying 135, 136
MDX 51, 73
MDX query 51, 52
measure properties
modifying 43
Merge Join transformation 106
Metro application
reports, developing 302, 303
Microsoft Accuracy Chart 205
Microsoft association rule
about 184-189
algorithm parameters 190, 191
Microsoft clustering algorithm 204
Microsoft Decision Tree
data mining solution, creating with 174-180
Microsoft Naïve Bayes algorithm 204, 205
Microsoft Time Series
future sales, predicting with 214-217
mining model 182
mining structure 181
mining variables 182
model
creating 125
creating, with DirectQuery storage mode 80, 81
Month attribute
order, changing 42, 43
Multicast transformation 106
Multi-Dimensional eXpression. *See* **MDX**
Multi-Dimensional SSAS
versus tabular SSAS 81, 82
multiple tables
hierarchy, creating from 71, 72

N

Naïve Bayes algorithm 172
NameColumn property 41
Named Calculation

creating 45
Named Query
about 46
using 46
Neural network algorithm 172
None relationship 49

O

ODBC destination 107
ODBC Source 103
OK button 129, 309
OLAP
about 27
need for 27-29
OLE DB Command transformation 106
OLE DB destination 106, 107
OLE DB Source 103
OnLine Transactional Processing (OLTP) 27
order
changing, of Month attribute 42, 43
OrderBy Attribute property 41
OrderBy property 41
ordering
applying, on data rows 234-237

P

package parameter 111
page property
changing 232-234
Parameterize 111
parameters
adding, to report 226-232
PerformancePoint
about 247, 248
configuring, in SharePoint 248-250
Dashboard Designer utility 250
PerformancePoint Dashboard Designer 262
PerformancePoint Services dashboards. *See* **PPS dashboards**
permissions
applying 135, 136
Pivot transformation 106
Power Map
about 285
data visualization, used with 285-292
URL 285, 286

PowerPivot 64
Power Query
 about 275
 self-service ETL, used with 276-285
Power Query Excel Add-in
 URL 276
Power View
 about 262
 data, filtering 273
 enabling, on Excel 263
 filter, using 273, 274
 map 266
 scatter chart 269
 used, for geographical data visualization
 266-269
Power View dashboard
 creating 264, 265
PPS dashboards
 fly features 256-258
Precedence Constraints 94
predictable variable 182, 204, 205
Predict button 317
prediction variable 212, 217
PredictProbability function 208, 213
PredictTimeSeries function 217
problem definition 181
Process Add mode 59
Process button 40
Process Clear mode 58
Process Clear Structure mode 59
Process Data mode 58
Process Default mode 58
Process Full mode 58
Process Index mode 59
processing
 about 57-59
 URL 58
processing mode 300
Process Structure mode 59
Process Update mode 59
Product Entity attribute 126
Profit Chart
 about 206
 best mining model, finding with 194-203
Progress tab 95
prospective bike buyers
 predicting 207-211

R

Raw File destination 107
Raw File Source 103
Recordset destination 107
Referenced relationship 49
relationship types
 data mining relationship 49
 Fact relationship 49
 Many to Many relationship 49
 None relationship 49
 Referenced relationship 49
 Regular relationship 49
report
 charts, adding 240
 deploying 242-244
 designing 304-307
 developing, in Metro application 302, 303
 developing, in web application 297-300
 developing, in Windows application 297-300
 expressions 237
 grouping 234
 page configuration 232
 page property, changing 232-234
 parameterization 226
 parameters, adding to 226-232
 printing 232
 sorting 234
report configuration
 changing, with ReportViewer Object 308-312
Reporting Services Configuration Manager 221
Report Manager
 about 221
 using 245
Report parameter 231
ReportParameter object 310
Report Server 221
Report Server Data Source (RSDS) 79
ReportViewer
 in web application 301
 in Windows application 301
ReportViewer Object
 report configuration, changing with 308-312
ReportViewer toolbar 301
ResultSet property 95
Row Count transformation 106
rules 166

S

scatter chart
about 269
time-based information, visualizing
with 270-272
SCD
about 84
type 0 24
type 1 25
type 2 25, 26
SCD transformation 106
Script Component transformation 106
Script Task 93
security
applying 135, 136
Select Members button 260
self-service ETL
used, with Power Query 276-285
Send Mail Task 93
Sequence clustering algorithm 173
SharePoint
PerformancePoint, configuring 248-250
single table
hierarchy, creating from 70, 71
Slowly Changing Dimension. *See* **SCD**
snapshot fact 22
snow flake schema 16
Sort transformation 106
Source component
about 103
ADO.NET Source 103
CDC Source 103
Excel Source 103
Flat File Source 103
ODBC Source 103
OLE DB Source 103
Raw File Source 103
XML Source 103
SourceFilePath parameter 110, 111
SQL Server Analysis Services engine 29, 30
SQL Server Data Tools (SSDT) 87
SQL Server destination 107
SQL Server Integration Services. *See* **SSIS**
SQL Server Management Studio (SSMS) 113
SQL Server Reporting Services. *See* **SSRS**
SQL Statement property 91

SSAS project
deploying 54-56
SSAS security
URL 31, 78
SSAS Tabular 64, 65
SSIS
about 10, 86
cleansing component, creating 166, 168
SSIS expressions
URL 105
SSIS package
executing, from catalog 114, 116
SSIS project
creating 87, 88
deploying 113, 114
SSRS
about 12, 219
architecture 220, 221
Expression editor 239, 240
Report Manager 221
Report Server 221
used, for creating first report 221-226
working, with charts 240-242
SSRS reports parameters
Dataset parameter 231
Report parameter 231
staging 84, 85
standardization
setting 160-162
Standardization 144
star schema 16
Start button 152
storage modes
about 79
model, creating with DirectQuery storage
mode 80, 81
URL 31
subscription view
creating 137, 138
synonyms
creating 160, 162

T

tabular project
creating 65, 66
measures, creating 68, 69

tabular security 77, 78
tabular SSAS
  versus Multi-Dimensional SSAS 81, 82
Term Lookup transformation 106
test set 183
time-based information
  visualizing, with scatter chart 269-272
time dimension
  URL 22
time intelligence functions
  used, in DAX 73-76
Time Series algorithm 173
TotalYTD function 76
training set 183
Transactional fact 22
transformation
  Aggregate transformation 105
  Audit transformation 106
  Conditional Split transformation 106
  Data Conversion transformation 105
  Derived Column transformation 105
  Fuzzy Lookup transformation 106
  Lookup transformation 106
  Merge Join transformation 106
  Multicast transformation 106
  OLE DB Command transformation 106
  Pivot transformation 106
  Row Count transformation 106
  SCD transformation 106
  Script Component transformation 106
  Sort transformation 106
  Term Lookup transformation 106
  Union All transformation 106
  Unpivot transformation 106
Transform process 83
type 0 24
type 1 25
type 2 25, 26

U

Union All transformation 106
Uniqueness 144
Unpivot transformation 106
Update button 317
user hierarchy 49

V

Variables 92
variables types
  input variable 182
  key variable 182
  predictable variable 182

W

web application
  reports, developing 297-300
  ReportViewer 301
Web Service Task 93
WebUI
  comparing, with Excel Add-in 123
Windows application
  reports, developing 297-300
  ReportViewer 301
WMI Data Reader Task 94
WMI Event Watcher Task 94

X

XML Source 103
XML Task 93
xVelocity 65

Z

zones 255

Thank you for buying
Microsoft SQL Server 2014 Business Intelligence
Development Beginner's Guide

About Packt Publishing

Packt, pronounced 'packed', published its first book "*Mastering phpMyAdmin for Effective MySQL Management*" in April 2004 and subsequently continued to specialize in publishing highly focused books on specific technologies and solutions.

Our books and publications share the experiences of your fellow IT professionals in adapting and customizing today's systems, applications, and frameworks. Our solution-based books give you the knowledge and power to customize the software and technologies you're using to get the job done. Packt books are more specific and less general than the IT books you have seen in the past. Our unique business model allows us to bring you more focused information, giving you more of what you need to know, and less of what you don't.

Packt is a modern, yet unique publishing company, which focuses on producing quality, cutting-edge books for communities of developers, administrators, and newbies alike. For more information, please visit our website: www.PacktPub.com.

About Packt Enterprise

In 2010, Packt launched two new brands, Packt Enterprise and Packt Open Source, in order to continue its focus on specialization. This book is part of the Packt Enterprise brand, home to books published on enterprise software – software created by major vendors, including (but not limited to) IBM, Microsoft and Oracle, often for use in other corporations. Its titles will offer information relevant to a range of users of this software, including administrators, developers, architects, and end users.

Writing for Packt

We welcome all inquiries from people who are interested in authoring. Book proposals should be sent to author@packtpub.com. If your book idea is still at an early stage and you would like to discuss it first before writing a formal book proposal, contact us; one of our commissioning editors will get in touch with you.

We're not just looking for published authors; if you have strong technical skills but no writing experience, our experienced editors can help you develop a writing career, or simply get some additional reward for your expertise.

Microsoft Silverlight 4 Business Application Development Beginner's Guide

ISBN: 978-1-84719-976-8   Paperback: 412 pages

Build Enterprise-Ready Business Applications with Silverlight

1. An introduction to building enterprise-ready business applications with Silverlight quickly.

2. Get hold of the basic tools and skills needed to get started in Silverlight application development.

3. Integrate different media types, taking the RIA experience further with Silverlight, and much more.

4. Rapidly manage business focused controls, data, and business logic connectivity.

What's New in SQL Server 2012

ISBN: 978-1-84968-734-8   Paperback: 238 pages

Unleash the new features of SQL Server 2012

1. Upgrade your skills to the latest version of SQL Server.

2. Discover the new dimensional model in Analysis Services.

3. Utilize data alerts and render reports to the latest versions of Excel and Word.

4. Build packages to leverage the new features in the Integration Services environment.

Please check **www.PacktPub.com** for information on our titles

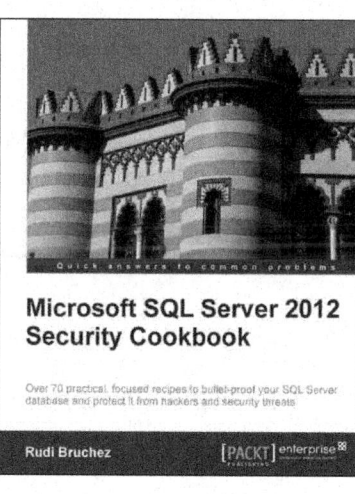
Microsoft SQL Server 2012 Security Cookbook

ISBN: 978-1-84968-588-7   Paperback: 322 pages

Over 70 practical, focused recipes to bullet-proof your SQL Server database and protect it from hackers and security threats

1. Practical, focused recipes for securing your SQL Server database.

2. Master the latest techniques for data and code encryption, user authentication and authorization, protection against brute force attacks, denial-of-service attacks, and SQL Injection, and more.

3. A learn-by-example recipe-based approach that focuses on key concepts to provide the foundation to solve real world problems.

Microsoft SQL Server 2012 Integration Services: An Expert Cookbook

ISBN: 978-1-84968-524-5   Paperback: 564 pages

Over 80 expert recipes to design, create, and deploy SSIS packages

1. Full of illustrations, diagrams, and tips with clear step-by-step instructions and real time examples.

2. Master all transformations in SSIS and their usages with real-world scenarios.

3. Learn to make SSIS packages re-startable and robust; and work with transactions.

4. Get hold of data cleansing and fuzzy operations in SSIS.

Please check **www.PacktPub.com** for information on our titles

CPSIA information can be obtained
at www.ICGtesting.com
Printed in the USA
FSOW03n0012301216
29042FS

9 781849 688888